MW01174690

Excel Shortcut Keys

Shortcut	Function	Shortcut	Function
F9	Calculate all worksheets	Ctrl +K	Insert Hyperlink
Ctrl +C	Copy	Ctrl +O	Open existing file
Ctrl +N	Create a new workbook	Ctrl +V	Paste
Ctrl +X	Cut	Shift + F3	Paste a function into a formula
Ctrl + F3	Define a range name	F3	Paste a name into a formula
Shift + F2	Edit a cell comment	Ctrl +P	Print default worksheet
F2	Edit the active cell	F4	Repeat the last action
Ctrl +F	Find	Ctrl +H	Replace
Shift + F4	Find next	Alt + Shift + F2	Save
Ctrl +1	Format Cells	Alt + F2	Save As
Ctrl +G	Go to	Ctrl +S	Save workbook
F5	Go to	F7	Spelling
F1	Help	Shift + F1	What's This

Note: For additional information on function and shortcut keys, open the Office Assistant and search for "Shortcut keys."

How to Select a Cell with the Keyboard

Press	To move...	Press	To move...
→	Right one cell	Ctrl + Home	First cell in worksheet
←	Left one cell	Ctrl + End	Lower right cell in worksheet
↓	Down one cell	PgDn	Down one screen
↑	Up one cell	PgUp	Up one screen
Ctrl + →	To right edge of current region	Alt + PgDn	Right one screen
Ctrl + ←	To left edge of current region	Alt + PgUp	Left one screen
Ctrl + ↓	To bottom edge of current region	Ctrl + PgDn	Next sheet
Ctrl + ↑	To top edge of current region	Ctrl + PgUp	Previous sheet

Standard Toolbar

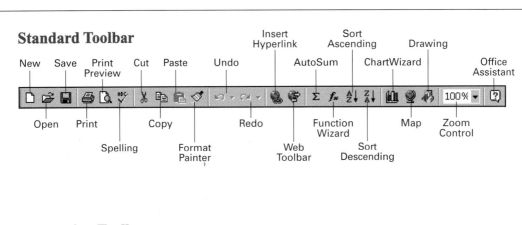

New, Open, Save, Print, Print Preview, Spelling, Cut, Copy, Paste, Format Painter, Undo, Redo, Insert Hyperlink, Web Toolbar, AutoSum, Function Wizard, Sort Ascending, Sort Descending, ChartWizard, Map, Drawing, Zoom Control, Office Assistant

Formatting Toolbar

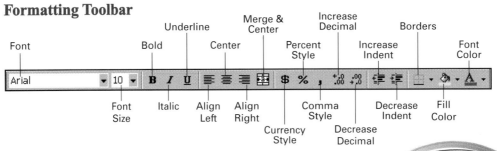

Font, Font Size, Bold, Italic, Underline, Center, Align Left, Align Right, Merge & Center, Currency Style, Percent Style, Comma Style, Increase Decimal, Decrease Decimal, Increase Indent, Decrease Indent, Borders, Fill Color, Font Color

DISCOVERY CENTRAL

DISCOVER
EXCEL 97

DISCOVER
EXCEL 97

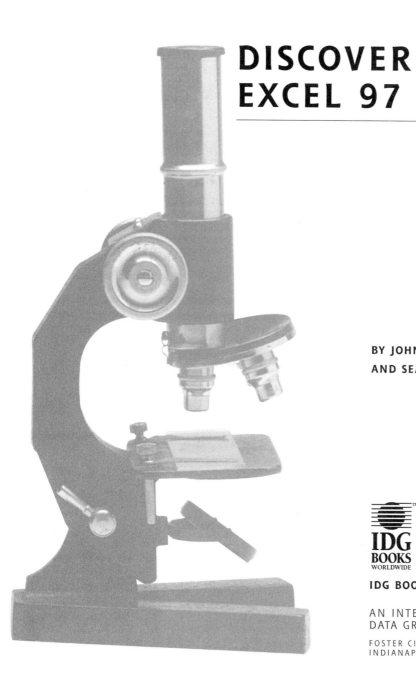

BY JOHN R. NICHOLSON
AND SEAN R. NICHOLSON

IDG BOOKS WORLDWIDE, INC.

AN INTERNATIONAL
DATA GROUP COMPANY

FOSTER CITY, CA • CHICAGO, IL •
INDIANAPOLIS, IN • SOUTHLAKE, TX

Discover Excel 97

Published by
IDG Books Worldwide, Inc.
An International Data Group Company
919 E. Hillsdale Blvd., Suite 400
Foster City, CA 94404

www.idgbooks.com (IDG Books Worldwide Web site)

Library of Congress Catalog Card No.: 96-79750

ISBN: 0-7645-3047-X

Printed in the United States of America

10 9 8 7 6 5 4 3 2

1B/QY/QZ/ZX/FC-IN

Distributed in the United States by IDG Books Worldwide, Inc.

Distributed by Macmillan Canada for Canada; by Contemporanea de Ediciones for Venezuela; by Distribuidora Cuspide for Argentina; by CITEC for Brazil; by Ediciones ZETA S.C.R. Ltda. for Peru; by Editorial Limusa SA for Mexico; by Transworld Publishers Limited in the United Kingdom and Europe; by Academic Bookshop for Egypt; by Levant Distributors S.A.R.L. for Lebanon; by Al Jassim for Saudi Arabia; by Simron Pty. Ltd. for South Africa; by Pustak Mahal for India; by The Computer Bookshop for India; by Toppan Company Ltd. for Japan; by Addison Wesley Publishing Company for Korea; by Longman Singapore Publishers Ltd. for Singapore, Malaysia, Thailand, and Indonesia; by Unalis Corporation for Taiwan; by WS Computer Publishing Company, Inc. for the Philippines; by WoodsLane Pty. Ltd. for Australia; by WoodsLane Enterprises Ltd. for New Zealand. Authorized Sales Agent: Anthony Rudkin Associates for the Middle East and North Africa.

For general information on IDG Books Worldwide's books in the U.S., please call our Consumer Customer Service department at 800-762-2974. For reseller information, including discounts and premium sales, please call our Reseller Customer Service department at 800-434-3422.

For information on where to purchase IDG Books Worldwide's books outside the U.S., please contact our International Sales department at 415-655-3172 or fax 415-655-3295.

For information on foreign language translations, please contact our Foreign & Subsidiary Rights department at 415-655-3021 or fax 415-655-3281.

For sales inquiries and special prices for bulk quantities, please contact our Sales department at 415-655-3200 or write to the address above.

For information on using IDG Books Worldwide's books in the classroom or for ordering examination copies, please contact our Educational Sales department at 800-434-2086 or fax 817-251-8174.

For press review copies, author interviews, or other publicity information, please contact our Public Relations department at 415-655-3000 or fax 415-655-3299.

For authorization to photocopy items for corporate, personal, or educational use, please contact Copyright Clearance Center, 222 Rosewood Drive, Danvers, MA 01923, or fax 508-750-4470.

 is a trademark under exclusive license to IDG Books Worldwide, Inc., from International Data Group, Inc.

ABOUT IDG BOOKS WORLDWIDE

Welcome to the world of IDG Books Worldwide.

IDG Books Worldwide, Inc., is a subsidiary of International Data Group, the world's largest publisher of computer-related information and the leading global provider of information services on information technology. IDG was founded more than 25 years ago and now employs more than 8,500 people worldwide. IDG publishes more than 275 computer publications in over 75 countries (see listing below). More than 60 million people read one or more IDG publications each month.

Launched in 1990, IDG Books Worldwide is today the #1 publisher of best-selling computer books in the United States. We are proud to have received eight awards from the Computer Press Association in recognition of editorial excellence and three from *Computer Currents'* First Annual Readers' Choice Awards. Our best-selling ...*For Dummies*® series has more than 30 million copies in print with translations in 30 languages. IDG Books Worldwide, through a joint venture with IDG's Hi-Tech Beijing, became the first U.S. publisher to publish a computer book in the People's Republic of China. In record time, IDG Books Worldwide has become the first choice for millions of readers around the world who want to learn how to better manage their businesses.

Our mission is simple: Every one of our books is designed to bring extra value and skill-building instructions to the reader. Our books are written by experts who understand and care about our readers. The knowledge base of our editorial staff comes from years of experience in publishing, education, and journalism — experience we use to produce books for the '90s. In short, we care about books, so we attract the best people. We devote special attention to details such as audience, interior design, use of icons, and illustrations. And because we use an efficient process of authoring, editing, and desktop publishing our books electronically, we can spend more time ensuring superior content and spend less time on the technicalities of making books.

You can count on our commitment to deliver high-quality books at competitive prices on topics you want to read about. At IDG Books Worldwide, we continue in the IDG tradition of delivering quality for more than 25 years. You'll find no better book on a subject than one from IDG Books Worldwide.

John J. Kilcullen

John Kilcullen
CEO
IDG Books Worldwide, Inc.

WINNER

*Eighth Annual
Computer Press
Awards ≥1992*

WINNER

*Ninth Annual
Computer Press
Awards ≥1993*

WINNER

*Tenth Annual
Computer Press
Awards ≥1994*

WINNER

*Eleventh Annual
Computer Press
Awards ≥1995*

IDG Books Worldwide, Inc., is a subsidiary of International Data Group, the world's largest publisher of computer-related information and the leading global provider of information services on information technology. International Data Group publishes over 275 computer publications in over 75 countries. Sixty million people read one or more International Data Group publications each month. International Data Group's publications include: **ARGENTINA:** Buyer's Guide, Computerworld Argentina, PC World Argentina; **AUSTRALIA:** Australian Macworld, Australian PC World, Australian Reseller News, Computerworld, IT Casebook, Network World, Publish, Webmaster; **AUSTRIA:** Computerwelt Osterreich, Networks Austria, PC Tip Austria; **BANGLADESH:** PC World Bangladesh; **BELARUS:** PC World Belarus; **BELGIUM:** Data News; **BRAZIL:** Annuário de Informática, Computerworld, Connections, Macworld, PC Player, PC World, Publish, Reseller News, Supergamepower; **BULGARIA:** Computerworld Bulgaria, Network World Bulgaria, PC & MacWorld Bulgaria; **CANADA:** CIO Canada, Client/Server World, ComputerWorld Canada, InfoWorld Canada, NetworkWorld Canada, WebWorld; **CHILE:** Computerworld Chile, PC World Chile; **COLOMBIA:** Computerworld Colombia, PC World Colombia; **COSTA RICA:** PC World Centro America; **THE CZECH AND SLOVAK REPUBLICS:** Computerworld Czechoslovakia, Macworld Czech Republic, PC World Czechoslovakia; **DENMARK:** Communications World Danmark, Computerworld Danmark, Macworld Danmark, PC World Danmark, Techworld Denmark; **DOMINICAN REPUBLIC:** PC World Republica Dominicana; **ECUADOR:** PC World Ecuador; **EGYPT:** Computerworld Middle East, PC World Middle East; **EL SALVADOR:** PC World Centro America; **FINLAND:** MikroPC, Tietoverkko, Tietoviikko; **FRANCE:** Distributique, Hebdo, Info PC, Le Monde Informatique, Macworld, Reseaux & Telecoms, WebMaster France; **GERMANY:** Computer Partner, Computerwoche, Computerwoche Extra, Computerwoche FOCUS, Global Online, Macwelt, PC Welt; **GREECE:** Amiga Computing, GamePro Greece, Multimedia World; **GUATEMALA:** PC World Centro America; **HONDURAS:** PC World Centro America; **HONG KONG:** Computerworld Hong Kong, PC World Hong Kong, Publish in Asia; **HUNGARY:** ABCD CD-ROM, Computerworld Szamitastechnika, Internetto online Magazine, PC World Hungary, PC-X Magazin Hungary; **ICELAND:** Tolvuheimur PC World Island; **INDIA:** Information Communications World, Information Systems Computerworld, PC World India, Publish in Asia; **INDONESIA:** InfoKomputer PC World, Komputek Computerworld, Publish in Asia; **IRELAND:** ComputerScope, PC Live!; **ISRAEL:** Macworld Israel, People & Computers/Computerworld; **ITALY:** Computerworld Italia, Macworld Italia, Networking Italia, PC World Italia; **JAPAN:** Computerworld Japan, Macworld Japan, Nikkei Personal Computing, OS/2 World Japan, SunWorld Japan, Windows NT World, Windows World Japan; **KENYA:** PC World East African; **KOREA:** Hi-Tech Information, Macworld Korea, PC World Korea; **MACEDONIA:** PC World Macedonia; **MALAYSIA:** Computerworld Malaysia, PC World Malaysia, Publish in Asia; **MALTA:** PC World Malta; **MEXICO:** Computerworld Mexico, PC World Mexico; **MYANMAR:** PC World Myanmar; **NETHERLANDS:** Computer! Totaal, LAN Internetworking Magazine, LAN World Buyers Guide, Macworld Netherlands, Net, WebWereld; **NEW ZEALAND:** Absolute Beginners Guide and Plain & Simple Series, Computer Buyer, Computer Industry Directory, Computerworld New Zealand, MTB, Network World, PC World New Zealand; **NICARAGUA:** PC World Centro America; **NORWAY:** Computerworld Norge, CW Rapport, Datamagasinet, Financial Rapport, Kursguide Norge, Macworld Norge, Multimediaworld Norge, PC World Ekspress Norge, PC World Nettverk, PC World Norge, PC World ProduktGuide Norge; **PAKISTAN:** Computerworld Pakistan; **PANAMA:** PC World Panama; **PEOPLE'S REPUBLIC OF CHINA:** China Computer Users, China Computerworld, China InfoWorld, China Telecom World Weekly; Computer & Communication, Electronic Design China, Electronics Today, Electronics Weekly, Game Software, PC World China, Popular Computer Week, Software Weekly, Software World, Telecom World; **PERU:** Computerworld Peru, PC World Profesional Peru, PC World SoHo Peru; **PHILIPPINES:** Click!, Computerworld Philippines, PC World Philippines, Publish in Asia; **POLAND:** Computerworld Poland, Computerworld Special Report Poland, Cyber, Macworld Poland, Networld Poland, PC World Komputer; **PORTUGAL:** Cerebro/PC World, Computerworld/Correio Informático, Dealer World Portugal, Mac*In/PC*In Portugal, Multimedia World; **PUERTO RICO:** PC World Puerto Rico; **ROMANIA:** Computerworld Romania, PC World Romania, Telecom Romania; **RUSSIA:** Computerworld Russia, Mir PK, Publish, Seti; **SINGAPORE:** Computerworld Singapore, PC World Singapore, Publish in Asia; **SLOVENIA:** Monitor; **SOUTH AFRICA:** Computing SA, Network World SA, Software World SA; **SPAIN:** Comunicaciones World España, Dealer World España, Macworld España, PC World España; **SRI LANKA:** Infolink PC World; **SWEDEN:** CAP&Design, Computer Sweden, Corporate Computing Sweden, Internetworld Sweden, it.branschen, Macworld Sweden, MaxiData Sweden, MikroDatorn, Natverk & Kommunikation, PC World Sweden, PCaktiv, Windows World Sweden; **SWITZERLAND:** Computerworld Schweiz, Macworld Schweiz, PCtip; **TAIWAN:** Computerworld Taiwan, Macworld Taiwan, Network World Taiwan, NEW ViSiON/Publish, PC World Taiwan, Windows World Taiwan; **THAILAND:** Publish in Asia, Thai Computerworld; **TURKEY:** Computerworld Turkiye, Macworld Turkiye, Network World Turkiye, PC World Turkiye; **UKRAINE:** Computerworld Kiev, Multimedia World Ukraine, PC World Ukraine; **UNITED KINGDOM:** Acorn User UK, Amiga Action UK, Amiga Computing UK, Apple Talk UK, Computing, Macworld, Parents and Computers UK, PC Advisor, PC Home, PSX Pro, The WEB; **UNITED STATES:** Cable in the Classroom, CIO Magazine, Computerworld, DOS World, Federal Computer Week, GamePro Magazine, InfoWorld, I-Way, Macworld, Network World, PC Games, PC World, Publish, Video Event, THE WEB Magazine, and WebMaster; online webzines: JavaWorld, NetscapeWorld, and SunWorld Online; **URUGUAY:** InfoWorld Uruguay; **VENEZUELA:** Computerworld Venezuela, PC World Venezuela; and **VIETNAM:** PC World Vietnam. 2/14/97

Welcome to the Discover Series

Do you want to discover the best and most efficient ways to use your computer and learn about technology? Books in the Discover series teach you the essentials of technology with a friendly, confident approach. You'll find a Discover book on almost any subject — from the Internet to intranets, from Web design and programming to the business programs that make your life easier.

We've provided valuable, real-world examples that help you relate to topics faster. Discover books begin by introducing you to the main features of programs, so you start by doing something *immediately*. The focus is to teach you how to perform tasks that are useful and meaningful in your day-to-day work. You might create a document or graphic, explore your computer, surf the Web, or write a program. Whatever the task, you learn the most commonly used features, and focus on the best tips and techniques for doing your work. You'll get results quickly, and discover the best ways to use software and technology in your everyday life.

You may find the following elements and features in this book:

Discovery Central: This tearout card is a handy quick reference to important tasks or ideas covered in the book.

Quick Tour: The Quick Tour gets you started working with the book right away.

Real-Life Vignettes: Throughout the book you'll see one-page scenarios illustrating a real-life application of a topic covered.

Goals: Each chapter opens with a list of goals you can achieve by reading the chapter.

Side Trips: These asides include additional information about alternative or advanced ways to approach the topic covered.

Bonuses: Timesaving tips and more advanced techniques are covered in each chapter.

Discovery Center: This guide illustrates key procedures covered throughout the book.

Visual Index: You'll find real-world documents in the Visual Index, with page numbers pointing you to where you should turn to achieve the effects shown.

Throughout the book, you'll also notice some special icons and formatting:

FEATURE FOCUS A Feature Focus icon highlights new features in the software's latest release, and points out significant differences between it and the previous version.

WEB PATH Web Paths refer you to Web sites that provide additional information about the topic.

TIP Tips offer timesaving shortcuts, expert advice, quick techniques, or brief reminders.

X-REF The X-Ref icon refers you to other chapters or sections for more information.

Pull Quotes emphasize important ideas that are covered in the chapter.

NOTE Notes provide additional information or highlight special points of interest about a topic.

CAUTION The Caution icon alerts you to potential problems you should watch out for.

The Discover series delivers interesting, insightful, and inspiring information about technology to help you learn faster and retain more. So the next time you want to find answers to your technology questions, reach for a Discover book. We hope the entertaining, easy-to-read style puts you at ease and makes learning fun.

Credits

ACQUISITIONS EDITOR
Ellen Camm

DEVELOPMENT EDITOR
Barbra Guerra

SENIOR COPY EDITOR
Barry Childs-Helton

COPY EDITORS
Tracy Brown
Robert Campbell
Katharine Dvorak
John Edwards
Nate Holdread

PROJECT EDITOR
John Pont

TECHNICAL EDITOR
Rebecca Halbasch

PRODUCTION COORDINATOR
Katy German

GRAPHICS AND PRODUCTION SPECIALISTS
Mario F. Amador
Vincent F. Burns
Renée Dunn
Ritchie Durdin
Ed Penslien
Christopher Pimentel
Dina F Quan
Mark Schumann
Elsie Yim

QUALITY CONTROL SPECIALIST
Mick Arellano

PROOFREADERS
Desne Border
Andrew Davis
Stacey Lynn
Candace Ward
Anne Weinberger

INDEXER
David Heiret

BOOK DESIGN
Seventeenth Street Studios
Phyllis Beaty
Kurt Krames

About the Authors

John R. Nicholson is a veteran computer user who has written several computer books about using PageMaker and Paradox. His work in the computer field also includes writing hardware and software reviews for a weekly computer magazine. Mr. Nicholson currently is an instructor in the Office Systems Technology program at Johnson County Community College in Kansas, where he was the 1995 Publication Award winner

Sean R. Nicholson owns New Horizon Hardware Consulting, which specializes in hardware upgrade and repair. He has published newsletters and written articles in the Branson Business Journal.

THIS BOOK IS DEDICATED TO OUR WIVES, PAMELA AND DEBORAH. THEY HAVE BEEN VERY PATIENT AS WE WORKED THROUGH DEVELOPING THIS BOOK FOR A NEW SERIES. IT IS ALSO DEDICATED TO: BECKY, ROB, MATT, MOLLY, JESSICA, KRISTOPHER, AND ASHLEY; BILL AND ELAINE; EILEEN, RICK, AND RYAN; PHIL AND GAYLE; PETE AND HELEN; AND VARIOUS OTHER MEMBERS OF OUR EXTENDED FAMILY, PARTICULARLY (IN ALPHABETICAL ORDER) DAVE, GAVIN, HELEN, RYAN, AND STEVE. JOHN EXTENDS SPECIAL THANKS TO GLENNA STITES FOR STARTING HIM ON HIS CURRENT ROAD TO INFAMY.

PREFACE

If you hate reading the sections at the beginnings of books as much as we do, you need to have an incentive to actually read the next few pages. Okay, here's the incentive: If you'll read this section, we *guarantee* to teach you the secret of how you can make a small fortune in the stock market. We are making the effort to write this preface; the least you can do is read it. (By the way, the secret's not at the end, it's hidden elsewhere.) So take a few minutes and learn how this book is constructed (beyond the paper and ink).

Discover Excel 97 is part of a new series of books from IDG Books Worldwide. The first question that comes to mind is, "Why do we need yet another series?" In case you don't realize it, IDG Books has several other series that include Excel books such as *Excel For Dummies, Dummies 101: Excel, Excel Bible*, and *Excel SECRETS*.

If you try to place the *Discover* series somewhere in that chain of series, it would probably fall close to the *...For Dummies* books. With the books in the *Discover* series, you get a different level of coverage of many features and lots of hands-on work. These books cover everyday computing tasks, and present them in a simple manner that focuses on giving you the building blocks with which you can meet your own computing needs.

Discover Excel 97 is written in a user-friendly manner (something you often hear about, but seldom see). You will find this book includes not only tips, warnings, and hands-on activities, but also humor. As is the case with most humor, you might not like all of it (but it got past the editors, so there must be at least a few funny things in the book).

Why Buy This Book?

If what you really need is a quick look at how Excel 97 can help meet your needs, and you don't want to wade through stacks of technical jargon, this is the book for you. Although an introductory level book, the topics it covers range from the basics of starting Excel through some very advanced features. Half of the problem when learning a program such as Excel is in understanding how its features can be used to quickly increase your productivity — and that is the focus of this book.

There is, of course, another reason to buy this book (no, not so that we can make more money, although that sure sounds like a good idea). You can get a complete overview of an extremely powerful and complex program. This book divides Excel into byte-sized (see, we told you there were bad jokes in here) slices of information that you can immediately put to use in your quest to become an Excel expert.

Assumptions

Everyone knows not to make assumptions, but in this case, some are required to keep this book under 1,000 pages. We assume that you understand the basics of working with Windows 95. If you don't, pick up a copy of *Windows 95 For Dummies* (Andy Rathbone, IDG Books).

We also assume that you don't know much, if anything at all, about Excel, and that you are ready to learn. We hope these assumptions are fairly accurate, although you may already be an Excel user who wants to learn about more of the available features in Excel, particularly those new to Excel 97.

The only way to learn Excel is by using it. You can have dozens of books sitting on your shelves, but unless you actually use the information in them, they are worthless to you. So as you work through this book, make sure that you are at your computer, so that you can read a little, and then see the feature in action.

Throughout the hands-on activities, you see steps listed in this format:

1. Type **42** and press Enter.

The characters in bold — in this case, the number **42** — should be entered exactly as shown. The preceding example tells you to enter the number 42 and then press the Enter key on the keyboard.

Choosing menu items

The following example shows how the hands-on activities instruct you to choose a menu item using the mouse:

1. Choose File → Save .

This means to point the mouse cursor at the File menu, click the mouse button, and then click the Save option. The terms *point* and *click* are further explained in the Test Drive.

Quick keys

You will also find quick-key references, such as Ctrl+S. This means to press and hold the Ctrl key on the keyboard, while you type the letter *S*. Quick keys are sometimes referred to as shortcut keys.

How Is This Book Organized?

This book is divided into five parts. The chapters in each part give you hands-on experience with related Excel features. By the way, the answer to the question "How do I make a small fortune in the stock market?" is an old, but often true saying, "Start with a large fortune."

Part I: Excel Basics

Before beginning the first chapter, you are given the opportunity to take a test drive of Excel. In the test drive, you see a few of the time-saving features that are explained in later chapters.

In Chapter 1, starting the Excel program is reviewed. Various parts of the Excel screen display are identified and explained. You learn to select menu commands and use the various toolbars. Saving your work for the first time and saving it after it is named is also covered. Brand new to Excel 97 is the Office Assistant, a fun help feature. The Office Assistant, as well as traditional methods of getting help are discussed. You learn to customize the Office Assistant in the Bonus Section of this chapter.

To know how you can use a program to increase your productivity, you need to have some idea of what the program is capable of doing. In Chapter 2, a sampling of tasks is offered. Data types are discussed. You are introduced to working with text, numbers, formulas, and functions. The Bonus Section offers a Baker's Dozen design questions to aid you in designing a good worksheet.

Chapter 3 shows you how to manage and protect your data on worksheets, in workbooks, and in briefcases. You learn to add, delete, rename, group, copy, and move worksheets. This chapter also discusses potential disasters and offers insight on how to avoid them (and how to recover from them if they happen). Briefcases are used to keep files up to date when sharing files with others or moving files between a laptop and a desktop computer. You learn how to protect your workbooks so that others can't make unauthorized changes. In the Bonus Section, you learn how to automatically save your workbook on a regular basis.

In Chapter 4, you look at how to format your worksheet data. Formatting cells, rows, and columns is discussed. In the Bonus Section, you see how to use Excel's automatic formatting features to easily and quickly format your worksheets with predeveloped formats.

Part II: Manipulating and Displaying Data

The second part of the book gives you some ideas for different ways to display and manipulate your data. You learn a number of shortcuts, as well as how to create charts.

The purpose of having a computer is to increase your productivity. In Chapter 5, you learn many shortcuts for entering data. Cutting, copying, and pasting data are introduced. You are shown how to limit the data input range, resulting in faster data entry. Microsoft's IntelliSense™ features, such as AutoCalculate, AutoComplete, AutoFill, and AutoSum, are introduced, as well as several other methods for saving time. You learn how to freeze parts of your worksheet on the screen, so when you scroll to another area of the worksheet, you can still see the row and column titles. The Bonus Section teaches you to customize the AutoFill option.

Chapter 6 shows you how to label your data and enter values in the worksheet. This chapter also provides an overview of working with formulas and functions. Function syntax is explained. In the Bonus Section, you learn to build more complex formulas.

In "Pretty Pictures: Creating Cool Charts," the final chapter of Part II, you begin by learning to use the Chart Wizard. A discussion of chart types guides you through choosing the best chart type for your needs. You also learn to edit and format the charts you create. In the Bonus Section, you learn to add graphics as indicators of data values in your charts.

Part III: Input and Output

In the third part of the book, input and output are examined. Input is important because the wrong input results in the wrong output. The output is important in ensuring that your viewers understand the information you are presenting to them.

Chapter 8 offers an overview of converting files from other spreadsheet programs. You learn the most common formats of data and how Excel uses the various formats. The chapter also introduces you to copying information from Word to Excel and from Excel to Word. The Bonus Section introduces you to the File Conversion Wizard.

In many cases, you need to print a copy of your worksheet. Before you can print a worksheet, however, you need to set up the specifications that Excel uses when printing your worksheet. In Chapter 9, you begin by creating a large, multiple-page worksheet. You then learn to set page specifications, margins, headers and footers, and other printing specifications. The Bonus Section shows you how to create permanent headers and footers for all future workbooks you create.

Chapter 10 covers the actual printing of the worksheets. You learn to use the Print dialog box to preview your work before sending it to the printer, to select a print area, to print nonconsecutive areas, and to create custom views. The Bonus Section in this chapter teaches you how to create and print worksheet ranges.

Unfortunately, Excel does what you tell it to do, not what you want it to do. In Chapter 11, you learn that numbers do lie. The order of operations within formulas and functions is reviewed. You learn how to avoid problems by using the Auditing toolbar. The three dangerous spreadsheet assumptions are explained.

You learn to sample your data to check for errors. In the Bonus Section, you learn to set data validation specifications, to help decrease the number of errors in your worksheet.

The final chapter of this part, Chapter 12, teaches you how to work with more than one worksheet at a time. You learn to evaluate users' needs for multiple worksheets, to copy and move worksheets, to insert and delete them, and to create a summary sheet. Grouped worksheets are discussed. These are used to save data entry time, and increase the accuracy of data entry. Linking worksheets is presented, and you learn to save your entire workspace (including all open workbooks) as a single file. In the Bonus Section, you learn to link workbooks, so that information for the current worksheet can be automatically retrieved from other workbooks.

Part IV: Enhancing Your Skills

Now that you understand the basics of Excel, you can explore even more creative ways to enhance your productivity. In Part IV of the book, you learn to create macros, use a database list, and create group projects.

Chapter 13 covers the three major time-savers in Excel: macros, templates, and styles. You learn what a macro is, how to record and play one, and how to edit and delete existing macros. Templates — worksheets that already contain formatting, formulas, functions, and text — are discussed. Templates offer you a place to begin, rather than having to create all of your workbooks from scratch. You learn to customize templates and save the changes for future use. The methods used for creating, assigning, modifying, and deleting styles are also presented. In the Bonus Section, you learn to add macros to both toolbars and menus.

Using Excel as a database is covered in Chapter 14. You learn what databases can do, and both the advantages and the limitations of using Excel as a database. This chapter covers inputting data using data entry forms, sorting the information, and selecting information based on specified criteria. The Bonus Section shows you how to sort your Excel workbook files.

Chapter 15 is all about working with other people. You learn to limit access to your files, to share files with others, and to track the changes that each person makes. You also learn how to accept and reject the changes that have been suggested by others. In the Bonus Section, you create personal views and print options for each user.

Part V: Real-Life Solutions

The final part of the book looks at some real-life solutions to problems or questions you may encounter on a day-to-day basis. Many of Excel's advanced features are presented in this part.

The major new feature of Excel 97 is its capability to create hyperlinks. In Chapter 16, you learn to move quickly between cells and ranges within the current worksheet or workbook, navigate among workbooks, and even how to use hyperlinks to access Internet data. You learn to create queries that retrieve information from the Internet and place it directly into your worksheets. In the Bonus Section, you learn to save your file as an HTML document, the common format for files stored on Internet sites.

Chapter 17 teaches you the basics of troubleshooting your worksheet and workbooks. You learn to use the Excel's validation tools, and to fix common error messages that you might see. In the Bonus Section, you learn to use the Microsoft Troubleshooters.

Appendix and Other Goodies

The appendix offers help on installing Excel. The Discovery Central card lists many shortcuts that you can use as an easy reference. This book is also thoroughly cross-referenced in the Index.

What's Next?

Where do you go from here? As Dorothy is told when beginning her trip in Oz, the best place to start is at the beginning, Our advice to you is the same. Sit down at your computer; get a cup of coffee, a soft drink, or some other libation (making sure you don't get it too near your computer) and take the Test Drive. From there, work through the chapters in sequence, or go to specific chapters that cover the help you need. Because each chapter's activities are independent of other chapters, you can start anywhere you want.

If you have any comments or questions about this book, you can reach us at:

John: jnichols@compuserve.com

jnichols@johnco.cc.ks.us

Wryterjccc@aol.com

Sean: newhorizon@compuserve.com

We would love to hear from you, especially if this book was helpful to you. If you have any complaints or suggestions for the next edition, please send them along, too. Let us know how you use Excel to increase your productivity, or how it is used in your organization. Now, sit back and enjoy the opportunity to *Discover Excel 97*.

Acknowledgments

Extra special thanks to Pamela Nicholson, who did the rough draft editing on everything we wrote (she has a really *nasty* red pen!), and to Becky Halbasch, the technical editor for the manuscript, who worked until all hours of the night so that we could get the project completed.

Special thanks and gratitude to our project editor, John Pont, who worked diligently and with a sense of humor in the completion of this project; also to Ellen Camm, Acquisitions Editor at IDG Books, who gave us the opportunity to work with IDG. Also at IDG Books, thanks to Greg Croy and Barb Guerra for their involvement with this series.

Thanks to John's agent, David Fugate at Waterside Productions for keeping things rolling, and to Maureen, who keeps the finances going.

CONTENTS AT A GLANCE

CONTENTS

6 NEW MATH: USING LABELS, VALUES, FORMULAS, AND FUNCTIONS, 137

7 PRETTY PICTURES: CREATING COOL CHARTS, 163

EXCEL 97 QUICK TOUR

W hen you want to get a feel for a new car, you take a test drive. I can't buy you a new car, but I'll be happy to take you for a quick tour of Excel. You don't have to do much except follow the directions, and I'll keep them simple. No technical jargon, just simple English. So for now, don't worry about RAM cram, disk drive average seek time, or screen refresh rate. (Oops, sorry about that. But if I accidentally use a term you don't know, look it up in the glossary at the end of the book.)

First Things First

I t helps if you have a computer, so you can follow along. Ideally, the computer should be plugged in and turned on. It also makes things simpler if you have Windows and Excel installed. If not, now is a good time to do all these things.

One of the first lessons to learn is that Excel often gives you a half-dozen ways to perform a task. In this Quick Tour, I take you through the most common steps, but later in the book I teach you some tricks that will really impress your boss.

Mousing Around

A quick overview of using a mouse is necessary at this point. Your mouse may have two or three buttons. Generally, the left mouse button is the primary button. If your mouse has three buttons, you use only the left and right ones for the activities in this book. (Your mouse may be programmed to perform a specific command when you click the center button, but that's a function of the mouse, not of Excel.)

The mouse should be resting on a mouse pad to the right of your keyboard and should be positioned parallel to the edge of the keyboard. Sliding the mouse up (moving it without pressing any buttons) results in the mouse cursor on the screen moving up. Sliding the mouse back toward you moves the cursor down. The shape of the cursor depends on the task being performed. Some of the shapes you see include an arrow; a hollow, thick plus sign; a cross-hairs; and a vertical line with horizontal arrows through it.

You need to know some terms in order to follow the instructions in this book (this should be just a review):

- **Point:** Move the cursor (by using the mouse) directly onto an object or the center of a cell.
- **Slide:** Move the mouse without pressing any buttons.
- **Click:** Press and release the main mouse button (normally the left one).
- **Double-click:** Quickly press and release the main mouse button twice. It is critical that you do not move the mouse while double-clicking. If a double-click doesn't work, try it again. It may take some practice, but you must master this skill to work with Excel.
- **Drag:** Position the cursor over the specified object, press *and hold* the main mouse button, and drag the mouse cursor to the new position. Release the mouse button. This generally results in a group of cells being highlighted or selected. In some cases, this action may move the selected object.

NOTE Most mouse clicking is done with the main mouse button. Always click the main mouse button (usually the left) unless I specifically tell you to right-click. (For lefties, if you have changed the Windows setup, the main mouse button is the *right* one.)

A NOTE FOR SOUTHPAWS:

If you are left-handed, you can place the mouse to the left of the keyboard, and you can change your setup so that the right-hand button becomes the primary button. The method you use to switch the main mouse button to the right button (instead of the left) depends on the mouse software you have installed. Generally you follow these steps:

1. Click the Windows 95 Start button.

2. Slide the mouse up to ⌐Settings⌐, and then right to highlight ⌐Control Panel⌐. Click ⌐Control Panel⌐. Windows opens the Control Panel dialog box.

3. Double-click the Mouse icon. The Mouse Properties dialog box opens.

4. In the Mouse Properties dialog box, look through the various tabs until you see the option for switching mouse buttons and then choose this option.

5. At the Mouse Properties dialog box, click the upper-right button (it contains an X). This is the Close button; it closes the dialog box.

6. At the Control Panel dialog box, click the upper-right button (it contains an X). This is the Close button; it closes the dialog box.

Starting Excel

f you are test driving a car, a key is helpful to get it started. In Windows, you don't need a key. To begin your journey, you simply click the Start button.

1. Move the mouse cursor (it looks like an arrow) onto the Start button in the bottom-left corner of the screen and click the primary button on the mouse.

   If the taskbar — the area in the Windows 95 screen that contains the Start button — isn't visible, someone has been playing with your computer. In this case, simply move the mouse cursor into the bottom of the screen and the task bar appears.

2. Slide the mouse pointer toward the top of the screen until ⌐Programs⌐ is highlighted. A list of programs is displayed.

3. Slide the mouse to the right and up or down until ⌐Microsoft Excel⌐ is highlighted, as shown in Figure 1.

4. Click once to open Excel.

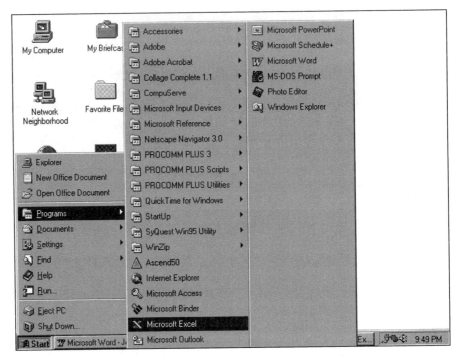

Figure 1 The Start button is one method used for starting Excel.

Excel is now open. Your screen should look similar to the one shown in Figure 2. (If it doesn't, someone may have already changed the screen to fit their needs.) Notice the group of six buttons in the upper-right corner of the screen. By clicking these buttons, you minimize and maximize the screen and close the Excel window. If either of the center buttons contains a single box rather than two boxes, click once on the button. Both center buttons should have two boxes displayed, and Excel should take up all of your screen (unless the task bar is showing, which you can ignore for now). Excel is now up and running, and you are ready to embark on your journey of discovery.

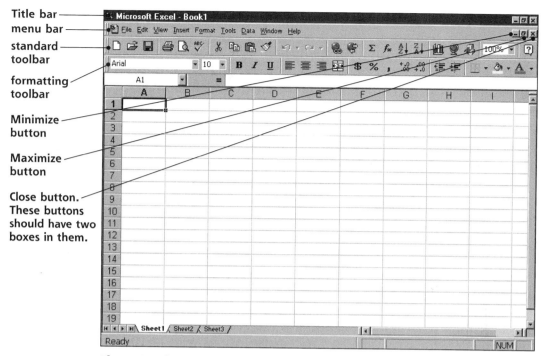

Title bar
menu bar
standard toolbar
formatting toolbar
Minimize button
Maximize button
Close button. These buttons should have two boxes in them.

Figure 2   The maximize buttons should contain two boxes.

A Few Words about Words

As much as it pains me (and probably you), you must become familiar with a few terms before you can continue to work in Excel. You need the following definitions to be able to complete the next activity:

* **Workbook:** The Excel file. It may contain multiple worksheets.

* **Worksheet:** The area in Excel consisting of many rectangular boxes (cells). By default, each new workbook contains three worksheets. You can change this number.

* **Cell:** One of the many rectangular boxes visible in a worksheet.

* **Row:** A horizontal group of cells. Each row is identified by a number.

* **Column:** A vertical group of cells. Each column is identified by a letter or letters.

* **Cell address:** A means for identifying a particular cell by the column letter and the row number. For example, the cell in the upper-left corner of the worksheet is A1. Excel displays the cell address of the active (highlighted) cell in the Name Box above column A.

✳ **Worksheet name:** The name of each worksheet, shown in the tab at the bottom of the sheet. By default, Excel names sheets as Sheet1, Sheet2, and so on.

Figure 3 shows the different parts of the screen. You can enter a variety of things in the cells that make up your worksheets: numbers, text, mathematical formulas, logos, and even pictures.

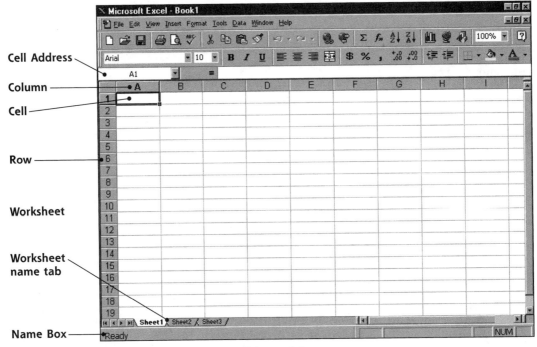

Figure 3 Important parts of the worksheet.

Getting a Move on

To enter data in a particular cell, you must make that cell active. To make a cell active (so that whatever you type goes in that cell), point to the cell with the mouse cursor and click once. As you learn later in this book, Excel offers many other ways to move around your worksheet.

TIP Windows 95 and Excel often provide several methods for performing a particular task. Rather than try to memorize all the different ways you can perform a task, try a few, find out which ones are easiest for you, and rely on them.

Now you can start to build your first workbook. It will be a simple one, requiring only a few explanations, but at least you can get an idea of what Excel is about.

Entering data

A1 is the *active cell*. You can tell because a heavy black line surrounds the cell and a tiny square box appears in the lower-right corner of the cell.

1. Make B1 the active cell by pointing with the cursor into the center of the cell and left-clicking.

   You can identify the active cell by looking directly above the A column heading. *B1* is displayed in the Name Box.

2. Type **Monday** in B1. *Do not press <Enter>.*

   You are going to have Excel automatically enter the days of the week across cells B1 through F1. In the lower-right corner of B1, you see a tiny box. This is called the AutoFill handle.

3. Move the cursor directly onto the AutoFill handle. The cursor changes to a cross-hairs.

4. Press *and hold* the main mouse button and drag to the right.

   As you move the cursor into cell C1, a small box appears displaying *Tuesday*. Continue to drag to the right until the cursor is in F1. Release the mouse button. Excel automatically enters the days for you, as shown in Figure 4. Excel has many shortcut features such as this.

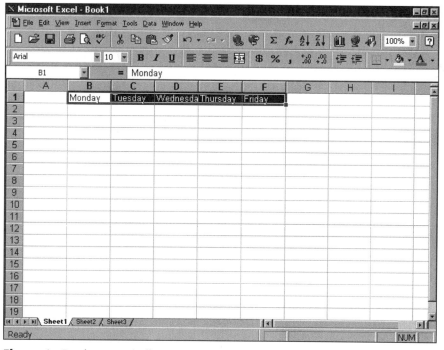

Figure 4 Excel automatically generates the days of the week.

Formatting data automatically

Another of Excel's time-saving features is the capability to automatically format data to best suit your needs. Notice that *Wednesday* in D1 doesn't quite fit. Also, when you enter numbers, they may not be in the desired format. In the following activity, you get a feel for a few of the ways in which Excel can format data for you.

1. Move the mouse cursor over the vertical line just to the right of D in the column heading.

    The cursor changes to a vertical line with horizontal arrows.

2. Double-click the mouse.

    The cell expands to accommodate the extra space needed by the word. If it didn't expand, that means that you either didn't click twice fast enough, or you moved the mouse while you were double-clicking. Try it again until the cell expands.

3. Click in A2, type **North**, and press <Enter>.

    The active cell automatically becomes A3. Pressing <Enter> is another way to move to a different cell.

4. Type **South** and press <Enter>.

5. Type **East** and press <Enter>.

6. Type **West** and press <Enter>.

7. Type **Daily Store Total** and press <Enter>.

    Notice that Daily Store Total doesn't fit into column A.

8. Move the cursor up to the right edge of the column A heading (the cursor again changes to a vertical line with double horizontal arrows) and then double-click to automatically adjust the width of the column.

9. Click in G1, type **Weekly Total**, and press <Enter>.

10. Adjust the column width so that the text fits in the cell. Your worksheet should now look like Figure 5.

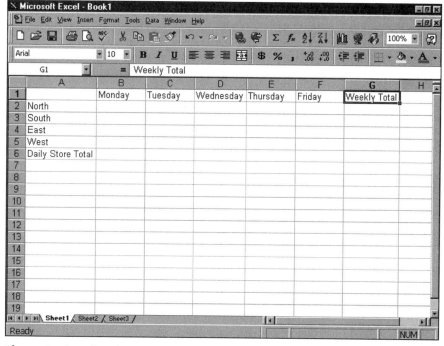

Figure 5 Store locations are typed into column A and a Weekly Total is added.

11. Enter the data shown in Table 1.

These are the daily sales for each store. Just type the numbers and periods. Do not add any commas or dollar signs. Excel doesn't display trailing zeros — for example, in Wednesday's sales amount for the North store — even though you enter them. You tell Excel to properly format the cells in the next step. Notice that I'm only having you format columns A through F. You format column G a little later in this Quick Tour (don't get impatient; you'll get to it).

TABLE 1 Daily Sales by Store

	Monday	Tuesday	Wednesday	Thursday	Friday
NORTH	1235.45	940.88	1173.50	1488.00	1360.92
SOUTH	1699.36	1822.57	1477.69	1966.37	1688.64
EAST	945.61	810.25	1042.63	1288.39	1028.94
WEST	547.36	859.73	772.98	974.56	899.37

12. Point to the center of B2, click and drag the mouse down and right until all the cells through F6 are highlighted.

    Remember, you must press and hold the main mouse button while you drag. As you drag the mouse, each of the cells is automatically highlighted (with the exception of B2). Don't worry about why B2 doesn't appear to be highlighted (I'll tell you that secret later). Just realize that as far as Excel is concerned, the entire block of cells from B2 through F6 is highlighted (or *selected*).

13. Move the cursor onto the button with the dollar sign.

    It is located on the formatting toolbar (the second line below the menu bar). A small box appears, indicating that this button selects *Currency Style*. The little box that appears when you move the cursor over a button is called a *tool tip*.

14. Click the Currency Style button to automatically format all of the highlighted data.

It is certainly a lot easier to format your numbers this way than to try to manually format each individual entry.

Automatically calculating totals

Another of Excel's spiffy (a highly technical term, which is actually beyond the scope of this book, but I wanted to impress you with my command of the English language) features is the capability to automatically calculate totals in a column or row. You don't even need to highlight the column or row that you want totaled. Excel guesses what you want, and usually guesses right. In the following activity, you get some hands-on experience using the AutoSum feature.

1. Click B6. The standard toolbar — that is, the first toolbar below the menu bar — contains an AutoSum button Σ .When you point at it, the tool tip displays *AutoSum*.

2. Click the AutoSum button.

    Excel assumes you want to total the column directly above the active cell. A moving box (sometimes called *marching ants*) surrounds the cells that Excel thinks you want totaled (B2 through B5). Excel inserts a formula, =SUM(B2:B5), into B6.

3. Because this is exactly what you want, press <Enter>. The total is displayed.

4. Click B6. Again, you see the small box in the lower-right corner of the cell (the AutoFill handle).

5. Drag it across until you reach F6 and then release the mouse button. Each column total is automatically generated.

6. Click G2. You still need to calculate the weekly total for each store.

7. Click the AutoSum button again.

   Because the selected cell is not below a column of information, Excel assumes that you want to total the row.

8. That is correct, so press <Enter>.

   Notice that the cell is automatically formatted, even though you did not include column G in the original currency formatting.

9. Click G2 again.

10. Drag the AutoFill handle down until the cursor is in G6 and then release the mouse button.

11. Click A1 to turn off the selection.

    As you can see in G6, the store sales for the current week totaled $24,023.20. Your worksheet should look like Figure 6. If your total is not the same, check each cell to see where you made your error.

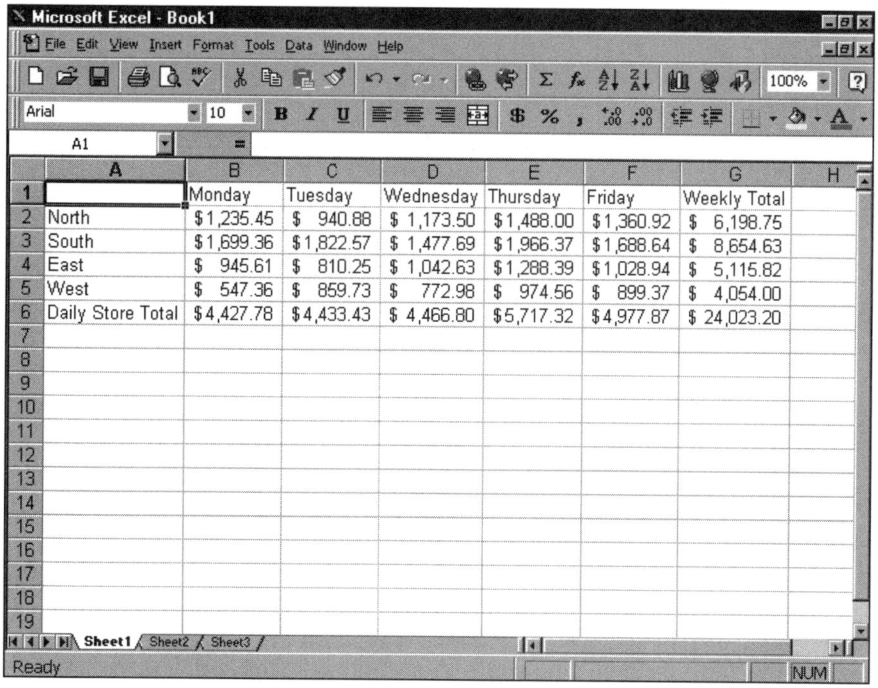

Figure 6 The completed worksheet.

TIP Notice that I assume *you* made a mistake, not the computer. The computer always does what *you tell it* to do — not what you *want* it to do. When you find the cell with the error, click it to make it the active cell, type the correct value, and press <Enter>. Excel automatically updates the totals.

12. Click C2, type **840.88**, and press <Enter>.

The new total, automatically calculated and displayed in G6, is $23,923.20. Doesn't this beat a hand-held calculator?

Saving your work

I assume you already understand the basics of working with Windows 95. (If not, you might want to begin with *Windows 95 for Dummies* from IDG Books Worldwide.) You should realize that until you save your data to a storage device (a floppy disk, a hard disk, or another source of permanent storage), your data remains in RAM (random access memory). When you turn off the computer, all of the data in RAM evaporates into thin air. (This feature is totally pollution free.) If you haven't saved your workbook (Excel's term for the file you created), you have to start all over again.

SIDE TRIP

In real estate, the three most important features are "location, location, and location." In computers, the three most important things to remember are, "save, save, and save." You can't save your work too often. Remember, you are only being paranoid if *they* aren't out to get you. If they *are* out to get you, you're being perceptive. You're not being paranoid about losing your data. Eventually, something bad will happen (like your spouse turns off the light switch that controls the socket your computer is plugged into). At that point, your choices are to retrieve the data that you have saved or to scream loudly and start all over again.

You need to save your work to a disk. By default, Excel saves your files in a folder called My Documents, located on the hard disk. However, you can create a new folder specifically for saving related files. In this next activity, you create a new folder specifically designed for the files (workbooks) you create throughout this book.

TIP From within Excel, a new folder can only be created from the Save As dialog box.

1. Choose File → Save As .

   As shown in Figure 7, Excel displays the Save As dialog box. The example shows three folders: Becky, JCCC, and JRN. The names of your folders, if any, will differ from those shown in the figure.

The Create New Folder button

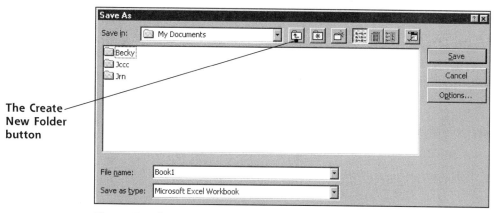

Figure 7 The Save As dialog box.

2. Click the Create New Folder button.

   (It looks like a file folder with a star *behind* it. When you point to the correct button, the tool tip displays *Create New Folder*.) Excel displays the New Folder dialog box. The text in the Name text box is already highlighted. *All* highlighted text is automatically deleted when you press any key.

3. Type **Discover Excel** and press Enter.

   The Save As dialog box is again displayed.

4. Double-click the Discover Excel folder.

   Discover Excel appears in the Save in text box.

5. Double-click in the File name text box.

   Book1 (the default workbook name) is highlighted.

6. Type **Exercise 1-1** and click Save.

   The workbook is again displayed. The Program Title Bar at the top of the screen now reflects the name of the new workbook: Exercise 1-1. The saved workbook with the completed worksheet is shown in Figure 8.

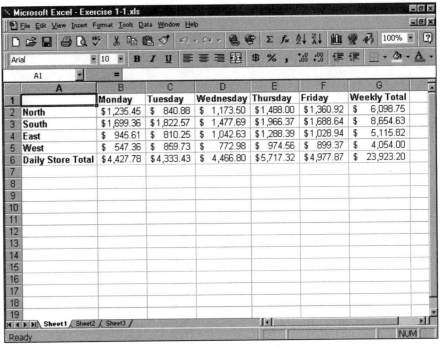

Figure 8 The completed worksheet, Exercise 1-1.

Printing your work

Several years ago, *those who know* (whoever that might be) proclaimed that computers would usher in the era of the paperless office. Other than the agent who refused to represent the Beatles because they were untalented, few predictions have proved to be so wrong. Once you have gone to the trouble of creating and saving your information, you probably want to get a hard copy (a printed copy) of it. Printing in Excel can range from the extremely simple, as in this next activity, to quite complex (as explained in the chapter about printing).

TIP **If you are sending your worksheet to a printer that is shared by several people, enter your name in A8.**

You may need to print your worksheet multiple times before it looks exactly like you want. (Excel has a print preview mode, discussed later, but while most users find it to be a very helpful feature, they still want to see how the final draft looks when it's printed.) Here's how you print the worksheet you've created in this Quick Tour.

1. Click the Print button (the fourth button on the standard toolbar).

It looks like a printer. (The standard toolbar is the one immediately below the menu bar.)

Always save your workbook prior to sending it to the printer. There is always a possibility that something will go wrong at the printer, so don't take a chance.

2. Retrieve your printed worksheet from the printer.

   (This instruction wasn't really necessary, but each activity must have a minimum of two steps. The problem is, printing a single copy of the worksheet is so simple it only requires a single step.)

Parking Excel (parallel parking not required)

Now that you have test-driven Excel, you need to put it "in the garage" (unless you plan to continue working through the following chapters in this book). When you close Excel, if you have changed your workbook since the last time you saved it, you are prompted to save the changes; otherwise, Excel simply closes.

Always close Excel, Windows 95, and any other open programs before turning off your computer. Otherwise, bad things could happen. (There is a popular book titled, *Why Bad Things Happen to Good Computers.* This explains the bad things, so I won't take up the room here.)

Excel can be exited in many ways. This activity shows you one way to exit.

1. Click the Excel program close button (in the top-right corner of the screen; an X marks the close button).

2. If you are prompted to save your work, do so. Excel is automatically closed.

Exiting Windows

Because I warned you to close Windows before putting your computer to bed for the night, you might want to know just how to do it. (Close Windows, not put your computer to bed.) As I said earlier, I expect that you know Windows 95 already, but a little extra instruction never hurts.

1. Click the Start button (in the lower-left corner of the Windows 95 screen).

   (Yes, that's right. In order to shut down the computer, you click the Start button. Don't ask me, I'm only the messenger.)

2. Choose Shut Down.

3. Click <Yes> in the Shut Down Windows dialog box, to shut down Windows 95. Windows 95 tells you when it is safe to turn off the power to your computer.

TIP If Windows doesn't tell you it's safe to turn off your computer after about three hours, go ahead and shut it off anyway. (Just kidding — if it doesn't shut down in a couple of minutes, something has happened, but it's probably nothing to worry about. Just turn the computer off.)

Summary

This concludes your Quick Tour of Excel. Now we can discuss financing. (Sorry, I got carried away with the new car analogy.) I hope it was a smooth ride. You may have hit a few potholes along the way, but I hope you found that Excel is easy to use. In the following chapters, you have plenty of opportunities to get additional hands-on experience with Excel. So, enjoy your new reputation as an Excel guru. Your knowledge will grow with each completed chapter.

PART ONE

EXCEL BASICS

THIS PART CONTAINS THE FOLLOWING CHAPTERS

Whether you are learning to play football, knit, play chess, or even drive a car, you must first understand the basics. In the first part of this book, you develop an understanding of the basic skills needed to use Excel 97. You learn how to start Excel, you become acquainted with the various parts of the Excel screen, and you explore Excel's help features, including the new Office Assistant (which can be anything from an animated paper clip to William Shakespeare). The Office Assistant watches how you work and offers tips based on your work habits. You can also ask it questions.

You are introduced to the different types of data used by Excel, and you find out how to work with text, numbers, formulas, and functions. This part of the book also covers management of your worksheets and workbooks. You discover numerous shortcuts for entering data, as well as methods for avoiding disasters (and recovering from the ones you can't avoid). Finally, you learn how to format your worksheets so that they display information in a pleasing and understandable manner.

Once you have mastered the basics of working with Excel, you can move on to other, more advanced features. By developing the basic skills described in Part I, you gain a solid base for exploring Excel's more advanced features.

In the late seventies, Excel for Windows was nowhere to be found. Back then, even the first, crude incarnation of Windows was almost a decade away. On top of all that, the type of machine that would eventually run Windows — the IBM PC — wasn't even invented yet!

Yet even without these household names, the computer industry was booming. One of the first microcomputers, the Apple II, was making news and slowly gaining popularity due to its ease of use. But when two graduate students wrote a program that took advantage of the Apple II's power, they ended up starting an industry that has been racing at a frenetic pace ever since.

In 1979, Dan Bricklin of Harvard and Bob Frankston of MIT combined their talents to create VisiCalc, the first spreadsheet program for microcomputers. Today, many people credit VisiCalc with being the sole reason that thousands of people bought the Apple II. Before 1979, many Wall Street analysts bought the Apple II, but at the time, there was little software that was useful for them. VisiCalc changed that. With this visual calculator, analysts could plot the performance of hundreds of stocks and analyze the data in seconds. Before VisiCalc, spotting trends took months; suddenly, an analyst with a computer could do it in minutes.

With that, the spreadsheet was born. And boy, would it grow.

When IBM introduced the PC in 1981, a small software company called Lotus was ready with a spreadsheet of its own. Beginning in the early eighties, Lotus 1-2-3 held the undisputed title of number-one spreadsheet for the DOS platform. Meanwhile, Microsoft, the little company whose DOS platform stood ready to command IBM's growing force of PCs, was concentrating on its other talent — creating software for the Macintosh. Microsoft Excel was gaining popularity for its graphical presentation, which fully utilized the Mac's paradigm-shifting look and feel.

On Microsoft's back burner was a new platform — one that would fit on top of DOS and make it graphical, similar to the Macintosh. Counting on big success with Windows, Microsoft programmed its popular Excel software to be compatible with that platform. But Lotus wasn't as quick to embrace Windows, and Excel quickly took off. On that platform, Excel has been the dominant spreadsheet ever since, and it shows no signs of slowing down.

CHAPTER ONE

DIVING IN

IN THIS CHAPTER YOU LEARN THESE KEY SKILLS

STARTING EXCEL   PAGE 20

UNDERSTANDING EXCEL'S SCREEN DISPLAY   PAGE 24

SELECTING MENU COMMANDS   PAGE 29

USING THE TOOLBARS   PAGE 32

SAVING YOUR WORK   PAGE 33

GETTING HELP FROM THE OFFICE ASSISTANT
    PAGE 36

GETTING HELP THE TRADITIONAL WAY   PAGE 39

C ongratulations on deciding to discover Microsoft Excel for Microsoft Office 97. That is quite a mouthful, so from here on, I just refer to the program as *Excel*. (You may also hear people use the term *Excel 8*.) By any name, Excel is the most popular spreadsheet for Windows, and according to informed sources (such as *moi*), it's one of the easiest to use.

You probably came to use Excel in one of five ways:

* You upgraded from a previous version.

* You decided you need a spreadsheet, and because Excel has such a great reputation, you decided to try it.

* You purchased a new computer with Microsoft Office 97 already installed.

* You bought Microsoft Office 97, which includes Excel.

* Your boss told you that you now have Excel on your computer, and you'd better learn to use it.

19

Regardless of the reason, you are in luck. This book is designed to help you quickly understand the basic features of Excel (and even some advanced ones). When you finish with this chapter, you'll have a feeling of what Excel is all about. In this chapter, you find out about the basics of working with Excel. You discover new ways to start the program, work with Excel's menus and toolbars, save files with existing or changed names, and get help by using both the Office Assistant and more traditional means.

If this is your first experience with a spreadsheet, you may feel a little lost at first. Don't worry; feeling a little lost is part of the great adventure of discovery.

Starting Excel

In the Quick Tour, you learned one basic way to start Excel.

The following hands-on activity reviews this method for starting Excel:

1. Click the Windows 95 Start button.

2. Click Programs .

3. Click the Microsoft Excel icon.

After Excel opens, close it by clicking the Close button in the upper-right corner of the screen. (This is the top button that has an X in it.)

As we mentioned in the Test Drive, Windows and Excel often give you more than one way to perform a particular task. The following are several other techniques for starting Excel.

Starting Excel by opening an existing workbook

Windows 95 is *document-centric.* In other words, Windows 95 lets you focus on the documents — for example, your Excel workbooks and your word processing files — instead of the programs that you use to work with those documents. This means that after you create a document and save it, you no longer have to manually open each program that is used to create the document. You can open an existing workbook directly from the Windows 95 desktop, and Windows automatically starts Excel and any other programs that were used to create the workbook.

Follow these steps to open an existing workbook and start Excel automatically:

1. Click the Start button.

2. In the submenu that's displayed, choose Documents .

Windows 95 displays a list of your most recently used documents. Depending on your screen resolution, you may see as many as 15 documents in this list.

TIP **If you open and view a document or a workbook but do not save it, Windows 95 doesn't display that particular document in the list of recently used documents.**

3. Click Exercise 1-1, the file that you created in the Quick Tour. Windows 95 starts Excel and opens the workbook.

4. Choose File → Exit to close Excel.

Starting Excel by using the Microsoft Shortcut bar

Describing the features and the exact location of the Microsoft Shortcut bar is difficult, because you can easily customize the bar and move it to a different location. By default, however, the Shortcut bar looks similar to the example shown in Figure 1-1 and is located in the upper-right portion of the screen.

Your Shortcut bar may be docked (placed) in the upper-right portion of the main Windows screen, or it may run vertically along the right side of the window. It may have fewer or more buttons than the example shown in Figure 1-1. For example, the vertical Shortcut bar in Figure 1-2 has buttons added for Word, Excel, PowerPoint, and Access. Clicking any one of these added buttons opens the corresponding program with a blank document, workbook, presentation, or table, respectively. In short, I don't have a clue as to how your particular Shortcut bar has been set up, but the one that's shown in Figure 1-1 should give you a good idea of what it may look like.

Figure 1-1 The default Microsoft Shortcut bar.

Figure 1-2 The Microsoft Shortcut bar with buttons added for opening other Office programs.

Starting Excel by using a workbook shortcut

If you regularly use a particular workbook, you can create a shortcut to that workbook, place the shortcut on your desktop, and use it to start Excel. One way to create a shortcut is by using Windows Explorer.

This activity shows you how to create a shortcut icon representing an Excel workbook and then place it on your desktop.

Follow these steps:

1. Click the Start button.

2. Highlight Programs .

3. Click Windows Explorer . As shown in Figure 1-3, Windows displays the Explorer program.

4. In the left window of the Explorer, double-click the My Documents folder (or whatever Excel is using for the default data folder).

Figure 1-3 The Windows Explorer program.

5. Double-click the Discover Excel folder that you created in the Test Drive. (If you are already in the Discover Excel folder, just ignore this instruction.) The Excel workbook that you created in the Quick Tour appears in the right window.

6. Right-click the workbook name, Exercise 1-1, and choose **Copy** from the pop-up menu that's displayed. Nothing appears to happen. (Remember, the term *right-click* means to click with the right — or secondary — button on the mouse.)

7. Minimize all open applications by clicking the minimize button *for each program.*

   Remember the three buttons in the upper-right corner of each window? The left button is the minimize button. Clicking it shrinks the window to an icon.

8. At an empty area on the Windows 95 desktop, *right-click* and then choose **Paste Shortcut** from the resulting pop-up menu. Your desktop should resemble Figure 1-4.

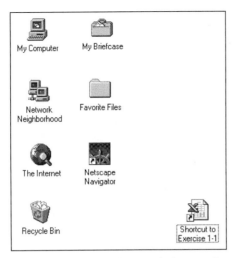

Figure 1-4 The desktop with the Exercise 1-1 shortcut icon.

After you place a shortcut icon on your Windows 95 desktop, you can simply double-click it to open Excel *and* the workbook.

SIDE TRIP

You can easily rename a shortcut as follows:

1. Click the shortcut, to select it.

2. Click the current name, to highlight it.

3. Type the new name for the shortcut.

To edit the name — rather than enter a new name — select the icon, click the name, click again to position the insertion point, and then edit by using Backspace, Delete, and the character keys as required. Press Enter when you have made the desired changes.

If you *double-click* the icon rather than single-clicking twice, you open Excel and the workbook.

Understanding Excel's Screen Display

In this section, we discuss the various elements of Excel's screen display. You can see these elements in Figure 1-5, which shows a blank workbook that is opened in Excel. If you have used Excel or other Windows 95 – based applications, you can skim through this section. If you are not familiar with all the terminology that is shown in Figure 1-5, read this section thoroughly. We use these terms throughout the rest of the book.

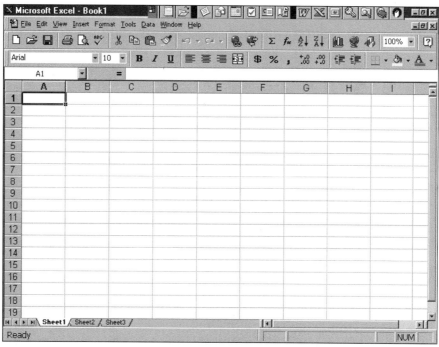

Figure 1-5 The major parts of the Excel screen display.

In Figure 1-5, both Excel and the workbook are shown in the maximized condition, which means that they take up the full screen. If your screen looks slightly different, check the two rows of buttons in the upper-right corner of your screen. The two middle buttons should each have two tiny boxes displayed. If not, click the button (or buttons) with a single box displayed. When both center buttons display two small boxes, both Excel and the workbook are maximized. We discuss these buttons in more detail later in this chapter.

Controlling windows

Both the program and the workbook Control menu icons are located in the upper-left corner of the screen. These icons (small pictures representing specific tasks) look like the icon for Excel. You can use them to control the size and location of the windows, and to close the workbook or Excel. In all likelihood, you will seldom use the Control menu icons, because Windows and Excel offer easier ways to accomplish the tasks that are performed by these icons.

If you click the upper icon, you open the *program* Control menu. It allows you to change the window size and perform other tasks. Clicking the *workbook* Control menu (in the menu bar line) opens the workbook Control menu.

TIP   By double-clicking the program Control menu icon, you close Excel and any open workbooks. If you double-click the worksheet Control menu, Excel closes the current workbook. If you haven't saved the workbook, you are prompted to do so before closing the workbook or Excel.

Understanding the Program title bar

The Program title bar lists the name of the program (in this case, Excel) and the name of the active workbook (file). If you have not yet saved the workbook, the title bar displays a name, such as Book1. This means that the workbook has not yet been saved with a name. (The displayed name may be Book2, Book3, and so on, depending on how many workbooks you have created since opening Excel. This name is only temporary, so don't worry about it.) After you save your workbook and name it, the designated name appears in the Program title bar.

Using the Office shortcut bar

You may not see the Office shortcut bar. (You — or someone else — may have removed it from the Windows Startup group.) The shortcut bar allows you to switch quickly among open Office applications, or to open other programs with the click of a button. Because switching among applications is also the purpose of the taskbar (at the bottom of the screen), many users choose to close the shortcut bar, to keep their screens less cluttered. Where required, the figures in this book display the Office shortcut bar. To keep the figures as simple as possible, however, we include the Office shortcut bar in only those figures that require it.

SIDE TRIP

The shortcut bar opens automatically each time that you start Windows. To close the shortcut bar, right-click the gray box with the four colored squares and choose [Exit] from the drop-down menu.

Minimizing Excel and the current workbook

In the upper-right corner of the screen, you can see two sets of three buttons. The upper set controls the display of Excel, while the lower set controls the display of the workbook. Each left-hand button resembles an underscore (_); these are the minimize buttons. Clicking the upper minimize button minimizes the entire Excel program (places it on the taskbar). You then see the Windows 95 desktop (unless you have another open program). Clicking the lower minimize button minimizes only the current workbook (and the worksheets that it contains).

Maximizing and restoring Excel and the current workbook

The middle button in each set of three buttons has two names: maximize or restore. These buttons are a little tricky to remember. If the icon is a single box, the button is called the *maximize* button. Clicking the maximize button causes Excel or the workbook to fill the entire screen. If the icon is two small boxes, it is called the *restore* button. Clicking the restore button returns Excel or the workbook to its previous size.

 TIP **If you want both Excel and the workbook to take up the maximum amount of space on your screen, make sure that both buttons contain two small boxes. This is the way that you should normally work.**

Closing Excel and any open workbooks

The right-hand button in this group is the close button. Clicking the upper close button closes Excel and all open workbooks. If any workbooks have been changed and not saved, Excel gives you the opportunity to save your changes. If you have already saved all changes, Excel and all open workbooks close automatically.

Clicking the *workbook* close button closes only the current workbook. If you haven't saved changes, Excel prompts you to save your changes prior to closing.

Taking a look at the menu bar

The menu bar is the starting place for performing many tasks within Excel. If you are accustomed to using the menu bar, you may find it a hard habit to break. In Excel for Windows 97, however, right-clicking allows you to access many of the available options without navigating multiple layers of menus. You find out more about the menu bar in "Selecting Menu Commands," later in this chapter.

Performing shortcuts by using the standard toolbar

Below the menu bar, you should see the standard toolbar (refer to Figure 1-5). If you don't see the standard toolbar, choose View → Toolbars → Standard.

By clicking a single button on the standard toolbar, you can accomplish a task that may otherwise take several clicks of the mouse. Pointing (without clicking) to any one of the buttons displays the *tool tip* for that button. (A tool tip is Excel's fancy way of telling you the button name). All tasks that you can perform from the standard toolbar can also be completed by using Excel's menus.

For example, to create a new workbook, click the first button on the standard toolbar (the tool tip says *New*). You can also perform the same task by choosing `File` → `New` from the menu bar.

Taking more shortcuts by using the formatting toolbar

Below the standard toolbar, you see another row of boxes and buttons known as the formatting toolbar. If you don't see the formatting toolbar, choose `View` → `Toolbars` → `Formatting`. (If the formatting toolbar is already visible, these commands close it.) This toolbar offers several buttons for formatting your worksheet. In the Quick Tour, you used the currency button to format several cells. As with the standard toolbar, all tasks that you can complete by using the toolbar can also be accomplished by using the menu bar commands.

Using the name box and the formula bar

Below the formatting toolbar is a bar that consists of two parts: the name box and the formula bar. The name box is on the left. Normally, it contains the address of the active cell. Later in this book, however, you discover how to name a cell or a group of cells. In this case, the name box shows the name that you have assigned to the selected cell(s).

To the right of the name box is the formula bar. This can be used to edit the information in the active cell. In older versions of Excel, you had to do your editing in the formula bar. Now, you can also edit directly in each cell. You may choose either method.

Row indicators

Row indicators begin with the number 1 and increase until the last row (65,536). Remember, each *horizontal* group of cells is called a row.

Column indicators

There are fewer columns available than rows. The columns are lettered from A through Z and then continue from AA to AZ, BA to BZ, until the last available column: IV. An Excel worksheet contains 255 columns and 65,536 rows (for a total of almost 17 million cells). If you need larger worksheets (*as if!*) you can use some pretty nifty tricks for combining multiple worksheets. With proper planning and organization, however, you shouldn't need to exceed the maximum number of rows or columns in your worksheets.

Using the vertical scroll bar

The vertical scroll bar allows you to see parts of the worksheet that are not currently visible on the screen. To scroll up and down through your worksheet, simply click the appropriate arrow on the vertical scroll bar. Remember that the scroll arrow points in the direction that you want to scroll. (If you want to see something farther down in your worksheet, click the down-scroll arrow.)

 When you scroll through a worksheet, the active cell does not change. If you create a new worksheet and then scroll down to row 5000, the active cell is still A1.

Using the horizontal scroll bar

The horizontal scroll bar works the same as the vertical scroll bar. Using the left and right scroll arrows, you can see columns to the left and right of the active cell. Like the vertical scroll bar, its use doesn't change the active cell.

Getting information from the status bar

At the bottom of the screen is the status bar. Excel uses this area to display various messages, as well as to indicate the sheet's current status.

What is a worksheet?

As you can tell from the preceding sections, Excel puts lots of stuff on your screen. But I still haven't told you about the most important part of Excel's screen display: the worksheet. The worksheet is the area that contains the cells in which you enter data. Notice that, by default, each workbook contains three worksheets, named Sheet1, Sheet2, and Sheet3.

Selecting Menu Commands

As you have already seen, Excel offers a multitude of ways to complete any task, and selecting menu commands is no exception. We show you a few of the more common ways to select the commands, but you may want to choose one or two, and then stick with them. Trying to memorize all the ways to complete any task is counterproductive.

You can drop down a list of available commands on the menu bar by using either the mouse or the keyboard. In the next two activities, you look at using both methods. The method that you choose may depend on where your hands are at the time (either already on the keyboard or on the mouse).

When you open a menu, you see a list of commands, and some contain special symbols:

* A right-pointing triangle indicates that choosing this command opens a submenu of additional options.
* An ellipsis (three dots) identifies a command that opens a dialog box.
* A quick-key command, such as Ctrl+N, shows you how to choose the command from the keyboard, rather than by using the mouse.

A command without one of these symbols is usually a *toggle* command. Clicking it once turns it on, placing a check mark next to it. Clicking again turns it off.

Choosing menu commands by using the mouse

After you learn to use the mouse, you may find it to be the easiest way to access commands. This is particularly true if you already have your hand on the mouse.

To use the mouse to choose menu commands, follow these steps:

1. Click File on the menu bar. A drop-down list of file options is displayed.

2. Move the mouse to Page Setup. Notice the ellipsis (three dots) next to the command. This indicates that clicking the option opens a dialog box.

3. Click Page Setup. Excel opens the Page Setup dialog box.

4. Click the close button in the upper-right corner of the dialog box. This closes the Page Setup dialog box.

5. Click File.

6. Move the mouse to Print Area. Notice the right-pointing triangle that is next to the option. This means that as you slide the cursor over the option (it isn't necessary to click), a pop-up list is displayed. Also, note the key sequence, Ctrl+P, next to the Print command. You'll use that shortly.

7. Click File to close the menu without making any choices.

8. With all menus closed, press Ctrl+P. This keyboard shortcut automatically opens the Print dialog box; you could also accomplish this by choosing File → Print from the menu bar.

9. Close the Print dialog box by clicking Cancel.

10. Click View. Notice the check mark that is next to Formula Bar. This is a toggle option.

11. Click Formula Bar . The menu closes, and the formula bar, directly below the formatting toolbar, is no longer visible.

12. Click View → Formula Bar . The formula bar is toggled back on.

Choosing commands by using the keyboard

If your hands are already on the keyboard, or if you simply prefer using keyboard commands, Excel allows you to access the menu bar by using the keyboard, as well as the mouse. Pressing Alt plus the underlined letter in the name of a menu opens that menu. After you open a menu, you don't need to hold Alt to choose an item in that menu. Simply type the letter that is underlined in the name of the menu item.

TIP **Often, the first letter of each command is underlined. These underlined letters are often referred to as *hot keys*. For example, to open the File menu, press Alt+F. In some cases, the first letter of a command is used for a different command, so another letter is underlined. For example, to open the Format menu, press Alt+O.**

To open a menu using keyboard commands, follow these steps:

1. Press the down-arrow key twice. A3 is now the active cell.

2. Press Alt+O (the letter, not the number zero) to open the Format menu. Make sure that you release the keys after the menu opens. The Cells option has an ellipsis next to it. At this point, no keys should be depressed.

3. Type **e**. Excel opens the Format Cells dialog box.

4. Press Esc to close the dialog box without making any changes.

5. Leave the workbook open.

TIP **If you were using the mouse, you could have clicked Cancel or the Close button rather than pressing Esc.**

Closing menus without making changes

To close an open menu, click outside of the menu area. You can also close a menu by pressing Esc. If you have several submenus open, you may need to press Esc several times. Each time that you press Esc, you close the current menu, and you are taken up one level. If you are in a dialog box, you can press Esc, click Cancel, or click the Close button to close the dialog box without making any changes.

TIP To quickly cancel all open menus, just click the main menu option again. For example, if you open the Edit menu and several successive submenus, just click Edit again.

Using the Toolbars

To perform a task on a specific group of cells, you must first select (highlight) those cells. For example, to boldface the text in cells B1 through D1, press and hold the left mouse button while the cursor is in B1, and then drag the cursor to D1. All cells (except for the first cell) appear in reverse (that is, white text on a black background). Even though the first cell isn't highlighted, it is still one of the selected cells.

In some cases, you don't need to select cells first. For example, to create a new workbook, simply click the New button. Buttons on the toolbars cannot be activated by using the keyboard; you must use the mouse.

This activity gives you an opportunity to use various buttons on the toolbars as shortcuts to tasks that are available through menu selections. If you still have Exercise 1-1 open, skip ahead to Step 3.

Follow these steps:

1. Click the Open button on the standard toolbar (it looks like a file folder).

2. Double-click Exercise 1-1.

3. Click B1 (Monday), hold the mouse button, and drag the cursor to G1 (Weekly Total). Release the mouse button.

4. Click the Bold button on the formatting toolbar. It is the first button in the formatting toolbar; it looks like a *B*.

5. Click A1 to turn off the selection. You could also press Esc to turn off the selection. Notice that all of the text in cells B1 through G1 is now boldfaced. Wednesday, in D1, just barely fits. You need to adjust the width of column D.

6. Move the cursor onto the vertical line to the right of the column D heading (the line between *D* and *E*). The cursor changes to a vertical bar with a horizontal, double-headed arrow.

7. Double-click. The column width is automatically adjusted.

8. Adjust the width of column G.

9. Using the instructions from the previous steps, boldface cells A2 through A6. Adjust the column width again so that all the text is visible. Your screen should look like Figure 1-6.

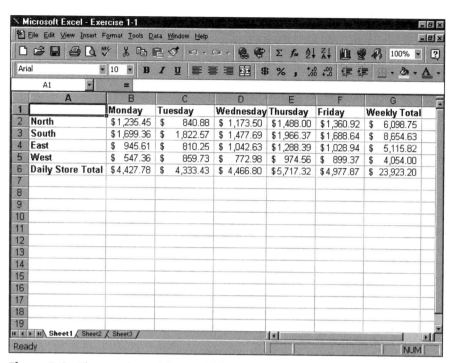

Figure 1-6 The sample worksheet, with boldfaced column and row titles.

10. Choose `File` → `Close`.

11. Click Yes when prompted to save the file.

Saving Your Work

It is imperative that you save your work every 5 – 10 minutes. Sometimes, the computer just locks up. If that happens, you can't do anything but turn the power off and reboot the machine. Any work stored in memory that wasn't saved to disk is placed in a burglar-proof box to which you don't have a key. (Just kidding. It really just disappears forever. Perhaps the RAM fairies take it.) The same thing can occur with a power surge or a drop in power.

The times that you forget to save your work are the ones that are most important. Here's a typical scenario:

Your boss points out that your worksheet includes an error that causes the worksheet to overstate total profit by $10,000. After many hours of troubleshooting, you find that parentheses are placed incorrectly in several cells that depend on each other. Having fixed all the offending cells, you rush to tell your boss that the problem is fixed. Meanwhile, a cleaning person comes into your office and accidentally kicks your computer's power cord out of the socket. He plugs it in, the computer restarts, and you come back to a Windows startup screen, rather than your Excel worksheet. As a result, the changes that you have made are gone to never-never land.

In reality, you may get lucky, and Excel may have saved some of your work. But don't count on it. Save regularly, and you will be fine.

Saving a file for the first time

It's a good idea to save your workbook immediately after creating it. That way, the workbook has a name, and it can't get mixed up with other files that may be in Excel's memory. The first time that you save a workbook, you name it by using the Save As dialog box.

Follow these steps:

1. Choose File → New . A new file is created. It is automatically assigned a name, such as Book1, Book2, and so on.

2. Choose File → Save As . Excel displays the Save As dialog box, which is shown in Figure 1-7. The Save in text box should show Discover Excel. If not, double-click the Discover Excel folder.

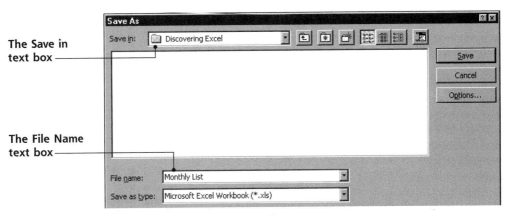

Figure 1-7   The Save As dialog box.

3. Type **Monthly List** in the File name text box.

4. Click Save. Excel saves the file and returns you to the worksheet. Notice that the new filename is now displayed in the Title Bar.

Saving a file using the existing name

After you have saved a file, there are several ways to update it, saving the latest version to the disk. Remember, if you don't save the file and the power goes off, you lose all work that was completed since you last saved the file.

To save your workbook if it already has a name, follow these steps:

1. Click B1.

2. Type **January**. *Don't* press Enter.

3. Drag the AutoFill handle to cell D1. February and March are automatically entered in cells C1 and D1, respectively.

4. Choose File → Save . Because the workbook already has a name, Excel automatically saves it over the existing copy of the workbook.

If you save a file without changing its name, Excel overwrites the existing file. If your work includes errors, Excel saves those errors in place of the original workbook, and you cannot recover the original. If you think that you may want to keep the original file intact, use the Save As command, and give the workbook a slightly different name, such as Monthly List A.

5. Drag the AutoFill handle from D1 to G1. April, May, and June are added as column heads.

6. Click the Save button on the toolbar. (The button looks like a floppy disk.) The file is saved, although it happens so quickly, you may not notice it.

TIP You can also save your workbook by pressing Ctrl+S. If the file is already named, you don't see any difference in the screen. If you haven't named your file, Excel automatically displays the Save As dialog box.

Filename rules

When you are running a Windows 95 (or later) program (such as Office 97), file-names can have as many as 255 characters, including the full path name. In reality, most screens show only the first 25 – 40 characters of the name, so you may want to keep your filename within those limits. You can use spaces, com-mas, and even multiple periods.

Filenames cannot include any of the following characters:

* forward slash (/)
* backslash (\)
* greater-than sign (>)
* less-than sign (<)
* asterisk (*)
* question mark (?)

* quotation marks ("")
* vertical bar (|)
* colon (:)
* semicolon (;)

TIP If you plan to share files with people who use versions of Excel prior to version 7 (Excel for Windows 95), consider keeping the filename to a maximum of eight characters with a suffix not exceeding three characters (for example, mybook10.xls); also, use no spaces and no periods.

The only punctuation that you should use is a hyphen or an underscore. If you give a file with a long name to a user of an older version of Excel, the filename that you assigned is cut short (*truncated,* if you prefer big words), and spaces and punctuation are removed. If you have two files such as *May Report for the North Store* and *May Report for the South Store*, Excel truncates the filenames to *mayrep~1.xls* and *mayrep~2.xls*. Better names, if you are sharing files, would be *MayNorth* and *MaySouth*.

Getting Help from the Office Assistant

B ecause the Office 97 or Excel 97 manual is not much help when it comes to solving problems, Microsoft has included online help information. As soon as you start the help function, the Office Assistant appears, as shown in Figure 1-8.

Although the manual that is included with Excel is rather skimpy, you can find a lot of technical support stored on your hard disk.

The Office Assistant is designed to help you find answers to your questions by following these steps:

1. Choose Help → Microsoft Excel Help . The Office Assistant appears.

TIP A shortcut to opening the Office Assistant is to press F1.

Depending on how your computer is set up, your Office Assistant may look different from the one that you saw in Figure 1-8. In the Bonus Section of this chapter, you learn to modify the Office Assistant to suit your taste.

2. Type **How do I save a file with a new name?** and click Search. Notice that while you are typing your questions, the Office Assistant is taking notes with its pad and pencil. Is Microsoft telling us that some tasks are better accomplished with a pad and pencil?

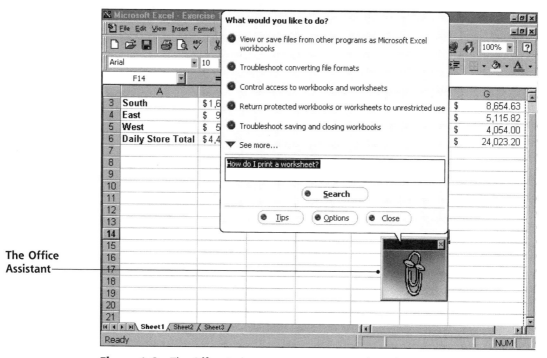

Figure 1-8 The Office Assistant answers your questions about Excel.

If the Paper Clip (Office Assistant) gets bent out of shape while searching for the appropriate topic, don't worry. Through the magic of computer animation, it returns to its normal self as soon as it is done searching. This is part of a group of features called Bells and Whistles.

Bells and Whistles are usually thought of as noncritical functions that make you say, "Gee whiz." The inclusion of a multitude of Bells and Whistles is imperative to our continuation as a solvent nation. Without them, we wouldn't need to upgrade our hard drives, sound cards, video accelerator cards, or even RAM. Just think of all the employees who would be out of work if you didn't upgrade your computer every two or three years (or is that months?). So, as you can see, Bells and Whistles serve a primary function in the continued economic growth of our great country.

When the search is complete, you see various options, as displayed in Figure 1-9. To see one of the help topics, click the blue button to the left of the topic. If more topics are available, click See more.

3. Click Save a workbook. The Save a Workbook help screen is displayed, as shown in Figure 1-10.

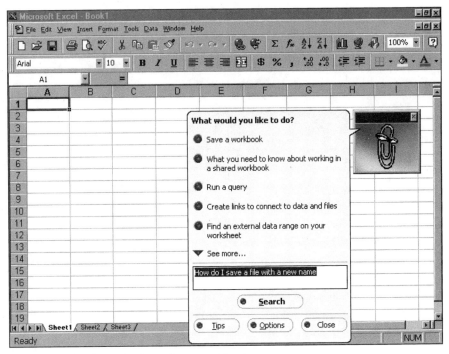

Figure 1-9 Help topics for saving a workbook.

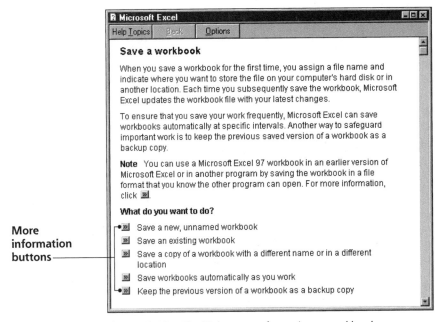

More information buttons

Figure 1-10 The Help screen for saving a workbook.

The help screen begins with an overview of the topic. If more specific help is desired, you can click any of the More Information buttons near the bottom of the screen. Each of these buttons opens an additional help screen with more specific information.

4. Click the More Information button to the left of Save a new, unnamed workbook.

5. Close the help screen when you are finished looking at the information.

TIP **If you aren't sure what a specific button or feature does, pressing Shift+F1 changes the cursor to a question mark. Click any button or choose any menu item to find out more about that object.**

Getting Help the Traditional Way

In addition to using the Office Assistant, you can also choose `Help` → `Contents and Index`. The Contents tab lists the help screens by topic. Clicking the Index tab gives you an index, just like in the back of this book.

As you may have already found out, an index doesn't always include exactly the information that you need to find. In that case, click the Find tab. Here you can type a word or phrase. Every help screen that contains that word or phrase is displayed in the Topics area. In Figure 1-11, I asked for help in password protection and then clicked Find Now. There may be many topics listed in the Click a topic panel. When the topics are listed, highlight one and click Display, or simply double-click the topic. When using the Find feature, it is usually best to be as specific as possible when typing the phrase.

TIP **Although Windows 95 or later help screens stay on top of the document so that you can easily view them, you may want to keep some instructions for future reference. Also, some instructions are lengthy and require lots of scrolling. To keep the instructions, or for easier use, print the help screen. To print a help topic, display it and choose `Options` → `Print Topic`. A complete copy of the topic is sent to the printer.**

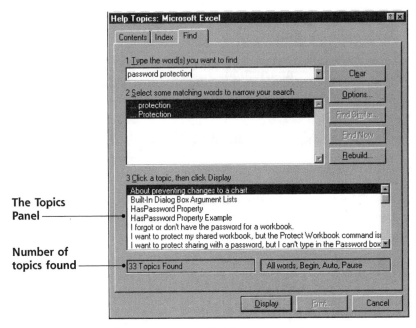

The Topics Panel

Number of topics found

Figure 1-11 The Find feature at work.

BONUS

Customizing the Office Assistant

Near the end of each chapter in this book, you find a Bonus section. This information is not really required for a basic understanding of how to use Excel, but it may make things easier for you. In this first Bonus section, you find out how to customize the Office Assistant. This skill is certainly not critical to using Excel, but it's a lot of fun and can impress your coworkers who don't know how to get those neat replacements for the Clippit Office Assistant. [If you are not familiar with Windows Explorer, you may want to read *Windows 95 for Dummies* by Andy Rathbone (IDG Books Worldwide, Inc.).]

Clippit is the default Office Assistant. However, you can choose from eight other characters to replace Clippit. Each Assistant has its own graphics and sound.

1. If the Office Assistant is open, click the Close box in the upper-right corner of the window. This is done so that you can begin by opening the Office Assistant. (We want to make sure that you are at the same starting place as we are.)

2. Press F1. Office Assistant appears.

3. Click the Options tab. The Office Assistant dialog box, shown in Figure 1-12, is used to set the various options for the Office Assistant. The Options tab is used to control how the Office Assistant responds. Your options may differ from those in the figure.

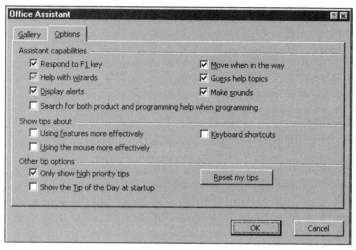

Figure 1-12   The Options tab of the Office Assistant dialog box.

4. Click the Gallery tab. By default, Clippit is the Office Assistant. The Gallery tab allows you to choose from several Office Assistants.

5. Click Next to see The Dot Office Assistant. Continue clicking Next until you get to Will (Shakespeare).

 NOTE   **Although you can see all the available Office Assistants, you must have your original Microsoft Office or Microsoft Excel 97 CD in the drive. By default, only Clippit is loaded to your hard disk.**

6. Click Back until you see Power Pup. Make certain that your Excel or Office CD is in the drive.

7. Click OK. After a few seconds, you return to Excel. Power Pup is now your guide.

8. If you don't like Power Pup, repeat the process and choose the Office Assistant that best fits your personality.

9. You may get tired of having the Office Assistant on the screen. If so, simply right-click the Office Assistant and choose **Hide Assistant** from the pop-up menu. Don't worry; any time that you want the Office Assistant back, just press F1 or click the Office Assistant button.

To load some or all of the Office Assistants (called Actors) to your hard disk at once, follow these steps:

1. Open Windows Explorer, and access the drive that contains your Office or Excel CD. Your screen should be similar to the one shown in the following figure. My CD-ROM drive letter is *E*. Yours may be some other letter.

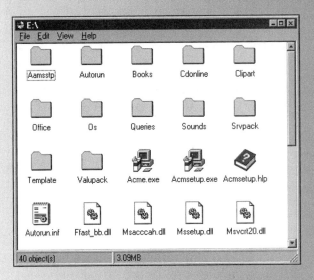

NOTE If your screen doesn't look like the figure, choose View → Large Icons .

2. Double-click the Office folder, and then double-click the Actors folder. Your screen should look similar to that shown in the following figure.

3. Click the first actor that you want to copy.

4. Press Ctrl, and click any other actors to be copied.

5. With all the desired actors selected, choose | Edit | → | Copy |.

6. Close the windows until you are back at the main Explorer window.

7. Double-click the Program folder, the Microsoft Office folder, the Office folder, and finally the Actors folder.

8. Choose | Edit | → | Paste |. After a few seconds, the actors are copied to the hard disk, and they are now available without having to insert the CD-ROM when you want to change the Office Assistants.

NOTE Again, if your screen doesn't look like the figure, choose | View | → | Large Icons |.

NOTE Notice that each actor consists of two files, one with an ACT extension and the other with an ACP extension. The latter files are only used to preview the actors in the Options dialog box for the Office Assistant.

WEB
PATH
If you would like different Actors, and you already know how to use the Internet, choose | Help | → | Microsoft on the Web | → | Microsoft Office Home Page |. For additional information about using the Internet with Excel, see Chapter 17.

CAUTION
The Mother Nature and Genius Assistants are only available from the CD-ROM version of Excel, not from the floppy disk version. To run these two Assistants, your video monitor and adapter must support at least 256 colors. For information on checking and resetting your monitor resolution, look in the Windows Help area (from Windows 95, not from within Excel).

X-REF

Summary

This chapter describes several ways to start Excel, including using shortcuts on the Windows 95 desktop. The method that you use depends on your personal preferences. You should now have a basic understanding of the various elements that are visible on the Excel screen. You can save a workbook with a new name or save one that already has a name. You can select menu commands by using either the mouse or the keyboard. Again, you may choose either method. The Office Assistant, a new feature in Excel 97, is available to help you solve problems. You can also get help using the commands on the toolbar.

At this point, you should have a general knowledge of how to control the basics of Excel. In the following chapters, you build on this knowledge, gradually becoming comfortable with all the basics of Excel 97.

CHAPTER TWO

WHY DO I NEED A SPREADSHEET?

IN THIS CHAPTER YOU LEARN THESE KEY SKILLS

One of my many hobbies is collecting old tools. They are mounted on walls throughout the house. A few years ago, I bought an old tool from an antique shop, but I had absolutely no idea of its purpose — and neither did the shopkeepers. It looked like a pitchfork, but not an ordinary one. Owning a tool without understanding its purpose seriously limits its usefulness. A spreadsheet can be the same way. You may have a general idea of its uses, but to really take advantage of its power, you need a complete grasp of the program.

NOTE I finally discovered that the mystery tool was used to break open and spread bales of hay. Now, as soon as I get a small ranch, I can put it to better use than as a decoration.

What Can a Spreadsheet Do for You?

When purchasing a spreadsheet program or committing the time to thoroughly learn it, the crucial question is, "What's in it for me?" Unfortunately, I can't answer that question for you. Only you know your specific needs. I can, however, tell you about the types of spreadsheets that you may want to develop. You can use spreadsheets for recording financial transactions, tracking inventory, and creating lists from which you can then retrieve specified data.

If you learn to use spreadsheets properly, Excel can make your work easier, more attractive, and most importantly, more accurate. However, don't get the idea that a spreadsheet is the ideal solution to all business problems. Although you can easily use Excel to accomplish simple word processing tasks (you set the width of a column to the width of the margins and turn on word wrap) and you can use Word to replicate some basic worksheet functions (such as creating tables that perform simple mathematical manipulations), each of these programs is best suited for its own specific function. Similarly, you can use Excel's List feature to create a database, or you can use Access, the Microsoft Office database, to perform mathematical operations. However, a database program such as Access is best suited for complex database tasks; for complex spreadsheet tasks, you should use a spreadsheet program such as Excel.

Although word processing, spreadsheet, and database programs share an overlap of features, it is important that you understand the basic features of each, and then choose the correct tool for your job. In some cases, you may need multiple tools. For example, if you need to do a mass mailing, you can use a database or a spreadsheet for storing your mailing list and then use a word processing program for creating your form letter.

SIDE TRIP

Using a word processing program, an administrative assistant at a regional hospital creates a directory that lists employee names, addresses, and phone numbers. When employees register to attend a training class, the administrative assistant must create a class list. Using the word processing program, this employee electronically copies the appropriate names and phone numbers from the employee directory and then pastes that information into the class list.

By using the same procedure — using the word processing program to electronically copy information from one document to another — the administrative assistant also generates confirmation letters regarding each employee's enrollment in a particular class. Although this approach is more efficient that manually typing each class list and confirmation letter, there are even more efficient ways to accomplish this task. For example, you can store the personnel information in a worksheet or a database, from which you can automatically generate class rosters and confirmation mailings.

A Sampling of Tasks

Any modern office processes and generates a vast amount of information. Examples include bulk mailing, inventory control, accounts receivable and accounts payable, financial reports, newsletters, and annual reports. You must analyze your routine tasks before you can decide which application (or applications) best suits your needs. For example, just because a task requires mathematical manipulation doesn't always mean that a spreadsheet is your best choice. Often you need a combination of several types of applications.

NOTE Simple tasks, such as balancing your personal checkbook, may be more quickly accomplished by pencil, paper, and a hand-held calculator than by designing a new spreadsheet. Although computers can often simplify tasks and reduce the time needed to complete them, inappropriate use is like renting a steam shovel to dig a hole for your rose bush.

First things first

When you only have a hammer, every job seems to need a hammer. When you only have a spreadsheet (or a word processor or a database), every task seems to be best suited to a spreadsheet (or a word processor or a database). Make a list of the jobs that you do, and evaluate how you keep your data. In some cases, the method that is used to complete a job is simply the way that it has always been done. Try to break that habit now. Evaluate all of your daily tasks, and decide which instrument is the *best* for manipulating the data in the way you need it.

In general, a spreadsheet is best used when you want to be able to ask, "What if . . .?" For example, what if I increase employee wages by five percent? What if I increase the cost of my ten most popular products by four percent? What if I add an extra holiday each year? How can that affect my bottom line? Excel shines at handling complex mathematical manipulations. Budgeting is another common use of a spreadsheet. Changing the budget for one department may reflect either positively or negatively on other departments.

Here are some sample ways that a spreadsheet program can be effectively used. Remember, these are only a few examples; spreadsheets have hundreds of other uses.

Inventory control

Although inventory control is probably best managed by a database program such as Access, not everyone has access to Access. Excel is an excellent alternative. For example, Figure 2-1 shows a sample worksheet that is used to track inventory of a small video store. Each row represents one title. Notice that the total value of current inventory is calculated in G2. The function that computes that value is shown in the formula bar, immediately above column B.

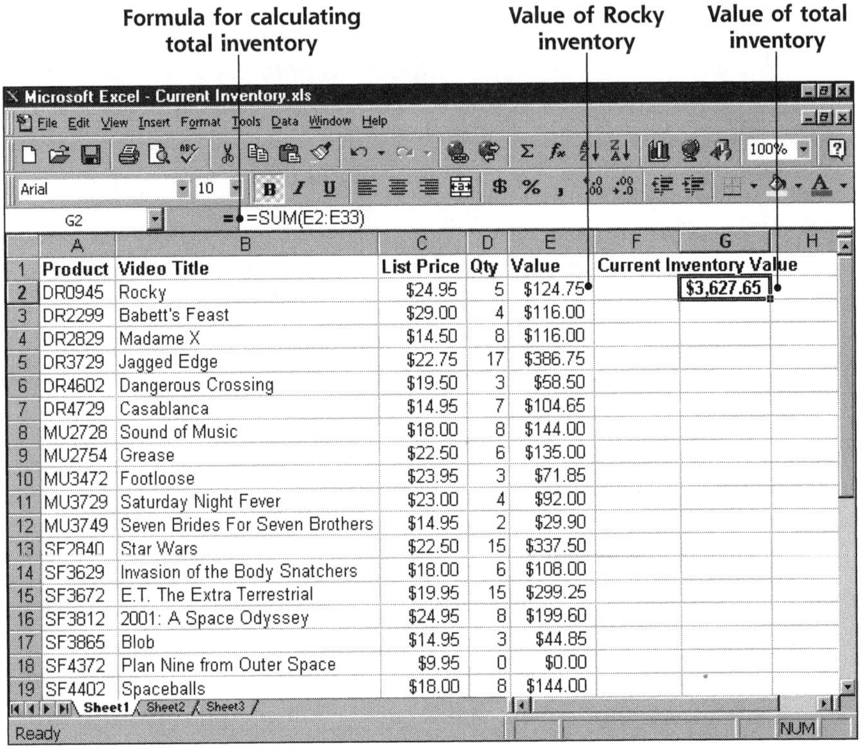

Formula for calculating total inventory   Value of Rocky inventory   Value of total inventory

Figure 2-1 An inventory for a small video store.

For each video, the first column (A) shows the product number for the tape. Column B displays the title of the video. Column C shows the list price. Column D lists the quantity on hand. The value in column E (the current value of the inventory for the video in that row) is automatically calculated. For example, the formula used to calculate the value of the *Rocky* tapes is =C2*D2 — that is, the amount in C2 multiplied by the amount in D2. This is a *formula;* you learn more about formulas later in this chapter.

In G2, a function tracks the current inventory value for *all* videos. A *function* is a shortcut for a complex formula. The function in G2 is =SUM(E2:E33), as shown in the formula bar. As a formula, it would be written =E1+E2+E3+E4+E5+..., resulting in a very long equation. The function =SUM(E2:E33) instructs Excel to total the values contained in cells E2 through E33. In other words, Excel sums all of the values that are contained in column E from row 2 through row 33. The current value of the entire inventory is $3,627.65, as shown in cell G2 of Figure 2-1.

Figure 2-2 shows that two copies of *Rocky* have been sold (the quantity has decreased from 5 to 3). In Figure 2-1, the total value of the *Rocky* video was $124.75.

The inventory value for the *Rocky* video automatically decreases to $74.85, and the total inventory value, displayed in G2, becomes $3,577.75. These calculations are done automatically, as soon as the new quantity is entered in cell D2.

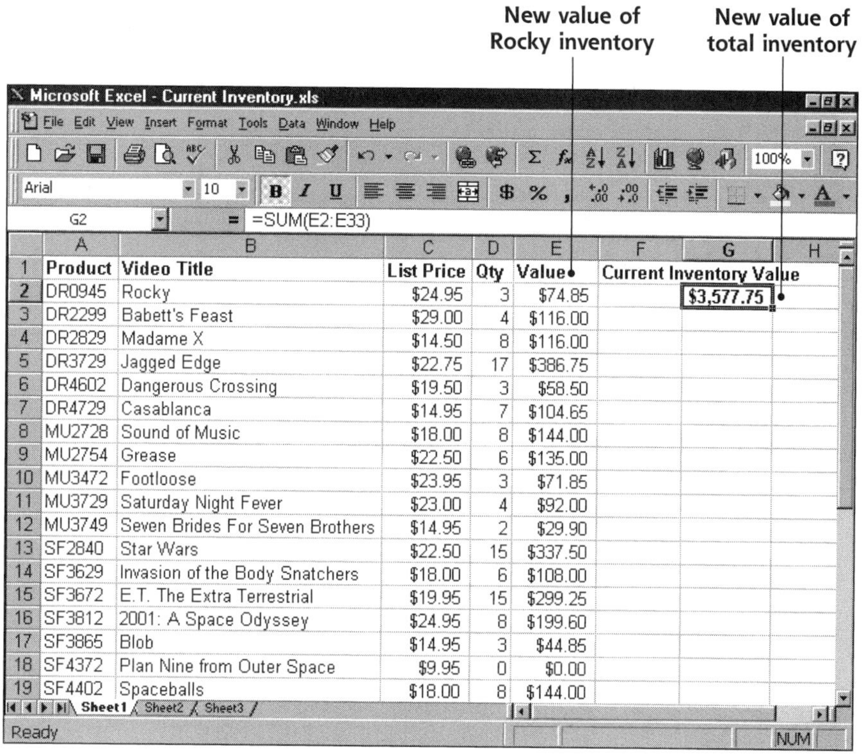

New value of
Rocky inventory

New value of
total inventory

Figure 2-2 Two *Rocky* videos have been sold; E2 and G2 are automatically updated.

Creating a simple inventory worksheet

Although the worksheet that we created in this activity is simple, it shows you some of the power of working with formulas.

Follow these steps to create a worksheet:

1. Open Excel.

2. In B1, type **Qty**.

3. In C1, type **List Price**.

4. In D1, type **Inventory Value**. You then need to AutoFit column D.

5. Move the cursor to the right edge of the column indicator. The cursor changes to a heavy vertical line that contains a horizontal line with left and right arrowheads.

6. Double-click to AutoFit the column.

7. In A2, type **Dog Feed**.

8. In A3, type **Chicken Feed**.

9. In A4, type **Cow Feed**.

10. In A5, type **Total**.

11. AutoFit column A.

12. In B2, type **50**.

13. In C2, type **12.50**.

14. In D2, type **=B2*C2** and press Enter. Don't worry about any of the formatting at this point. You take care of that shortly.

15. In B3, type **75**.

16. In C3, type **15**.

17. In D3, type **=B3*C3** and press Enter.

18. In B4, type **25**.

19. In C4, type **18**.

20. In D4, type **=B4*C4** and press Enter.

21. In B5, type **=B2+B3+B4** and press Tab.

22. Create similar formulas for columns C and D.

23. Move the cursor to C2, press and hold the left mouse button, and drag down and to the right until D5 is highlighted. Release the mouse button.

24. Click the dollar sign ($) on the toolbar.

25. Click A1.

26. Save the file in the Discover Excel folder as Feed Inventory.

    Your worksheet should look like the one shown in Figure 2-3. The total value in D5 should be $2,200.00. If not, check your values and formulas.

27. Leave Excel open for now.

Customer contact information

Figure 2-4 shows one method for tracking your customers. Each customer's information is contained in a single row (remember that a row is a horizontal group of cells). Although the worksheet is not currently in any identifiable order, it is a simple matter for Excel to alphabetize based on any column (a vertical group of cells).

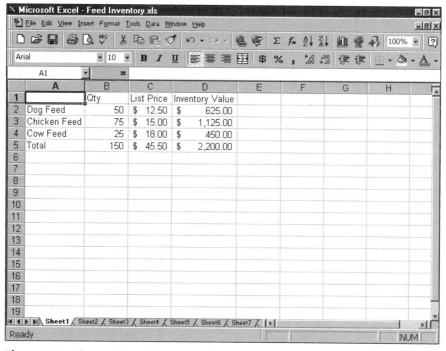

Figure 2-3 The worksheet is properly formatted and contains the correct formulas.

	First	Last	Address	City	State	Zip	Phone
1	First	Last	Address	City	State	Zip	Phone
2	Charles	Robert	564 Highlight Drive	Overland Park	KS	66210	(913) 555-2211
3	Hadley	William	66512 Morgan	San Remo	CA	94451	(818) 555-5571
4	Smith	Joanie	95 Central Drive	Lakeside	CA	94002	(818) 555-9337
5	Williamson	Barry	22 Santa Paula Road	Woodland Hills	CA	91367	(818) 555-3482
6	Forester	Dustin	991 San Remo Drive	Overland Park	KS	66212	(913) 555-3008
7	Gray	Bailey	44679 East 104th Avenue	Morgansville	CA	94404	(818) 555-9771
8	Halbasch	Pamela	3256 South Grape Street	Leavenworth	KS	66057	(913) 555-6691
9	Smith	Samatha	566 Main Street	Billings	CA	92298	(818) 555-4473
10	Climber	Joanie	244 Nicobar	Olathe	KS	66061	(913) 555-3886
11	Garey	Sean	111 Kansas Avenue	Los Angeles	CA	90210	(818) 555-9951
12	Allen	Robert	524 Hargis Lane	Leavenworth	KS	66056	(913) 555-4466
13	Adams	Matthew	7314 Booth	Santa Rosa	CA	95588	(818) 555-7359
14	Kiowa	Molly	5124 Marigold Lane	Elizabeth	CO	80101	(303) 555-6672
15	Griffith	Kristopher	1700 Chaparral	St. Cloud	FL	32769	(407) 555-5591
16	Hickey	Jessica	1920 Doral Court	Pittsburg	KS	66762	(913) 555-3104
17	German	Ashley	13558 Anteres	Lafayette	CO	80026	(303) 555-8872
18	Carrier	Heidi	6300 Owensmouth	Mission	KS	66202	(913) 555-8564
19	Norman	Rebecca	6208 Reinholdt Way	Fulton	MO	65251	(816) 555-3006

Figure 2-4 A sample customer contact list.

Personnel information

In Figure 2-5, you can see a sample personnel file for a small company. In addition to the information that is already entered in the worksheet, you may want to track the date of performance appraisals, termination dates, dates and amounts of raises, or even additional personal information such as home phone numbers.

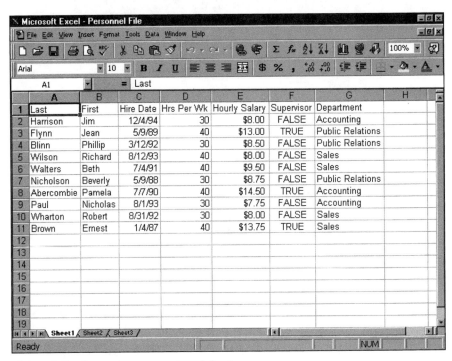

Figure 2-5 A sample personnel worksheet.

Sales information

Figure 2-6 shows a sample worksheet for tracking yearly sales by state. A column graph is included, which makes it very easy to see the difference between the yearly sales for the various states.

Other sample worksheets

The figures in the preceding sections provide samples of simple worksheets that you soon find out how to build. They should give you some ideas of different ways to use worksheets. The Excel program includes several samples of more complex worksheets that you can view. You can even use these samples as starting points for creating your own worksheets. They can be found, by default, in C:\PROGRAM FILES\MICROSOFT OFFICE\OFFICE\EXAMPLES\SAMPLES.XLS.

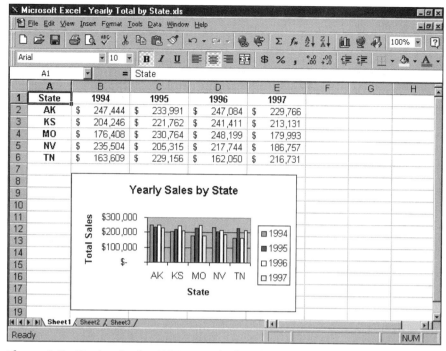

Figure 2-6 Yearly sales for 1994–1997 broken down by state.

How Do You Decide Which Application to Use?

As we mentioned earlier, Excel can perform many tasks that are best suited to Word and Access. How, then, can you decide which application is the best for your particular need? It would be nice if there were an easy answer, but there isn't. Deciding when to use Word shouldn't be much of a problem. Basically, you use Word when you are dealing with text and graphics. However, choosing between Excel and Access is a little more difficult. The best question to ask is, "What do I want as an end result?" If you want to sort and select complex data, your best bet is Access. If you want to manipulate numbers (finances, statistics, and so on), your choice should be Excel.

What Can You Put in a Spreadsheet?

You may think that numbers are the only things that you enter into worksheet cells. They are the most common form of spreadsheet data. However, in addition to numbers (values), you can also place many other things in your worksheet — for example, text (sometimes called labels), formulas to perform mathematical manipulations, functions (shortcuts for formulas), dates, charts, pictures, and buttons.

Although most worksheets consist of only text and values, some of the other items that we've mentioned make the worksheet more user friendly, performing calculations automatically. Other items, such as charts and pictures, can help make the worksheet easier for the viewer to interpret.

Handling Different Data Types

Excel stores data in a variety of ways — most commonly as text or numbers. You can format text and numbers in many ways. With text, you can change the alignment, the font, the size, and various type characteristics. You can also format numbers in many different ways — currency, scientific, and integer, to name a few. In general, Excel tries to guess how you want the data to be formatted. In most cases, Excel is correct. But in some cases, as you soon see, it guesses incorrectly.

Of course, Excel lets you do more than simply format your text and numbers. For example, you can compare things, sort information, and perform complex calculations. The following sections describe the types of data that Excel handles.

Working with text

As mentioned earlier, text is only one type of data that can be entered into Excel. Text doesn't always just consist of alphabetic characters. It can include punctuation, spaces, and even numbers. The uses for text may differ. For example, a particular cell may be a name (John), a column label for a report (North), or a product ID number (A204BZ6). In some cases, cells may contain numbers that you want to have treated as text (in other words, you don't need to perform mathematical calculations on them).

By default, hyphenated numbers are *usually* assumed to be text unless you tell Excel differently. Social security numbers and telephone numbers are good examples of numbers that are treated as text. You wouldn't want to perform mathematical operations on either of them.

When you type a telephone number, a social security number, or some other combination of text and mathematical symbols, Excel usually treats it as text. One exception involves dates. If you type **2-2-76**, Excel interprets it as a date and displays it in the default date format (for example, as 2/2/76). Because Excel treats this entry as a date, you can perform mathematical operations using the information in this cell. If you want Excel to treat this entry as text rather than as a date, type the value and then choose Format → Cells . This opens the Format Cells dialog box, as shown in Figure 2-7. Excel assumes that the entry is a date, so the Date category is highlighted. On the Number tab in the Category panel, select Text to format the cell as text. The formatting then returns to the way that you originally entered the date.

The Category panel

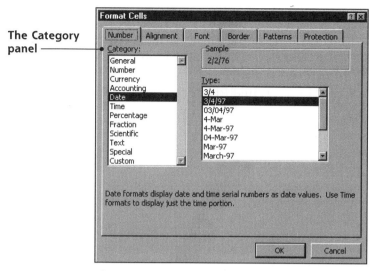

Figure 2-7 The Format Cells dialog box.

NOTE   As a shortcut to formatting entries that look like dates as text, begin your entry with a single quotation mark ('). For example, Excel automatically treats '2-2-76 as text. When you print your worksheet, Excel doesn't print the quotation mark.

If you format dates as text, you cannot perform mathematical operations with them.

Working with numbers

In earlier versions of Excel (and other spreadsheets), when you tried to store numbers as text (such as a telephone number), you would get the mathematical answer. For example, if you entered **555-1234** and pressed Enter, Excel displayed the value –679 (the result of subtracting 1,234 from 555). Excel now stores hyphenated numbers as text unless they are preceded by an equal sign (=). Entering **=555-1234** still produces –679. Without an equal sign, Excel treats the entry **555-1234** as text.

If you enter a number into a cell with no other characters (including punctuation), Excel usually treats it as a number. If you start the entry with a minus sign or a plus sign, Excel treats the entry as a negative or positive number. If the entry begins with an asterisk or a single quotation mark, Excel treats it as text. If you have spaces following the number, Excel still treats it as a number.

Although you can precede numbers with a variety of symbols, you can't start any entry with a forward slash (/). This holdover from Lotus 1-2-3 programming activates the menu, just as though you had pressed Alt.

If you need to begin a cell text entry with a forward slash, a plus sign, a minus sign, or an equal sign, first type a single quotation mark. This alerts Excel to treat the following characters as text, even though they may look like a menu request, a negative number, or a formula (discussed shortly). Although the single quotation mark shows in the formula bar, it does not show when the worksheet is printed.

Aligning text and numbers

By default, all text is aligned at the left edge of the cell (called left justified), and all numbers are aligned to the right side of the cell. By using the justification buttons on the toolbar, you can change the alignment to left, center, or right, regardless of the data type. Figure 2-8 shows the justification buttons.

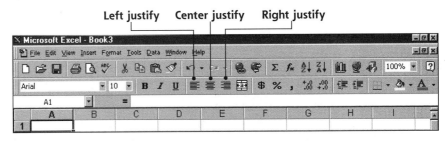

Figure 2-8 The justification buttons on the toolbar.

Justifying text

Using the Feed Inventory workbook that you created in the previous activity, you can now change the justification of the text (labels).

Follow these steps:

1. Highlight cells A1 to A5.

2. Click the Center justification button on the toolbar. Notice that all labels in column A are now centered.

3. Highlight cells B1 to D1.

4. Click the Center justification button on the toolbar. The column titles are now centered. Notice that all values in B2 through D5 are still right aligned.

5. Save the workbook.

Working with formulas

Excel stores not only numbers and text but also *formulas.* In an earlier activity, you wrote a few formulas without knowing exactly what you were doing. Here, you look a little deeper into formulas. Formulas can be either simple or complex. For example, you can have a formula that adds the contents of C1 to the contents of C2:

```
=C1+C2
```

Or you can have a formula that sums the contents of C1 to C5:

```
=C1+C2+C3+C4+C5
```

You can also use other mathematical symbols in formulas:

```
=C1*C2+(C3/C4)
```

The asterisk means multiply, and the forward slash means divide.

 A formula must begin with an equal sign, or Excel treats it as text.

When you work with formulas, remember that the formula is *stored* in the cell, but the answer is *displayed.* As shown in Figure 2-9, when you make a cell containing a formula active, the formula itself appears in the formula bar, whereas the answer to the calculation is displayed in the cell. The active cell (C3) displays the answer to the formula. This formula is displayed in the formula bar.

Changing the value in C1 or C2 changes the displayed value for C3, but the formula remains the same. By default, Excel recalculates any affected areas of the worksheet after each entry.

Sometimes, formulas can be more complex. For example, to find the sum of C1 through C10, the formula would be as follows:

```
=C1+C2+C3+C4+C5+C6+C7+C8+C9+C10
```

If you are calculating the results of many cells, typing the formula in this manner could be time consuming and very prone to errors. For example, if column C contained 1,000 test scores and you wanted to sum them, imagine the difficulty of typing the formula using the previous example. This is where functions are useful.

Working with functions

A *function* is really just a shortcut for a formula. For example, `=Sum(C1:C1000)` adds the contents of cells C1 through C1000. (A colon indicates a range of cells.) As you can see, this is much easier than typing a formula to accomplish the same task.

A function *always* begins with an equal sign, followed immediately by the name of the function, a left parenthesis, a combination of cells (or ranges of cells), and mathematical operators; the function ends with a right parenthesis.

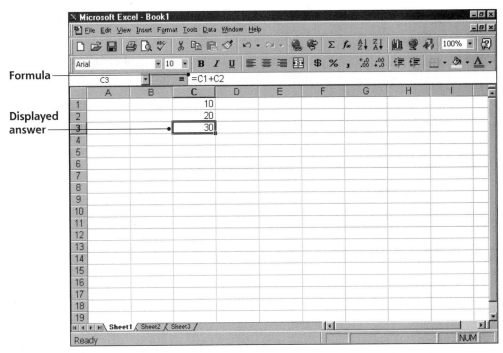

Figure 2-9 The formula bar lists the formula; the cell displays the result.

As with a formula, the cell containing the function displays only the answer to the calculation. When the cell is active, the function itself is displayed in the formula bar. You learn more about formulas and functions as you read each chapter, but Chapter 5 provides a thorough discussion of both, and Chapter 6 examines some of the more complex formulas and functions.

Creating simple functions

Although you discover more about functions in later chapters, this activity gives a brief introduction to their use. The Feed Inventory workbook should still be open.

Follow these steps:

1. If this workbook is not open, open it now.

2. Highlight cells B5 to D5 and press Delete. All of the formulas are cleared, and the cells are blank.

3. In B5, type **=SUM(B2:B4)** and press Tab to move to the next cell.

   As soon as you press Tab, the value, 150, is displayed in B5. This is the same value as when the formula =B2+B3+B4 was entered in B5.

TIP You can use the AutoFill feature to copy the formula to the other cells.

4. Click B5. The AutoFill handle is the small box in the lower-right corner of the active cell.

5. Drag the AutoFill handle to D5. The total in C5 should be $45.50. D5 should show $2,200.00.

6. Close Excel unless you are not going to move on to the next chapter immediately.

BONUS

This bonus section provides a baker's dozen of questions to ask before designing your worksheet. If you have the answers, you can most likely create a spreadsheet that meets or exceeds your needs and expectations. After completing this chapter, don't expect to be able to answer all of these questions. However, when the time comes to design your own worksheet, make sure that you review these questions. They can save you a lot of time.

Ask yourself these questions:

1. Who will be using the worksheet?

If it is only you, it may not be necessary to add instructions as comments on the worksheet. If other people will access the worksheet, you may need to protect certain parts from change or even hide them so that other users can't see them. For example, you may have a column for Salary that you don't want other users to see. In that case, you want to hide the column. You learn how to hide information later in this book.

2. What data will you be using to develop your worksheet?

You need to determine whether the data is already available. If it is not, you may have to input data from several different sources.

3. What is the format for the data that you will be receiving?

If you will be getting data from other users, you need to make certain that it is in a format that you can use; you want to avoid re-entering all of the data manually.

4. Do you have access to all of the data needed to complete your worksheet?

   If not, figure out who has the data and how you can gain access to it. Your processing of the data may require approval from higher authorities in the organization.

5. How are you going to manipulate the data?

   You may need to create only a few simple formulas, or you may need to retrieve data from multiple worksheets before it can be processed.

6. What methods are you going to use to ensure that all the data has been correctly entered and that all of your formulas are correct?

7. What reports are required and by whom?

   Depending on how the reports are to be used, you may need to summarize the information before printing a report, or you may be able to simply print the worksheet in its entirety.

8. Which automatic features can you use to minimize data entry errors?

9. Do you need to design multiple levels of outlines for the data so that you can easily expand or collapse it to fit the needs of the person(s) reading the report?

10. Can charts and graphs help interpret the information without giving an invalid picture?

    If so, decide which types of graphs and charts you need.

11. Based on the results of manipulating this data, what decisions are going to be made?

    If no decisions are to be made based on a report of this data, you should question whether you really need to create the report. The decisions that are made dictate the type and the amount of data that must be collected.

12. Is there some way to flag problem areas for immediate attention?

    For example, you may decide to print problem areas in a different color or in a different style or font.

13. Finally, how are you going to acquire ongoing feedback and evaluation of your worksheet and reports?

    If others are going to be using the reports, make sure that the information that you provide is helpful and not redundant.

Summary

Spreadsheets can be used for many different types of needs. Examples of common uses of spreadsheets include inventory control, customer contact, personnel information, and sales reports. Worksheets can contain many types of objects. Text can be labels for data, names, and product identification numbers. You can also enter numbers that are formatted as text (such as social security numbers and telephone numbers).

Numbers are common in worksheets. Numbers can be manipulated using either formulas or functions. Numbers are normally right aligned within a cell, while text is left aligned. However, by using the justification buttons on the toolbar, you can change the justification of text or numbers as you desire. Excel has many uses, and at this point, you have barely scratched the surface of its capabilities. As you move through subsequent chapters of this book, you begin to feel more comfortable with the variety of features offered by Excel.

MANAGING FILES AND AVOIDING DISASTERS

IN THIS CHAPTER YOU LEARN THESE KEY SKILLS

When searching for a file in a colleague's file cabinet, you may have some difficulty finding what you need. We all have a filing method that make sense to us but not necessarily to others. Even using standard filing procedures, do you file a letter by its date, by the sender, by the receiver, or by the subject? What if the letter contains more than one subject?

Luckily, Excel offers excellent file-management tools. You can easily create new folders to hold related documents. Unlike in Windows 3.1, you can now create folders inside of folders, which makes grouping your files easy. In a previous chapter, you learned how to create a shortcut on the Windows desktop. If you have an Excel file that you want to keep in more than one place, you can create a shortcut in a new folder.

Even within a workbook, you may find that you want to keep related information together. You do this by using multiple worksheets inside a single workbook.

Perhaps the most important part of this chapter focuses on how to avoid losing your work and what to do if it happens anyway (which is almost assured, given the nature of computers). If you lose a file that you've just created, it's probably not a major loss. But losing a file that has taken you months to create can be a disaster and may even directly affect your future employment.

Manipulating Worksheets

By default, Excel for Office 97 comes with three worksheets in each workbook (Excel for Office 95 has 16). Having more than one worksheet in a workbook simplifies the task of creating a summary worksheet. For example, you may have a sales report for each of four stores (with each store having its own worksheet). This way, you can easily print individual store reports. To summarize the information from the individual worksheets, you can add a fifth sheet to the workbook.

In addition to adding and deleting worksheets, you can rename them. You can even group them so that anything you type in a cell in one sheet is duplicated in the same cell in all the other worksheets. This is called *grouping* worksheets.

Adding worksheets to a workbook

Adding worksheets is fairly simple, but you need a bit of mathematical ability if you want to add more than a few worksheets. If you need many sheets, arrange them in sets of worksheets or workbooks. For example, if you are tracking the sales for 100 stores, you may divide the stores into 10 different regions and give each region its own worksheet or workbook (depending on the complexity of the data).

Previous versions of Excel limit you to a maximum of 256 worksheets per workbook (depending on the version of Excel you were using). The current maximum is determined by the amount of available RAM. If you create too many worksheets, Excel crashes, and you lose any work that you haven't saved. To test this, I added 1,535 worksheets before crashing; another time, I added 3,071. In reality, most workbooks don't need more than about a dozen sheets.

Because it's easier to add worksheets than to tell you how to do it, this activity gives you experience in adding one and multiple worksheets to a workbook.

Follow these steps:

1. Open Excel. A new workbook is displayed. The Sheet1 tab is already highlighted, so it is the active worksheet.

2. Press and hold Shift, and click the Sheet3 tab.

3. Choose `Insert` → `Worksheet`.

   You now have six worksheets. Notice that Excel inserts Sheet4 through Sheet6 *prior to* the first selected worksheet, and Sheet4 now becomes the active worksheet.

NOTE To double the number of worksheets, you would press Shift, click the Sheet3 tab, and then choose `Insert` → `Worksheet` again. For this activity, however, you only want to add four more worksheets.

4. Press Shift, and click Sheet1. Four worksheet tabs are now selected.

5. Choose `Insert` → `Worksheet`.

   Excel inserts the four new worksheets prior to the first selected worksheet (in this case, Sheet4). Your screen should be similar to Figure 3-1. The tabs for sheets 1, 2, and 3 are hidden to the right of Sheet6.

TIP If you know exactly (or even approximately) how many worksheets you want in a workbook *before* you create it, choose `Tools` → `Options` and click the General tab in the Options dialog box. Set the Sheets in new workbook option to the number that you want, close the dialog box, and create a new workbook. Remember to reset the option after creating the new workbook, or Excel creates all future workbooks with that number of sheets.

6. Leave the workbook open for now.

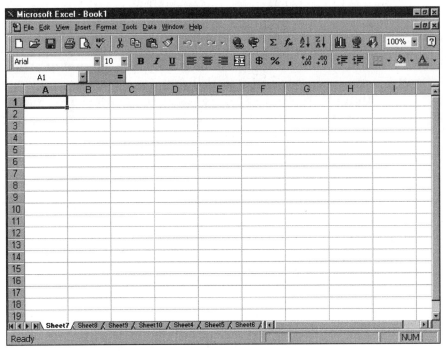

Figure 3-1 The total number of worksheets is increased to 10.

Deleting worksheets

As this activity demonstrates, deleting worksheets is easier than adding them. Sheet7 should be the active sheet.

Follow these steps:

1. If Sheet7 isn't the active sheet, click the Sheet7 tab.

2. Hold Shift, and click the tab for Sheet10.

3. Choose **Edit** → **Delete Sheet** . You are prompted to confirm that you want to delete the worksheet(s), as shown in Figure 3-2.

TIP To select multiple sheets that are contiguous (next to each other), click the first sheet's tab, hold Shift, and click the last sheet's tab. All sheets between the two are highlighted. To select noncontiguous sheets, click the first sheet's tab, hold Ctrl, and click the tabs for any other sheets that you want to select. After you've selected the desired sheets, you can delete them.

Figure 3-2 Excel displays this warning (confirmation) box when you attempt to delete any worksheet.

Excel displays a warning when you try to delete a worksheet. Remember, all of the data contained on the worksheet is also deleted. If deleted sheets contain links to other worksheets or workbooks, you find errors when you examine the other worksheets or workbooks.

4. Click OK to delete the sheets.

5. Close the workbook without saving.

Renaming worksheets

By default, worksheets are given names such as Sheet1, Sheet2, and Sheet3. If you are using multiple worksheets in a workbook, it is helpful to give each one a more descriptive name. You must rename each worksheet individually; you can't rename multiple sheets at one time.

This activity shows how to rename a worksheet.

Follow these steps:

1. Click the New button on the toolbar to create a new workbook.

2. Choose Insert → Worksheet . Excel inserts a single worksheet, Sheet4, prior to the current worksheet.

3. Double-click the Sheet4 tab. The tab is shown in reverse (black background with white letters).

TIP To edit (rather than replace) the name, *double-click* the tab, click the tab once more to drop the insertion point, and then edit as usual.

4. Type **Region 1**.

5. Rename the remaining sheets as **Region 2** through **Region 4**. Press Enter after renaming each worksheet.

6. Choose File → Save As . Excel displays the Save As dialog box.

7. Select the Discovering Excel folder.

8. Type **REGIONAL SALES** in the File name text box.

9. Click Save.

TIP If you have many worksheets, *right-click* any of the sheet-scrolling buttons (located to the left of the first worksheet tab), and you see a list of all tab names. To activate a sheet, simply click its name.

Grouping worksheets

When you have several worksheets that need to have the same row or column labels, use the group feature to save time and increase accuracy. After you group a set of worksheets, anything that you do to any of the sheets is replicated on all of the sheets.

In this exercise, you create similar worksheets for all four of the sales regions. By using the group feature, you save many keystrokes and ensure greater accuracy. The Region 4 tab is still active.

Follow these steps:

1. Hold Shift, and click the Region 1 tab. Notice that all four sheets are now selected, and a Group message is displayed in the Program Title bar.

2. In B1, type **January**.

3. AutoFill the months from B1 to M1. You do this by dragging the AutoFill handle to the right until you see December in the small box that follows your cursor. (When you get to the right edge of the screen, keep moving the mouse to the right.) Release the mouse button.

4. Press Home to cancel the selection and return the cursor to A1. The columns for September to December may not be visible. Use the scroll bar at the bottom of the screen to see the parts that are hidden.

5. In A2, type **North** and press Enter.

6. In A3, type **South**.

7. Add **East** and **West** entries to A4 and A5, respectively.

8. Press Ctrl+Home to move the cursor back to A1. Your worksheet should look like the example shown in Figure 3-3.

If you click the tab for the active worksheet in the group, the group feature is *not* turned off. Click any other tab to turn off the group feature.

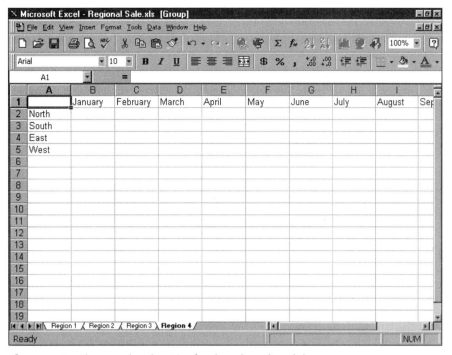

Figure 3-3 The completed entries for the selected worksheets.

9. To ungroup the sheets, click any of the first three worksheet tabs.

10. Click each sheet in turn to see the changes that you made. All worksheets have the same text in the same cells. In the next chapter, you learn to format cells and add formulas and functions to grouped worksheets.

11. Leave the workbook open for the next activity.

Copying and moving worksheets

In some instances, you may need to copy or move worksheets. You can copy and move individual sheets or grouped sheets.

COPYING WORKSHEETS

You have been so incredibly successful (saving your boss thousands of dollars through the appropriate use of Excel) that your company has expanded to a new region. To include it in your workbook, you could just add a sheet and type the headings. An easier way, however, is to simply copy one of the existing worksheets.

Copying a worksheet is a matter of selecting it and using the copy command. When you copy a sheet, the original remains intact.

Follow these steps:

1. Click the worksheet tab for Region 1.

2. Choose [**Edit**] → [**Move or Copy Sheet**] to display the Move or Copy dialog box, as shown in Figure 3-4.

   Because you are copying the sheet to the current book, leave the default name in the To book text box. The Before sheet panel allows you to insert a copy of the current worksheet prior to any existing worksheet in the workbook. In the Before sheet panel, Region 1 is already highlighted. Normally, you would select (move to end), but you need to practice moving a sheet in the next exercise.

Figure 3-4 Use the Move or Copy dialog box to move or copy a worksheet.

3. Click the Create a copy option in the lower-left corner of the dialog box. If you don't specify this option, the worksheet is *moved,* not copied.

4. Click OK. You now see another sheet. The tab name is Region 1 (2). It is a copy of the Region 1 worksheet.

5. Using the skills that you gained in the earlier activities, rename the tab as Region 5. Press Enter to complete the name change. The new sheet is in the wrong position, but you remedy that in the next activity.

6. Save the workbook.

NOTE To copy multiple worksheets, select the ones that are to be copied. If they are contiguous, click the first tab, hold Shift, and click the last tab. If they are not consecutive, click the first tab, hold Ctrl, and click the tab for each sheet to be added to the group. When the group is complete, copy the worksheets as you normally would.

MOVING WORKSHEETS

Moving worksheets involves almost the same process as copying them. The difference is that when a worksheet is moved, the original worksheet is deleted. When you copy a worksheet, you have two identical copies of the worksheet. When you move it, you have only one sheet, but it is in a different location.

As with copying worksheets, you can move groups of sheets to other workbooks or you can move them within the current workbook.

You move a sheet because you need to rearrange the worksheet order without adding or deleting any worksheets. As you notice in this activity, this process is nearly identical to copying a worksheet.

Follow these steps:

1. If the Region 5 tab is not active, click the tab to activate it.

2. Choose Edit → Move or Copy Sheet Excel displays the Move or Copy dialog box.

3. In the Before sheet panel, click (move to end).

4. Click OK. The sheets are now in the correct order.

5. Save the workbook.

 NOTE **You can also move a sheet by selecting its tab and dragging it to a new position. As you drag, you see a downward-pointing triangle between each pair of sheets. Release the mouse button to drop the dragged sheet between the two existing sheets.**

Avoiding Disasters (and Recovering from the Unavoidable)

This section deals with possible problems and their remedies, focusing on some of the more common problems that you may encounter when using Excel. Chapter 18 covers troubleshooting in depth.

Losing your work

One of the most common problems with any computer application is completing a section of work and then having it disappear. Although the explanation for the disappearance may range from the mundane (accidentally pressing Delete) to the mysterious (it was there when I got up to get coffee), there are ways to prevent data loss and to recover the data if, indeed, you do lose it. (We believe in data burglars — gnomes who lurk in every office and regularly steal data for their diet.)

SAVE YOUR WORK REGULARLY

Save your work approximately every five minutes. You can do this by pressing Ctrl+S or by clicking the Save button on the toolbar. This simple task can save you many hours of headaches. After you do it for a while, it becomes a natural part of your data entry.

BACK UP YOUR FILES

Always make a backup copy of your files on a floppy disk or a tape backup device. Keep the backup files at a separate location. (If thieves steal your computer, they are probably going to take anything that's near the computer.)

SIDE TRIP

Years ago, we worked in an older office building that had an antiquated sprinkler system. A small fire set off the sprinklers in the janitor's room. Unfortunately, the fire also set off the sprinklers in our computer lab. That was a major disaster — we lost not only the equipment, but also all of our data.

Even if your files are automatically backed up to a network server every night, we still recommend making backups of your data to floppy disks. You can fit lots of files on a single disk, and you gain peace of mind from knowing that you always have another copy of your data.

SIDE TRIP

A university hospital had all of its financial information, covering four years, on a hard disk. The data entry personnel weren't worried about backing up, because they had printouts of all the information. We asked how long it would take to re-enter all of the data if it were lost, and after careful consideration, we were told, "Weeks." Soon thereafter, we learned that backup systems seemed like a good idea after all.

SAVE YOUR DATA TO A FLOPPY DISK

If you are on a network, you may assume that your data is automatically backed up when the network is backed up each night. However, if you are saving your data to a local hard disk, the data may not be being backed up. A simple way to cure this problem is to back up the data to a floppy disk. If you are familiar with the Windows Explorer, you can also use it to copy your files to a floppy disk.

A good method to ensure that your data remains safe is to back it up to a floppy disk. This activity shows one way to do it.

Follow these steps:

1. Save the Regional Sales workbook to the hard disk.

2. Place a floppy disk in your disk drive, and choose File → Save As . Excel displays the Save As dialog box.

3. In the File name text box, type **A:\Regional BU**. If your backup drive is other than A, substitute its letter in the filename. For example, if your backup drive is B, type **B:\Regional BU** in the File name text box.

4. Click Save.

5. Close the workbook. If any other workbooks are open, close them.

Deleting a workbook

Using the right mouse button in Excel, it is a simple task to delete a workbook. However, you may delete a workbook and then change your mind. At other times, a workbook may be deleted without your realizing it, and when you look for it, the workbook isn't there.

Before you can delete a workbook, you *must* close it. If you try to delete an open workbook, you get an error message that tells you access to that file is denied.

Follow these steps to delete a workbook:

1. Choose File → Open . The Discover Excel folder, containing Regional Sales, is displayed.

2. Move the cursor to the workbook name (Regional Sales), and *right-click* it. As shown in Figure 3-5, Excel displays a drop-down shortcut menu.

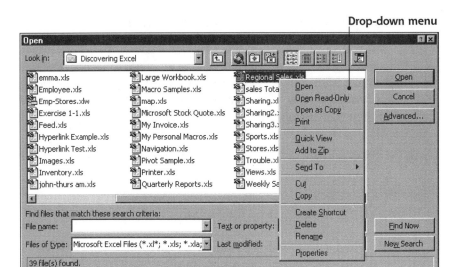

Drop-down menu

Figure 3-5 Excel displays a drop-down menu when you right-click the name of the workbook.

3. Choose [**Delete**]. As shown in Figure 3-6, Excel displays the Confirm File Delete dialog box.

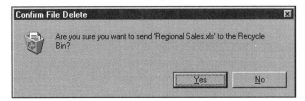

Figure 3-6 The Confirm File Delete dialog box.

 NOTE The displayed dialog box is the default under Windows 95, using the Windows 95 Recycle Bin as the storage place for your deleted files. If you have added a program that replaces the Recycle Bin — for example, Norton Utilities — your dialog box may differ slightly.

4. Click Yes to delete the workbook. The workbook is no longer displayed.

5. Click Cancel to close the Open dialog box.

Recovering a workbook

If you accidentally delete a workbook, it isn't necessarily a disaster, particularly if you try to recover it *right away.* The easiest way to learn about file recovery is for you to recover a file that you purposely delete.

In this activity, you recover the workbook that you previously deleted.

Follow these steps:

1. Minimize Excel by clicking the Program Title bar minimize button (the third button from the right). Excel is removed from your screen and is placed in the taskbar at the bottom of the screen (if your taskbar is visible). You should now see the Windows desktop on your screen.

2. If any other programs are open, minimize them now. On the Windows desktop, you see an icon for the Recycle Bin. (If you have replaced the Recycle Bin with another program, such as Norton Utilities, the name of the icon may be different. It probably looks like either a trash can or a shredder.)

3. Open the Recycle Bin by double-clicking it. The Recycle Bin dialog box, shown in Figure 3-7, is displayed. The files are probably arranged alphabetically, by name.

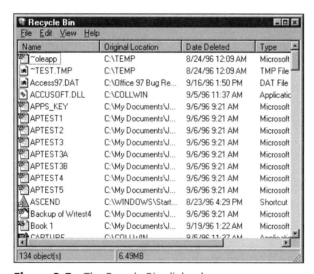

Figure 3-7 The Recycle Bin dialog box.

To change the order in which the files are displayed, choose View → Arrange Icons, and then choose the order in which you want to have them arranged.

4. If necessary, scroll down until you see Regional Sales.

5. *Right-click* the filename, and choose Restore from the resulting pop-up menu. The file is removed from the Recycle Bin dialog box.

6. Close the Recycle Bin by clicking the Close button in the Program Title bar of the Recycle Bin. (The button contains an *X*.)

7. If the taskbar is not visible, move the cursor to the bottom of the screen. Move the cursor onto the Microsoft Excel button (you may not be able to see all of the text), and click the button to return Excel to your screen.

8. Choose File → Open . Regional Sales has been recovered.

9. Double-click it to open it. The workbook should appear intact.

If you left the computer after you deleted the file and someone emptied the Recycle Bin, you need a more specialized utility program to recover the file.

Recovering a worksheet

If you accidentally delete a worksheet from a workbook, the Undo feature does *not* restore it. Before you delete any worksheet, always save the workbook.

About every half-hour, save your workbook by using the Save As command to add a letter (perhaps *A* or *B*) to the end of the filename. By using slightly different names for saving your workbook at various stages, you give yourself a means for undoing major errors that you may make in creating your workbook. If you discover a large mistake, you can go back to an earlier version of the file without having to start over again.

If you realize that you have incorrectly deleted a worksheet, close the file *without saving it.* Reload the file. You lose any work that you have done since you last saved, but that may be a better solution than having to rebuild an entire worksheet.

If you save a file with the same name as an existing file on the disk (for example, by choosing File → Save , clicking the Save button on the toolbar, or pressing Ctrl+S), the current file overwrites the existing file, and the existing file is no longer recoverable.

If you accidentally save a small or empty workbook with the name of an existing large workbook, a computer specialist may be able to recover most of your work. It could be very time consuming and expensive, but if it's a large workbook, it may be worthwhile to try to save the file.

Recovering a workbook that doesn't load into Excel

If your workbook doesn't load into Excel, it probably means that the file is damaged. Your hard disk may need repairs, or the file may not have been saved properly. (Possible causes include a power outage or brownout, the physical failure of your hard disk, and failure to properly shut down your computer.) Sometimes files are damaged for no apparent reason (probably the data burglar again). You can try recovering the file with a utility program, such as Norton Utilities. Norton Utilities includes a tool that tries to repair your file.

Do not use any disk utilities that are designed for earlier Windows versions. This could make things even worse. If you upgrade from an earlier version of Windows to Windows 95, you need to buy new disk utility programs and virus checkers.

Using Briefcase to Keep Files Updated

I f you share files on a network, share files between your laptop and your desktop computer, or use multiple computers, you should use the Briefcase to automatically keep the files up to date on both computers.

The first time that you open Briefcase, you see the Welcome to the Windows Briefcase instruction screen, as shown in Figure 3-8. You only see it the first time that you run Briefcase.

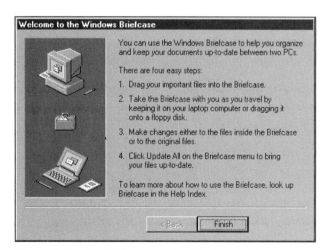

Figure 3-8 The Welcome to the Windows Briefcase instruction screen.

TIP To see the Welcome screen again, *right-click* any blank area of the Windows desktop and select New → Briefcase . Double-click the new Briefcase icon to open the new Briefcase. The Welcome screen is displayed again. After you are done viewing the screen, close the new Briefcase, *right-click* it again to open the pop-up menu, and choose Delete . At the Confirm Folder Deletion dialog box, click Yes.

A Briefcase is only automatically installed when you choose a portable installation or a custom installation and select the Briefcase option. Create a new Briefcase by *right-clicking* any blank area of the Windows desktop and selecting New → Briefcase from the pop-up menu that's displayed.

NOTE To use the Briefcase between computers, the computers must be connected, either by a network or a direct cable.

For additional information about Briefcase, open a Briefcase, choose Help → Help Topics , and search for Briefcase. Click the first option, Accessories: Using Briefcase to keep files up to date.

TIP To print a copy of the Briefcase Help topic, choose Options → Print Topic .

Protecting Workbooks

As long as we're talking about protection, this is a good place to mention workbook protection. To password-protect a workbook, choose File → Save As and click the Options button in the Save As dialog box. As shown in Figure 3-9, Excel displays the Save Options dialog box.

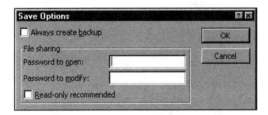

Figure 3-9 The Save Options dialog box.

The File sharing panel offers three options:

* The first option requires a password for opening the worksheet. If you set a password in this dialog box, the workbook cannot be opened without the password.

* If you choose the Password to modify option, the workbook can be opened without a password but can't be changed unless a password is entered.

* The final option is Read-only recommended. When this option is checked and the file is opened, Excel displays the warning box shown in Figure 3-10. The box says that the file should be opened as read-only

unless you need to modify it. Click Yes to open as read-only or No to open and make changes to the worksheet.

Figure 3-10 The read-only information box.

BONUS

Automatically Saving Your Workbook

The AutoSave feature appears in the last section of this chapter for three reasons: First, because I want to emphasize the need to *save, save, save* when you are working with data; second, because it's a nifty feature with which to end the chapter; and third, because it doesn't always work. It's just an insurance policy against losing your data.

Add-ins are extra programs than not everyone may want to use or programs that are used infrequently. When you turn them off, they don't get removed from your hard disk; you can easily turn them back on. Some add-ins take a lot of RAM (the computer memory that helps determine how fast your computer works). If you load too many add-ins and don't have a lot of RAM, or are running several other programs at the same time, you may find that your computer slows to a crawl. To maintain your computer's speed, use only the add-ins that you need.

Because AutoSave is an add-in feature, it isn't active by default. You need to activate it before it works for you.

Follow these steps:

1. Choose Tools → Add-Ins .

2. To set the AutoSave feature, click it, as shown in Figure 3-11.

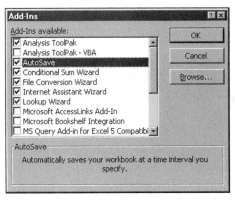

Figure 3-11 The Add-Ins dialog box. The AutoSave feature must be checked to be active.

3. Click OK to close the Add-Ins dialog box.

4. Choose **Tools** → **Auto Save** to display the AutoSave dialog box, as shown in Figure 3-12.

   By default, AutoSave only saves the active workbook every ten minutes and prompts you before doing so. You can vary the default time, turn on the option to save all open workbooks, and turn off the prompt option. This automatically saves your file every ten minutes (or whatever interval you specify).

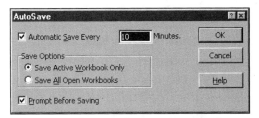

Figure 3-12 The AutoSave dialog box.

5. Click OK to close the AutoSave dialog box.

6. Close Excel without saving any open workbooks.

If you have several large workbooks open, you may find that saving all workbooks every ten minutes becomes too time consuming. In that case, turn off the AutoSave feature by choosing **Tools** → **Add-Ins** and turning off the AutoSave option.

Summary

Using Excel's worksheet and workbook tools, you can perform several tasks. You can easily add or delete worksheets from a workbook. You can rename individual worksheet tabs so that they are easier to identify. By grouping files, you can save duplicate entries of labels or other items on the worksheets. If you need to add a worksheet similar to one that already exists, you can copy it to a new position, rename it, and make the changes. You can move a worksheet either through the Move/Copy command or by dragging the name tab of the worksheet to the new position.

Using the Windows 95 Recycle Bin, you can easily restore workbooks that have been accidentally or purposely deleted. The Briefcase feature is used to make sure that when you are working with multiple computers, you are always working with the most updated version of the workbook. You can easily add a password to protect your workbook from unauthorized access. Finally, using an add-in feature, you can set Excel to automatically save your work on a regular basis.

CHAPTER FOUR

SPRUCING UP YOUR WORKSHEET

IN THIS CHAPTER YOU LEARN THESE KEY SKILLS

4

Buying a car can be a major commitment of your time, not to mention your money. What do you consider when purchasing a car? I consider price (you need a starting point, and that's mine!), warranty, gas mileage, the salesperson ("Here, kick the tires."), and the car's functional features. The car's looks also interest me. Is the interior in good shape? What color is the car? How is the driver's console arranged? How many cup holders does the car have? (Do you get the feeling that I'm obsessed with cup holders? I am.) I may even look at the hubcaps (to make sure that they can't be stolen). To summarize, in addition to price, I look at two distinct classes of details: functions and features.

So far, this book has dealt mainly with the functional aspects of Excel — how it works. Now it's time to take a closer look at Excel's features: specifically, how to change a worksheet's appearance so that it is not only easy to read but also presented in a way that enhances the viewer's interpretation of the information.

In this chapter, you explore some of Excel's formatting features. Formatting features are ways of making the worksheet *look* different, even though it contains the same information. We can't possibly cover all the formatting features in a single chapter, so instead we focus on the ones that can save you the most time and effort. In subsequent chapters, you examine additional formatting features of Excel.

What is Formatting?

A car that runs well but looks as though it is held together with rubber bands and chewing gum may be a good investment, but appearances can affect your perception of the car's value. The same holds true for a worksheet. It may contain all the required information, but if the data is difficult to interpret, the viewer may not give the worksheet the professional attention it deserves.

Two aspects of a worksheet's appearance — or *formatting* — affect the viewer's interpretation of the worksheet's worth. First, is the worksheet easy to read? (For example, does the worksheet have column widths that allow you to view all of the data in each column? Is the text easy to read? Are borders used to divide the contents into groups?) Second, can you easily retrieve the needed information?

SIDE TRIP

We have seen Excel users (as well as users of other software) spend hours making a worksheet look nice. However, closer examination reveals that the worksheet contains numerous errors in data and formulas. There is a fine line between formatting for greater readability and formatting to impress the reader with your formatting skills. Accuracy comes first; then format the worksheet so that it is readable.

Formatting Cells

You can change the appearance (formatting) of cells in many ways. Before you can format a cell or a group of cells, you must select (or highlight) the cell(s) that you want to change. You format the selected cells by using the Format Cells dialog box.

Creating a sample worksheet

Before you can format a worksheet, you need to have a worksheet to format. (That's why we're writing this book.) In the following activity, you build a simple worksheet, and in subsequent activities, you format it.

Follow these steps:

1. In B1, type **Test 1**.

2. Before pressing Enter, drag the AutoFill handle to E1. Test 2 through Test 4 are automatically entered.

3. In F1, type **Total** and then press Enter.

4. In G1, type **Percent** and press Enter.

5. In A2 through A4, type **Ann**, **Bob**, and **Cathy**.

6. In A5, type **Average**.

7. Enter Ann's scores in row 2: **93**, **89**, **91** and **85.5**.

8. For Bob's scores in row 3, type **88**, **76.5**, **82**, and **88**.

9. For Cathy's scores in row 4, type **79.5**, **90**, **83.5** and **85**.

10. In B5, type **86.3333**.

11. In C5 through E5, type **85.1666**, **85.5**, and **86.1666**.

12. In F2, type **=B2+C2+D2+E2**.

13. Without pressing Enter, drag the AutoFill handle to F4.

14. In G2, type **=F2/400** and drag the AutoFill handle to G4. This divides the total score for each student by the total number of points.

In the following step, do *not* type an equal sign before the text.

15. In A7, type **2-12-97** and press Enter. The date is changed slightly and now reads 2/12/97. Notice that it is right-aligned (meaning that Excel is treating it as a number) even though you did not enter an equal sign. Excel treats the entry as a date, rather than text, and dates are considered to be numbers.

16. Press Ctrl+Home to make A1 the active cell.

17. Save the workbook in the Discover Excel folder as TEST SCORES. Your worksheet should look like the example in Figure 4-1. At this time, the default format is applied to the cells. You begin formatting cells in the next activity.

18. Click the Print button on the toolbar.

19. Leave the workbook open for the next activity.

Formatting by the numbers

Numbers can be displayed in many different ways. The default is General, which really means that the entry has no special formatting. By default, text is left-aligned and numbers are right-aligned. Also, trailing zeros in the numbers are not displayed. In many cases, your worksheet is more easily interpreted if the numbers are formatted.

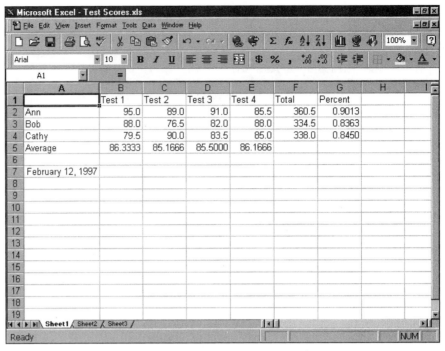

Figure 4-1 The worksheet after the data has been entered.

The formatting that you apply depends on how you want the reader to interpret the information in your worksheet. The following activity shows several types of number formatting.

Follow these steps:

1. Select B2 through E4. Excel highlights the selected cells.

2. Choose **Format** → **Cells** . The Format Cells dialog box is displayed. The Number tab, shown in Figure 4-2, should be visible. If any other tab is visible, click the Number tab to make it active. Notice that the Sample panel shows 93 — the contents of the first cell in the selection — formatted as specified by the current setting of General in the Category panel. Below the Sample panel you see a description of how the number is formatted with the current Category selection. By default, all numbers are formatted as General.

3. Click Number in the Category panel. The Number option changes formatting significantly, as shown in Figure 4-3. The Sample panel now contains 93.00. The default number format is two decimal places, no comma separator for numbers greater than 1,000, and negative numbers shown in black with a minus sign. Although Figure 4-3 isn't in color, the second and fourth choices in the Negative numbers panel are displayed in red.

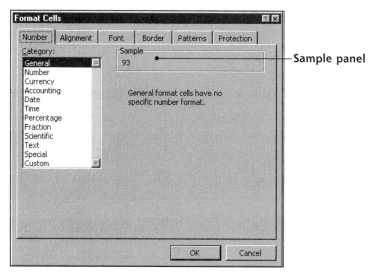
— Sample panel

Figure 4-2 Use the options on the Number tab to format selected numbers.

4. Click OK to close the dialog box. The selected numbers now appear with two decimal places.

5. Click ⫶₀ (the Decrease Decimal button); this is the sixth button from the left on the formatting toolbar. All the selected numbers now have only one decimal place. You could have changed this on the Number tab, but we wanted to show you a shortcut.

6. Select G2 through G4, and click **%** (the Percent Style button) on the formatting toolbar. The values are automatically displayed as percentages with no decimal places.

7. Click ⫶₀ (the Increase Decimal button) on the formatting toolbar, and then click it again. The numbers are now formatted as percentages with two decimal places.

8. Select B5 through E5, and click the Decrease Decimal button. All numbers are now displayed with *three* decimal places, including the number in D5, which had only one decimal place to begin with. This is because Excel works from the number that has the *most* digits displayed after the decimal point.

9. Click the Decrease Decimal button again. The numbers in B5 through E5 now have two decimal places. Again, you could change this on the Number tab of the Format Cells dialog box.

10. Select A7, the date, and then choose **Format** → **Cells**.

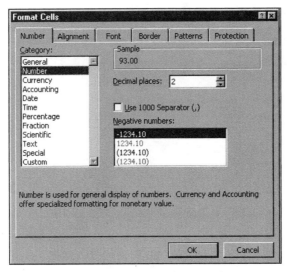

Figure 4-3 The Number tab when Number is selected in the Category panel.

Excel knows that this should be a date, so Date is already highlighted in the Category panel, as shown in Figure 4-4. The Sample panel shows the current format.

11. Scroll through the date formats in the Type panel, and click the format in the Type panel that displays the date as February 12, 1997 in the Sample panel.

12. Click OK to close the dialog box.

13. Select A9, type **5432.10**, and press Enter. You haven't seen how money is formatted, so a brief overview is in order.

14. Right-click A9, and choose Format Cells from the pop-up menu. This is a shortcut to opening the Format Cells dialog box. Look at the example in the Sample panel. The number currently has a General format.

15. Click Currency in the Category panel. In Figure 4-5, notice that the options look similar to the number options shown earlier in Figure 4-3. The second and fourth Negative numbers are still in red. In the Symbol drop-down list, you can choose the currency symbol that you want to use. Symbols from many countries are available.

16. Click Accounting in the Category panel. You can no longer choose the formatting for negative numbers. Negative numbers now appear in parentheses, in black type. Using the accounting format, all decimal points in a column are aligned.

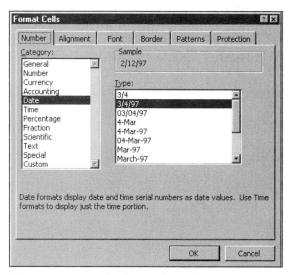

Figure 4-4 Date has been selected in the Category panel.

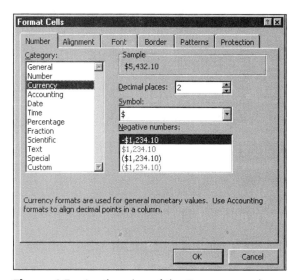

Figure 4-5 Another view of the Category panel.

TIP If negative numbers are involved in the display, decimal points may not line up within a column. You must use the Accounting format to align the decimal points.

TIP The Currency and Accounting formats differ in another way. In the Currency format, the dollar sign (or selected symbol) appears immediately to the left of the number. Using the Accounting format, the symbol appears at the far left edge of the cell.

17. Click OK to close the Format Cells dialog box. A9 should be the active cell.

18. Press Delete. This removes the cell contents but not the formatting.

 TIP To remove the contents *and* all formatting from a cell, choose Edit → Clear → All.

19. Press Ctrl+Home to make A1 the active cell.

20. Save the file, and leave the workbook open for now.

Justifying your worksheet

Another word for alignment is *justification*. Both terms refer to the manner in which Excel positions numbers or text within a cell. The Alignment tab of the Format Cells dialog box lets you specify how the data is placed within a cell or a group of cells. This tab contains three basic panels: Text alignment, Text control, and Orientation. Although the panels refer to text, the alignment changes the position of any data in the cell or selected cells (including numbers, which are generally right-aligned). Changing the alignment of the data in a cell does *not* change its data type. If you have a number in a cell, and you left-align it (so that it looks like text), it is still formatted as a number.

The formatting toolbar includes buttons for aligning data to the left, the center, and the right as well as for merging a group of cells and centering the text that they contain. Figure 4-6 shows these buttons.

ALIGNING DATA IN YOUR WORKSHEET

In some cases, you may not want the default alignment of right for numbers and left for text.

To change the alignment to fit your needs, follow these steps:

1. Select B1 through G1.

2. Right-click and choose Format Cells from the pop-up menu. Excel displays the Format Cells dialog box.

3. Click the Alignment tab. Figure 4-7 shows the Alignment tab. The options are broken down into three panels: Text alignment, Text control, and Orientation. By default, text is left-aligned. Using the Horizontal drop-down list, you can choose from several options.

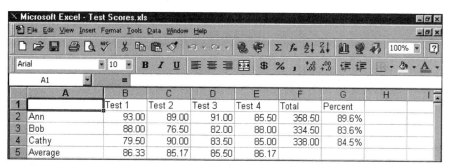

	A	B	C	D	E	F	G	H	I
1		Test 1	Test 2	Test 3	Test 4	Total	Percent		
2	Ann	93.00	89.00	91.00	85.50	358.50	89.6%		
3	Bob	88.00	76.50	82.00	88.00	334.50	83.6%		
4	Cathy	79.50	90.00	83.50	85.00	338.00	84.5%		
5	Average	86.33	85.17	85.50	86.17				

Figure 4-6 Basic alignment can be accomplished by using the buttons on the formatting toolbar.

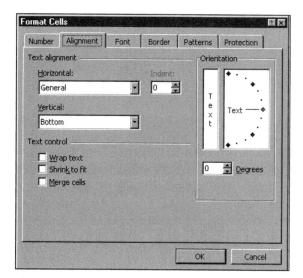

Figure 4-7 The Alignment tab of the Format Cells dialog box.

4. Drop down the Horizontal list, and choose Center. Justify stretches the text between the cell edges. The Fill option fills the cell with the character that it contains. For example, if you type an asterisk in a cell and apply Fill alignment, the cell fills with asterisks. Narrowing or widening the column adjusts the number of asterisks automatically.

TIP If you choose Left (Indent) in the Horizontal drop-down box, the Indent spin button box becomes active. You use this setting to specify the number of characters (*not* inches) that the selected entries should be indented from the left edge of the cell, based on the current font and size.

5. Drop down the Vertical list, and choose Center. This controls the *vertical* position of the text within the cell. If you choose Justify, the text is stretched vertically to fit the cell height.

6. Click OK to close the dialog box. The selected text is centered both horizontally and vertically within the cells.

The Text control panel offers three choices: Wrap text, Shrink to fit, and Merge cells. Wrap text causes Excel to work like a word processor, wrapping the text to the next line if it doesn't fit within the cell width.

TIP If Wrap text is not enabled, when text exceeds the width of the cell, it spills over into the next cell *if the next cell is empty.* If the next cell is not empty, the text is cut off. However, if you select the cell with the cutoff text and look in the Formula bar, you can see that the text is still intact. It just isn't fully displayed in the cell.

FEATURE FOCUS The Merge cells option is new in Excel for Microsoft Office 97. Cells can be merged either horizontally or vertically. If more than one cell is selected and the Merge cells option is selected, the selected cells merge into a single cell, with the cell address set as the left or the top address of the group of cells.

The Orientation panel is used to slant the text. In the right box of the Orientation panel, you can specify the desired orientation by dragging the red diamond up or down.

Before moving on, we need to discuss one more alignment feature: Merge and Center. This option is used to center selected text across a number of selected cells.

MERGING CELLS AND CENTERING THE TEXT THAT THEY CONTAIN

You may want to center text across several cells. This is particularly helpful for setting up a title.

To add a title to your worksheet, follow these steps:

1. Right-click A1 and choose Insert from the pop-up menu. Excel displays the Insert dialog box.

2. Click the Entire row option button, and then click OK. An entire row is inserted.

3. In A1, type **Word Processing 101** and press Enter. Notice that the text spills over into B1.

4. Select A1 through G1.

5. Click the Merge and Center button (just to the right of the Align Right button on the formatting toolbar). Notice that the heading — Word Processing 101 — is centered across the selected range of cells (A1 through G1).

 Cells A1 through G1 become a *single* cell, with the address A1. Any formulas referring to B1 through G1 return errors.

6. Save the workbook by pressing Ctrl+S. Leave it open.

Giving your text a facelift

You may want to make certain text stand out in some way: make it larger or smaller; change what it looks like; add bold, italics, or underlining; or change the color. All these changes can be accomplished from the Font tab in the Format Cells dialog box, as shown in Figure 4-8.

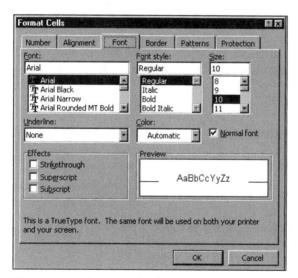

Figure 4-8 The Font tab of the Format Cells dialog box.

A *font* is an appearance given to a group of characters. The two most common fonts are Times (or a variation, such as Times New Roman or Times New Roman PS) and Helvetica (or similar fonts, such as Arial and Univers).

Font size in Excel is measured in *points*. As we mentioned earlier, one inch equals 72 points. A character that is a half-inch high is 36 points, and an 18-point character is approximately one-quarter inch high. By default, character size in Excel is 10 points (0.72 inches high). Today, all computer programs use points to measure font size.

To change any of the font characteristics of an *entire* cell or cells, select the cells and set the font characteristics. To change *individual* characters within a cell, first select the characters and then set the font characteristics.

Many of the options on the Font tab of the Format Cells dialog box are also available from the formatting toolbar. In the next activity, you get a chance to use both.

This activity gives you a chance to change some of the font characteristics on your worksheet. Cell A1 should still be selected.

Follow these steps:

1. Click **B** on the toolbar. All of the text in A1 is bolded.

2. Choose **Format** → **Cells** . Excel opens the Format Cells dialog box.

3. Click the Font tab.

4. Scroll through the list of available fonts, and click Century Schoolbook, if it's available. The Preview panel shows what the font looks like. If you don't have Century Schoolbook, select another font.

5. Scroll through the list of available font sizes, and click 18.

 TIP Unlike the font choices, which you must select from a list, you can enter a size directly into the Size box. For example, 15 points is not an option, but you can enter it directly into the Size box.

6. Drop down the Underline list. Notice that you can choose from single or double underline, or single or double accounting underlining. Single and double underlines cut through the descenders (the parts of letters that extend below the imaginary line on which capital letters sit). For example, regular underlining cuts off the bottoms of the letters *g* and *y*. The accounting underline is moved down farther so that the bottom of the letters is not cut off.

7. Click None for Underline choice.

8. Click OK to close the dialog box. Notice that A1 now contains text that has been formatted as Century Schoolbook, 18 points, and bold.

9. Select A3 through A6, and click both the Bold and the Italic buttons on the toolbar. The text is boldfaced and italicized. These buttons act as toggles. If you click them a second time, boldface and italics are turned off. For now, leave them on.

10. Select B2 through G2, and click the Bold button.

11. Save the workbook, and leave it open.

Getting to the border

You may want a cell or group of cells to stand out from other data in the worksheet. You can accomplish this by adding borders.

Figure 4-9 shows the Border tab in the Format Cells dialog box. The Border tab lets you set borders for a single cell or for groups of cells.

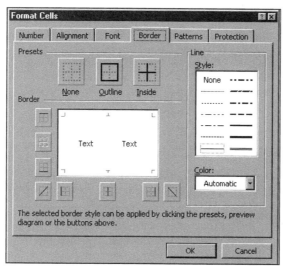

Figure 4-9   Use the Border tab in the Format Cells
dialog box to place lines around the
edges of a cell or a group of cells.

By default, all borders are turned off. To turn on all borders for a single cell, or only the outside borders for a group of cells, select the cell(s) and click the Outline option. If a group of cells is selected, the entire group is surrounded by a single border. If multiple cells are selected, you can also choose the Inside option. This adds borders between the individual cells in the group. Borders for a cell or a group of cells can also be set individually in the Border panel. Border line styles can be varied, as can border color.

SIDE TRIP

By default, the gridlines show only on the screen and are not visible when you print the worksheet. Gridlines can be printed by turning on the Gridlines option in the Print panel on the Sheet tab of the Page Setup dialog box.

New to Excel for Office 97 is the diagonal border feature. This places a diagonal line from the upper-left corner of the cell(s) to the lower-right, or from the upper-right to the lower-left.

Figure 4-10 shows several different borders that are set around individual cells and groups of cells. The gridlines have been turned off so that you can see the cell borders. (A1 doesn't contain a border; it is the active cell.)

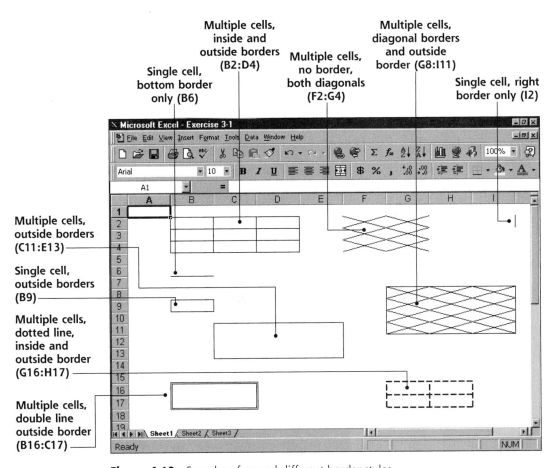

Figure 4-10 Samples of several different border styles.

This activity offers several opportunities for you to format cell borders using different commands. Remember that, by default, no borders appear around cells.

Follow these steps to format cell borders:

1. Choose `Tools` → `Options`. Excel displays the Options dialog box.

2. On the View tab in the Windows options panel, turn off the Gridlines option (click to remove the check mark) and click OK. Turning off the gridlines makes it easier to see the borders that you create.

3. Right-click A1, and choose `Format Cells` from the pop-up menu. Excel displays the Format Cells dialog box.

4. Click the Border tab.

5. In the Style panel, choose the evenly broken border (the fourth selection in the right column). Then click Outline, and click OK.

If you click Outline first and *then* select the border, the border does not change.

6. Click A8. This gives you a better view of the border around A1. You can't see the top or left edges of the border, but if you click the Print Preview button on the toolbar, you can see that the border should print properly.

7. Select A3 through G5, right-click the selected cells, and choose `Format Cells`. Excel displays the Format Cells dialog box. The Borders tab is displayed, because it was the last one that you used.

8. In the Style panel, choose the heaviest line, and then click Outline.

9. Now choose the thinnest line (first column, last row), and click Inside.

10. Click OK.

11. Click A1 to view the borders.

12. Save the workbook, and leave it open.

Adding background patterns and colors

Patterns are helpful for setting particular groups of information aside or for drawing the viewer's attention to specified cells. By default, cells do not contain any patterns or colors. You use the Patterns tab to control the color and the pattern that are applied to a selected cell or group of cells. Figure 4-11 shows the Patterns tab in the Format Cells dialog box.

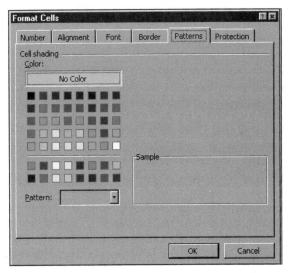

Figure 4-11 The Patterns tab in the Format Cells
dialog box.

 NOTE Notice that in the group of available shading colors, a line separates
the top 40 colors from the bottom 16. If your display is set to 256 colors
or greater, these all appear as solid colors, and some of them seem to be
the same color. If your display is set to 16 colors, only a few of the 56
colors are solid; the others appear as combinations (such as blue and
yellow dots to make a greenish color). If your *printer* supports only 16
colors, choose from the lower 16 colors. If it supports 64 colors or
greater, you can use any of the colors as shading.

By clicking any color in the Color area, you assign that *background*
color to the selected cells. Clicking Pattern opens an additional box of
choices, as shown in Figure 4-12. Clicking a pattern in the upper area
sets the pattern. By default, the pattern lines are black. Clicking a color
sets the color for the pattern lines (*not* the background).

CAUTION With the default setting (no pattern), if you select a pattern color
without selecting a pattern, no pattern is added to the selected cells.

Setting patterns can help draw the viewer's eye to important information. In
the next activity, you add color to the worksheet title in A1 and a pattern for the
Average scores. A1 is still the active cell.

Follow these steps:

1. Right-click and choose Format Cells . The Border tab of the Format Cells
dialog box is displayed, because this is the last tab that you used in this
dialog box.

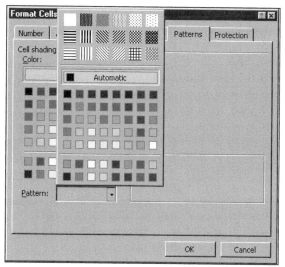

Figure 4-12 In this area, you can set patterns in a selected cell or group of cells.

2. Click the Patterns tab. This tab, shown earlier in Figure 4-11, is displayed.

3. Click Yellow in the Color panel (third column, bottom row).

4. Click OK. The background of A1 is now yellow. This *doesn't* print as yellow unless you have a color printer.

5. Select A6 through E6, right-click, and choose Format Cells from the pop-up menu.

6. On the Patterns tab in the Format Cells dialog box, choose the cream background color (sixth row, third column) and then click the Pattern drop-down list. The Pattern selections, shown earlier in Figure 4-12, are displayed.

7. Choose the pattern in the upper-right corner (a few black dots with a white background).

8. Click OK to apply the pattern.

9. Click A1 so that you can see the applied pattern.

10. Save the workbook.

Applying patterns to cells can make the data difficult to read. Apply patterns sparingly.

Formatting Rows

Rows are horizontal groups of cells. You can format individual rows or a group of rows. You can change the row height, tell Excel to automatically set the row height, and even specify whether to hide or display rows. When you assign formatting to a row (or rows), *all* cells in that row (or rows) take on the formatting.

Setting row height

As with all vertical measurements in Excel, row height is measured in points (one inch equals 72 points). By default, the text in Excel is 10 points high, and the rows are 12.75 points high. Most of the text that you regularly read is 10 or 12 points high.

You can set row height in several ways. Choosing  displays the Row Height dialog box, as shown in Figure 4-13. From this dialog box, you can enter the desired row height (with an accuracy of $1/100$ of a point).

Figure 4-13 Use the Row Height dialog box to set the height for selected rows.

You can also change row height by dragging the bottom row boundary line (the black line *under* the row indicator at the left of the screen). As you drag the boundary line, a small box appears, specifying the current row height (in points).

 TIP **To change the height of several rows at once, select the rows and then drag any of the boundary lines. All selected rows are enlarged or condensed to the desired size.**

To set all the rows in a worksheet, click the Select All button (to the left of the column A indicator and above the row 1 indicator). Then set the size by using the Row Height dialog box or by dragging any boundary line.

Follow these steps to set the default row height for all rows in a workbook:

1. Click the first worksheet tab, press Shift, and then click the last worksheet tab. This groups the worksheets.

2. Click the Select All button, and then make the desired change by using the Row Height dialog box or by dragging any boundary line.

Because the worksheets are grouped, any change that you make to one sheet is reflected in all the other sheets.

Using AutoFit

You can also AutoFit rows. If you select a row or rows and then choose `Format` →
`Row` → `Auto Fit`, Excel adjusts the selected row height(s) to accommodate the
tallest cell in the row(s). If you subsequently decrease a font size, you need to
AutoFit the row again; the row height doesn't adjust automatically.

TIP **For a shortcut to AutoFit the height of selected rows, you can double-
click the bottom boundary of any selected row.**

Hiding and unhiding rows

To hide a single row or a group of rows, follow these steps:

1. Select the row (or rows).

2. Choose `Format` → `Row` → `Hide`.

Excel hides the selected row(s). Although the numbers of hidden rows are
hidden, the remaining visible rows are *not* renumbered.

Follow these steps to unhide rows that you've hidden:

1. Select the rows above and below the hidden rows.

2. Choose `Format` → `Row` → `Unhide`. The hidden rows again appear.

Although hiding rows does not prevent a competent worksheet user from
unhiding them (unless you protect the worksheet with a password), this command lets you keep unneeded rows out of sight. Later in this book, you find out
about Excel's outlining feature. This offers a better way to hide and unhide rows
without having to select them each time.

Putting it all together: formatting rows

Your worksheets look more professional if you include interesting titles and meaningful headings.

To format rows for titles and headings, follow these steps:

1. Create a new workbook, and select row 1 by clicking the row indicator.

2. Choose `Format` → `Row` → `Hide`. The first row is hidden from view.

3. Try to unhide row 1 by selecting row 2 and choosing `Format` → `Row` →
   `Unhide`. Notice that row 1 is *not* visible. To unhide a row, you must select
   the rows above *and* below the hidden row. You have only one choice for
   unhiding row 1.

4. Click the Select All button, and choose `Format` → `Row` → `Unhide`. Row 1 is again visible.

5. Click A1 to turn off the selection.

6. In A1, type **Monthly Summary** and press Enter.

7. Using the skills that you acquired earlier in this chapter, center the text across A1 through D1 and then click E1 to turn off the selection.

8. Click A1 again, and set the font size to 24 by dropping down the size box and clicking 24. Notice that Excel automatically adjusts the row height.

9. Add height to the row by clicking the boundary indicator for row 1 and dragging down until it is approximately 40 points (don't worry if it's not exact). This adds extra space to the top of the cell.

10. AutoFit the row size to the font size by double-clicking the boundary indicator for row 1. Excel automatically adjusts the row height.

11. Close the workbook without saving it.

Formatting Columns

You format columns (vertical groups of cells) in much the same way as you format rows. You can set the width (instead of the height) to a specific value (it is 8.43 by default), choose to AutoFit the selected columns, and hide or unhide selected columns.

You can also change the standard width of all columns in the worksheet by choosing `Format` → `Column` → `Standard Width`. The value that you enter in the Standard Width dialog box, shown in Figure 4-14, represents the average number of digits that the column holds *at the default font and size*. To reset all columns that have not been formatted with a specific width, select any cell and set the standard width. Columns with custom widths are *not* affected.

Figure 4-14 The Standard Width dialog box.

TIP   To reset all column widths, including columns that have been customized, click the Select All button and choose `Format` → `Column` → `Standard Width`. In the Standard Width dialog box, enter the new value and click OK. To set the standard width for all worksheets in a workbook, group all of the worksheets and then set the standard width.

BONUS

Automatic Excel Formatting

The bonus section of this chapter deals with Excel's AutoFormatting features. To see some of the features at work, you use a fairly simple sample file so that you don't have to do much typing.

Excel can automatically format an entire worksheet or any selected cells in any of 15 prerecorded formats. The format that you choose depends on how you have laid out your worksheet.

You can use the AutoFormat feature in any existing worksheet. You may want to complete your worksheet *before* applying AutoFormat.

In this activity, you develop a simple worksheet and then apply various AutoFormats to see how this feature works.

Follow these steps:

1. Create a new worksheet by choosing File → New , and click OK.

TIP **You can also use either of two shortcuts to create a new workbook: Click the New button on the Standard toolbar or press Ctrl+N.**

2. Save the new workbook in your Discover Excel folder with the filename AutoFormat Example.xls.

3. Enter the information shown in Table 4-1, using the AutoFill feature to enter the month names and the AutoSum feature to generate the totals.

   Don't enter the totals manually — we list them in Table 4-1 just to show you what they should be. (A1 is actually blank.) Figure 4-15 shows the sheet before any formatting has been applied.

4. To see the formatting more easily, turn off the screen gridlines. You do this by choosing Tools → Options . Then, on the View tab, turn off the Gridlines option.

5. Select the table by dragging from A1 to E6. The table must be selected before you can apply AutoFormatting.

6. Choose Format → Auto Format . As shown in Figure 4-16, Excel displays the AutoFormat dialog box. The Simple option is already highlighted.

7. Click OK.

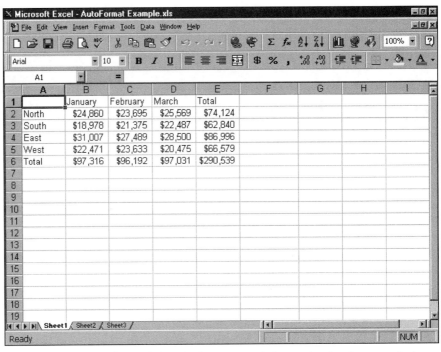

Figure 4-15 The Sales worksheet before automatic formatting has been applied.

TABLE 4-1 Data To Be Entered in A1 through E6

Row	Column A	Column B	Column C	Column D	Column E
1		January	February	March	Total
2	North	$24,860	$23,695	$25,569	$74,124
3	South	$18,978	$21,375	$22,487	$62,840
4	East	$31,007	$27,489	$28,500	$86,996
5	West	$22,471	$23,633	$20,475	$66,579
6	Total	$97,316	$96,192	$97,031	$290,539

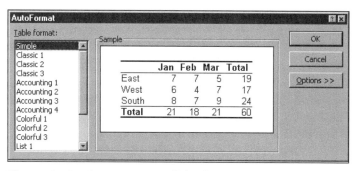

Figure 4-16   The AutoFormat dialog box.

8. Increase the zoom by typing **150** in the Zoom box and pressing Enter. Click A8 so that you can see the formatting more easily. You probably need to AutoFit column E. Your sheet should look like the one shown in Figure 4-17.

TIP In some cases, you may need to adjust the zoom, and even some column widths, to see all of the data. If a cell is filled with pound signs (####), you have more data than the column width can handle. You can AutoFit the column by double-clicking the right column boundary in the column heading.

9. Change the AutoFormat to Accounting 1. To do this, reselect the table, choose Format → Auto Format , click the Accounting 1 option, and then click OK. Click A8 again to turn off the selection. Your screen should look like Figure 4-18.

10. Change the AutoFormat to 3D Effects 1. To do this, choose Format → Auto Format , click the 3D Effects 1 option, and then click OK. Your screen should look like Figure 4-19.

11. Select other AutoFormats as desired.

12. When you are finished, close Excel and save the changes to your workbook.

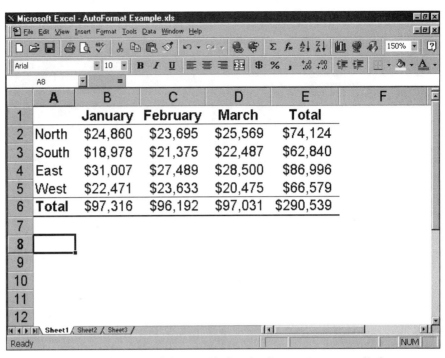

Figure 4-17 The sample worksheet, with the Simple AutoFormat applied.

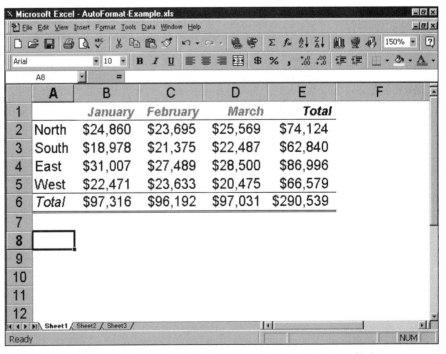

Figure 4-18 The worksheet, with the Accounting 1 AutoFormat applied.

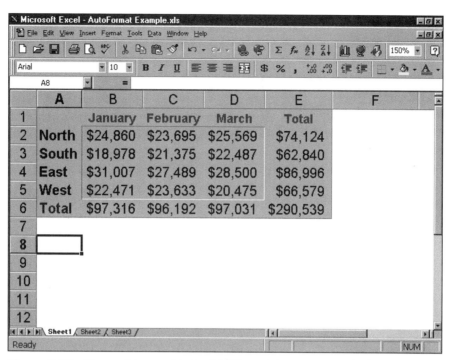

Figure 4-19 The worksheet, with the 3D Effects 1 AutoFormat applied.

Summary

Ensuring that your worksheet looks good is sometimes almost as important as ensuring its accuracy. By using the formatting features that are included with Excel, you can boldface, italicize, and underline text. You can change the text's horizontal and vertical alignment, change the size and color of the text, and even center text across a selected group of cells. A professional-looking worksheet helps convince the viewer that you are indeed a professional.

MANIPULATING AND DISPLAYING DATA

THIS PART CONTAINS THE FOLLOWING CHAPTERS

One of the most powerful features in Excel 97 is its capability to monitor how you work and then offer automated solutions. For example, if you type **Monday** in one cell, you can automatically insert subsequent days of the week in neighboring cells simply by clicking and dragging an AutoFill handle. And as you enter data into a cell, Excel checks your typing to see if it matches previously entered data, offering suggestions on how to finish the entry without additional typing. In this part of the book, you work with various Excel features such as these, learning how to streamline the process of entering data into your worksheets.

You also delve deeper into formulas and functions, mastering numerous shortcuts for making calculations. Excel offers a multitude of features that make mathematical manipulation easy. You'll be astounded by the ease with which Excel handles complex formulas.

To display your data in the most effective manner, you learn how to use Excel charts. Excel's charts are dynamic — as you make changes to the numbers in your worksheet, Excel automatically updates the chart. In this part, you gain a basic understanding of which types of charts are useful in specific situations. You even find out how to add graphics to your charts.

"Computers are too expensive." "We can't afford more software." "Computers steal jobs that real people used to have."

These accusations against technology are nothing new. Since the Industrial Revolution, technology and automation have had a mighty task in proving their worth, and workers have looked at technological "progress" with a cautious eye. And for good reason. After all, one of the reasons for having computers in the first place is to do the work of people — only faster and more efficiently than people could do it.

Computer industry pundits, however, have made broad statements in defense of their industry. In fact, some have said that for every job that a computer takes from a person, it creates four jobs in return. You might be wondering, "After the computer technician, where are the other three jobs?"

That's a good question. But keep in mind that the jobs don't always reappear in the same company as the jobs that were taken. But those jobs will not leave the state.

Sean Fahey, the Deputy Director of Commerce's Office of Development Finance, will see to that. The Department of Commerce works hard to bring new economic opportunities to Indiana, and one of the jobs of Sean and his staff is to analyze data to decide the most appealing place in Indiana for companies to set up shop.

Thanks in large part to Microsoft Excel, Sean is looking pretty good these days.

Sean uses Excel to analyze and evaluate data pulled from the state's massive Microsoft Access database. "When we look for the ideal county for a company to locate," Sean says, "there are dozens of factors we must consider. For example, what is the unemployment rate in the various counties that are vying for the company's attention? Which county has the type of workers that will most benefit the organization? Do the counties have a good record of sticking to their budgets? When companies like General Motors or Toyota are prepared to spend a billion dollars to build a plant, they want to know these things."

Thanks to Excel, Sean can find that information — fast. And timing is critical. "If ten counties in another state have already prepared their proposed financial packages, and I need another week to sort through data, I look like a fool." Fortunately for Hoosiers, that's not the case. In the last year, Toyota and AK Steel have each announced plans to build plants in the state, a combination that promises to bring over 1,700 new jobs and nearly $2 billion to Indiana. Of course Sean can't give all the credit to Excel. "Having good, smart people is the most important thing. But if you give them the right tools, you're way ahead."

FASTER AND EASIER: SHORTCUTS FOR ENTERING DATA INTO YOUR WORKSHEETS

IN THIS CHAPTER YOU LEARN THESE KEY SKILLS

In the olden days of computers (way back in the early 1980s), many computers were bigger than compact cars, and their sole purpose was to store vast amounts of information. To operate those clunkers, some poor soul had to sit at a keyboard and enter the same repetitive (and redundant) information over and over again. Luckily, modern computers allow you to avoid such mundane tasks through the use of data-entry shortcuts.

Cutting, Copying, and Pasting

To paraphrase Robert Fulghum, you learned most of your really important skills in kindergarten. Excel reinforces your cutting and pasting skills. Proper cutting (or copying) and pasting greatly reduces the amount of time that you spend entering data. Instead of entering the same information over and over, you simply enter the information once and then — by cutting (or copying) and pasting — place it into as many other cells as you need to.

Figure 5-1 shows the Cut, Copy, and Paste buttons on the Standard toolbar — often your most-used buttons.

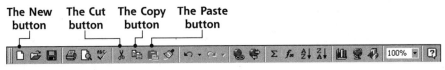

Figure 5-1   The Standard toolbar.

Cutting data

Cutting data means removing the information from one or more cells. You can then place this information in another cell or cells. When you cut data, Excel surrounds your data with a *marquis* (a box that looks like marching ants) until you specify where the data should be pasted or until you select another cell. After you paste the data into the specified destination, Excel removes it from the original cell(s).

You can cut data by using several methods. The simplest method is to select the data and then click the Cut button on the toolbar. This highlights the data from the selected cell(s) and prepares it for pasting.

You can also cut data by using the appropriate quick-key command. Select the data that you want to cut, and press Ctrl+X.

TIP   **Excel also allows you to *drag and drop* data from one cell (or group of cells) to another. To do this, simply click and hold your mouse button on the border of a cell or group of cells (be sure that you don't grab the AutoFill handle), drag the border of the cell(s) to the new destination, and then release the button.**

Copying data

Copying data is similar to cutting. However, copying leaves the data in the original cells and places a duplicate of the information in the selected destination cells. After the data is copied, it remains surrounded by a marquis until you specify where it should be pasted, select another cell, or press Esc.

To copy data, simply select the cells and click the Copy button on the toolbar. You can also use the quick key, Ctrl+C.

TIP   **You can also copy (rather than cut) by using the drag-and-drop feature in combination with the Ctrl key. On the keyboard, press and hold Ctrl, highlight the cells that you want to copy, and drag the borders of the cells to the new location.**

Pasting data

After you cut or copy your data (and the data is surrounded by a marquis), you tell Excel where you want the data placed by selecting destination cells. To paste, simply select the desired destination cell(s) and then click the Paste button on the toolbar. Excel places the cut or copied data into the selected cell(s). You can also paste data by using the appropriate quick keys (Ctrl+V or Shift+Insert).

TIP Excel's [Edit] → [Paste Special] option allows you to choose a specific part of the cut or copied data to paste. You may want to paste only the formula in the cell or possibly just the formatting specifications. The Paste Special option gives you the power to decide exactly which parts of the selection to paste.

Putting it all together: cutting, copying, and pasting

This activity provides practice in cutting, copying, and pasting. To see the difference between cutting and copying, you first cut text and place it in another location, and then you copy it to the original location.

Follow these steps:

1. Open Excel and a new workbook.

2. Enter the data that is shown in Figure 5-2. Name the three worksheets North, South, and East.

 Don't use the AutoFill feature to create the dates. Enter them manually, or the date is increased one day each time, not one month at a time.

3. Save the file in your Discover Excel folder as Sales Total.

4. On the North worksheet, select A1 through A8.

5. Right-click the selected cells, and then choose [Cut] from the pop-up menu.

   Notice that Excel surrounds the selection with a marquis. Unlike Word and other Windows programs, Excel does *not* remove the selection from its original position until you paste it (or move the highlight to another cell).

6. Click the South tab.

7. If A1 isn't selected, click it.

8. Click the Paste button on the toolbar. (You can also just press Enter.)

9. AutoFit column A to adjust the column to the correct size.

10. Click the North tab. Notice that the data has been *moved.* The original cells are now blank.

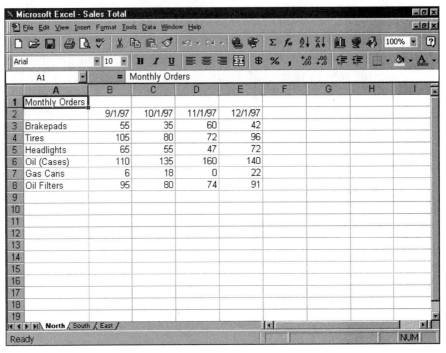

Figure 5-2 Data for cutting, copying, and pasting.

11. Click the South tab again, and select A1 through A8.

12. Click the Copy button on the toolbar.

13. Click the North tab.

14. Instead of clicking the Paste button, press Enter. (You also could right-click and select **Paste** from the resulting pop-up menu.)

15. Click the South tab again. Notice that the data is still there, because it was copied, rather than cut.

16. Click the North tab once more, and AutoFit column A.

17. Click A1, and then save the workbook. Leave it open for the next activity.

Limiting the Data Input Range

When you know that you need to work with only a limited number of cells, there are advantages to limiting the range of cells in which you can enter data (also known as the *data input range*). To specify which cells you plan to use, you simply highlight them.

After you highlight a group of cells, you can move through the highlighted area in the following ways:

- ✳ Press Tab to move to the next cell.
- ✳ Press Shift+Tab to move to the previous cell.
- ✳ Press Enter to move down one cell.
- ✳ Press Shift+Enter to move up one cell.

Don't use the mouse or the arrow keys when entering data into a restricted range. Doing so automatically turns off the data input range.

If you accidentally turn off the data input range, just highlight the range again, press Tab or Enter to move to the next cell in the range, and continue entering the data.

The best way to understand the advantages of restricting a data input range is by gaining some hands-on experience This activity demonstrates the advantages of working with a limited data input range.

Follow these steps:

1. Using the skills that you learned in the previous activity, *copy* B2 through E2 on the North sheet, and paste these cells into the South sheet. Be sure to paste them in the same location, and click in any other cell to cancel the selection.

2. On the South worksheet, highlight B3 through E8. The 24 cells that are shown in Figure 5-3 are now your *limited* data input range.

3. In B3, type **60** and press Tab.

4. In C3, type **48** and press Tab.

5. In D3, type **75** and press Tab. Oops! That last entry should be 78.

6. Press Shift+Tab to move to the previous cell, and then type **78**.

7. Press Tab, and type **101.**

8. Press Tab again to move to cell B4 in the next row.

5

SIDE TRIP

In a word processor, when the cursor reaches the end of a line, it automatically moves to the beginning of the next line. To reach the end of a row in Excel, you have to press Tab hundreds of times. By selecting a data input range, when you tab to the end of a row in the selection, you are moved to the beginning of the next row in the selection.

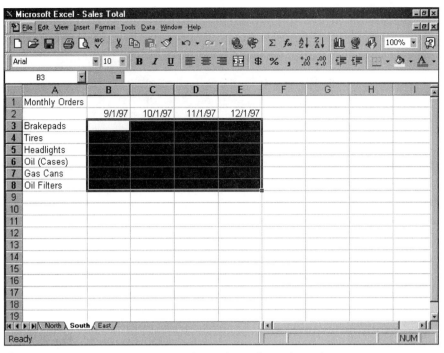

Figure 5-3 The data input range is limited to cells B3 through E8.

9. Continue to enter the data that is shown in Figure 5-4, and move from cell to cell by pressing Tab, Shift+Tab, and Enter (if you need to move down one cell) until you have entered all of the data.

10. Click Save, and leave the workbook open.

So what are the advantages of limiting your data entry field? You can scroll from the last cell in a row to the first cell in the next row simply by pressing Tab, and you can scroll from the last cell in a column to the first cell in the next column by pressing Enter. This saves you both time and keystrokes.

TIP When you are in the last cell of the last row, pressing Tab or Enter moves you to the upper-left cell of the selection. To enter data *outside* the limited area, press any arrow key or click with the mouse.

SIDE TRIP
The instructions in the preceding steps demonstrate that we will *never* become surgeons. Can you imagine a surgeon who says, "Oops"?

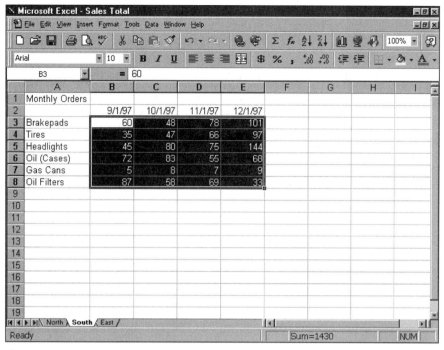

Figure 5-4   Enter the data into the selected data range.

Making Sense of Excel's IntelliSense™ Features

E
xcel for Microsoft Office 97 includes features that can help you reduce the time spent entering data and calculating numbers. These shortcut features are known as Excel's IntelliSense. You have already worked with AutoFill, so you know how helpful these features can be.

Excel has the following IntelliSense features:

* AutoCalculate sums or performs other mathematical manipulations on selected cells.

* AutoComplete anticipates your intended typing before you complete it.

* AutoCorrect replaces abbreviations with words or phrases and automatically corrects commonly misspelled words.

* AutoSum sums a row or column of cells.

* AutoFill fills cells with a series of data and copies formulas and values in a single step.

* Pick Lists alphabetizes information in a column, allowing you to click an entry to select it for the current cell.

Keeping a running total by using AutoCalculate

AutoCalculate is a handy tool for finding the sum, the average, or some other mathematical information for a selected set of values without entering a formula into the worksheet. By simply selecting a range of cells, you can have Excel keep a running sum of the values in those cells.

Look at the status bar in Figure 5-5. The AutoCalculate box displays the sum of Brake pads sold during the four-month period in the South store.

You can also use AutoCalculate to perform several other mathematical manipulations. Right-click the AutoCalculate box to display the AutoCalculate menu that is shown in Figure 5-6. In addition to Sum, this menu offers several other AutoCalculate options:

* None turns off the AutoCalculate feature.
* Average calculates the mean (average) of the selected values.
* Count counts the number of cells in the selection.
* Count Nums counts the number of selected cells that contain values (blank cells or cells with text are not included in the results).
* Max displays the highest value in the range.
* Min displays the lowest value in the range.

This activity demonstrates the different options that are included in the AutoCalculate feature.

Follow these steps:

1. On the South worksheet, drag across B6 through E6. The sum, 278, is automatically displayed in the AutoCalculate box on the status bar.

2. Right-click the AutoCalculate box to display the AutoCalculate menu.

3. Choose None. The AutoCalculate box is now empty.

4. Right-click the AutoCalculate box, and select Average. The average number of cases of oil sold each month during the four-month period is 69.5.

5. Right-click the AutoCalculate box, and choose Count. Excel displays Count = 4. This is the number of cells in the selected range.

6. Highlight A6 through E6, and select Count Nums from the AutoCalculate menu. Notice that even though you selected five cells, the answer is Count Nums = 4. The newly selected cell, A6, doesn't contain a value.

7. Try the Max and Min options.

8. When you are finished, reset AutoCalculate to Sum. Leave the workbook open.

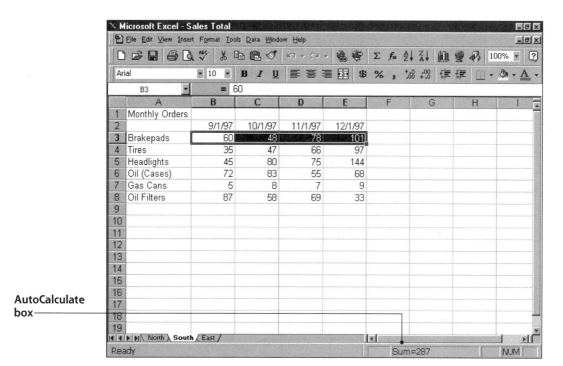

AutoCalculate box

Figure 5-5 By default, Excel's AutoCalculate keeps a running sum of selected cells.

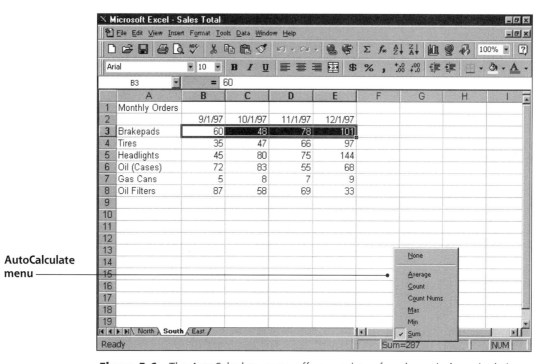

AutoCalculate menu

Figure 5-6 The AutoCalculate menu offers a variety of mathematical manipulations.

Saving keystrokes by using AutoComplete

Imagine how much easier data entry would be if only Excel could read your mind. Although Excel can't quite do that, it can anticipate what you are typing and can often complete the entry for you. The AutoComplete feature can save many keystrokes and thus give you more time to work on the important strokes of life (backstroke, golf stroke, different strokes, and so on).

Using AutoComplete, Excel looks at all of the other entries in the *column* in which you are working and compares those entries to what you are typing. If Excel finds a similar entry, it completes the current entry for you.

TIP   **Excel looks up the current column only as far as the first blank cell that it encounters. If you need to leave a cell blank, enter all of the other information in the column first (leaving no blank cells) and then move the appropriate cells down to make room for the blank cell.**

After AutoComplete fills in an entry, you can decide whether it is what you really want. If the entry is correct, simply press Enter, and the data is entered. If the entry is not what you want, continue typing, and AutoComplete removes the incorrect data.

This activity shows how to speed up data entry by using AutoComplete.

Follow these steps:

1. Click A9.

2. Type **Oil F**. AutoComplete doesn't display an entry when you type **Oil**, because the entry could be Oil (Cases) or Oil Filters. When you add a space and the letter *F*, Excel completes the entry, as shown in Figure 5-7.

3. Press Enter.

4. Click A9 *after* the entry Oil Filter, and revise the entry to read Oil Filters (Cases).

5. Click A9, and press Delete to clear the cell.

6. Save your workbook, and close it.

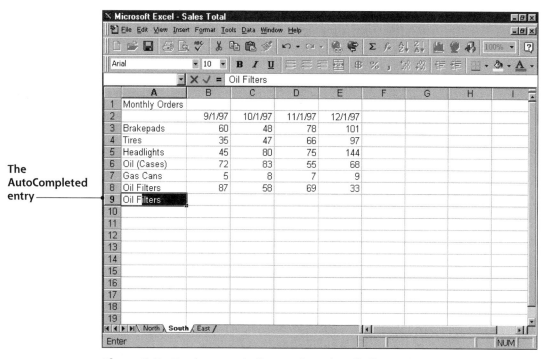

The AutoCompleted entry

Figure 5-7 Excel automatically completes the Oil Filter entry.

Be sure that your data is spelled correctly. If you type **National** in one cell and **Naitional** in another cell, AutoComplete must wait for the *third* character before it can complete the data for you.

If you decide that you don't want an entry in the cell in which you are typing, simply press Esc to cancel the entry.

Avoiding mistakes by using AutoCorrect

AutoCorrect is a lifesaver for those of us who aren't expert typists. Excel automatically changes misspelled words to the correct spelling — for example, replacing *thier* with *their* — without even running a spell check. AutoCorrect also allows you to create nifty little icons by using keystrokes. For example, typing a lowercase *c* in parentheses — (c) — creates a copyright symbol, ©. You must use a lowercase character.

If you're like me, you consistently misspell the same words. You can add these words to AutoCorrect by using the AutoCorrect dialog box that is shown in Figure 5-8. Open the AutoCorrect dialog box by choosing **Tools** → **Auto Correct** . Enter the word as you usually misspell it, and then tell Excel the correct spelling. AutoCorrect is activated when you type a space, enter a punctuation mark, or move to another cell.

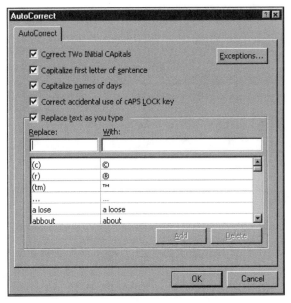

Figure 5-8 Use the AutoCorrect dialog box to enter custom abbreviations or to mark words that you commonly misspell.

AutoCorrect does not correct *all* misspellings, just those that are relatively common. Remember to always run a spell check just to be safe. Also, AutoCorrect does not eliminate the need for proofreading your material. For example, it replaces *thier* with *their*, but you might really mean *there*.

In addition to correcting misspellings, AutoCorrect offers the following options:

* Correct TWo INitial CApitals
* Capitalize the first letter of sentence
* Capitalize names of days
* Correct accidental use of cAPS LOCK key

The last of these options is perhaps the handiest AutoCorrect feature. If you accidentally turn on Caps Lock or forget to turn it off after you are finished with it, you end up with a paragraph that looks like this:

tHIS IS A PARAGRAPH THAT WE TYPED WITH THE cAPS lOCK KEY ACCIDENTALLY LEFT ON. aNY TIME THAT WE PRESS THE sHIFT KEY, A LOWERCASE LETTER IS TYPED.

In Excel, as soon as you begin to type the preceding paragraph — by typing **tHIS** and pressing the spacebar — Excel not only uses the proper case for the word that you typed, but it also automatically turns off Caps Lock. This is one of our favorite features (probably because we often make this mistake).

TIP AutoCorrect's Caps Lock feature does not work properly if the sentence begins with a single letter or number. For example, the entry *a HOLIDAY WISH.* is not automatically changed until after the period. And for the phrase *I'LL BE THERE.*, AutoCorrect fixes only the *I* but not the rest of the sentence. Remember, AutoCorrect's Caps Lock feature works properly only if the sentence begins with two or more consecutive characters.

You can turn off any AutoCorrect options by removing the corresponding check mark from the AutoCorrect option box.

Using and customizing AutoCorrect

Learning to use and customize AutoCorrect can save you a lot of time. In this activity, you find out how AutoCorrect works as well as how to customize it.

Follow these steps:

1. Create a new workbook by clicking ☐ on the toolbar.

2. In A1, type **It is thier ball**. As soon as you type **thier** and press the space bar, Excel automatically corrects the word.

3. Press Esc to cancel the entry.

4. While you are still in A1, type **IntelliSense(tm).** As soon as you type the period, Excel automatically converts the *tm* to a trademark symbol.

5. Press Enter, click A1, and press Delete. This clears the contents of the cell.

6. Open the AutoCorrect dialog box by choosing Tools → Auto Correct . Scroll through the list to see the entries that are included by default. Notice that the misspelled word is listed on the left, with the corrected spelling shown on the right.

   You can also use AutoCorrect to automatically expand abbreviations.

7. In the Replace text box, type **de**.

8. In the With text box, type **Discover Excel for Office 97**.

9. Click Add, and then click OK.

10. In A1, type **de** and press Enter. Remember to use this feature any time that you need to type phrases on a regular basis.

11. Close the workbook without saving it.

Saving steps by using AutoFill

AutoFill is another feature that tries to anticipate your data-entry needs. You have used it previously to fill consecutive series, such as Store 1, Store 2, and so on, as well as the months of the year. By grabbing the AutoFill handle in the lower-right corner of a selected cell or group of cells and dragging, you can enter data without typing.

AutoFill can fill in repetitive data, or it can anticipate your needs and follow a pattern that you have established. The way in which AutoFill works depends on the cell or the group of cells that you select. Table 5-1 shows the original cell contents and the results of AutoFilling to one or more cells.

Although you have worked with AutoFill in previous chapters, this activity gives you additional practice with the feature.

Follow these steps:

1. Create a new workbook.

2. In B1, type **1st Quarter** and press Enter.

3. Click B1 again, and then drag the AutoFill handle to I1. Notice that after 4th Quarter in E1, Excel is smart enough to begin again with 1st Quarter in F1.

4. Type **Jan** in A3, and then AutoFill to C3. Notice that Excel abbreviates the months exactly as you typed the first one.

5. With the cells still highlighted, press Delete to clear the cell contents.

6. Type **January** in A3, and then AutoFill to C3. Excel automatically enters the months in the form that you used in A3.

7. Close the workbook without saving it.

 TIP To AutoFit several columns at once, select them, right-click the selection, and choose Format → Columns → Auto Fit Selection .

Using AutoSum

AutoSum allows you to total a group of cells by selecting the cell below or to the right of the cells and then clicking the AutoSum button Σ on the toolbar. Excel looks at the numbers either above or to the left of the active cell to make a suggestion for the cells that you want to sum. If these aren't the cells that you want, simply reselect the correct cells.

TABLE 5-1 AutoFill Contents and Results

Contents	Results
A VALUE IN A SINGLE CELL	The value is copied to all other AutoFill cells that you select.
VALUES IN MULTIPLE CELLS	Excel calculates the difference between the first two original cells and then AutoFills the selected cells accordingly.
A FORMULA IN A SINGLE CELL	The formula is copied to AutoFill cells.
A DAY OR DATE IN A SINGLE OR MULTIPLE CELLS	Dragging a day or date AutoFills the selection with corresponding days or dates. The formatting is copied with the AutoFill.
A MONTH IN A SINGLE OR MULTIPLE CELLS	Dragging a month or months AutoFills the selection with the corresponding month or months.
A WEEK IN A SINGLE OR MULTIPLE CELLS	Dragging a week or weeks AutoFills the selection with the corresponding week or weeks.
PLAIN TEXT IN A SINGLE OR MULTIPLE CELLS	The text is copied exactly to the AutoFill selection.
NUMBERED TEXT IN A SINGLE OR MULTIPLE CELL	Text such as `Quarter 1` becomes `Quarter 2`, `Quarter 3`, and so on. Text such as `1st Quarter` becomes `2nd Quarter`, `3rd Quarter`, and so on.

This activity shows how AutoSum works.

Follow these steps:

1. Open Sales Total workbook, and click B9 on the South tab.

2. Click the AutoSum button on the toolbar. Cells B3 through B8 display the marquis. B9 shows the formula `=SUM(B3:B8)`.

3. Press Enter. The result, 304, is the number of items that were sold in the South store during September.

4. Click F3, and then click the AutoSum button. The marquis surrounds B3 through E3.

5. Press Enter. As shown in Figure 5-9, F3 lists the total number of Brake pads that were sold by the South store during the four-month period. You can also use AutoFill to copy formulas.

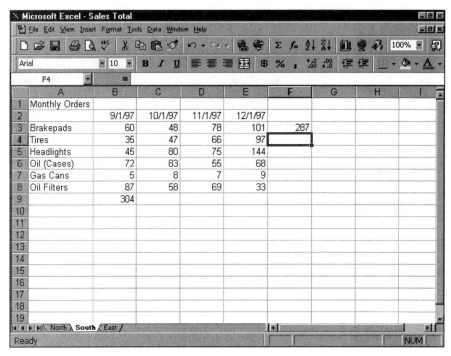

Figure 5-9 B9 shows the number of items that were sold during September. F3 shows the number of Brake pads that were sold during the four-month period.

6. Click F3, and drag the AutoFill handle down to F8.

7. Click B9, and drag the AutoFill handle to E9. Your screen should now look like Figure 5-10.

8. Type **Total** in F2. Also type **Total** in A9. In the next step, you AutoFormat the table.

9. Select A1 through F9, choose ` Format ` → ` Auto Format `, select the 3D Effects 1 format, and click OK.

10. Click A1 to turn off the selection. Your table should be formatted as shown in Figure 5-11.

11. Save the file, and close the workbook.

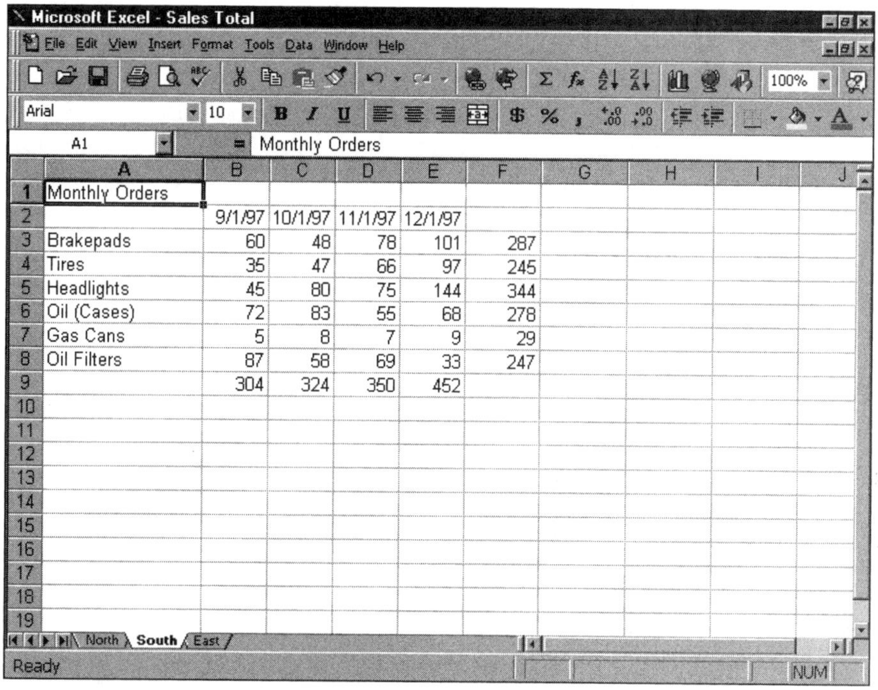

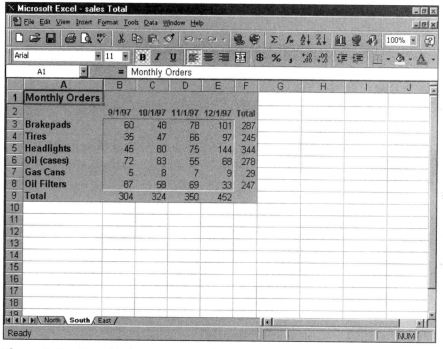

Figure 5-10 Use AutoFill to copy the totals formulas to other cells.

Figure 5-11 The table is AutoFormatted with the 3D Effects 1 option.

Entering data by using a Pick List

One last IntelliSense feature is the Pick List. In Figure 5-12, ten first and last names have been entered, along with their order numbers. By clicking the cell in which you want to make the *next* entry and then right-clicking, you can choose Pick From List from the pop-up menu that Excel displays. Excel responds to this command by displaying an alphabetized list of all cell entries, as shown in Figure 5-12. You can then click the name that you want to enter in the cell. Duplicates are not shown, and you may need to scroll through the list before making your selection.

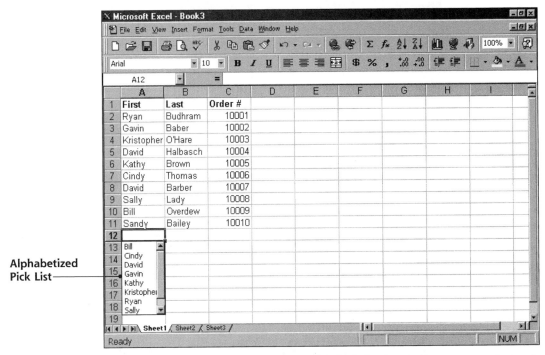

Figure 5-12 The Pick List is displayed in alphabetical order. Duplicates are not displayed.

 If you have entered both the first and the last name in a *single* cell, the Pick List is alphabetized by the *first letter* in the cell, not by the first letter of the last name.

Freezing Parts of the Screen

When working with a large workbook, one potentially irritating problem is that every time you scroll to the right to enter data, your row headings move out of sight. Likewise, when you scroll down, your column headings disappear. This makes it difficult to ensure that you are entering the data in the correct cells.

Excel overcomes this problem by enabling you to freeze portions of the screen that you want to keep in sight at all times. For example, imagine that you are working on the data in Figure 5-13.

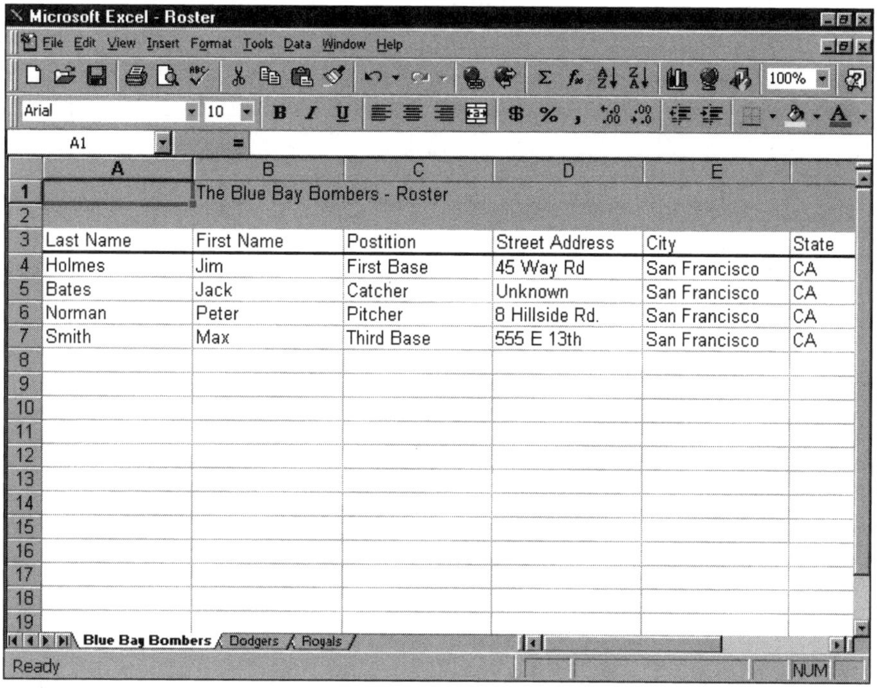

Figure 5-13 Not all of the columns are visible on the screen at the same time.

The last column shown on the screen is the State column. However, two more columns are off the screen: Zip and Phone Number. As shown in Figure 5-14, without any parts of the screen frozen, every time that you scroll over to Phone Number, the first three columns scroll off to the left, where you can't see them. This makes it difficult to make sure that you are entering the correct phone number in the right cell.

Additionally, if you scroll down past row 21, the column headings scroll up and are not visible, making it even more difficult to ensure that the data is being entered into the correct cell.

To alleviate this problem, you can freeze certain rows or columns to make sure that the data is entered correctly. In Figure 5-13, row 3 is the important row. The important columns contain the First and Last Names (columns A and B). To make sure that these always stay visible, you can freeze them.

To freeze portions of the screen, select the cell *below* the row that you want to freeze and to the *right* of the column that you want to freeze. For example, if you want to freeze row 3 and columns A and B, as shown in Figure 5-15, you must select the cell below row 3 and to the right of column B (cell C4).

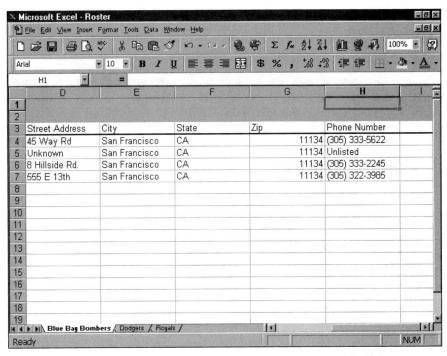

Figure 5-14   With no columns frozen, important columns can scroll off the screen to the right or left.

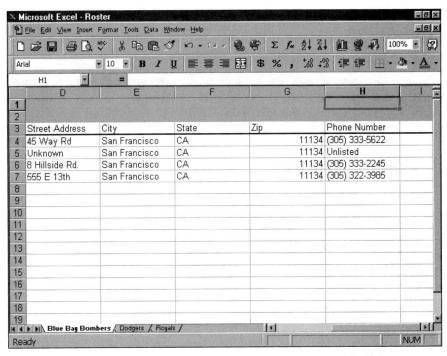

Figure 5-15   The rows above and the columns to the left of C4 are frozen.

Depending on the size of your monitor and its resolution, you may be able to see more or fewer columns and rows on the screen at one time than are shown in the figures.

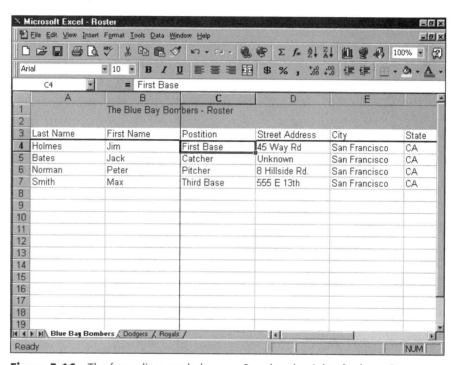

Figure 5-16   The freeze lines are below row 3 and to the right of column B.

After you select cell C4, choose | **Window** | → | **Freeze Panes** |. Excel places a line to the right of column B and below row 3, as shown in Figure 5-16.

Now, when you scroll to the right, the Last Name and First Name columns remain in sight. And when you scroll down, the column headings remain in sight.

Be sure that you select the cell to the *right* and *below* the columns and rows that you want to freeze. If you want to freeze a row but not a column, select the cell in the first column under the row that you want to freeze.

If you want to freeze a column but not a row, select the cell in the first row to the right of the column that you want to freeze.

This activity shows you how to freeze the columns and rows that you want to always display.

Follow these steps:

1. Create a new workbook by clicking the New button on the toolbar.

2. Type **January** in B2.

3. Grab the AutoFill handle of cell B2 and drag it to M2. This enters the next 11 months.

4. Type **Store 1** in A3.

5. Drag the AutoFill handle of cell A3 to A22. Excel AutoFills these cells with consecutive Store numbers.

6. Type **25** in M22. As you scroll over to column M, notice that your row headers scroll off the screen. Your column headers also disappeared when you scrolled down to row 22, as shown in Figure 5-17.

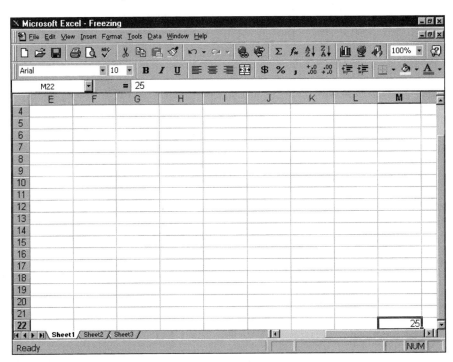

Figure 5-17   Both the row and column headers have scrolled off the screen.

7. Select B3. This is the cell that is below the column header row and to the right of the row headings.

8. Choose ⌐Window¬ → ⌐Freeze Panes¬. A bold horizontal line appears under the column header row, and a vertical line appears to the right of the row headings.

9. Scroll over to cell M22. Notice that the row and column headings remain visible at all times, as seen in Figure 5-18.

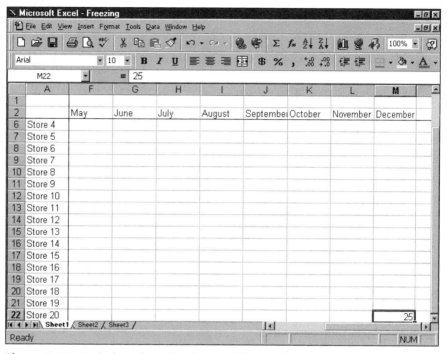

Figure 5-18 Both the column headings and the row headings remain in view.

10. To unfreeze the panes, choose Window → Unfreeze Panes .

11. Close the workbook without saving it.

TIP You can simplify the process of freezing panes by adding the Freeze Panes button to your toolbar as follows:

1. Choose View → Toolbars → Customize , and select the Commands tab.

2. In the Categories box, select Windows and Help.

3. Drag the Freeze Panes button onto your toolbar.

Whenever you want to freeze a portion of the screen, select the cell below and to the right of the area that you want to freeze, and click the Freeze Panes button. Clicking the button a second time removes the freeze.

BONUS

Customizing the AutoFill Option

Excel's AutoFill feature also allows you to create custom lists that you can insert by using the AutoFill handle. Just as Excel enters the days of the week when you type Monday and drag the AutoFill handle, you can specify what data Excel should enter when you enter specific data.

For example, you may work with several different businesses for which you enter data into workbooks on a regular basis. Instead of typing each business's name, you can set up a custom series of information that consists of all the names of the businesses. When you type the first name and drag the AutoFill handle, Excel fills in the rest of the names.

This activity shows you how to develop a custom series of information and then apply the AutoFill feature to a worksheet.

Follow these steps:

1. Create a new worksheet by choosing `File` → `New` and clicking OK.

2. Choose `Tools` → `Options`, and click the Custom Lists tab, as shown in Figure 5-19.

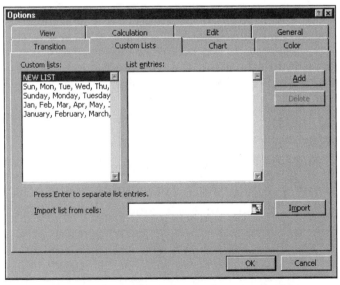

Figure 5-19 The Custom Lists tab of the Options dialog box.

3. In the Custom lists panel, highlight NEW LIST.

4. Click the List entries panel, type **Northwest Automotive**, and press Enter.

5. While your are still in the List entries panel, create entries for Western Parts, Billings Auto Parts, and Auto Parts R Us, pressing Enter after each entry.

6. Click Add. Your list then moves into the Custom lists panel.

7. Click OK.

8. In your new worksheet, type **Northwest Automotive** in cell B2 and press Enter.

9. Grab the AutoFill handle in B2, and drag it down to B5.

10. AutoFit the column. Figure 5-20 shows the results.

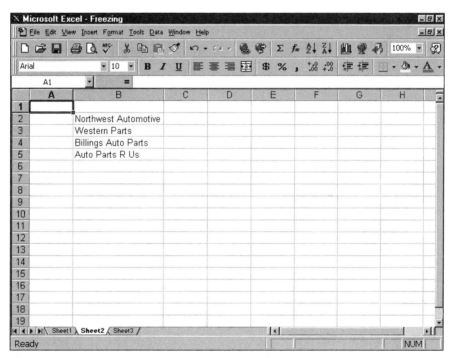

Figure 5-20 Excel automatically fills in the company names.

11. Close the workbook without saving it.

12. Close Excel.

Using a customized series and the AutoFill handle can save you time by entering data that you would otherwise have to type repeatedly. Additionally, it reduces the chance of spelling errors and missed entries.

TIP AutoFill also has a shortcut menu that gives you greater control over AutoFill's actions. Instead of using the *left* mouse button to drag the AutoFill handle, try using the *right* button. After dragging the handle over the area to be filled, a menu appears offering several AutoFill options, as shown in Figure 5-21.

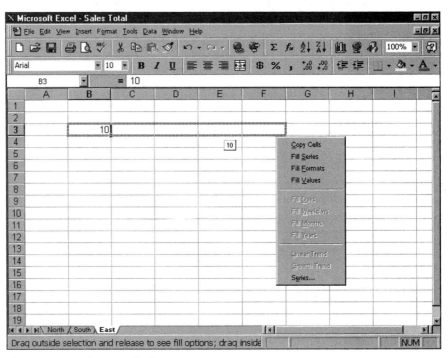

Figure 5-21 The AutoFill shortcut menu.

From this shortcut menu, you can copy the cells, fill the cells with a series, format the cells in the same way as the first cell, or choose from several other options.

Summary

Excel's data-entry shortcuts are designed to make your work more productive. By saving keystrokes and anticipating your needs, Excel reduces the time that you spend on tedious data entry. Perhaps one day computers will anticipate that we would rather have them do *all* the work and just mail us our paychecks every Friday.

CHAPTER SIX

NEW MATH: USING LABELS, VALUES, FORMULAS, AND FUNCTIONS

IN THIS CHAPTER YOU LEARN THESE KEY SKILLS

I remember buying my first calculator. (For that matter, I remember buying my first six-transistor radio.) The calculator handled addition, subtraction, multiplication, and division. (The square root button had not yet been invented.) By the time I got to college, I had my very own, full-function, statistical calculator. Although the calculator hanging from my belt clearly marked me as a card-carrying nerd, I couldn't have gotten through my statistics class without it. In much the same way as I came to rely on my hand-held calculator, you may soon wonder how you ever got by without Excel's number-crunching capabilities.

Although worksheets contain many different elements, four of these are critical to successful worksheets: labels, values, formulas, and functions. In this chapter, you take a look at each of these elements and get some practice in using them. So sit back (hopefully at your computer), and follow along as you find out even more about what Excel can do.

Labeling Your Data

Your clothes usually have one or more labels to identify the fabric content, the size, the manufacturer, and the cleaning instructions. Some clothing articles have labels to tell you who inspected the garment (you can call the company and complain to Inspector 152!). The point is that labels provide information. (I've had to throw away more than one mattress because someone tore off the tag — illegally, I might add.) Worksheets have labels, too. Without labels, the numbers in a worksheet are meaningless.

Labels are nothing more than text that describes the various parts of the worksheet. For example, the first row of the worksheet in Figure 6-1 lists the days of the week. The first column contains the names of the employees. At the intersection of a day of the week and an employee name, you can see a value (a number) representing that employee's daily sales total. Without the day and name labels, the values are meaningless.

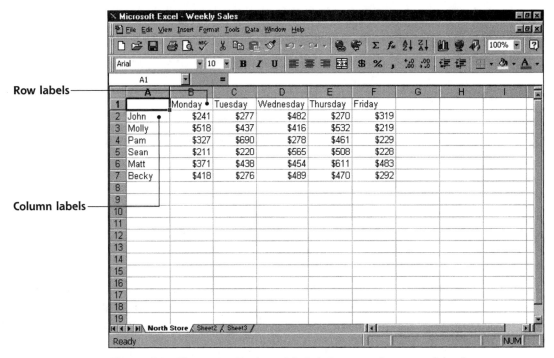

Figure 6-1 The row and column labels help you make sense of the data.

Understanding how Excel handles labels

Excel treats nearly any cell entry that doesn't begin with a plus sign or an equal sign as a label. Even if the cell entry appears to be a mathematical equation, unless it begins with one of those two signs, Excel treats it as text. For example, 555-9999 is treated as text.

As you learned in the chapter on formatting, there are some exceptions. If you enter **3–2**, Excel interprets it as March 2. If you put a plus sign or an equal sign in front of the 3, Excel enters a value (1) in the cell and displays the formula (=3-2) in the formula bar.

If you type **3–2**, Excel displays March 2. If you then realize your error and type =3–2 or +3–2, you get 1-Jan. The cell was automatically formatted as a date when you first entered the data. The new answer is 1, and because the cell is formatted as a date, 1-Jan appears in the cell. To display the correct answer (1) return the cell formatting to General.

If you type **3–13**, Excel enters this as a label. This is not a possible date (there is no 13th month), and because no equal or plus sign precedes the data, Excel sees it as a label and displays 3-13.

Entering labels

This activity shows how to enter and format labels.

Follow these steps:

1. Open a new workbook.

2. Type **Monday** in B1.

3. Use the AutoFill feature to enter the rest of the weekdays in C1 through F1.

4. Type **John** in A2.

5. In cells A3 through A7, enter the other names that are shown in Figure 6-2. Adjust the column width where necessary.

6. Click the Row label for row 1.

7. Click **B** (the Bold button) on the toolbar, and then click ▤ (the Center button) on the toolbar. The labels in row 1 are now formatted as bold and centered.

8. In the same way, format the labels in column A as bold (but not centered).

9. Change the Sheet1 tab name to North Store.

10. Save the file in your Discover Excel folder as Weekly Sales. Your screen should look similar to Figure 6-3.

11. Leave the workbook open for the next activity.

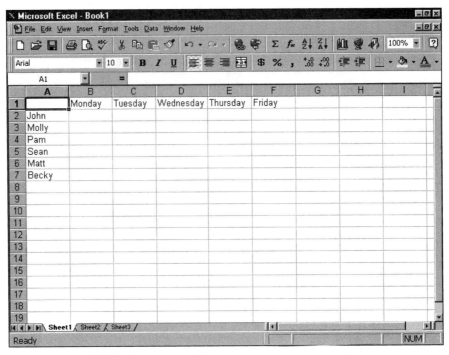

Figure 6-2 Labels for the new worksheet.

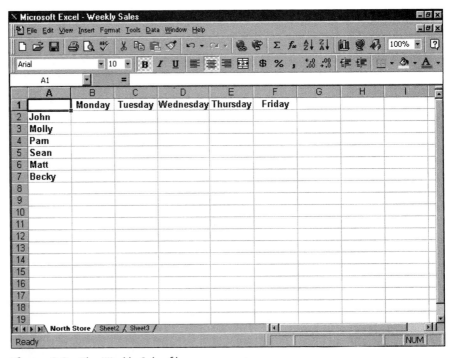

Figure 6-3 The Weekly Sales file.

Entering Values in Your Worksheet

Some spreadsheet users don't have values — at least not ethical ones (present company excepted, of course). The values that we discuss in this section are simply numbers. I leave the ethics of spreadsheet use to other writers.

You already have some experience with entering values into cells. Values can contain only numbers, commas, and decimal points. You only enter a decimal point if it is required.

TIP Don't include special formatting — for example, dollar signs and commas — when you enter values into your worksheets. Enter the values first, and then apply any necessary formatting. For example, to insert $11,050.50 into a cell, type **11050.5** and then format the entry by clicking the toolbar buttons that specify Currency Style and the desired decimal precision.

When you enter a value into a cell, the formula bar displays the value. If you enter a formula (we discuss formulas in the next section of this chapter), the formula *results* appear in the cell. You can tell whether a cell contains a value by clicking the cell and looking in the formula bar. If you see a formula, the cell doesn't contain a value.

If you are manually entering values into a worksheet, double-check your work and then give it to another person to check. For some of our statistical work, we have as many as five people proof the data, and we sometimes still find problems. Accuracy is imperative in spreadsheet work. Without accuracy, your data is meaningless. Even worse, you may make important decisions based on erroneous information.

Inserting Random Numbers into Your Worksheet

This activity shows how to make your worksheet look realistic without having to type many numbers. You use Excel to automatically generate random numbers.

Follow these steps:

1. Choose Tools → Add-Ins .

2. In the dialog box that's displayed, select the Analysis ToolPak option. This loads several new functions called *add-ins*. Add-ins are extra

functions that Microsoft felt not everyone needs all the time (they take up RAM). Add-ins are only loaded as needed.

3. Click OK.

4. Click B2, and type **=randbetween(200,700)**. This Excel function (randbetween) generates a random number. The random number falls in the range of values that is defined by the two numbers enclosed in the parentheses.

5. Press Enter. Excel places a random number in the cell.

6. Click B2. Note that the Formula bar still displays =RANDBETWEEN(200,700), even though the cell contains a number.

7. AutoFill B2 through F2. Excel enters random numbers in the selected cells. The cells are still selected.

8. Drag the AutoFill handle *down* to F7. Excel fills the cells with random numbers between 200 and 700.

NOTE Each time that you enter a number, Excel recalculates the worksheet. When your worksheet contains random numbers, Excel generates *new* random numbers each time it recalculates the worksheet. You need to change the random number formulas to values; otherwise, the values constantly change.

9. Press F9 to manually recalculate the sheet.

   Notice that all of the numbers change. To convert them to values (rather than random-number formulas), you need to Copy and Paste Special the contents of the cells. (The Paste Special command allows you to paste just part of the data — in this case, the numbers that are currently in B2 through F7.) Make sure that the cells are still selected.

10. Click 📋 (the Copy button) on the toolbar.

11. Choose Edit → Paste Special . Excel displays the Paste Special dialog box, shown in Figure 6-4.

12. Click Values, and click OK.

13. Click in any other cell to cancel the selection.

14. Click B2. The formula bar now displays the *value* that B2 contains, rather than the randbetween function. Click in other cells to see that they also now contain values.

15. Format the cells as currency values by selecting B2 through F7 and then clicking the Currency Style button. To decrease the number of decimal places, click 🔲 (the Decrease Decimal button) twice.

Figure 6-4 The Paste Special dialog box can be used to change randomly generated numbers to permanent values.

16. Click A1. Your screen should be similar to Figure 6-5; however, your values are going to be different.

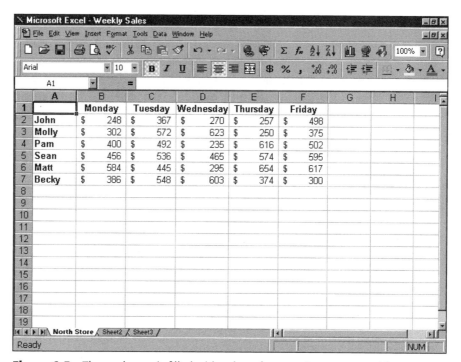

Figure 6-5 The work area is filled with values, formatted as currency with no decimal places.

17. Save your work, and leave the workbook open for the next activity.

Understanding Formulas

A *formula* performs calculations or comparisons using the data in your worksheet. Formulas perform operations such as addition, multiplication, and comparison of worksheet values; they can also combine values. A cell entry such as 60 is a value. On the other hand, =6*10 is a formula. Formulas can contain values, mathematical commands, or references to other cells within the same worksheet, other worksheets, or even other workbooks.

Examining some sample formulas

Formulas range from very simple (such as =5+2) to somewhat complex (such as =A1*5/(.65*B10)+H12) to very complex. As an example of a complex formula, a Weekly Sales Total worksheet may contain the following formula, which totals the sales figures for each employee for each day of the week, from each of four stores:

```
='[Weekly Sales.xls]North Store'!$G$8+'[Weekly Sales.xls]South
    Store'!$G$8+'[Weekly Sales.xls]East Store'!$G$8+'[Weekly
    Sales.xls]West Store'!$G$8
```

This formula includes references to cells in four different worksheets from another workbook. The formula actually performs a very simple mathematical operation: adding the contents of those cells. The formula is complex because it uses values from several different worksheets that are not part of the current workbook.

Creating formulas

You can create formulas by typing cell references or by pointing to cells. If you are working in one simple sheet, you may be able to type the references, but in more complex sheets, it is much easier to point and click or drag.

This activity shows you how to create formulas by typing and using a combination of keyboard and mouse actions.

Follow these steps:

1. In G1 on the North Store worksheet, type **Total**. Because you formatted the row earlier, the text is automatically bold and centered.

SIDE TRIP

According to Webster's dictionary, the plural of formula is *either* formulas or formulae. It is generally easier to talk about formulas rather than formulae, and Microsoft uses *formulas* as the plural, so that's the term that we use.

2. Click G2, and then type **+B2+C2+D2+E2+F2**. The cell references can be uppercase or lowercase characters. Excel automatically converts all cell references to uppercase.

3. Press Enter to see the result. Your screen should be similar to Figure 6-6, although your actual values will differ.

The formula bar———

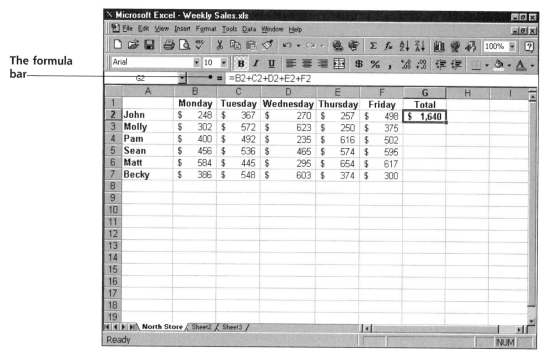

Figure 6-6 The formula bar displays the formula for adding the values contained in B2 through F2.

4. Click G2. Write down the value in this cell for later comparison. Check your formula in the formula bar for accuracy.

TIP To double-check your answer, you could use a calculator. A simpler way is to use the AutoCalculate feature that you learned about in Chapter 5. Drag across B2 through F2. The answer appears in the AutoCalculate box, as shown in Figure 6-7. Because the values in the cells of your worksheet differ from those shown in the figure, compare the results in the AutoCalculate box with the sum in G2 of *your* worksheet. These values should be the same.

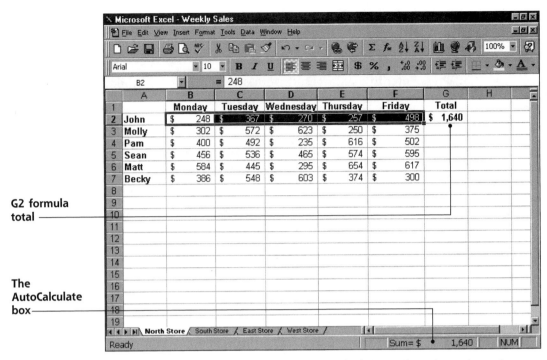

Figure 6-7 Use the AutoCalculate box to verify that your formula produces the correct result.

5. Click G2 and press Delete to delete the formula. Now you can create the same formula by pointing and clicking.

6. Type = and click B2.

7. Type + and click C2.

8. Continue in this manner until you have added D2, E2, and F2 to your formula.

9. Press Enter to complete the formula. Compare the result to the answer that you wrote down after Step 4. The results should be identical.

10. Save your work, and leave the workbook open for the next activity.

Getting It Right: Formula Syntax

Despite the belief of many that the term *syntax* refers to the penalty paid for inappropriate actions, syntax is actually the study of well-formed formulas of a logical system and the set of rules that generate such a system. For example, using sentence syntax *ball forward* doesn't follow the syntax of a well-formed sentence. *The quarterback passed the ball forward to the receiver.* contains all of the elements of a well-formed sentence.

In Excel, formula syntax is the structure or order of the elements in a formula. Formulas follow a specific syntax that includes an equal sign (=) followed by the elements to be calculated (the operands) and the calculation operators (such as +, –, *, and /). Each operand can be a value that does not change (a constant value), a cell or range reference, a label, a name, or a worksheet function. We discuss functions a bit later in this chapter.

Confirming your results

By default, Microsoft Excel calculates a formula from left to right, starting with the equal sign (=). You can control how calculation is performed by changing the syntax of the formula. For example, the answer to =5+11 is obviously 16. But what is the answer to =30/5-2? Because Excel calculates a formula from left to right, the answer is 4. If you expected 10 as the answer, you may be in for a shock. The correct syntax for calculating the answer 10 would be =30/(5-2). It is imperative that you understand the order of operation within a formula, because results vary depending on how the formula syntax is created. Remember, Excel does what you tell it to do, not what you want it to do!

Understanding Excel's order of operation

Without getting too deep into the order of operation of a formula, you need to keep the following rules in mind when creating formulas:

* Excel evaluates a formula from left to right.
* Each formula must begin with an equal sign.
* Any elements that are enclosed in parentheses are evaluated first.
* Multiplication and division are performed *before* addition and subtraction.

Any time that you create a formula, you should have test data for which you know the correct answer *in advance*. Then, when you enter the actual data, your results should be correct. Forgetting a single set of parentheses could cause your entire worksheet and all associated worksheets, workbooks, graphs, and charts to be incorrect. For more information about the order of operation within formulas, use the Office Assistant to search for *order of operation*.

Copying formulas

Copying formulas is simple, but the results may not be exactly what you expect. For example, in the previous activity, you created the formula =B2+C2+D2+E2+F2 in G2. What happens if you copy that formula from G2 to G3? Take a look.

In this activity, you see the results of copying a formula from one cell to another.

Follow these steps:

1. Click G2.

2. Right-click, and then select [Copy] from the pop-up menu.

3. Click G3 and press Enter to paste the copy into G3. You could also right-click and select [Paste] or click the Paste button on the toolbar.

4. Compare the values in G2 and G3.

   If the formula had been copied exactly, the results in G3 would be the same as in G2. Notice that they are different. That is because the formula was *not* copied exactly. The formula in the Formula bar now reads =B3+C3+D3+E3+F3. Excel automatically adjusts the row number to create the new formula.

5. Save your work, and leave the workbook open for the next activity.

Giving directions

There are two ways to give directions: relative and absolute. If we're standing at the corner of First and Main Streets and you ask us how to get to the post office, we can say, "Go two blocks north and one block east." This is a *relative* reference; it is relative to our current position. If we're at the corner of Second and Broadway and we give you the same instructions, you don't find the post office. The relative instructions are good only from the original position.

We could also tell you that the post office is located at Third and Broadway. This is an *absolute* reference. Regardless of where we are standing in the city, the position of the post office at Third and Broadway doesn't change, and the instructions are good. As the previous activity shows, you have to be very careful when you give Excel directions. If you don't give the right directions, your formulas probably aren't going to produce the correct results.

USING RELATIVE REFERENCES

When you write a formula in Excel, it is not really written as it appears. In the previous example (=B2+C2+D2+E2+F2) the cell locations are actually relative. That is, the purpose of the formula in G2 is to add the contents of the five cells to the left of the cell that contains the formula.

By default, Excel copies formulas as *relative references*. In other words, the formula in G2 adds the contents of the five cells that are directly to the left of G2. When you copy the formula to G3, Excel automatically updates the row numbers, resulting in the answer that you really want: the total of the cells in row 3. In most cases, you want Excel to automatically update the references in the formula. In some cases, however, you may want to refer to an exact cell or group of cells. That's when you need an absolute reference.

USING ABSOLUTE REFERENCES

When you want to refer to one specific cell or group of cells, you need to designate it as an *absolute cell reference*. In a formula, an absolute cell reference is marked with a dollar sign ($).

To create an absolute reference to a cell, use a dollar sign next to both the column address and the row address. For example, an absolute formula in H2 is =G2*$I$1. When you copy the formula from H2 to H3, the new formula is =G3*$I$1. The relative part of the formula changes (G2 becomes G3), whereas the absolute part of the formula ($I$1) is copied exactly.

CREATING RELATIVE AND ABSOLUTE REFERENCES IN FORMULAS

In the previous activity, you created a worksheet to track the daily sales of employees in the North Store. You created a single formula that totals the sales for John. This activity shows how to copy that formula and then create and copy a formula for calculating bonuses.

Follow these steps:

1. Click G3.

2. Right-click, and choose Copy from the pop-up menu.

3. Drag down until G4 through G7 is highlighted. Press Enter. The relative formula in G3 is copied into G4 through G7. In the following steps, you create a formula for calculating bonuses.

4. Type **Bonus** in H1.

5. Type **.02** in I1.

6. Click H2.

7. Type **=G2*I1** and press Enter. This shows the correct bonus.

8. Right-click H2, and select Copy from the pop-up menu.

9. Click in H3 and press Enter.

   Notice that no bonus is displayed. This is because the formula in H3 is *relative*. Look at the Formula bar for H3. It reads =G3*I2. Because I2 doesn't contain a value, no bonus is given. You need to correct the formula in H2.

10. Click H2.

11. Click to the right of the asterisk in the formula bar to drop the insertion point.

12. Change the formula to read =G3*$I$1. Press Enter.

13. Click H2.

14. Right-click, and select `Copy`.

15. Highlight H3 through H7. Press Enter. Look at the formulas in H3 through H7. They all refer to I1 as the cell from which to retrieve the bonus percentage. Only the row references for the first part of the formula change from cell to cell.

TIP Here is a secret that Microsoft doesn't tell you. When the cursor is in a cell reference in the formula bar, pressing F4 acts as a four-way toggle. For example, if the cell reference is G2, pressing F4 changes it to $G$2. Pressing it again changes the reference to G$2. Pressing once more changes it to $G2. Pressing F4 a fourth time returns the reference to G2. This is actually a holdover from Lotus 1-2-3, but it works.

16. Save the file, and leave it open for the next activity.

Understanding Functions: An Overview

A function is a built-in formula shortcut in Excel. According to Microsoft, functions are predefined formulas that perform calculations by using specific values (called *arguments*) in a particular order (called the *syntax*). Excel provides hundreds of built-in functions.

Assume that you want to add cells in B2 through B100. Imagine typing **=B2+B3+B4 . . . +B100**. Instead, you can use Excel's SUM function. SUM is one of the most commonly used functions. Rather than typing the cell references from B2 to B100, you can type **=SUM(B2:B100)** and press Enter. Table 6-1 shows other common functions.

Remember that the functions shown in Table 6-1 are but a *few* of the available functions. However, unless you know how to use the functions and are able to interpret their results, don't use them. For example, unless you are a statistician, you probably aren't going to use the KURT (kurtosis) function. To see a list of the available functions, choose `Insert` → `Function` to display the Paste Function dialog box shown in Figure 6-8.

TABLE 6-1 Common Functions

Function	Description
AVERAGE	Calculates the average of a selected group of cells
RANDBETWEEN	Returns a random number between the numbers that you specify
COUNT	Counts the number of cells containing information
ROUND	Rounds a number to a specified number of digits
COUNTIF	Counts the number of cells in a range that meet the specified criteria
SQRT	Returns the square root of a number
IF	Returns one value if specified criteria are met and another if they are not met
SUMIF	Sums only those cells that meet specific criteria
MAX	Returns the maximum value of selected cells
TRIM	Removes all spaces from a selected group of text, except for single spaces between words
MIN	Returns the minimum value of selected cells
UPPER	Converts a selected group of text to uppercase characters
RAND	Returns an evenly distributed random number between 0 and 1
VALUE	Converts a selected group of text representing a number into a value

Entering functions

The left panel of the Paste Function dialog box lists categories. The first category is Most Recently Used. When you select this category, the Function name panel lists the most recently used function. When you select All in the Function category panel, the Function name panel lists all functions. You can use the scroll arrows to see all the choices.

Below the All category is a list of several categories of related functions. For example, if you click Statistical in the Function category panel, only the statistically related functions are displayed in the Function name panel. This makes finding specific functions easier.

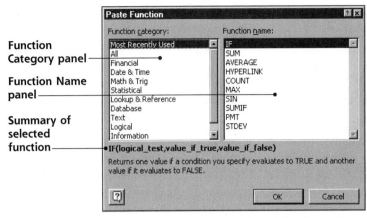

Function Category panel

Function Name panel

Summary of selected function

Figure 6-8 The Paste Function dialog box offers many functions that are included in Excel.

Below the two panels is a description of how the selected function works. First, the syntax of the function is shown, including various arguments that are either required or optional. *Arguments* are values that Excel uses in evaluating the function. You find out more about them in the next section of this chapter. Below the function syntax is a brief explanation of the function's purpose.

You now have a chance to enter a few simple functions so that you can see how they work. This activity shows how to use functions to create summary information.

Follow these steps:

1. Click B9, and type **High Sale**.

2. Click B10, and type **Low Sale**.

3. Click C9, type **=MAX(**, and click B2. Remember, the Max function finds the largest value in a selected group of cells.

4. Drag to highlight B2 through F7. Officially, you need to complete the function by closing the parentheses.

5. Instead, press Enter. Excel automatically inserts the closing parenthesis and completes the function for you.

FEATURE FOCUS Excel 97 monitors how you type functions and automatically corrects 15 different types of errors, such as not typing a closing parenthesis.

6. Click C9 again. The formula bar automatically completed your function. C9 displays the maximum value for any cell in the range.

7. Click C10, type **=MIN(**, and click B2.

8. Drag down and right until F7 is highlighted. Press Enter. C10 displays the minimum value of B2 through F7.

9. Save the file, and leave the workbook open.

Creating a formula by using the Formula Palette

When you create a formula that contains a function, the Formula Palette helps you enter worksheet functions. To display the Formula Palette, click the equal sign (=) in the formula bar. When you are ready to enter a function into your formula, choose it from the Function Name drop-down list at the left side of the formula bar.

The Formula Palette is a new feature to Excel 97. This activity shows how to create formulas using it.

Follow these steps:

1. Click A8, type **Daily Total**, and press Enter.

2. AutoFit column A so that the new text fits.

3. Click B8 and then click the Equal sign in the formula bar. This displays the Formula Palette that is shown in Figure 6-9.

4. Drop-down the Function Name box, and click **Sum**.

   The palette changes, as shown in Figure 6-10. The first series of cell addresses are automatically entered into the Number 1 text box. They should be B2 to B7. If you need to change the addresses, you can do so at this point.

5. Click OK to accept the formula shown in the formula bar. Your worksheet now includes the first daily sales total, as shown in Figure 6-11.

6. AutoFill B8 through G8. Row 8 now contains all of the totals for the daily sales.

7. Save the file, and leave the workbook open.

Function
Name box
(at the left
edge of the
formula bar,
where the
cell address
is normally
displayed –
currently
contains "IF")

Formula
Palette (the
new bar
beneath the
formula bar)

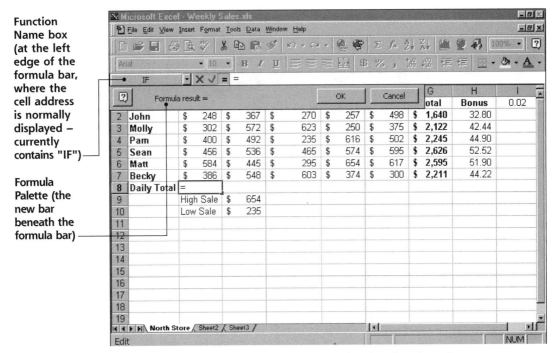

Figure 6-9 Use the Formula Palette to enter functions into formulas.

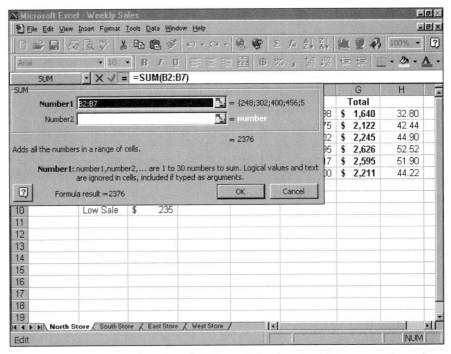

Figure 6-10 The Formula Palette includes a dialog box in which you can input the appropriate values.

![Excel spreadsheet: Microsoft Excel - Weekly Sales.xls]

Cell B8 formula bar: `=SUM(B2:B7)`

	A	B	C	D	E	F	G	H	I
1		Monday	Tuesday	Wednesday	Thursday	Friday	Total	Bonus	0.02
2	John	$ 248	$ 367	$ 270	$ 257	$ 498	$ 1,640	32.80	
3	Molly	$ 302	$ 572	$ 623	$ 250	$ 375	$ 2,122	42.44	
4	Pam	$ 400	$ 492	$ 235	$ 616	$ 502	$ 2,245	44.90	
5	Sean	$ 456	$ 536	$ 465	$ 574	$ 595	$ 2,626	52.52	
6	Matt	$ 584	$ 445	$ 295	$ 654	$ 617	$ 2,595	51.90	
7	Becky	$ 386	$ 548	$ 603	$ 374	$ 300	$ 2,211	44.22	
8	Daily Total	$ 2,376							
9		High Sale	$ 654						
10		Low Sale	$ 235						
11									
12									
13									
14									
15									
16									
17									
18									
19									

Sheet tabs: North Store / Sheet2 / Sheet3

Figure 6-11 Calculating daily sales totals.

Getting It Right II: Function Syntax

Syntax for functions is a little more difficult than for formulas, partly because each function has its own syntax. However, by using the Paste Function dialog box and the Formula Palette, the task becomes a little easier. The major problem with using functions is that you have to understand how they work in real life. The SUM function is fairly easy to understand. It simply totals the values of a selected group of cells. For example, `=SUM(A1:A10)` consists of three separate parts:

* The equal sign, which identifies the entry as a formula
* The function name (so that Excel knows the type of operation that you want to perform)
* A set of information, in parentheses, indicating the range of values to be summed

Other formulas containing functions are more difficult to understand. For example, to evaluate the skewness of a group of values, the formula is `=SKEW(number1, number2...)`. Excel's description of the skew function is *Returns the skewness of a distribution: a characterization of the degree of asymmetry of a distribution around its mean.* If you are a statistician, this makes sense to you, because you already know about the distribution of random scores around a bell-shaped curve. Skewness indicates that one of the two tails of the curve contains more cases than the other tail. Although this is helpful to a statistician for describing the distribution of values, the function isn't applicable to most of your data.

The syntax of a function is tied in with the syntax of the formula in which you use that function. It must follow specific rules:

* A function is part of a formula, so the formula must begin with an equal sign.
* The function itself must begin with the function name.
* The function name is followed by a left parenthesis and then the appropriate arguments.
* The formula ends with a right parenthesis.

Arguments can be numbers, text, cell references, or various other types of information that are beyond the scope of this chapter. The argument that you designate must produce a valid value for that argument. Arguments can also be constants, formulas, or even other functions.

Arguments, then, are simply values or references to cells containing values. Take a quick look at another commonly used function.

Using functions to make decisions

The IF function decides which of two values to place in a cell by evaluating the arguments that you supply to this function. Basically, if the arguments meet specified criteria, one answer is placed in the cell. If the specified criteria are not met, another answer is placed in the cell.

This activity gives you an opportunity to see the IF function at work.

Follow these steps:

1. Copy the names in A2 through A7 to A12 through A17.

2. Press Esc to turn off the marquis.

3. Click B12.

4. Type **=IF(G2>2500,"Great","OK")**. Press Enter.

   The IF function contains three arguments, separated by commas. The first part is the condition being tested. In this case, is G2 greater than 2500? If it is, the function prints Great in the cell. If G2 fails the test, the next part of the function (OK) is printed. In the example, because John's sales are less than $2,500, OK is entered into the cell. Because the values in your worksheet are based on random numbers, your results of the IF function may vary.

5. Click B13. Now you use the Paste Function dialog box to create the same function.

6. Choose `Insert` → `Function` to display the Paste Function dialog box.

7. In the Function category panel, choose Logical.

8. In the Function name panel, choose If.

9. Click OK. As shown in Figure 6-12, Excel displays the Function Palette. Three arguments are required: Logical_test, Value_if_true, and Value_if_false.

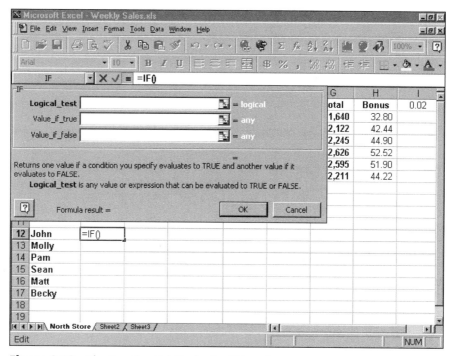

Figure 6-12 The Function Palette for the If function.

10. In the Logical_test text box, type **G3>2500**. Notice at the right side of the text box, the True or False condition has already been evaluated. It is False.

11. Press Tab to move the insertion point to the Value_if_true text box.

12. Type **Great**.

13. Press Tab to move to the Value_if_false text box.

14. Type **OK**.

15. Press Tab again. Notice in the formula bar that the quotation marks were automatically added to Great and OK. The result of the function is displayed in the bottom left corner of the Formula Palette.

16. Click OK. B13 is already highlighted. Now you can copy the formula to B14 and see if it works.

17. Right-click B13, and choose `Copy` from the pop-up menu.

18. Right-click B14, and choose `Paste`

19. Press Esc to cancel the selection. The G3 location was automatically changed to G4 because the formula is a *relative* reference.

20. Copy B14 to B15 through B17. Don't forget to cancel the selection. If everything works correctly, your worksheet should be similar to (but not exactly like) Figure 6-13.

21. Save the file, and leave the workbook open.

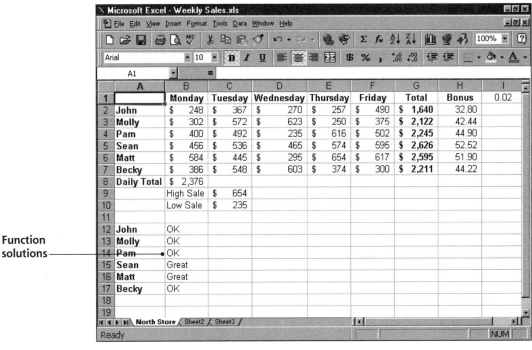

Function solutions

Figure 6-13 The IF functions in cells B12 through B17 automatically categorize the sales amounts as `OK` or `Great`.

/NOTE Earlier in the Hands-On activities in this chapter, you generated random numbers for your worksheet. Therefore, the salespeople who did *Great* or *Good* in your worksheet probably differ from those shown in the figure. Check to make sure that everyone with sales of more than $2,500 has `Great` next to his or her name in Column B and that the rest have `OK`. It is possible, although unlikely, that all have `Great` or all have `OK`.

Entering functions

As you have discovered in this chapter, you can enter functions in one of three ways: manually, using the Function Palette, or from the Paste Function dialog box (which actually uses the Function Palette).

When you manually enter a function, you may forget to include all of the arguments. If so, you get an error, similar to the one shown in Figure 6-14. If you leave out a critical part of the function when using the Paste Function dialog box or the Formula Palette, you also get an error. However, because you can see all of the arguments that are needed to complete the function, you are less likely to make an error than when typing a function manually.

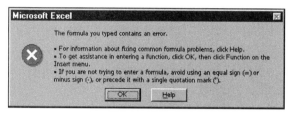

Figure 6-14 An error box is displayed when a formula or function is incomplete.

 TIP Unless the function is simple and you are familiar with its syntax, use the Paste Function dialog box or the Formula Palette to make your entries.

BONUS

Building Fancier Functions

I f you open the Office Assistant, type **Function**, and click Search, you find several areas of help, none of which explain the individual functions in detail. You must take another path to find out how to use individual functions, what they are used for, which arguments they must contain and which are optional, and how and when they should be used.

This activity steps you through the process of getting additional help in understanding how functions work. Any time that you aren't sure exactly what a function does, return to this activity for additional information.

Follow these steps:

1. Choose `Help` → `Contents and Index` . This takes you to the Help Topics dialog box, which contains three tabs.

2. Click the Find tab.

   The first time that the Find tab is used, you see a dialog box asking if you want to create a minimal or complete index. The complete index includes words such as *and* and *the.* If the dialog box that asks if you want to create a minimal or complete index isn't displayed, skip to Step 5.

3. Leave the option at minimal, and click OK. The next dialog box provides additional information that is totally unimportant.

4. Click Finish.

   The computer works anywhere from several seconds to several minutes (depending on the speed of the computer, available RAM, and hard disk speed). When it is complete, you see a tab similar to the one shown in Figure 6-15.

5. In the Type the word(s) you want to find text box, type **Function** and then click Find Now.

   If needed, you could scroll through the Select some matching words to narrow your search text box to narrow the topic. Scroll through the Click a type, then display list box, and choose the category of functions about which you need additional information.

6. Double-click Functions in the Click a topic box, and then click the Display text box. The Functions dialog box is displayed.

7. Click About Statistical Functions. The About Statistical Functions help window is displayed, as shown in Figure 6-16.

   You can scroll through the list of statistical functions until you see the one that you want.

8. Click the button next to the AVERAGE worksheet function.

   Figure 6-17 shows the first portion of the help screen for the AVERAGE function. You can scroll through it to see the information or choose `Options` → `Print Topic` to send the entire topic to the printer for later reference.

   Every function is documented in this way. This makes it possible to examine a function to see if it is applicable to your data.

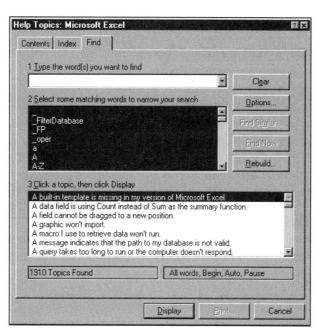

Figure 6-15 The Find tab of the Contents and Index dialog box.

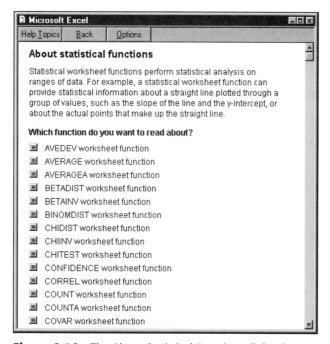

Figure 6-16 The About Statistical Functions dialog box.

Don't use a function if you don't understand how to use the function manually. That way, you can find out whether it is appropriate to your specific situation.

9. Click the Close box in the upper-right corner of the Help window to close the help feature.

10. Close the workbook, and close Excel.

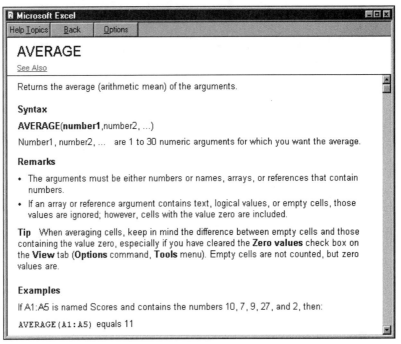

Figure 6-17   The Average screen is displayed, telling you how to use the function and its arguments, and when it's most appropriate to use the function.

Summary

Without labels, values, formulas, and functions, Excel would be like a car without a motor. These are the tools that you use to make Excel do the job for which it is designed. An understanding of how these features work together is what separates the novice spreadsheet user from the master. By understanding their purposes and appropriate interactions, you can become the master of the spreadsheet.

magine life without pictures — no television, no Mona Lisa, and worst of all, no computer games (a pleasing thought to my wife). Life would be pretty boring without visual images.

Charts and graphs are the visual tools that make Excel worksheets exciting. Think about the reaction that you would get from your boss if you submitted a report filled with endless pages of data. In my experience, you usually get a reaction like, "Thanks, I'll get to this later," and your boss tosses the product of your hard work on top of a never-ending to-do pile. On the other hand, if you submit a chart explaining your data, the response is usually something like, "Holy cow, sales are up 20%?!?"

By learning to use charts effectively, you can make your worksheets easier to understand and, therefore, more likely to be read.

NOTE By definition, charts and graphs are both visual representations of data. This chapter uses the word *chart* to refer to both charts and graphs because this is the term that's used by Excel.

Understanding Charts

Think of charts in much the same way as you view the various items in your wardrobe. If you look in your closet, you probably find many different ways to represent yourself. Each outfit says something different about you (ball gown or tux, sweater and jeans, your favorite sweats, and so on).

Charts are the wardrobe for your data. Excel offers several different types of charts, so you can visually represent your data in a variety of ways. The right style of chart depends on the message that you want your chart to convey. Choosing the wrong style, however, can project false images of your information and thus give the reader an inaccurate impression (which can be as dangerous as wearing your favorite old sweats to a business meeting with the CEO).

The first step in understanding how to use charts is to examine the different types of charts and their attributes. Each chart type has its own common use as well as advantages and disadvantages. Understanding how each type of chart works can aid you in your selection and ensure that the chart you choose best represents your information. Before we get into the details about Excel's various chart types, however, you need to learn a couple important terms.

Presenting a Few Points about Data Points and Data Series

To correctly design and interpret charts, you must understand the difference between data points and data series. A *data point* is a specific value, usually corresponding to a specific point in time. For example, the number of cars a dealership sells during June constitutes a single data point on a sales chart. Looking at the complete sales chart for a full year, the 12 data points make up a single *data series* (the total number of cars sold during the year).

However, charts often depict several, smaller categories of data. For example, a car dealership may track the number of trucks and luxury, mid-price, and economy cars sold each month. The number of trucks sold during a single month is a data point, while the number of trucks sold for the entire year is a data series. A *data series,* then, is a combination of related data points.

 TIP Data points are sometimes also called *data items.*

As another example, you may think of each group of coins in your pocket as a data point. (You could plot the number of pennies, nickels, dimes, and quarters that you have in your pocket.) If you plot these values over a period of a week, the number of pennies becomes a data series, as does the number of nickels, dimes, and so on.

In this chapter, you read a lot about data points and data series, so it's important that you understand the difference between these two terms. Understanding these terms now saves a lot of confusion during the remainder of this chapter.

Creating a Chart by Using the Chart Wizard

One of the most useful tools offered by Excel for Office 97 is the improved Chart Wizard. By following the Chart Wizard's simple step-by-step process, you can quickly display your data in eye-catching charts. The following activity shows you some of the Chart Wizard's basic features.

To create a chart and customize it with labels and titles, follow these steps:

1. Open Excel and a new workbook.

2. Save the file in your Discover Excel folder as Books.xls.

3. In A4, type **Books Read**.

4. In C3, type **January**.

5. As shown in Figure 7-1, drag the AutoFill handle to fill C3 through H3 with the months.

6. Enter the following values in C4 through H4, respectively: **4**, **6**, **5**, **7**, **7**, and **8**.

7. Select C3 through H4.

8. Click ▥ (the Chart Wizard button) on the toolbar. Excel displays the Chart Type dialog box (Step 1 of 4 in the Chart Wizard).

9. Under Chart type, select Column. The Chart Wizard displays the corresponding Chart sub-types.

10. Under Chart sub-type, select Clustered Column with a 3-D visual effect (the first chart in the second row).

11. Click Next to move to Step 2 of the Chart Wizard.

12. Make sure that the Rows radio button is selected, and click Next to move to Step 3 of the Chart Wizard.

13. Click the Titles tab.

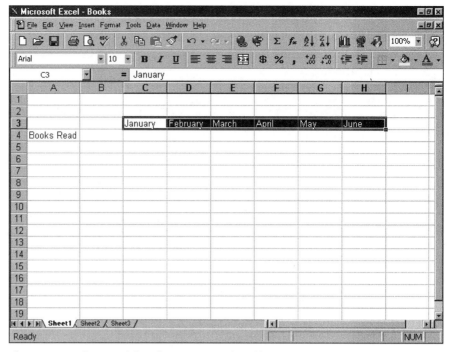

Figure 7-1 The month headings are completed by using the AutoFill handle.

14. Type **Books Read** in the Chart title box, and then press Tab.

15. Type **Month** in the Category (X) axis box, and press Tab. This places a title under the *x* axis.

16. Type **Number of Books** in the Value (Z) axis box. As shown in Figure 7-2, this places a title along the *z* axis.

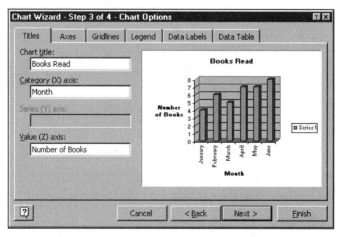

Figure 7-2 The chart's title and the labels for the axes are entered in the Titles tab of the Chart Options dialog box.

17. Click the Legend tab, and click Show legend to remove the check mark next to this option, as shown in Figure 7-3. This turns off the legend. You don't need a legend for this chart, because the chart depicts only one data series.

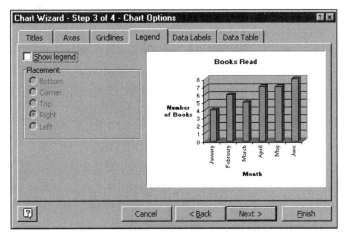

Figure 7-3 Use the Legend tab to turn off or to modify placement of the legend.

18. Click Next to move to Step 4.

19. Sheet 1 is already selected as the object in which the chart is to be placed, so click Finish. Excel places the chart in the worksheet.

20. Click the chart's border, and drag the sizing handles on the chart until all the labels are readable.

21. Save the file, and leave the workbook open for the next activity.

When resizing the chart, make sure that you click the chart's border; otherwise, you may select the data box.

Picking the Right Chart

With dozens of chart types available in Excel, how do you know which one to choose? It's a lot like the clothes analogy that we mentioned earlier in this chapter. Until someone tells you that you shouldn't wear sweats to a job interview or a tuxedo to a swimming party, you don't really know.

Perhaps one of the simplest and best books on charts is *How to Lie with Charts,* by Gerald E. Jones (Sybex). If you need to use charts on a regular basis, this incredibly fun and informative book can serve as a top-notch reference tool.

Jones shows how you can present the same information in a variety of ways, leading to several different interpretations of the same data.

In the following sections, we describe a few of the many charts that are available in Excel. Although we can't possibly cover the full range of Excel's charting options, we can put you on the right track toward creating professional-looking charts.

Line charts: You have to draw the line somewhere!

Line charts are the most simple of Excel's chart types. A line chart shows the changes in data over evenly spaced intervals. Although line charts most commonly plot data in intervals of time (measured in minutes, hours, days, months, years, and so on), the intervals can represent changes in temperature (degrees), weight (pounds, drams, and so on), and other types of evenly plotted data. Excel plots each piece of your data on the line chart using a horizontal (*x*) axis and a vertical (*y*) axis, with the *x* axis reflecting intervals and the *y* axis showing the data value that corresponds to each interval.

You can use line charts to track trends and predict what will happen in the future. For example, as demonstrated by Figure 7-4, by plotting weekly reading habits for the six months on a line chart, you can predict how many books you may read in future months.

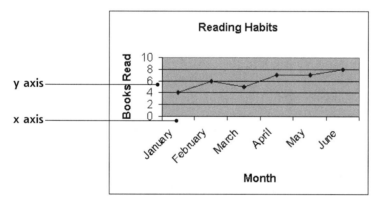

Figure 7-4 Line charts can help you make predictions about the future.

Line charts only work properly if the intervals between the data are *even*. If the data has uneven gaps, the chart does not accurately reflect trends.

Prediction is scientific guessing. In other words, you may be right more often than if you flip a coin, but then again, a coin is sometimes better than scientific guessing for predicting the future. That's why gambling is never a sure thing (unless you own a casino). For the Reading Habits chart, the predictions depend on how you interpret the data. Here are two possibilities:

✳ We read less in the winter than in the summer, so the number of books that we read in July and August continues to be high, tapering to a low in December.

✳ Overall, we are reading more each month, so the end of the year has one of the highest numbers of books read.

As you can see, depending on which interpretation you make, the end of the year prediction can be very different. Always try to present your data as accurately and completely as possible, and be ready to explain any unusual fluctuations.

CREATING A SIMPLE LINE CHART

This activity guides you through the process of creating a line chart by using Excel's Chart Wizard.

Follow these steps:

1. Delete the previously created chart. It is already selected, so just press Delete.

As soon as you delete the chart, the selection area surrounding the data is removed. You don't need to select the entire data area; just select any cell containing data.

2. Select C3 through H4.

3. Click the Chart Wizard button on the toolbar. Excel displays the Chart Type dialog box.

4. On the Standard Types tab in the Chart Type panel, choose Line. As shown in Figure 7-5, Excel displays many different types of line charts in the Chart sub-type panel.

5. Select the option entitled Line with markers displayed at each data value (the first chart in the second row of the Chart sub-types panel).

TIP When you choose a chart sub-type, the description box that is located directly below the chart examples gives you a brief description.

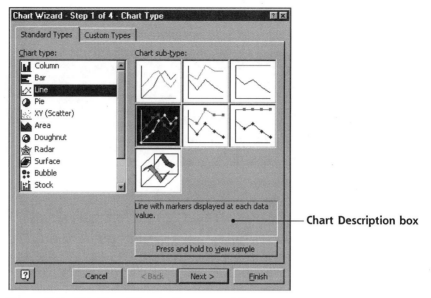

Chart Description box

Figure 7-5 The Chart Wizard offers many different types of line charts.

FEATURE FOCUS As shown in Figure 7-6, clicking Press and hold to view sample displays a sample of what your data should look like using the highlighted sub-chart.

6. With the Line chart sub-type highlighted, click Next. The Chart Wizard moves to Step 2 and displays your line chart.

7. Click Next to move to Step 3, Chart Options. The Chart Options step allows you to customize your chart.

8. On the Titles tab, type **Books Read** in the Chart title box.

9. Press Tab to move to the Category (X) axis box.

10. Type **Month** and then press Tab to move to the Value (Y) axis box.

11. Type **Number of Books Read**. Because you have only one data series, you don't need a legend.

12. Click the Legend tab, and turn off the Show legend option.

13. Click Next to move to Step 4, the Chart Location dialog box. You use the Chart Location dialog box to position the chart either on the current worksheet or on a new worksheet.

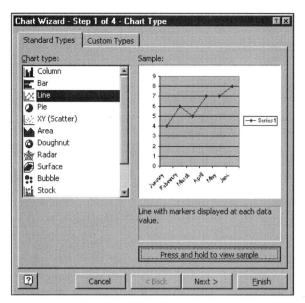

Figure 7-6 Excel for Office 97 can give you a preview of how your data is going to be displayed using the current chart type.

14. You want to place your chart as an object in the current worksheet (the default), so click Finish to return to the worksheet.

15. Enlarge the chart by dragging the lower-right sizing handle until you can see the names of the months. Your chart should look like the example shown in Figure 7-7.

16. Click Save, and leave the workbook open.

COMMON USES OF LINE CHARTS

When you want to show a numerical trend over a specified period of time, a line chart often offers the most effective means for doing so. For example, professionals such as stock brokers use line charts to display trends in stock prices, while businesses use line charts to show profit and loss trends. As the preceding hands-on activity shows, individuals can also use line charts to track personal information. For example, you could track the number of calories consumed per day, the number of miles run per week, or the number of hours that you spend in front of the computer each day.

T I P   Excel includes seven different styles of line charts, including one 3-D style.

ADVANTAGES OF LINE CHARTS

The primary advantage of line charts is their simplicity. As long as you can match data with a specific point in time, line charts provide you with a valuable forecasting tool. Additionally, line charts allow you to look both forward and backward. Assuming that you have continued to enter data at regular intervals in the past, you can compare your present situation with previous data and predict future trends based on that comparison.

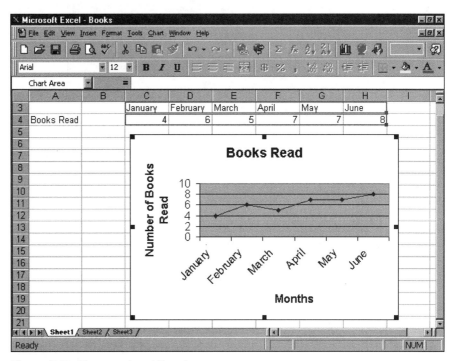

Figure 7-7 The completed line chart.

DISADVANTAGES OF LINE CHARTS

The biggest disadvantage of line charts is the need for even time intervals. If the time intervals between data points are not exactly the same (for example, weekly, monthly, or yearly), the chart does not accurately depict the trend in a series of data points. It is therefore imperative that the time intervals are equal when you use a line chart.

GETTING THE MOST FROM YOUR LINE CHART

The most important rule in making line charts work for you is to keep your data simple. Line charts offer a quick and easy means for representing uncomplicated data. Additionally, it is important to update your data on a regular basis, ensuring that the categories on the *x* axis are evenly spaced. By doing this, you create a tool that helps you accurately analyze past activities and forecast future trends.

Area charts: charting unmapped areas

Area charts have similar applications to those of line charts. An area chart provides not only a clear comparison of the values in several related data series but also a concise picture of the overall trend for the entire collection of data. For example, you can use an area chart to analyze your reading habits just as you did by using a line chart, but you can also display the number of books read by category. In Figure 7-8, the top line of the chart shows the total number of books read, while each band represents the value for a particular type of book.

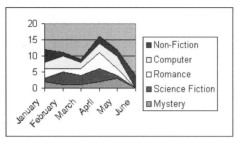

Figure 7-8 Area graphs display how your data series relate to each other and allow you to see the overall trend.

COMMON USES OF AREA CHARTS

Area charts are commonly used to show the consumption of resources. For example, an area chart displaying your reading habits shows how many books you've read during a specific time. Area charts can also be used to show information such as energy consumption, number of hours worked by employees, or the quantity of orders processed by a sales representative.

ADVANTAGES OF AREA CHARTS

As with line charts, area charts are relatively easy to create. Their advantage over the line chart comes from the capability to show relationships between the different data series as well as the entire collection of data. For presenting the big picture, area charts are better than line charts, because all the different data series can be seen at the same time, and their individual roles within the whole can be visualized.

For example, you may be interested in analyzing the performance of each member of your sales team, but your boss may not care whether one specific salesperson excelled. Your area chart can show your boss that the efforts of the team as a whole resulted in increased sales but still allow you to analyze each salesperson's performance.

DISADVANTAGES OF AREA CHARTS

The disadvantages of area charts are similar to those of line charts. If the data is not entered over even intervals, area charts tend to provide a false image. Figure 7-9 demonstrates how data that is entered over uneven intervals in an area chart can cause both the individual data and the data as a whole to be misrepresented.

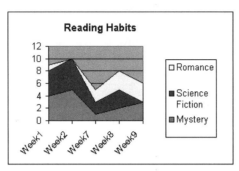

Figure 7-9 By entering data at uneven intervals, a false image is projected. What happened in Weeks 3–6?

GETTING THE MOST FROM YOUR AREA CHARTS

The use of colors can really make an area chart stand out. While each band or color should make its data series stand on its own, the color should not separate a data series from the rest of the chart. For example, in a chart that uses light blues and greens for the data series, a bright yellow band would alienate its data series from the rest of the chart. However, if you have a specific reason to highlight one data series, a contrasting color can be effective.

TIP Excel offers six different styles of area charts. Figure 7-10 displays Excel's area chart sub-types, including three 3-D styles.

Belly up to the bar (charts)

One of our most vivid memories from elementary school is a book-reading competition known as the Read-a-thon. (You may have guessed by now that we read a lot!) The school kept track of the number of books that each student read over a period of time and displayed the results on a giant bar chart. We remember competing fiercely to advance our marker past our classmates' by reading anything that we could get our hands on. As we reminisce about the contest, we find it funny that we don't remember what the prize was, but we sure remember that big bar chart on the gym wall. Bar charts are often used to visually display ongoing competitive data — such as sales contests — or to show your progress toward meeting a goal — such as the United Way contribution goal.

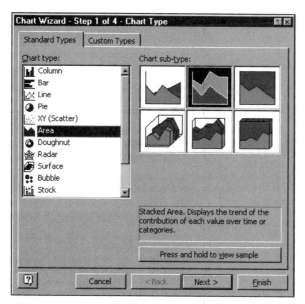

Figure 7-10 Excel's area charts can help you compare individual data series while showing each data series' contribution to the whole.

Excel offers six types of bar charts. As shown in Figure 7-11, you can place the data series side by side or stack them end to end to show each bar's contribution to the total.

Excel's different types of bar charts do more than let you choose how you want your data to look. The 100% stacked bar chart style shown in Figure 7-12 and the stacked bar chart style shown in Figure 7-13 look nearly identical in the Chart sub-types dialog box. However, the 100% stacked bar chart plots data on a percentage scale, while the stacked bar chart plots numerical values.

COMMON USES OF BAR CHARTS

Bar charts are most often used to show how data series compare to each other. One of the most common uses of bar charts is in competitions between multiple contestants. As seen in Figure 7-14, the bar chart produces the impression that contestants in the Read-a-thon are trying to win, even though the readers may not be in competition with each other.

ADVANTAGES OF BAR CHARTS

As emphasized before, a bar chart can be a useful tool for creating a sense of competition. Creating this sense of competition can motivate a sales staff, encourage students to read, or achieve numerous other objectives. Remember, the purpose of your chart is to emphasize the results of the data. If a bar chart shows that a salesperson has fallen behind the rest of the sales team, your chart may inspire that salesperson to work harder.

Bar charts are a great tool for motivating people. Use these charts when you know that the viewers are in a competitive mood. Your chart may encourage those who are not in the lead to make the extra effort necessary for overtaking their rivals.

Figure 7-11   Excel offers several types of bar charts.

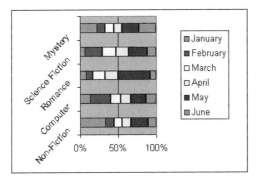

Figure 7-12   The 100% stacked bar chart gives you a chart with the data labeled on a percentage scale.

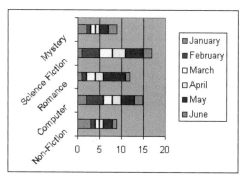

Figure 7-13 The stacked bar chart style depicts your data using the numeric values in your data series.

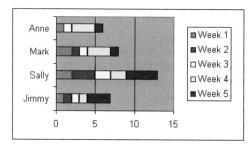

Figure 7-14 The bar chart gives the impression that the data series represent scores in a competition.

DISADVANTAGES OF BAR CHARTS

Bar charts can be used to misrepresent data — for example, using a technique known as creating *cumulative* bars. To do this, the chart designer plots the first series of data, adds the second series of data to the first series, and then plots the sum as the second bar on the chart. Although the chart is labeled correctly and its data is accurately displayed, the use of cumulative bars tricks the viewer into thinking that the second data series is bigger than it really is.

GETTING THE MOST FROM YOUR BAR CHARTS

A well-designed bar chart creates an image of a race in which each bar (data series) is trying to get ahead. The goal for the chart is to show how one or more bars in the chart lead the others over a period of time.

Call 'em column charts

Column charts are similar to bar charts. In fact, the only difference between the two is that bar charts display data horizontally, and column charts display data vertically. Now you may be thinking, "Wait a minute, doesn't that mean that a bar chart is just a column chart on its side?" Right you are!

So why do you need two different types of charts that display the same data? Although the two charts may display the same information, each can produce an entirely different impression for the viewer. Bar charts tend to create the feeling that one bar *is ahead* of the others, while column charts give the impression that one column *has more* than the others (a seemingly minor detail, but one that can make the difference between a good presentation and a blockbuster presentation).

 When choosing a chart style, remember that the feeling the chart evokes in the viewer is just as important as how well the chart presents your data.

COMMON USES OF COLUMN CHARTS

Column charts have similar uses to those of bar charts. Like bar charts, column charts are used when you want to compare one set of data to another. However, the upward progression of data in a column chart can create a sense of optimism for the person viewing the chart. For this reason, companies often use column charts to show growth over a period of time. Column charts can also be used to depict an increase in event participation, as shown with the Read-a-thon example in Figure 7-15.

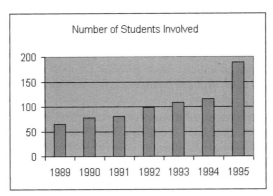

Figure 7-15 This column chart generates the feeling that participation will continue to increase.

ADVANTAGES OF COLUMN CHARTS

Column charts give the viewer a sense of the volume of data involved. Where bar charts emphasize the *progress* of data over a specified time period, column charts help the viewer understand the changes in quantity rather than the change in time.

DISADVANTAGES OF COLUMN CHARTS

Column charts are not your best bet for comparing large amounts of data. As shown in Figure 7-16, column charts tend to get crowded and lose their effectiveness when they display too much data. A line chart is usually more effective for displaying vast numbers of data points.

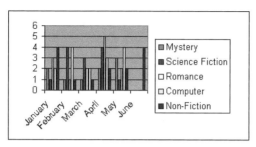

Figure 7-16 When you add too much data, column charts become difficult to read.

GETTING THE MOST FROM YOUR COLUMN CHARTS

Once again, keep it simple. Charts are not meant to boggle and bedazzle; they're meant to inform. Cluttered column charts can be confusing. Try to have less than five data series. If you have any more than that, you risk crowding the chart and losing the viewers' attention.

TIP When you need to emphasize the volume of your data, but have a lot of data to fit on a chart, group the data into similar categories and create a stacked column chart. Like an area chart, a stacked column chart, such as the example in Figure 7-17, allows the viewer to analyze the big picture while comparing each individual data series.

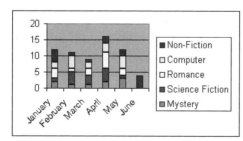

Figure 7-17 Stacked column charts can represent vast quantities of data without causing confusion.

Have a slice of pie (charts)

Pie charts tend to be the most eye-catching of the chart styles. Their simple yet informative format allows the viewer to compare slices of data and understand their relation to the whole. In contrast to most other chart types, pie-chart values are usually stated in percentages. This allows the viewer to understand how each data series contributes to the whole.

COMMON USES OF PIE CHARTS

Pie charts usually depict the proportions in which resources are allocated to a certain activity. For example, a pie chart may break down the allocation of time in a person's day, showing segments for eating, sleeping, and working. Businesses use pie charts for depicting information that is related to budgets, human resources, and project development. The pie chart in Figure 7-18 compares Read-a-thon participation levels for several elementary schools.

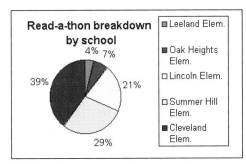

Figure 7-18 Pie charts allow the viewer to understand how each data series relates to the whole.

ADVANTAGES OF PIE CHARTS

The biggest advantage of pie charts is that they are easy to read — if they are constructed properly. You can use various color combinations and segment the chart in a number of ways to call the viewers' attention to important details. As shown in Figure 7-19, you can segment (or call out) portions of the chart to emphasize each data series' importance.

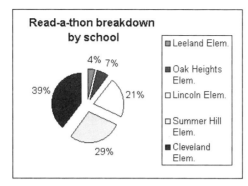

Figure 7-19 Segmenting the pie chart calls attention to the individual portions of the chart.

DISADVANTAGES OF PIE CHARTS

Pie charts are often used incorrectly. For example, creating a pie chart that shows *values* rather than percentages defeats the purpose of the pie chart. The pie chart should show how each slice of the pie contributes to the pie as a whole. When you use values rather than percentages, the viewer doesn't know what role the wedges play in relation to the whole. For example, the pie chart in Figure 7-20 shows the number of students from each school, but it doesn't tell you what percentage of the pie each school represents.

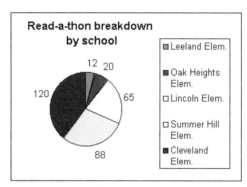

Figure 7-20 This pie chart shows the individual values for each slice.

GETTING THE MOST FROM YOUR PIE CHARTS

When creating a pie chart, remember that the purpose of the pie chart is to show each slice of data as a percentage of the whole pie. If you need to show the value of the data, use a bar chart or a column chart. Additionally, don't try to crowd a pie chart with numerous data series. Pie charts can become nearly impossible to read when the data labels are squished (a highly technical term used by chart designers) into a tiny amount of space. A good rule of thumb is to limit your pie charts to no more than five slices. This ensures that the viewer doesn't get eye strain trying to figure out the meaning of your chart.

2-D or not 2-D

Not only does Excel offer numerous chart types, but you can also choose to display most of these types in either 2-D (two-dimensional) or 3-D (three-dimensional) formats. Both formats have advantages and disadvantages that you should consider when selecting a chart.

A 2-D chart is easy to read. A simple bar chart can say a lot about your data with little explanation. This simplicity, however, can also be a disadvantage. Imagine the reaction of prospective clients when they compare your elementary 2-D bar chart to your competitor's dazzling 3-D bar chart. Although both charts may show the same data, the 3-D chart may influence the client because of the visual impact that it creates.

When choosing between a 2-D and a 3-D chart, analyze the time constraints that have been placed on your presentation. (Do you have 20 minutes or 2 minutes?) Then decide which style best reflects your data. If simplicity is your goal, use a 2-D chart. If you want to add a little pizzazz, choose a 3-D chart.

Editing Charts

After you create your chart, you can customize it to fit your needs. You can alter many aspects of the chart, including its size, color, and appearance.

When editing a chart, remember: Keep it simple. Too many changes in the chart's format can render it difficult to read.

SIDE TRIP

Keep in mind that *more sophisticated* does not necessarily mean *better* or *more accurate*. In many cases, a presentation must be given under hurried circumstances. Therefore, the less time that you have to spend explaining your chart, the better it is for you and the viewers.

Changing the type of chart

If you need to change your chart after you create it, Excel allows you to return to the Chart Wizard and change the chart options instead of starting from scratch. *Right-click* the chart and choose `Chart Type` from the pop-up menu that Excel displays.

This activity shows how to change your chart's type after you have created the chart.

Follow these steps:

1. *Right-click* any white space in your Books Read chart. As shown in Figure 7-21, Excel displays a pop-up menu.

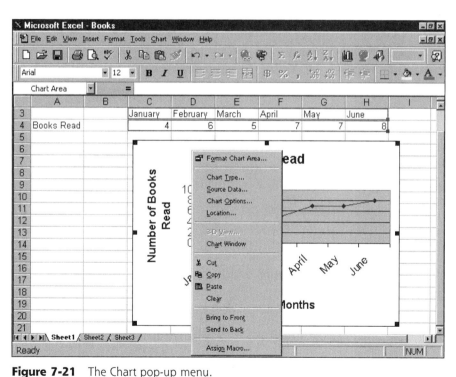

Figure 7-21   The Chart pop-up menu.

CAUTION
Be sure that you do not right-click any part of the chart that contains data. This opens the pop-up menu for editing and formatting the data within the chart, not the chart itself.

2. Choose Chart Type . As shown in Figure 7-22, Excel displays the Chart Type dialog box, which allows you to choose a new type of chart.

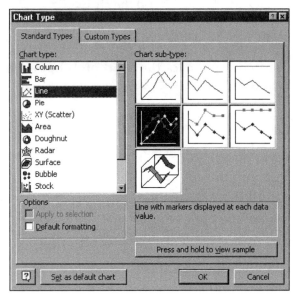

Figure 7-22 You can specify a different chart type in the Chart Type dialog box.

3. Click Pie, and choose the first pie chart in the Chart sub-type panel.

4. Click OK. Excel changes your chart into a pie chart, but all the chart's labels are deleted.

5. Right-click the white space again, choose Chart Type → Line , choose the fourth sub-type, and click OK. Chart titles are once again displayed.

6. Leave the workbook open.

Changing the sizes of the chart and the chart objects

NOTE You can change the size of your chart in several ways. Before changing the size of the chart and the objects that it contains, you need to decide which part of the chart you want to resize. Are the objects within the chart (such as the legend) too small? Is the chart itself too big? Or, do you need to enlarge the frame around the chart?

The following activity shows how to change the size of your chart and the objects that it contains.

Follow these steps:

1. Click any white space in the chart. As shown in Figure 7-23, Excel places sizing handles (small boxes) around the chart frame.

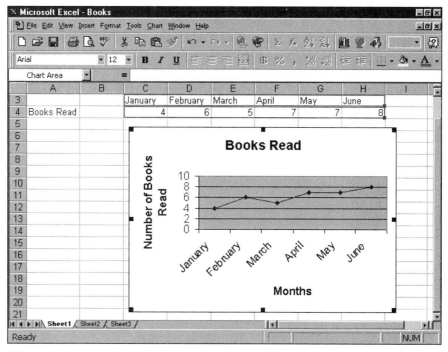

Figure 7-23 When you click the chart's white space, Excel places sizing handles around the chart frame.

2. Experiment with changing the size of the chart. Dragging any of the eight sizing handles resizes the chart accordingly.

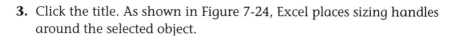

New to this version of Excel, as you point to each object inside the chart, Excel displays a tool tip that identifies the object.

3. Click the title. As shown in Figure 7-24, Excel places sizing handles around the selected object.

4. Drag the lower-right sizing handle. Notice that the title is *not* resized, but rather moved.

5. Click the Undo button to undo the move.

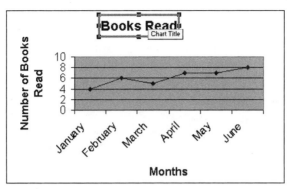

Figure 7-24 Excel displays sizing handles around the selected object — in this case, the title.

Unlike all other objects in Excel, chart titles cannot be resized by dragging the sizing handles. This only moves the box. The only way to change the title's size is to select the text and change the size of the font.

Moving a chart

To move a chart, select it and then click and drag anywhere on the chart's border until you have the chart in the desired location. Do not drag the sizing handles; this simply resizes the chart, without moving it.

Formatting Charts

Excel also enables you to change the formatting of your chart, including attributes such as the font and the border color. If you right-click the white space of the chart and then select Format Chart Area from the pop-up menu, Excel opens the Format Chart Area dialog box shown in Figure 7-25. Use this dialog box to select a new font or pattern.

Changing the text within your chart

Excel allows you to change the chart title and the axis labels used in your chart. Click the text in your chart, and Excel places a border around the selected text, just as it would for any selected object in the chart. You can now click to drop your cursor anywhere in the text and make the necessary changes. After you make the changes, press Enter, and Excel updates your chart.

TIP You can remove data from your chart by either deleting the data from the worksheet or by selecting the chart and dragging the blue border surrounding the data in the worksheet so that it does not include the data.

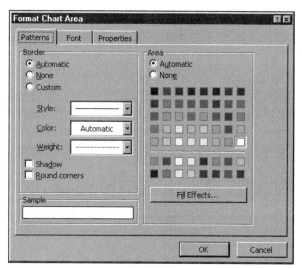

Figure 7-25 Use the Format Chart Area dialog box to change the font or the pattern that is used in your chart.

Adding new data to your chart

As your data changes, you need to update your chart to reflect the new data. Adding the new data to your chart is a relatively simple process.

To insert new data into your chart, follow these steps:

1. In cell I3 of the example worksheet, type **July**.

2. In I4, type **7**. As shown in Figure 7-26, even though you entered the data into the worksheet, Excel does not update the chart to include the new data.

NOTE When the chart is selected, Excel places a blue border around the data that is selected in your chart. This blue border does *not* extend to the newly entered data and thus indicates that the chart does not reflect the new data.

3. Select the chart by clicking any white space.

4. On the worksheet, drag the AutoFill handle from H4 to I4 so that it includes the new data. As shown in Figure 7-27, once the border surrounds all the data from C3 to I4, Excel automatically updates your chart to reflect the new data.

5. Save the file, and close the workbook.

The AutoFill
handle

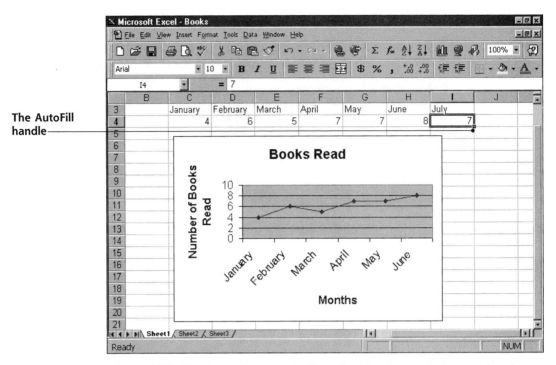

Figure 7-26 Excel doesn't automatically update the chart to depict new data that
you enter in the worksheet.

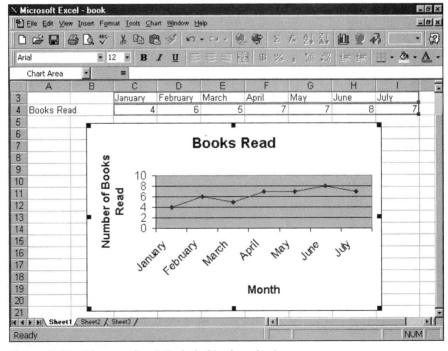

Figure 7-27 The new data is included in the selection.

BONUS

Adding Graphics as Indicators

You can also spice up your charts by replacing those boring columns or bars with your own graphics. Nothing catches a viewer's eye more than graphics that lend themselves to the presentation, as shown in Figure 7-28.

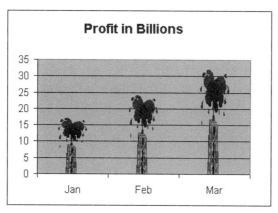

Figure 7-28 Catch the viewer's eye by using graphics to replace columns or rows.

NOTE **You can use graphics that come with Excel, or you can create graphics by using programs such as Microsoft Draw, CorelDRAW!, or Microsoft Paint (which is provided with Windows 95).**

To replace columns or bars with graphics, follow these steps:

1. Create a new workbook.

2. In A1, type **Jan**.

3. Drag the AutoFill handle to C1. Cells B1 and C1 are filled with Feb and Mar.

4. In A2 through C2, type **17**, **24**, and **32**.

5. Select A1 through C2.

6. Click the Chart Wizard button on the toolbar. Excel displays the dialog box for Step 1 of the Chart Wizard.

7. Accept the defaults, and click Next. Step 2 is displayed.

8. Accept the defaults in Step 2, and click Next. Step 3 is displayed.

9. Type **Profit in Billions** in the Chart title text box of the Title tab. (Hey, as long as this is fictitious, we're going for the gold!)

10. Click the Legend tab.

11. Click Show legend, to turn off the legend.

12. Click Next. Excel displays the final step of the Chart Wizard.

13. Click Finish.

14. Save the file in the Discover Excel folder as Graphic Chart. Your worksheet should look like the example shown in Figure 7-29. The chart is already selected (it has sizing handles around its edge).

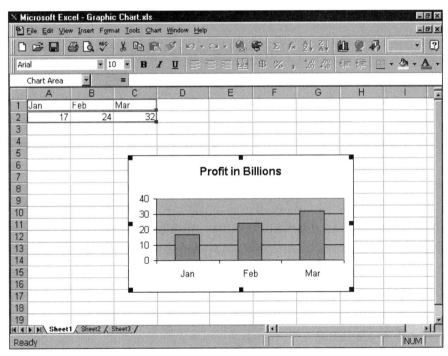

Figure 7-29 Your workbook should look like this.

15. Click in any of the three columns. All three columns are selected.

16. Choose | Insert |→| Picture |→| From File |. Excel displays the Insert Picture dialog box, as shown in Figure 7-30. Yours probably looks different.

17. Double-click the Office Popular folder. It is probably located at C:\ProgramFiles\MicrosoftOffice\Clipart\Popular.

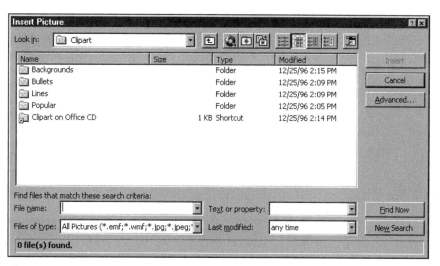

Figure 7-30 The Insert Picture dialog box.

18. Scroll through the graphics, and double-click Oildrill.wmf. The columns are automatically replaced with pictures of oil wells. Each one is the height of the previous column.

TIP If you are using columns, use graphics that have a vertical orientation. If you are using bars, use graphics with more of a horizontal orientation. They look better in your chart.

19. Click the edge of the chart to select it, and then drag the bottom-center sizing handle down to make the chart taller. (The chart looks more impressive that way.)

TIP If you have the CD version of Excel or Office, you can also choose the Clipart on Office CD folder for access to an extensive set of clip art. The CD must be in the drive before you double-click the folder.

20. Save the file, and close Excel.

TIP After clicking a column the first time, you can click it once more (don't double-click or you open the Format dialog box). That selects only the single column. Add your graphic. Click each remaining column, adding a different graphic to each.

One final word about using graphics in your charts. (This is a kind of a reverse *Dare to Compare*.) In previous versions of Excel, you could stack the graphics on top of each other (so that you may have ten oil wells stacked on top of each other, instead of one being really tall one). This feature is no longer available. Only a single graphic can be used to represent each column or bar. We think this is a loss and have told Microsoft that it's on our wish list to be replaced in the next version of Excel. So if you see it there, you know what incredible power we have with Microsoft.

Summary

Charts are an exciting way to help viewers understand and appreciate your data. Remember that the style of chart that you choose is just as important as the data within the chart. By keeping your charts simple and clear, you can increase the effectiveness of your presentation.

You may have heard the phrase *garbage in, garbage out*. That is, unless the data you enter into Excel is accurate, and your formulas and functions perform exactly as you want them to, Excel's output is worse than useless — it is *wrong*. The chapters in this part of the book help you to ensure that Excel produces the results you want.

You learn how to transfer data from other programs into Excel, making sure that the formulas convert properly. You find out how to transfer data between Excel worksheets and Word documents. You also work with the File Conversion Wizard, a simple tool to help you translate files into a format that Excel can understand.

Although you see your worksheet on your monitor, the final product of most worksheets is a hard copy — a printed copy of the worksheet. This part shows you how to adjust the printer settings — including headers, footers, margins, and page breaks — to get the output that is most helpful to you.

In perhaps the most important chapter in this book — Chapter 11, Numbers Do Lie! — you learn that Excel does what you tell it to do, not what you want it to (oh, darn!). You discover how to use Excel's tools to ensure that you get what you want.

In some cases, you may want to share workbooks with others. By sharing data, worksheets, and workbooks, you can increase productivity, and ensure that everyone has access to the latest data.

Microsoft Excel, the same spreadsheet that you and I use, is the same thing that the real number crunchers use to work on the hard stuff. Brian Croxford, a financial analyst for a major electronics company, is one of those "real number crunchers." He keeps Excel constantly running on his machine, because he once calculated that despite the additional resources needed to keep the program active, the relative cost of reloading the software would slow his productivity just enough to cause a slight trade imbalance with various Pacific Rim countries.

Like most mathematical whizzes, Brian sometimes talks over the heads of average people. His job, in his own words, "involves using Excel to calculate Net Present Value (NPV) and Internal Rate of Return (IRR) on projects, calculate amortization schedules for tooling and depreciation schedules for fixed assets, and format data for upload into our product costing software."

I was already impressed, but he wasn't finished. "Of course, I should probably also mention that I have to sort and subtotal and create pivot tables from downloads of data from our corporate accounting systems, create charts and format data for presentations to management, create product cost estimating worksheets, and perform what-if scenarios and sensitivity analyses for manufacturing planning."

Brian's manufacturing plant makes everything from car stereo buttons to electronic airbag switches. He uses Excel to help determine which of those products his company should make, where it should make them, and how much it should charge the customer (although the actual customer is General Motors, the car buyer is the ultimate customer). As a result, the price you pay for your GM car is directly related to the information that Brian crunches with Excel spreadsheets.

He does all this with Excel? The same thing I use to balance the checkbook? "Sure. Not only has Excel been an asset to the corporate world, it has been an asset to this great nation and quite possibly the entire global economic system."

There was a chance that he was exaggerating, but only he could calculate the odds of that.

CHAPTER EIGHT

IN WITH THE OLD: CONVERTING WORKSHEET FILES

IN THIS CHAPTER YOU LEARN THESE KEY SKILLS

Fitting a square peg into a round hole seems easy when compared to the stress and frustration of importing worksheets that were created by another application. Just as it may be simpler to go to the hardware store and buy a round peg to fit the round hole, you may find it easier to retype the data and formulas and then reapply the formatting, rather than try to convert files that were created in programs other than Excel.

However, each new version of Office gets a little better at handling *alien worksheet* files (that is, worksheets that were created by other spreadsheet programs, not those created on other planets). However, if you have experienced the pain of file conversion, you know that when trying to import files, the more complex they are, the higher the likelihood that you are going to experience problems.

You may need to convert a non-Excel file into an Excel file for any of several reasons:

* You have some data stored in another format (perhaps a table in a Word document), and you want to use that data in an Excel spreadsheet.
* You need to convert files that colleagues created in programs other than Excel.
* You switched to Excel from another spreadsheet program in which you created some critical files.

Depending on the type of file that you are converting, the process may be as simple as opening the document, or on the other end of the scale, it may be an experience to be avoided whenever possible.

You must consider the issue of file conversion *before* you make the transition to a new program. This rule applies to most types of programs that you use (for example, word processing, spreadsheet, or database). By testing various files to see just how well they convert, you can save yourself a great deal of time and aggravation when you begin mass conversion.

In this chapter, you create a worksheet, format it, and save it in various file formats. You use Microsoft Word to examine some of these files and see how each of them is saved. You also get some practice at converting a non-Excel document to one that Excel can read.

Understanding Why You Need to Convert Files

You may encounter serious problems when converting from one file type to another. You may lose formatting, formulas, and functions. If the original worksheet contains macros, they may not function as expected after you import the file. For these reasons, you should carefully consider whether you really need to convert a file that was created in another program.

You may not need to convert all alien files to Excel for Office 97. If you don't use a file on a regular basis, you may decide not to convert it, particularly if conversion is difficult. Instead, consider saving a copy of the *original program* on your hard disk, where you can access it as needed.

If you don't need to perform any more calculations on a worksheet, a hard copy may be sufficient. As a rule, don't convert files that you aren't going to be using on a regular basis, unless conversion can be automated (more about that later).

Displaying File Extensions

By default, a title bar in Windows 95 shows a file's name but *not* its extension. (Windows 95 doesn't think you need to see the extension; in most cases, you probably don't.) Because you need to see the extensions for the files that you work with in this chapter, the following activity shows you how to display file extensions in Windows 95.

In this activity, you display the DOS file extension that is attached to each filename. This setting is a toggle — clicking it turns it on or off.

Follow these steps:

1. Minimize any windows so that the Windows Desktop is visible.

2. Double-click the My Computer icon. (It's probably in the upper-left corner of your screen.)

3. Choose View → Options . Excel displays the Options dialog box.

4. Click the View tab. Figure 8-1 shows the View tab of the Options dialog box.

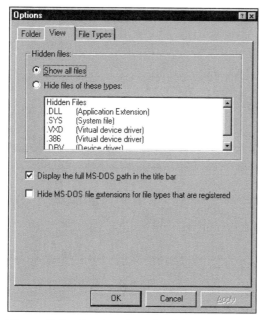

Figure 8-1   Use the View tab of the Options dialog box to turn the DOS file extensions on or off.

5. Click the Show all files option button.

6. Make sure that a check mark appears next to the option entitled Display the full MS-DOS path in the title bar. If necessary, turn on this option by clicking its check box.

7. Make sure that the check box next to the option entitled Hide MS-DOS file extensions for file types that are registered *does not* contain a check mark. If necessary, turn off this option by clicking its check box. Your display should match the example shown in Figure 8-1.

8. Click OK to close the Options dialog box.

9. Close the My Computer window.

10. Maximize Excel. When you open a file, Windows 95 displays the file's full name (including the extension) in the title bar.

Creating a Sample Worksheet

Before you can convert a spreadsheet, you need to have something to convert. To see the changes that are made when the file is saved in different formats, you need to create a sample formatted worksheet that you can then save in various formats.

You use this sample worksheet throughout the rest of this chapter to see how changes are made when files are saved in different formats.

Follow these steps:

1. Open Excel if it is not already open.

2. In B1 on a new worksheet, type **January**.

3. Drag the AutoFill handle to G1 (June).

4. In A2 through A5, type **North**, **South**, **East**, and **West** (one entry in each cell).

5. Boldface and center the month names.

6. Boldface the store locations (North, South, East, West). In the next few steps, you fill the data cells with random numbers.

7. Choose Tools → Add-Ins , and make sure that the Analysis ToolPak option box contains a check mark.

8. Click OK.

9. Click B2, type **=Randbetween(2500,5000)**, and press Enter.

10. Drag the AutoFill handle from B2 through G2, and then release the mouse button.

11. Drag the AutoFill handle from G2 through G5. The entire range fills with random numbers and remains selected.

Remember, these cells now contain formulas for creating random numbers, and the values change each time that the worksheet is recalculated. You need to change these formulas to permanent values.

12. Highlight B2 through G5.

13. Right-click, and choose Copy from the resulting pop-up menu.

14. Right-click, and choose Paste Special . Excel displays the Paste Special dialog box.

15. Click Values, and then press Enter.

16. Click B2. Notice in the formula bar that the selected cell now contains a value rather than the Randbetween formula.

17. In H1, type **Total**.

18. Boldface and center this entry.

19. Select H2 through H5, and click the AutoSum button on the toolbar. Because you selected more than one cell, Excel generated the AutoSum as soon as you filled the cells. You did not need to double-click the AutoSum button to generate the values.

20. Select B2 through H5, click the Currency Style button on the toolbar, and then click the Decrease Decimal button twice (as opposed to double-clicking it).

21. Highlight A2 through A5.

22. Right-click, and choose Copy from the pop-up menu.

23. Click A8, and press Enter.

24. Click B8, type **=IF(H2>20000, "Great","Good")**, and then press Enter.

25. Click B8 again, and drag the AutoFill handle down to B11. Your worksheet should be similar to the example shown in Figure 8-2. Your values are going to be different (because they were randomly generated), and the labels in B8 through B11 may differ.

By default, the standard column width is 8.43. Before saving the file as Formatted Text, you need to set the width to a whole number.

26. Select columns A through H.

27. Choose Format → Column → Width .

28. In the Column Width dialog box, type **10** and then click OK.

29. Save the file in the Discover Excel folder as Sales Example. Don't close the workbook yet, because you're going to save it shortly as different file types so that you can see what happens.

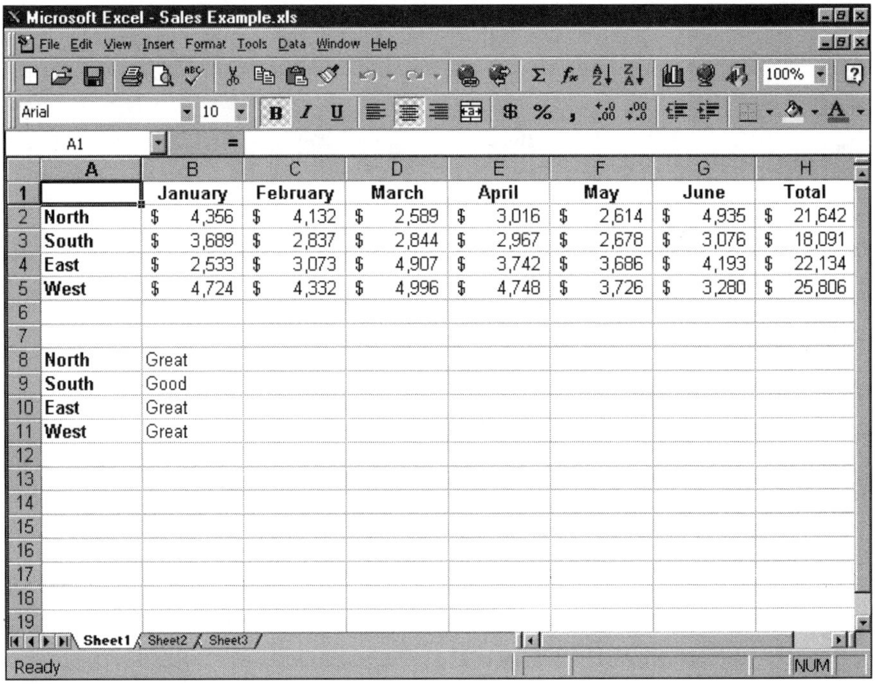

Figure 8-2 The completed worksheet.

Working with Different File Formats

Files fall into two general classes: *proprietary* and *nonproprietary*. Each program (for example, Excel) has its own proprietary format — the specific structure that the program normally uses to save data. In other words, the format that Excel uses for storing your files differs from the formats that are used by other programs, such as Lotus 1-2-3 or Corel Quattro Pro. However, Lotus and Corel have their own *filters* — small programs that convert Excel's files into the formats that are used by 1-2-3 and Quattro Pro. Likewise, Excel has filters that let you import files from most proprietary formats.

Because Excel knows how to handle supported proprietary formats, the following method is preferable for converting other worksheet types to Excel. To convert a spreadsheet file that was created in a program other than Excel, your best bet for converting that file into an Excel worksheet is to make sure that the file is stored in a proprietary format that Excel supports. If so, Excel can usually open the file with no input from you. However, you still may lose some formatting and formulas.

Most programs can also open and save files using nonproprietary formats. Think of nonproprietary formats as a common ground for moving files from one application to another. (The mathematically minded reader may think of nonproprietary formats as a lowest common denominator. Such formats allow you to import and export data among various programs, but they don't always maintain all the formatting and other special features that you pack into your files.) Nonproprietary formats are general formats that nearly all programs can understand. Depending on the format that you import, however, you may lose some or all of the formatting, *and* you may lose all formulas.

Working with proprietary formats

Excel can read several proprietary formats:

* Lotus 1-2-3
* Lotus Symphony
* Corel Quattro Pro
* Borland dBASE II, III, IV, and V for Windows
* Microsoft Works

As we mentioned, Excel can usually open these file types without asking you for any input. Excel opens these types of files by using the appropriate filter.

NOTE If the appropriate filter was not installed when you installed Excel, you need to run the setup program again and install the required filter. Appendix B describes installation and the setup program.

Working with nonproprietary formats

A nonproprietary format is used to save files in a general format that nearly any program can read. For example, Excel can't directly read Smart spreadsheet files, so you must save a Smart spreadsheet in some other (nonproprietary) format before you can import it into Excel.

You may think that it would be better to store a file in a nonproprietary format, because many programs recognize such a format. However, when you convert files from nonproprietary formats, you often lose formatting and other functions. The conversion filters for proprietary formats generally do a much better job of translating the data than do nonproprietary filters.

Several nonproprietary formats are in general use:

* **Delimited files.** These simple text files use specified characters to organize data into columns and rows. A tab or a comma separates one cell from the next, and a carriage return marks the end of each row. All

formatting and formulas are lost when you save a spreadsheet as a delimited file.

- ✳ **DIF (Data Interchange Format) files.** This format is less common than the delimited file. Although most formulas are changed to values, some formatting is retained.

- ✳ **SYLK (Symbolic Link) files.** This is the preferred format for exporting and importing files between Excel and unsupported spreadsheet programs. Most formulas are retained, but most text formatting is lost. Some border formatting may change, and most page setup formatting is lost.

In a comma-delimited file, the data in any cell containing a comma must be placed in quotation marks *before* saving. For example, if a cell contains a city, a state, and a zip code, you need to enclose the data in quotation marks, like this: **"Kansas City, MO 64108"**. Otherwise, Excel reads the data as two cells, one containing **Kansas City** and the other containing **MO 64108**. For this reason, tab-delimited text files are more common than comma-delimited files.

After a quick hands-on activity to create a tab-delimited file, you can take a look at what happens when you save an Excel file in delimited format, as well as what such a file looks like when Excel imports it.

SAVING AN EXCEL WORKSHEET AS A TAB-DELIMITED FILE

Excel should still be open, with the Sales Example file displayed. In this activity, you save the Excel file as a tab-delimited file.

Follow these steps:

1. Choose `File` → `Save As`. Excel displays the Save As dialog box. The Discovering Excel folder should already be open.

2. Click the drop-down arrow in the Save as type list box, and choose Text (Tab delimited) (*.txt).

3. Click Save to save the worksheet as a tab-delimited file.

A warning box is displayed, telling you that the selected file type saves only the *active* worksheet. To save all of the worksheets in a workbook that contains multiple worksheets, you must save each sheet individually.

4. Click OK to save the file in tab-delimited format.

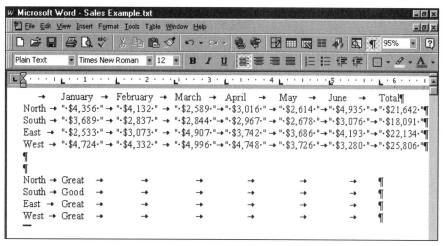

Figure 8-3 The tab-delimited file when it has been imported into Microsoft Word.

5. Choose **File → Close** . Excel displays a warning box to inform you that the file is not in Microsoft Excel 97 format. You are asked whether you want to save your changes.

6. Click No to confirm that you don't want to save the file in Excel format.

IMPORTING A TAB- OR COMMA-DELIMITED FILE

To open a tab- or comma-delimited file in Excel, you must use the Text Import Wizard. This tool converts the file so that Excel can read it. The Text Import Wizard consists of three steps. Each step offers an opportunity to specify how Excel imports the file. In most cases, the defaults are adequate for importing the file.

TIP Comma-delimited files often have a CSV extension. This stands for *comma-separated values.*

To import a tab-delimited file using the Text Import Wizard, follow these steps:

1. Choose **File → Open** . Excel displays the Open dialog box.

2. Click the drop-down arrow in the Files of type list box, and scroll up or down until you can click Text Files (*.prn, *.txt, or *.csv).

3. Double-click Sales Example.txt to open the text file.

As shown in Figure 8-4, Excel displays Step 1 of the Text Import Wizard. This step allows you to choose whether the original data is in Delimited or Fixed width format. You can change the beginning import row and the original file type. A preview of your data is shown in the bottom half of the window.

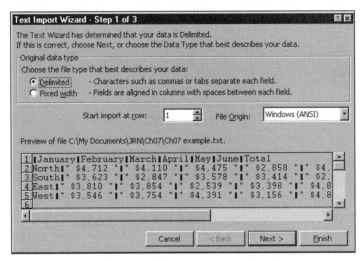

Figure 8-4 The first step of the Text Import Wizard.

4. Make sure that the Original Data Type is set to Delimited. Leave the start row at 1 and the file type as Windows (ANSI). (ANSI is an abbreviation for ANother Stupid set of Initials — just kidding, it's yet another format that you don't need to understand.) The bottom half of the dialog box displays an example of how your data should look. You can use the scroll bars to make sure that all your data is there, but nothing else can be changed in this dialog box.

5. Click Next to move to Step 2 of the Text Import Wizard. As shown in Figure 8-5, this step allows you to set the delimiter. Tab is the most common delimiter that is used in a text file, with comma in second place. You can also use semicolons, spaces, or another character to mark the end of each cell. The Treat consecutive delimiters as one option is unchecked. By default, Excel treats consecutive delimiters as empty cells. The Text Qualifier identifies the characters that surround text (as opposed to values).

6. Click Next to move to the final step of the Wizard, as shown in Figure 8-6. The Column data format can be General, Text, or Date. For this activity, make sure that the General option is selected in the Column data format panel. To set a *specific* column format, click the column heading and apply the format. You can also choose not to import specific columns by selecting them and clicking Do not import column (Skip). Your screen should look like Figure 8-6.

7. Click Finish to display the imported text.

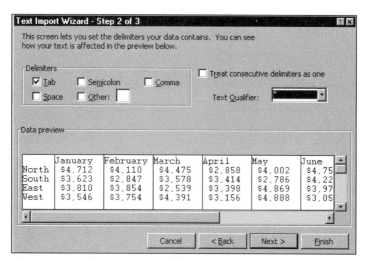

Figure 8-5 The second step of the Text Import Wizard.

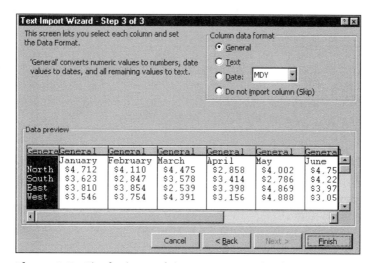

Figure 8-6 The final step of the Text Import Wizard.

8. Choose Tools → Options . The Options dialog box is displayed. In the following step, you set Excel to display the *formulas* in each cell, rather than the normally displayed *results* of the formula.

9. On the View tab in the Windows option panel, click the Formulas option box and click OK. Your worksheet may not look exactly like Figure 8-7.

We AutoFitted the columns so that you can see all of the worksheet at once. Notice that all the formulas have been changed to values, and the column and text formatting (boldfacing and alignment) has been lost.

10. Choose **File** → **Close** , and click No to close the file without saving it.

	A	B	C	D	E	F	G	H
1		January	February	March	April	May	June	Total
2	North	4712	4110	4475	2858	4002	4757	24914
3	South	3623	2847	3578	3414	2786	4226	20474
4	East	3810	3854	2539	3398	4869	3976	22446
5	West	3546	3754	4391	3156	4888	3059	22794

Figure 8-7 The Formulas option is turned on to see that the formulas have been changed to values.

RECOGNIZING THE LIMITATIONS OF DELIMITED FILES

Although it is nice to be able to read a text file from another spreadsheet program, tab- and comma-delimited files have their limitations. As the preceding activity shows, character formatting, such as boldfacing is lost; column formatting, including centering and column width, is also lost; and all formulas are changed to values. Any links to other worksheets or workbooks are also lost when the file is saved in a delimited format.

WORKING WITH DIF FILES

Although DIF files differ significantly from delimited files in structure, you get approximately the same results when you import a DIF file — that is, you lose most of the formatting and formulas that the original file contains. Column widths and number formats are saved.

WORKING WITH SYLK FILES

SYLK files are the preferred method for exporting and importing files between Excel and unsupported spreadsheet programs such as Informix Smart. SYLK files transfer most formulas and worksheet formatting intact.

SIDE TRIP

Sometimes Excel refers to *SYLK* files; other times, it refers to *Sylk* files. There doesn't seem to be any logic to this, so I use *SYLK*.

Keep the following points in mind when saving your worksheet as a SYLK file:

* When saving a file in SYLK format, you can save as many as 255 characters per cell.

* If an Excel function is not supported by the SYLK format specifications, Excel calculates the function and saves the result as a value.

* Rotated text, merged cells, and horizontal and vertical text alignment are lost. Font color may change.

* All borders are converted to single lines, and cell shading is set to a dotted gray shading.

* Manual page breaks and page setup information (including orientation, margins, and headers and footers) are lost.

* Any embedded charts or other objects are lost.

TIP If you have entered cell notes in an Excel file and saved it as a SYLK file, the notes are saved, but they only appear if you reopen the file in Excel.

Importing from and Exporting to Word Tables

You may sometimes enter data into a Microsoft Word table, rather than an Excel worksheet. Although Word tables can perform some functions of a worksheet, their capabilities are limited. For example, you can create formulas in a Word table, but they are not automatically updated. Word tables can also be used to perform merges of form letters or labels. Although Microsoft Graph can be used to create graphs from Word tables, graph type selection and customizing options are limited.

Copying a table from Word to Excel

You can easily copy a table from Word to Excel, but a warning is in order. If you create formulas in Word, only the *values* are copied, not the *formulas*. However, because any formulas that Word creates are extremely simple, you don't have much trouble rewriting the formulas in Excel.

TIP Formatting numbers as currency is next to impossible in Word. However, if you place dollar signs in front of the numbers and import them into Excel, they are *automatically* formatted as currency.

To complete this activity, you must have Word installed.

To copy a table from Word into Excel, follow these steps:

1. Minimize Excel by clicking the *program* minimize button.

2. Open Word. A blank Word document is automatically created.

3. Click ▦ (the Insert Table button) on the toolbar, and then drag down and to the right to highlight a 3 × 3 table. Word creates an empty table containing three rows and three columns.

4. Enter the following data, including the dollar signs.

$500	$750	$400
$825	$950	$1045
$680	$880	$725

5. Highlight the data, and click the Copy button on the toolbar.

6. Minimize Word by clicking its minimize button. Word is reduced and placed in the taskbar. Leave Word open; you need it again in the next activity.

7. Click Excel in the Windows taskbar.

8. Create a new worksheet by clicking the New button on the toolbar.

9. Click the Paste button on the toolbar. The table appears as shown in Figure 8-8. Notice that the pasted cells are automatically formatted as currency.

	A	B	C
1	$500	$750	$400
2	$825	$950	$1,045
3	$680	$880	$725

Figure 8-8 The Word table is copied into Excel, with currency formatting automatically applied.

10. Close the Excel worksheet without saving it. Leave Excel open.

Copying a table from Excel to Word

You can copy a selected range of cells from Excel directly into Word — a table is automatically created to hold the Excel data. If you format the data as currency in Excel, the formatting carries into Word.

Although the numbers *appear* to be formatted as currency, they are actually text with spaces between the dollar sign and the values. Unless all your values are of equal length, you may find that the decimal points don't line up. This is because Word inserts spaces following the dollar sign. If you use a *proportional font* (a font in which some letters occupy less space than others), such as Times Roman, the numbers may not line up.

The following activity takes you in the opposite direction from the previous activity.

To copy the data from an Excel worksheet and move it into Word, follow these steps:

1. Open Sales Example.xls (the original worksheet that you created in the first activity of this chapter).

2. Select A1 through H11.

3. Click the Copy button on the toolbar.

4. Click the Word icon in the taskbar. It isn't necessary to minimize the applications. Even if they are full-size, their icons appear in the taskbar, and clicking a program's icon brings the program back to full size.

5. If the table is still highlighted, click the paragraph mark that's below the table.

6. Click the Paste button on the toolbar. Word automatically places the data in a table. The Word table gridlines are displayed, as shown in Figure 8-9. The gridlines demonstrate that the data was actually placed into a table, rather than as text separated by tabs.

TIP   If you do not see any gridlines, someone has turned off that option. To turn it back on, choose `Table` → `Show Gridlines` .

¤	January¤	February¤	March¤	April¤	May¤	June¤	Total¤
North¤	$····4,356	$····4,132	$····2,589	$····3,016	$····2,614	$····4,935	$····21,642
South¤	$····3,689	$····2,837	$····2,844	$····2,967	$····2,678	$····3,076	$····18,091
East¤	$····2,533	$····3,073	$····4,907	$····3,742	$····3,686	$····4,193	$····22,134
West¤	$····4,724	$····4,332	$····4,996	$····4,748	$····3,726	$····3,280	$····25,806
North¤	Great¤						
South¤	Good¤						
East¤	Great¤						
West¤	Great¤						

Figure 8-9   The Excel data is automatically entered into a Word table.

7. Exit Word without saving the file.

8. Leave the Excel file open. You use it again in the Bonus section of this chapter.

BONUS

Using the File Conversion Wizard

Excel for Office 97 contains another goodie called the File Conversion Wizard. Using it, you can convert individual files or multiple files. Excel guides you through the conversion process by asking you a series of questions.

To use the File Conversion Wizard to convert files from one format to another, follow these steps:

1. Choose **File** → **Save As** . Excel displays the Save As dialog box.

2. Drop down the Save as type list and choose WK3 (1-2-3) (*.wk3).

3. Save the file as Sales Example.wk3 in the Discover Excel folder.

4. Close the file *without* saving it.

5. Click the New button on the toolbar. To run the File Conversion Wizard, you must be in a *blank* workbook.

6. Choose **Tools** → **Wizard** → **File Conversion** . As shown in Figure 8-10, Excel displays the first step of the File Conversion Wizard.

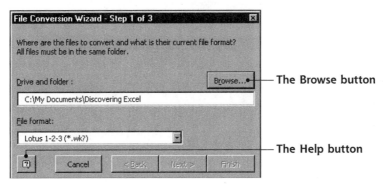

Figure 8-10 Use the first step in the File Conversion Wizard to set the folder containing the files to be converted and the type of files that you are converting.

7. If necessary, change the settings in your dialog box so that it looks like the example in Figure 8-10.

If you need help, click the Help button in any of the three screens of this Wizard. If necessary, use Browse to locate the drive and the folder that contain the file(s) that you want to convert.

8. Click Next to move to Step 2 of the Wizard, as shown in Figure 8-11.

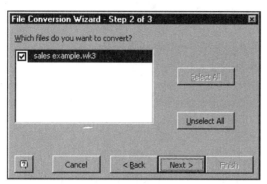

Figure 8-11   Use the second step of the File Conversion Wizard to choose the file or files that you want to convert.

9. Choose the file that you want to convert (Sales Example.wk3). Using the File Conversion Wizard, you can convert as many files as you want in a single step, provided that they are all of the same file type. To select a group of contiguous files, click the first file, press and hold Shift, and click the last file. To select nonconsecutive files, press and hold Ctrl, and click each of the files to be converted.

TIP   **To convert similar file types that are located in multiple folders, use Windows Explorer to move all the files to a common folder and then run the File Conversion Wizard.**

10. Click Next to move to the final step of the File Conversion Wizard, which is shown in Figure 8-12.

11. Using Browse, select the *destination* folder for the converted file (it should still be Discover Excel).

TIP   **To create a new folder, click New Folder.**

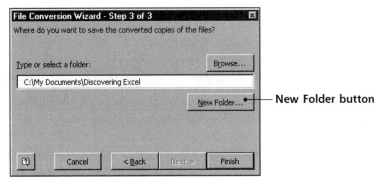

Figure 8-12 In the final step of the File Conversion Wizard, you specify the folder in which you want the converted files to be saved.

12. Click Finish to complete the conversion.

The converted file is *not* automatically opened. Rather, you see a report that is similar to the one shown in Figure 8-13. The file is now an Excel file, and you open it as you would any other Excel workbook.

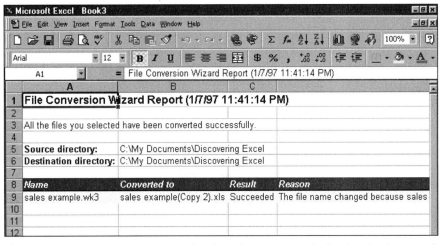

Figure 8-13 The File Conversion Wizard produces a report indicating that it created a new workbook.

NOTE Notice in B9 of the File Conversion Wizard Report that the name of the file is changed to Sales Example(Copy 2).xls. In column D, you can see that the name was changed because Sales Example.xls was already in the folder.

WEB PATH For shareware, begin by looking at:

`http://www.shareware.com`

This site contains thousands of shareware programs. You can use the search feature on the Web site to search for *file converter.*

Summary

Remember, file conversions seldom go smoothly. Plan plenty of extra time to convert your existing files, and admit when it's going to be faster to retype the entire worksheet than try to convert it. If you need more help in converting files, begin with the online help files that are in Excel.

CHAPTER NINE

GET READY, GET SET: GO TO PAGE SETUP

IN THIS CHAPTER YOU LEARN THESE KEY SKILLS

When you buy a house, you take it *as is*. After moving in, you may decide that you want to change the landscaping (perhaps adding sod, trees, and plants), the garage (adding a workbench and some storage space), or the room that you use as an office (rewiring it for a direct Internet connection). You seldom like everything about your new house exactly as it is. Instead, you find that customizing your setup makes your new home more efficient and better suited to your tastes.

Just as you tailor your new house to fit your needs, you may need to make some changes in the setup of your worksheet. Before you print your worksheet, you may decide that you want to change to the default way in which Excel prints the pages. For example, the default page orientation is *portrait* (the page is taller than it is wide). If you need to place more columns on a single page and are not as concerned with how many rows fit on each page, you may change the page orientation to *landscape* (the page is wider than it is tall).

Regardless of how you want to set up your page, Excel is flexible enough to meet almost any need. In this chapter, you modify many of the page settings, and you get tips on customizing a worksheet page to fit specific needs.

Creating a Large Sample Worksheet

Before you can change the page setup, you need to have something to work with. So far, the worksheets that you've developed have been fairly small. To see the various functions of the Page Setup dialog box, you need to develop a worksheet that is too large to fit on one page.

In this activity, you use some of the automatic features in Excel to create a large sample worksheet so that you can experiment with various page setup features.

Follow these steps:

1. Open Excel. A new workbook is displayed.

2. Save the file in the Discover Excel folder as Large Workbook.

3. In A2, type **Store 1** and press Enter.

4. Click A2, and then AutoFill A3 through A76.

5. Press Ctrl+Home to move the cursor back to A1.

6. Click B1, type **January** and then AutoFill B1 through M1.

7. Choose **Tools** → **Add-Ins**, and select the Analysis ToolPak.

8. Click OK.

9. Click B2, type **=Randbetween(5000,10000)**, and press Enter. This generates a random number between 5,000 and 10,000.

Make certain that you *don't* put commas in the numbers 5000 and 10000. If you do, Excel displays a #Value! error message.

10. AutoFill B2 through M2. This fills the selected cells with random numbers between 5,000 and 10,000.

11. Drag the AutoFill handle from M2 to M76.

    Cells B2 through M76 are now filled with random numbers. Because these cells contain random number formulas, the numbers are regenerated each time that the worksheet is recalculated. You need to change the formulas to values. Cells B2 through M76 should still be selected.

12. Click the Copy button on the toolbar. Excel places a marquis (a line of marching ants) around the selected cells.

13. Choose **Edit** → **Paste Special**. Excel displays the Paste Special dialog box.

14. Click Values, and then click OK. The selected cells now contain values rather than random number formulas.

15. Press Esc to turn off the marquis selection.

16. Select columns A through N, and then choose Format → Column → Width. Excel displays the Column Width dialog box.

17. Type **10** and click OK. This sets the column width for the selected columns.

18. Select row 1 and click the Center and Bold buttons on the formatting toolbar. All the months are boldfaced and centered.

19. Select N1 and type **Total**.

20. Select N2 and click the AutoSum button twice. This places a formula for summing B2 through M2 in N2.

> **TIP** If any cells contain pound signs (#) instead of numbers, you need to AutoFit the column. The pound signs mean that the numbers are too wide for the columns.

21. AutoFill N2 through N77.

22. Select B2 through N77, click the Currency button on the formatting toolbar, and then click the Decrease Decimal button twice.

23. Select row 77 and click the Bold button on the formatting toolbar.

24. Click A77 and type **Total**.

25. Click B77 and then double-click the AutoSum button.

26. AutoFill B77 through N77. The amount in N77 may not fit. You may need to AutoFit the column again.

27. Click the Save button on the toolbar.

28. Press Ctrl+Home to make A1 the active cell.

Your worksheet should look similar to Figure 9-1. *Your values will be different.* To see the entire worksheet, choose 25% in the Zoom box. If you printed your worksheet now, it would cover four pages.

29. If you changed the zoom to 25%, return it to 100%.

30. Save the workbook, and leave it open for the next activity.

Zoom box

	January	February	March	April	May	June	July
Store 1	$ 6,104	$ 8,368	$ 9,562	$ 6,793	$ 6,844	$ 7,488	$ 8,909
Store 2	$ 7,415	$ 5,979	$ 5,613	$ 7,118	$ 6,749	$ 8,225	$ 8,235
Store 3	$ 9,063	$ 6,651	$ 9,051	$ 5,401	$ 8,806	$ 5,045	$ 7,353
Store 4	$ 7,853	$ 6,351	$ 8,829	$ 7,636	$ 9,815	$ 6,072	$ 8,967
Store 5	$ 5,737	$ 8,308	$ 6,739	$ 7,385	$ 6,553	$ 5,280	$ 7,219
Store 6	$ 7,959	$ 8,618	$ 8,532	$ 7,061	$ 8,159	$ 5,692	$ 6,090
Store 7	$ 7,826	$ 5,087	$ 8,572	$ 5,755	$ 6,234	$ 7,759	$ 7,642
Store 8	$ 8,817	$ 8,268	$ 9,334	$ 5,232	$ 6,485	$ 7,475	$ 7,148
Store 9	$ 8,673	$ 7,236	$ 6,830	$ 6,066	$ 8,204	$ 7,534	$ 6,264
Store 10	$ 9,515	$ 6,105	$ 7,517	$ 9,149	$ 5,458	$ 9,094	$ 8,105
Store 11	$ 5,370	$ 5,778	$ 8,576	$ 9,333	$ 7,591	$ 8,775	$ 7,486
Store 12	$ 9,266	$ 7,483	$ 9,835	$ 9,405	$ 6,824	$ 6,167	$ 5,413
Store 13	$ 8,165	$ 5,064	$ 7,534	$ 9,464	$ 7,502	$ 8,535	$ 9,308
Store 14	$ 8,983	$ 5,001	$ 7,949	$ 7,855	$ 5,276	$ 5,440	$ 6,678
Store 15	$ 9,856	$ 5,045	$ 8,037	$ 9,314	$ 8,654	$ 8,730	$ 5,181
Store 16	$ 7,062	$ 9,695	$ 8,855	$ 9,813	$ 8,073	$ 8,256	$ 6,705
Store 17	$ 8,756	$ 6,393	$ 5,102	$ 7,097	$ 5,317	$ 5,922	$ 9,397
Store 18	$ 9,891	$ 6,716	$ 5,265	$ 9,186	$ 9,590	$ 9,818	$ 8,626

Figure 9-1   The completed Large Worksheet is only partially visible at 100% zoom.

Setting Up Your Page

B efore you print your worksheet, you need to set the page specifications by using the Page Setup dialog box that is shown in Figure 9-2. To display this dialog box, choose **File** → **Page Setup**.

The Page Setup dialog box has four tabs: Page, Margins, Header/Footer, and Sheet. These tabs offer options for controlling how Excel prints a worksheet.

Taking command of the page setup

In addition to OK and Cancel, each tab in the Page Setup dialog box has the same three command buttons located along the right side of the dialog box: Print, Print Preview, and Options. Each button opens a corresponding dialog box.

The Print dialog box allows you to specify which pages to print, the number of copies, and other print-related options. The Print Preview dialog box displays the worksheet *exactly* as it will print. This feature is covered in depth in the following chapter. The third command button, Options, displays the Printer Properties dialog box that is shown in Figure 9-3. Your screen may look slightly different, depending on your type of printer.

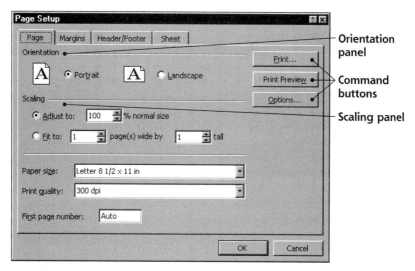

Orientation panel

Command buttons

Scaling panel

Figure 9-2 The Page tab of the Page Setup dialog box.

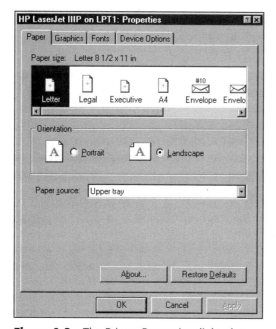

Figure 9-3 The Printer Properties dialog box.

You use the Printer Properties dialog box to directly change the *default* printer settings. Unless you are an advanced computer user, you shouldn't change these settings, because they affect the settings in *all* Windows-based programs. For example, choosing Landscape orientation from this dialog box sets the default for all printed material to landscape. Instead, when you need to print a document in landscape orientation, set the Landscape option from the Page tab of the Page Setup dialog box. This affects only the current workbook.

Setting page specifications

You use the Page tab of the Page Setup dialog box (shown previously in Figure 9-2) to set the physical specifications of the page. The available options for paper size and print quality depend on your printer. Printer specifications are installed when you install the software for your printer.

You can set several options on the Page tab:

* **Orientation.** Choose either Portrait (the page is taller than it is wide) or Landscape (the page is wider than it is tall). You often print spreadsheets in landscape mode, because this allows you to display more categories (columns) on a page than rows.

* **Scaling.** Use the Adjust to box in the Scaling panel to reduce or increase the size of the worksheet by a given percentage. Excel also has an automatic fit option called Fit to. You can tell Excel to automatically reduce the worksheet to fit a specific number of pages wide by a specific number of pages tall.

Be careful when using the Fit to option. Excel decreases the font size and margins until the worksheet fits on the specified number of pages. If the worksheet *nearly* fits on a specific number of pages, this option is helpful. Otherwise, the printed worksheet may be reduced too much and thus become unreadable.

* **Paper size and Print quality.** Available options are determined by your printer. If you have a high-quality printer, such as the Hewlett-Packard V SI, you can print pages as large as 11 inches by 17 inches. The higher the number of dots per inch (dpi), the better the clarity of the worksheet when it is printed. Most laser printers print at 300 dpi. However, newer ones can also print at 600 dpi or even 1,200 dpi.

The higher the dpi, the longer a worksheet takes to print. Also, printing at a higher dpi uses more toner with a laser printer or more ink with an inkjet printer.

This activity shows you how you change the orientation of your printed pages from portrait (the default) to landscape so that you can see more columns on your page.

Follow these steps:

1. Choose `File` → `Page Setup`. Excel displays the Page tab of the Page Setup dialog box, unless you have used another tab since you started Excel. If the Page tab isn't displayed, click it.

2. Click Landscape in the Orientation panel. Notice that the option button to the left of the Landscape option is now black. The Portrait option button has been automatically deselected.

3. Leave the Page Setup dialog box open for the next activity.

Setting margins

Figure 9-4 shows the Margins tab of the Page Setup dialog box. Regardless of the paper orientation, Excel has a default setting of 1 inch for the top and bottom margins and 0.75 inches for the left and right margins.

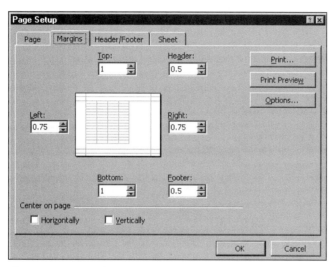

Figure 9-4 Use the Margins tab to set the four margins and the position of any headers and footers.

By default, the headers and footers on each page are positioned 0.5 inches from the top and bottom *of the page* (not from the margins). The check boxes in the Center on page panel allow you to center the worksheet vertically and horizontally on the page (between the margins). If neither of the option boxes is checked, the worksheet is aligned to the top and left margins. The two Center on page options are check boxes. This means that none, either, or both can be selected at the same time.

For most printers, all margins must be at least 0.25 inches. This gives the printer room to move the paper through the printing path. Your printer may require even wider margins. Check your printer manual to confirm the minimum margin requirements.

In this activity, you change the margins for your worksheet and center it both vertically and horizontally on the page.

Follow these steps:

1. Click the Margins tab in the Page Setup dialog box.

2. Use the spin buttons to set the top and bottom margins to 1.5 inches, and the left and right margins to 1.25 inches.

   As you click each spin button, the margin increases or decreases by 0.25 inches. However, you are not limited to increments of 0.25 inches. You can also double-click any of the margin values and enter a specific value directly into the text box.

3. Click the Horizontally and Vertically option boxes to center the worksheet on the page.

4. Using the spin buttons, set the Header and Footer values to 1 inch.

   This merely sets the position of the headers and the footers. If you do not specify text for the headers or footers, as described in the following section, your page does not display headers or footers. The Margins tab should now look like Figure 9-5.

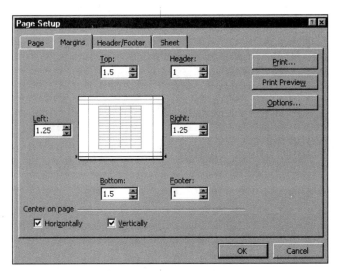

Figure 9-5   The new settings for the Margins tab of the Page Setup dialog box.

5. Leave the Page Setup dialog box open for the next activity.

Creating headers and footers

Next, decide whether you want headers and footers on your page. For example, you may want to print a title at the top of each page, and a page number and the date at the bottom of each page. Figure 9-6 shows the Header/Footer tab of the Page Setup dialog box. The text boxes for the header and footer are blank, indicating that your worksheet has no headers or footers. By default, Excel doesn't print headers or footers.

Zoom box

	A	B	C	D	E	F	G	H
1		January	February	March	April	May	June	July
2	Store 1	$ 6,104	$ 8,368	$ 9,562	$ 6,793	$ 6,844	$ 7,488	$ 8,909
3	Store 2	$ 7,415	$ 5,979	$ 5,613	$ 7,118	$ 6,749	$ 8,225	$ 8,235
4	Store 3	$ 9,063	$ 6,651	$ 9,051	$ 5,401	$ 8,806	$ 5,045	$ 7,353
5	Store 4	$ 7,853	$ 6,351	$ 8,829	$ 7,636	$ 9,815	$ 6,072	$ 8,967
6	Store 5	$ 5,737	$ 8,308	$ 6,739	$ 7,385	$ 6,553	$ 5,280	$ 7,219
7	Store 6	$ 7,959	$ 8,618	$ 8,532	$ 7,061	$ 8,159	$ 5,692	$ 6,090
8	Store 7	$ 7,826	$ 5,087	$ 8,572	$ 5,755	$ 6,234	$ 7,759	$ 7,642
9	Store 8	$ 8,817	$ 8,268	$ 9,334	$ 5,232	$ 6,485	$ 7,475	$ 7,148
10	Store 9	$ 8,673	$ 7,236	$ 6,830	$ 6,066	$ 8,204	$ 7,534	$ 6,264
11	Store 10	$ 9,515	$ 6,105	$ 7,517	$ 9,149	$ 5,458	$ 9,094	$ 8,105
12	Store 11	$ 5,370	$ 5,778	$ 8,576	$ 9,333	$ 7,591	$ 8,775	$ 7,486

Figure 9-6   Use the Header/Footer tab of the Page Setup dialog box to select preformatted headers and footers or to create customized headers and footers.

FEATURE FOCUS   In previous versions of Excel, the default header displays the worksheet name and the default footer displays the current page number. In Excel for Office 97, by default both headers and footers are blank.

Using preformatted headers and footers

Excel comes with more than a dozen preformatted headers and footers. You can see the available selections by using the Header or Footer drop-down list. Figure 9-7 shows a sample list of preformatted headers. (Unless the name of your company is Creative Consultants, your options look slightly different from those shown in the figure.)

To use a preformatted header or footer, drop down the list and select an option. Excel automatically enters the selected text into the header or footer text box.

CAUTION   What appears in the text box may not be exactly what you see when you print. (There isn't enough room to show all the area for the header or footer, so if some of your text is long, it may appear to overlap other information in the header or footer.) Use the Print Preview option to check your headers and footers before printing.

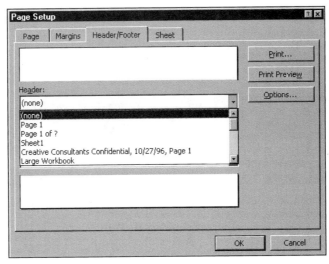

Figure 9-7 Sample preformatted header options. Footer options are similar.

Creating custom headers and footers

In addition to using preformatted headers and footers, you can create customized headers and footers by clicking Custom Header or Custom Footer. Excel responds by displaying either the Header dialog box or the Footer dialog box. Figure 9-8 shows the Header dialog box.

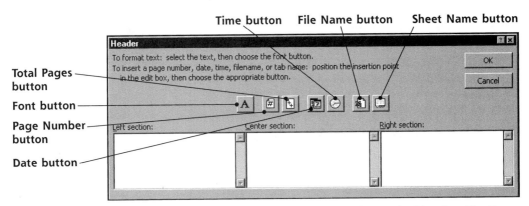

Figure 9-8 Use the Header dialog box to create customized headers. The Footer dialog box looks the same.

FEATURE FOCUS Excel 7 does *not* offer Tool Tips in most dialog boxes. Excel for Office 97 does offer Tool Tips. To access them, right-click the dialog box feature for which you need help and then left-click the What's This message.

Notice that in Figure 9-8, the header section is divided into three parts: Left section, Center section, and Right section. Text or fields entered in the Left section are automatically justified to the left margin. Text or fields in the Center section are centered between the margins. Text or fields in the Right section are justified to the right margin.

You can use any combination of text and buttons to create a custom header or footer. All the buttons except Font are used to insert *dynamic* (changing) information into the header or the footer:

✽ The Page Number button prints the current page number.

✽ The Total Pages button prints the *total* number of pages in the document.

✽ The Date and Time buttons insert dynamic *fields* rather than text. Dynamic information is automatically updated as required, as opposed to static information, which remains constant. For example, if you click the Date button, Excel places a date field at the insertion point. Each time that you print the worksheet, Excel prints the *current* date (rather than the date on which the header was created).

✽ The File name and Sheet name buttons insert the current workbook name and worksheet name, respectively.

TIP **If you don't want the date (or other field information) updated each time you print, simply type a specific date, time, or other required information in the section box rather than inserting one of the field commands.**

Figure 9-9 shows an example header. The Left section contains the filename, and the Center section displays the sheet name. Notice that field names begin with an ampersand (&) and are followed by the appropriate command name contained in brackets.

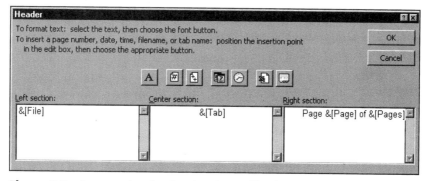

Figure 9-9   A custom header showing the workbook name, the worksheet name, the page number, and the total number of pages.

You have already seen the Header dialog box. The Footer dialog box is nearly identical. To create both a custom header and a custom footer, follow these steps:

1. Click the Header/Footer tab in the Page Setup dialog box.

2. Click Custom Header. Excel displays the Header dialog box.

3. Type your name in the Left section.

4. Tab to the Center section, and click ![File Name button] (the File Name button). Notice that the workbook name is *not* inserted. Instead, the *field* for the workbook name (&file) is placed at the insertion point.

5. Tab to the Right section box, and click ![Date button] (the Date button). As in the Center section, only the field is displayed, not the actual date. Figure 9-10 shows the Header dialog box with your custom header.

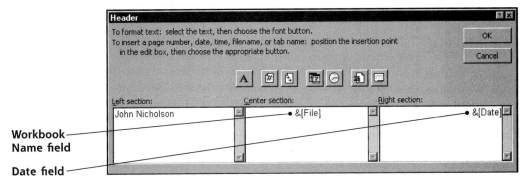

Figure 9-10   The custom header that you created should look similar to this. Your name may be different!

6. Select all of the text in Center section, and click [Times New Roman ▼] (the Font button). Excel displays the Font dialog box.

7. Set the Size to 18 points. You do this by double-clicking the value in the Size text box and typing **18**, or by clicking the down-arrow in the drop-down list and choosing 18.

You can only select one header or footer section at a time. If you want to change the font in all three sections, you must change each section individually.

8. Click OK to close the Font dialog box.

9. Click OK to close the Header dialog box. As shown in Figure 9-11, the header *text* (not the field codes) appears in the Header text box as well as in the Header drop-down list.

10. Click the Footer drop-down list. The selections for the footer are the same as those for the header.

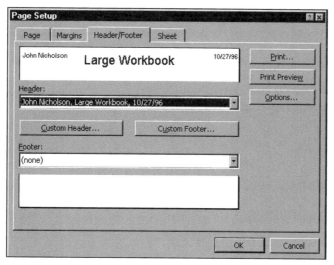

Figure 9-11 The Header panel shows the text (not the field names) of the custom header that you created.

11. Click (none) at the top of the drop-down list to close the drop-down list without making any changes.

12. Click Custom Footer. Excel displays the Footer dialog box.

13. Drop the insertion point in the Center section.

14. Type **Page** (be sure to type a space after the word), and click ⊞ the Page Number button.

15. Type another space, type **of**, type another space, and then click ⊞ the Total Pages button. The Footer dialog box should now look like Figure 9-12.

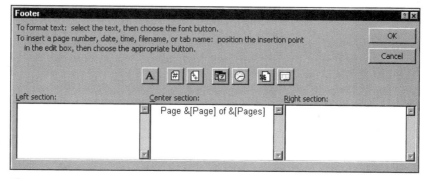

Figure 9-12 The Footer dialog box, showing your custom footer.

16. Click OK to close the Footer dialog box.

17. Click OK to exit the Page Setup dialog box.

18. Save your work, and leave the workbook open for the next activity.

Setting up your sheet

Figure 9-13 shows the Sheet tab of the Page Setup dialog box. The options in this tab directly affect the appearance of the printed worksheet. The Sheet tab has four panels: Print area, Print titles, Print, and Page order.

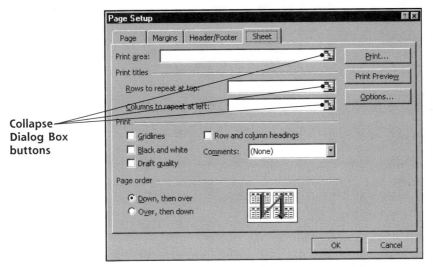

Figure 9-13 The Sheet tab of the Page Setup dialog box.

FEATURE FOCUS Notice the Collapse Dialog Box buttons at the right side of the text boxes for Print area, Rows to repeat at top, and Columns to repeat at left. The Collapse Dialog Box button is a new feature of Excel for Microsoft Office 97. Clicking one of these buttons collapses the dialog box to a single line and allows you to select an area on your worksheet by clicking and dragging. Figure 9-14 shows a collapsed dialog box. To restore a collapsed dialog box to its full size, simply click the Collapse Dialog Box button at the right side of the text box.

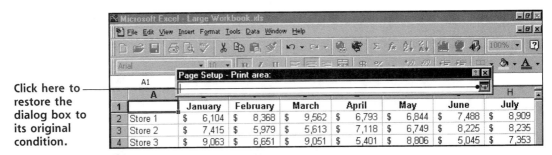

Figure 9-14 The collapsed dialog box for selecting the print area.

TIP Buttons like the one on the right side of the Print area text box are always called Collapse Dialog Box buttons, even when clicking one of them restores the dialog box to its full size.

Setting the print area

The Print area text box allows you to specify the range of cells that you want to print. Type the upper-left cell address of the print area, a colon, and the lower-right cell address. Each cell address must be preceded with a dollar sign ($). Remember, these are absolute references. (Chapter 6 describes the difference between absolute and relative references.) For example, typing **$A$1:$F$10** prints all cells between A1 and F10.

In earlier versions of Excel, you could select the range to print and then choose `File` → `Print Area` → `Set Print Area`. In Excel for Office 97, highlighting a range of cells before displaying the Sheet tab of the Page Setup dialog box makes no difference; the Print area text box remains blank.

Setting print titles

The Print titles panel (shown in Figure 9-14) is used to print the column letters and row numbers. It also contains Collapse Dialog Box buttons.

TIP Headers print *above* the top margin on each page, while the Rows to repeat at top option prints *at* the top margin. Likewise, the Columns to repeat at left option prints *at* the left margin, not outside it.

Choosing print options

The five print options allow you to control several characteristics of the printed page:

* **Gridlines.** By default, gridlines (gray cell dividers) are *not* printed. To print lines between cells, select the Gridlines option.

* **Black and white, or Colors.** These options only apply if you have a color printer. Click the Black and White option to cause all screen colors to print as black and white.

* **Draft quality.** This option increases print speed. Excel does not print gridlines and graphics.

* **Row and column headings.** This option causes the column letters to be printed across the top of the sheet and the row numbers to be printed down the left side of the worksheet.

✳ **Comments.** This option lets you print any notes that you've added to cells. You can choose to print comments at their actual position in the worksheet, or you can choose to print them all on a separate page at the end of the worksheet. To select a Comments option, drop down the list and make a selection.

Specifying the page order

You use the final option on the Sheet tab to specify the order in which multiple pages print when you send the worksheet to the printer. By default, page 2 is the area of the worksheet contained directly *below* page 1. By choosing Over, then down, page 2 becomes the area directly to the *right* of page 1.

Putting it all together: setting sheet options

In this activity, you set the print area to print the information for only the first 25 stores. Column A (the store names) is repeated at the left edge of each page, and row 1 (which lists the months) is printed along the top of each page. The gridlines are turned on.

Follow these steps:

1. Open the Page Setup dialog box by choosing File → Page Setup .

2. Click the Sheet tab of the Page Setup dialog box.

3. Click the Collapse Dialog Box button to the right of the Print area text box.

4. On the worksheet, drag from A1 to N26. Notice, as you drag, that the *absolute* addresses for the range that you select are automatically entered in the Print area text box. You can tell that they are absolute references because each contains dollar signs.

5. Click the Collapse Dialog Box button to restore the Page Setup dialog box to its original size.

6. In the Rows to repeat at top text box, type **$1:$1**.

7. In the Columns to repeat at left text box, type **$A:$A**.

Note that Steps 6 and 7 show the proper form for selecting only one row or column. Any ranges that are typed directly into the Rows to repeat at top text box or the Columns to repeat at left text box must include *absolute* references to both the starting *and* the ending row(s) or column(s). Otherwise, you receive an error message when you try to print.

8. Click the Gridlines option box to select printing of the gridlines.

9. In the Page order panel, choose Over, then down. Your Sheet tab should look like the example shown in Figure 9-15.

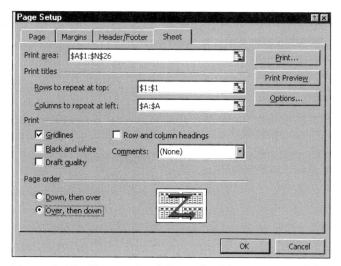

Figure 9-15 The completed Sheet tab of the Page Setup dialog box.

10. Click Print Preview to see your worksheet before sending it to the printer.

   Your worksheet should look like Figure 9-16. Notice that the worksheet page-breaks after September, rather than breaking at the end of the first half-year, where you may logically prefer the break. In the next chapter, you find out how to adjust page breaks.

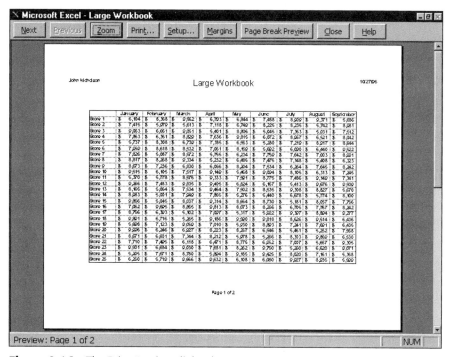

Figure 9-16 The Print Preview dialog box.

11. Make sure that your printer is turned on, and then click Print to open the Print dialog box.

12. Click OK to send a copy of both pages to the printer.

13. Close the worksheet, and save any changes. *Do not close Excel yet.*

BONUS

Creating Permanent Headers and Footers

As mentioned earlier in this chapter, Excel no longer provides a default header or footer. Most long-time users of Excel cheer this change. The default — worksheet name for the header and page number for the footer — was almost useless.

Now, through the magic of this book, you can create your own default headers and footers. These defaults do not affect any workbooks that you have already created, but they will be in effect for any workbooks that you create in the future.

Using the following method, you can also reset the defaults for other workbook and worksheet settings, such as font, size, column width, and orientation. Instead of changing the settings in the Header/Footer tab, select any tab in the Page Setup dialog box, make your changes, and continue the following instructions, starting at Step 15.

To create default headers and footers to be used with all new worksheets that you create, follow these steps:

1. Click the New button.

2. Choose `File` → `Page Setup` to open the Page Setup dialog box.

3. Click the Header/Footer tab.

4. Click Custom Header. Excel displays the Header dialog box.

5. Type your name in the Left section.

6. In the Center section, click the File Name button.

7. In the Right section box, click the Date button.

8. Click OK to close the Header dialog box.

9. Click Custom Footer. Excel displays the Footer dialog box.

10. Drop the insertion point in the Center section.

11. Type **Page** (be sure to type a space after the word), and then click the Page Number button.

12. Type another space, type **of**, type another space, and click the Total Pages button.

13. Click OK to exit the Footer dialog box.

14. Click OK to exit the Page Setup dialog box.

15. Choose File → Save As . Excel displays the Save As dialog box.

16. Drop down the Save as type list box, and choose Template.

    The Save in text box is automatically set to Templates. Templates are used to create default worksheets that already contain specific settings and data. Templates are discussed further in Chapter 13.

17. Drop down the Save in list box, and set the path for saving your template.

    For example, if you have installed Office in the default directory, set the path to C:\Program Files\Microsoft Office\Office\Excel\XLStart. To do this, click the C drive icon, double-click the MSOffice folder, double-click the Office folder, and then double-click the XLStart folder.

TIP   **If you haven't used the default installation folders, click Start on the taskbar and click Find → Files or Folders . In the Named text box, type xlstart and click Find Now. The In Folder information shows you where the folder is located.**

18. Type **Book** in the File name text box. For the defaults to be changed, you must save the revised workbook in the XLStart folder as a template named Book.

19. Click Save.

20. Exit Excel. For the template to take effect, you must restart Excel.

21. Start Excel.

22. Choose File → Page Setup to open the Page Setup dialog box.

23. Click the Header/Footer tab. You should see the custom header and footer that you created.

24. Click OK.

25. Exit Excel.

To reset the original defaults, simply delete BOOK.XLT, the file that you created in this activity. If you want to change the defaults, load BOOK.XLT, make the changes, and save it again as a template. Close Excel and restart it to activate the changes.

Summary

In this chapter, you discovered how to set up the page that is printed as an Excel worksheet. By mastering the setup of the pages, you can easily create custom reports. By changing the defaults in Excel, you can save time and energy as well as increase the formatting consistency of your reports. Changing the page setup is simple, but many users fail to take advantage of the opportunity to design pages in ways that best suit their needs.

CHAPTER TEN

OUT WITH THE NEW: PRINTING WORKSHEETS

10

IN THIS CHAPTER YOU LEARN THESE KEY SKILLS

N ow that you've created brilliant worksheets by using Excel's newest features, what do you do with your masterpieces? Most likely, you want to print them. Whether you create a weekly report, a presentation for the board of directors, or just a simple worksheet, at some time, you probably need a hard copy of your data. *Hard copy* refers to a printed version of your material, *not* the television show.

Talking to Your Printer

C hoosing File → Print opens the Print dialog box, which you use to specify information such as the desired number of copies, the quality of the print, and the printer that you are using.

235

SIDE TRIP

It is wise to maintain an updated hard copy of the data in your files. If you lose files because of hard disk crashes, defective floppy disks, or power surges, an up-to-date hard copy greatly simplifies the process of re-entering your data.

Unlike other programs such as WordPerfect, Excel does not open the Print dialog box when you click (the Print button) on the toolbar. Clicking the Print button in Excel (or any other Microsoft program) prints a single copy of the current worksheet, using the default settings from the Print dialog box.

As shown in Figure 10-1, the Print dialog box contains four panels. A border surrounds each panel, and a title appears in the upper-left corner of each panel. Each panel provides information about the current setup for your printer and Excel. By understanding the role that each panel plays in your print job, you can greatly reduce the number of copies of your worksheet that end up in the recycling bin.

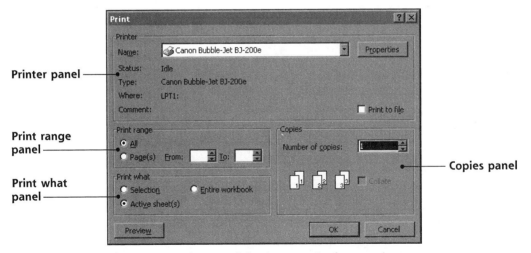

Figure 10-1 The Print dialog box contains four panels.

Choosing printer options

The Printer panel in the Print dialog box allows you to specify the printer that you are using as well as the desired quality of the printout. If you have only one printer installed, the Name box at the top of the dialog box displays only the single printer. If your computer is on a network with multiple printers or if you have more than one printer attached to your computer, the Name box offers you a drop-down list from which you can choose a printer.

The Printer panel also displays information about the printer that you select:

* The Status line tells you whether the printer is busy or idle.

* The Type line is supposed to tell you what type of printer you have (for example, bubble jet, laser, or fax), but it actually just mimics the information that is provided to you in the Name box.

* The Where line identifies the port to which the printer is connected.

* The Comment line displays comments regarding the selected printer.

* The Print to file check box allows you to choose whether to print directly to your printer or to a file. Once a file is created, you can use it to print the workbook at a later time. To print directly to the printer, this box *must* remain unchecked.

TIP **Most computers use LPT1 as the default printer port. However, you usually attach fax/modems to one of the available COM ports. Because the Printer panel lists your fax/modem as a printer choice, you can send worksheets to the fax/modem instead of the printer.**

The final item in the Printer panel is the Properties button. Click this button to examine the specific properties of your printer. The Properties dialog box offers two tabs: Paper and Graphics. This dialog box is specific to each printer, so the Paper and Graphics options differ from printer to printer. The Properties dialog box for your printer may not look quite like Figure 10-2.

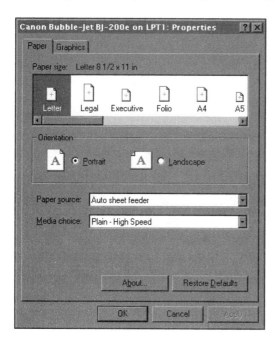

Figure 10-2 The Properties dialog box is used to modify the paper and graphics settings for your printer.

The Paper tab in the Properties dialog box allows you to choose the following settings:

* Paper size
* Orientation (portrait or landscape)
* Paper source
* Media choice (just a fancy phrase for the quality of print)

The Graphics tab of the Properties dialog box offers varying resolutions of the printed graphics. Generally, the higher the resolution, the sharper the quality of your printed charts and pictures.

Many laser printers are now set to print at 600 dots per inch (dpi) by default. Inkjet printers may be set to 720 dpi. Setting your printer at this high resolution can slow the print speed of your documents *considerably*. Additionally, printing at high resolution wears out your laser cartridge, ink cartridge, or printer ribbon much faster than a lower resolution. A resolution of 300 dpi or 360 dpi provides you with clear, crisp graphics in a much shorter time.

SIDE TRIP

I keep the following sign above my desk to provide a constant reminder of the hazards of technology:

> ### WARNING!
>
> This machine is subject to breakdowns during periods of critical needs.
>
> A special circuit in the machine called a "critical detector" senses the operator's emotional state in terms of how desperate he or she is to use the machine. The critical detector then creates a malfunction proportional to the desperation of the operator. Threatening the machine with violence only aggravates the situation. Likewise, attempts to use another machine may cause it to malfunction. (They belong to the same union.) Keep cool and say nice things to the machine. Nothing else seems to work.
>
> Never let anything mechanical know that you are in a hurry.

Selecting your printer and print settings

I n this activity, you create a sample file and then print it. You learn to how select a printer and adjust the print settings.

Follow these steps:

1. Open Excel, and save the blank file in your Discover Excel folder as Printer.

2. Choose Tools → Add-Ins , and make sure that a check mark appears in the Analysis ToolPak check box.

To use the Randbetween function, the Analysis ToolPak must be active.

3. In A1, type **=Randbetween(0,25)** and press Enter.

4. AutoFill A1 through Z1.

5. AutoFill Z1 through Z75. Excel fills the selected cells with random numbers between 0 and 25.

6. *Right-click* the selected data series, and choose Copy from the pop-up menu.

7. *Right-click* the active data series again, and choose Paste Special from the pop-up menu. Excel displays the Paste Special dialog box.

8. Click the Values button, and then click OK. Excel replaces the random number formulas with values.

9. Press Esc to cancel the marquis selection.

10. Click A1 to turn off the selection.

11. Save the file.

12. Choose File → Print . Excel displays the Print dialog box.

13. In the Printer panel, select the printer that you want to use.

14. Click Properties. Excel displays the Properties dialog box.

15. Set the paper size to Letter and the orientation to Portrait.

16. Click the Graphics tab. Figure 10-4 shows the Graphics tab.

17. Make sure that the resolution is set to either 300 or 360 dpi, and then click OK. Excel closes the Properties dialog box and returns to the Print dialog box.

Spin buttons —

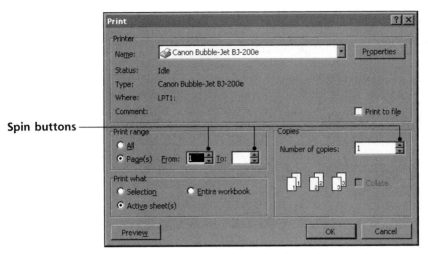

Figure 10-3 The Print dialog box is used to set print specifications.

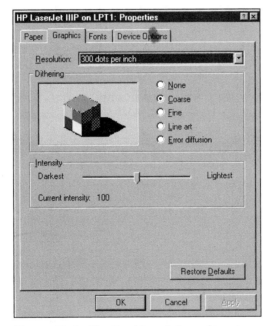

Figure 10-4 The Graphics tab is used to set printer resolution for graphics.

TIP Use the spin buttons in the Print range and Copies panel to easily specify the pages that you want to print and the desired number of copies.

18. Click OK to print your worksheet. The Print dialog box closes, and in a few seconds, your worksheet appears at the printer.

19. Leave the worksheet open.

The printer and print settings that you chose in this activity are now the default settings. In other words, these settings remain in effect until you alter them by repeating the process that you just completed, even if you exit and restart Excel. Changing the printer options in this way also affects other programs that use the printer.

Printing specific pages

The Print range panel in the Print dialog box (shown earlier in Figure 10-3) allows you to choose which pages of the worksheet you want to print. You specify the desired pages by entering the appropriate page numbers in the From box and the To box, or by clicking the spin buttons to increase or decrease the desired page numbers. Unlike Word, Excel doesn't let you directly print nonconsecutive pages.

TIP **When you click in either the From box or the To box, Excel automatically assumes that you *don't* want to print the entire document and moves the black dot from the All option button to the Page(s) option button.**

To select a print range, follow these steps:

1. Choose File → Print . Excel opens the Print dialog box.

2. Type **2** in the From box, and then press Tab.

3. Type **2** in the To box.

4. Click OK. Excel prints only the second page of your worksheet.

5. Leave the workbook open.

Telling Excel what to print

You use the Print what panel to specify exactly what you want to print:

* To print only highlighted cells, click the Selection button.
* To print only the sheet(s) that you have been working on, click the Active sheet(s) button.

✳ To print all the worksheets in the workbook, click the Entire workbook radio button.

TIP More than one worksheet can be active if the worksheets are grouped. You learn more about grouping in Chapter 12, which discusses working with multiple worksheets.

Telling Excel how many copies to print

Use the Copies panel to tell Excel exactly how many copies of your document you want to have printed. You can specify the desired number of copies by entering a value in the Number of copies box or by clicking the spin buttons. Checking the Collate box tells Excel to collate each copy when you print multiple copies.

TIP The Collate option is only important when you need to print more than one copy of a multipage document. When you select Collate, Excel builds a picture of page 1 and sends it to the printer. Excel then builds page 2 and sends it to the printer. This continues until Excel has printed all pages of the first copy. Then Excel starts over at page 1 to print the next copy. If you turn off the Collate option, Excel builds page 1 and sends multiple copies of that page to the printer. Then it builds page 2 and sends multiple copies of that page to the printer. This is much faster than having the document collated, particularly if you are printing many copies of a document. However, you then have to collate by hand.

TIP If you are printing many copies, it may be cheaper and faster (as well as easier on your printer) to print only an original and then photocopy it.

Previewing the Printed Worksheet

Print preview is a handy tool for saving time and paper. Before you actually print, Excel offers the option to display your work on your screen *exactly* as it is to appear on paper. You can open the Print Preview window by clicking ▣ (the Print Preview button) on the toolbar or by clicking Preview in the Print dialog box.

Zooming in and out

As shown in Figure 10-5, Print Preview displays a page showing your data as it appears when printed. Print Preview automatically displays the entire page. You can zoom in on your text by placing your cursor (a magnifying glass) on the section that you want to examine more closely. Then, left-click the mouse or click Zoom on the Print Preview toolbar. To return to the full-page view, simply click again or click Zoom again.

Next page button —

Previous page button —

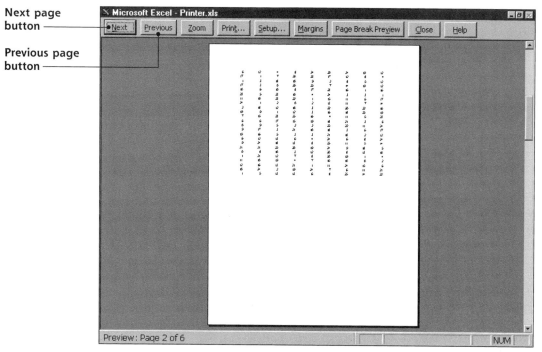

Figure 10-5 The Print Preview screen lets you see your work exactly as it is to be printed.

Moving between pages

While you're in Print Preview, the toolbar at the top of the screen (see Figure 10-5) offers you different views of the document. To scroll down one page, click Next. To scroll up one page, click Previous. You can also scroll up or down by pressing PgUp or PgDn on your keyboard, or by using the arrow keys.

NOTE If your worksheet contains only a single page, the Next and Previous choices are grayed (unavailable).

Previewing your work

This activity gives you a chance to view your work before printing. Although you already know what it looks like when printed (from the previous activities), this gives you a chance to try a few of the options.

To view your work before printing, follow these steps:

1. Click ▣ (the Print Preview button) on the toolbar. Excel displays the Print Preview window. The cursor becomes a magnifying glass, and the first page of the file is displayed. Notice that when you see a full page at a time, the numbers look like they don't line up. When you zoom in, you see that they actually do line up. In the full-page view, some lines, borders, or other objects may not appear, or they may appear broken. You can zoom in to make sure that they are OK.

2. Click the center of the page. The view zooms in so that the detail is clearer. Click again to return to the full-page view.

3. Click Next on the toolbar. Page two of the worksheet is displayed.

4. Click Next twice, and then press PgDn twice to move to the last page of the worksheet. You can move among the worksheet pages by using the keyboard arrow keys or PgUp, PgDn, Home, and End. Or you can click the Next or Previous buttons on the Print Preview toolbar. Notice that the Next button is now grayed.

5. Leave the Print Preview window open.

Changing the page setup

By clicking Setup on the Print Preview toolbar, you open the Page Setup dialog box, which lets you modify the page layout, the margins, the headers and footers, and the sheet settings for your worksheet. Chapter 9 provides complete coverage of the options in the Page Setup dialog box.

Setting your margins

To show column and page margins, click Margins on the Print Preview toolbar. You can adjust a margin or a column by dragging it to the desired location. As you drag a column or margin guide, its current position is displayed in the lower-left corner of the status bar near the bottom of the screen.

 Setting columns and margins from the Print Preview window is *not* the most accurate method. To ensure that you place the margins *exactly* where you want them, set your margins by using the Margins tab in the Page Setup dialog box. By using exact measurements for your margin and column settings, you can ensure consistency from worksheet to worksheet or from workbook to workbook.

Displaying page breaks

To help ensure that your printout looks exactly as expected, Excel for Office 97 offers a new feature called the Page Break Preview. This feature displays your worksheet with the page breaks, showing where each new page begins. You can access the Page Break screen in two ways:

* From normal view, choose View → Page Break Preview . Excel displays the Page Break screen.

* From the Print Preview window, click Page Break Preview on the Print Preview toolbar. This closes the Print Preview window and displays the Page Break screen.

As shown in Figure 10-6, the Page Break Preview now shows exactly where each page ends and the new one begins on the worksheet. The page breaks are shown as broken horizontal and vertical lines across the screen. To return to normal view, choose View → Normal .

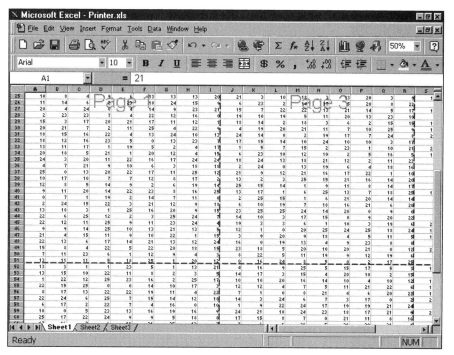

Figure 10-6 The Page Break Preview feature lets you see each page break in your worksheet.

TIP When calculating the page breaks, Excel places the maximum number of rows or columns on a page, which may make the worksheet break in an undesirable location. While in Page Preview, you can move the page breaks by dragging them *up* or *left* to their new location. This allows you to easily control which information stays together on a page. Ordinarily, you can't drag the page break line *down* or *right* to include more rows or columns because they simply don't fit on the page when printed. However, if the pages aren't completely filled with columns or rows, you may be able to drag down or right.

Changing page breaks

In older versions of Excel, setting page breaks could be a painful experience. In this activity, you learn to use the new dragging method of repositioning page breaks. The Print Preview screen is still displayed.

Follow these steps:

1. Click Page Break Preview on the Print Preview toolbar.

2. Click the horizontal broken line indicating the horizontal page break, and drag it up to row 50.

   Notice that the page break indicator becomes a solid line. This indicates that you have manually placed the page break. If you have cells selected, your page break lines normally show in yellow; with no cells selected, they are in blue.

3. Click the vertical broken line at the right edge of column I and drag it one column to the right. In this case, you have enough room on the page to move the page break to the right and include one more column.

4. Scroll up and down, as well as left and right, until you have viewed all of the pages.

5. Choose View → Normal to return to normal page view.

6. Leave the worksheet open for the next activity.

Printing your worksheet

Now that you have previewed your worksheet and reset the page breaks, you are ready to print the worksheet. You should always take the time to preview your document before sending it to the printer. Continually reprinting a document with only minor changes needlessly ties up the printer and wastes both time and resources. Using Print Preview can save you lots of time, paper, and grief from coworkers.

TIP   **Keep an extra toner cartridge, inkjet cartridge, or printer ribbon on hand. Computers seem to be able to sense when you are working on an important project and are under strict time constraints. It is during these times that the cartridge dries up (usually around midnight, just after all the stores have closed).**

Always save your workbook *before* sending it to the printer. Although you seldom experience problems with printing, this also seems to be the most common time for the program to lock up, which means that you lose anything that you haven't saved.

Previewing and printing your changed worksheet

Before sending your work to the printer, preview it to make sure that it looks like what you want.

To preview your work, follow these steps:

1. Save the workbook.

2. Click the Print Preview button on the toolbar. Excel displays the Print Preview window.

3. Browse through the various pages to see where they are to break when printed.

4. Click Print on the Print Preview toolbar. The Print dialog box opens.

5. Click OK. The file is sent to the printer, and you are returned to the normal viewing mode.

6. Leave the workbook open for the next activity.

Selecting the Print Area

In many cases, you do not need to print the entire worksheet. By specifying a *print area*, you tell Excel which parts of your worksheet you want to print. To define a print area, you simply select the area that you want to print and then choose File → Print Area → Set Print Area. After you set the print area, Excel surrounds it with a dashed box, as shown in Figure 10-7.

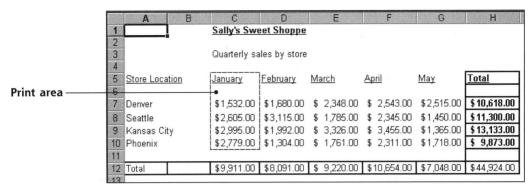

Print area

Figure 10-7 Excel places a dashed line around the selected print area.

Until you clear the print area specifications or set a new print area, Excel prints *only* the data within this print area. To clear the print area setting, choose File → Print Area → Clear Print Area .

Setting and clearing a print area

To set a print area, follow these steps:

1. Select A1 through D7.

2. Choose File → Print Area → Set Print Area . This sets the selected cells as the print area.

3. Click the Print Preview button on the toolbar. Excel displays only the series of cells that you designated to print.

4. Click Print on the Print Preview toolbar. Excel opens the Print dialog box.

5. Make sure that your settings are correct, and then click OK. Excel prints the specified area.

6. Choose File → Print Area → Clear Print Area . This clears the print area setting.

7. Save the changes, and leave the workbook open.

Adding a Set Print Area button to your toolbar

If you often use the Set Print Area command, you may want to add a button to your toolbar that automatically sets the print area for you. Adding a button to the toolbar is fairly simple, and it can save you a lot of time and effort.

Any time that you make changes, preview the document. A small change in the worksheet may create a big change in the way that the document is printed. Be certain that the correct print range is specified. We once sent a 95-page document to the printer because we forgot to make sure that the print range was correct. Unfortunately, our boss sent her two-page document to the printer right after ours, and she had to wait while our 95-page error finished printing. This was *not* a good way to learn the value of Print Preview.

10

To add a button to the toolbar, follow these steps:

1. Choose View → Toolbars → Customize . Excel displays the Customize dialog box.

2. Click the Commands tab. Figure 10-8 shows the Commands tab in the Customize dialog box.

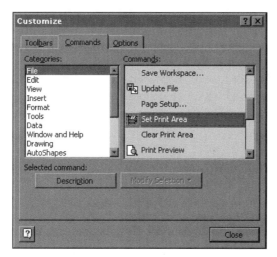

Figure 10-8 The Customize dialog box is used to add commonly used command buttons to your toolbar.

3. In the Categories panel, choose File.

4. In the Commands panel, scroll down until you see Set Print Area.

5. Drag the icon onto your toolbar, between the Underline button and the Left justify button.

NOTE This action increases the width of the toolbar, so some of your buttons may move to the next line.

6. Close the Customize dialog box. The toolbar now includes a Set Print Area button. In the following steps, you remove this button from the toolbar.

7. Choose View → Toolbars → Customize to open the Customize dialog box.

8. Remove the Set Print Area button by dragging the button *off* the toolbar.

9. Close the Customize dialog box.

10. Leave the workbook open for the next activity.

Printing nonconsecutive ranges

By setting the print area as described in the preceding sections, you print one consecutive group of data. But what if you need to print groups of data that are not in consecutive areas? You can define a print area that includes *noncontiguous* (how's that for a fancy term?) ranges of cells by pressing Ctrl while you select the various ranges that you want to print. Excel places a dashed border around each selected range.

 Although Excel includes each of the selected ranges in the print area, they are *not* printed on the same page. Even if you hide columns to make the ranges appear adjacent to one another, Excel prints each range on a separate page.

The following activity shows you how to select a print area in which all the ranges of cells aren't next to each other (in other words, they're noncontiguous).

Follow these steps:

1. Select A1 through D7.

2. Press Ctrl, and select K1 through N7.

3. Continue pressing Ctrl, and select U1 through X7.

4. Release Ctrl.

5. Choose File → Print Area → Set Print Area .

6. Click the Print Preview button on the toolbar. Notice that only the first data series prints on the first page. The other two series print on individual pages, even though they would all fit on a single page.

7. Click Close.

8. Close and save the workbook.

TIP If you want to print your nonadjacent ranges on one page, copy the ranges to a separate worksheet and place them next to one another. Then select all of the ranges as one print area, and print that print area.

Creating One More Worksheet

To complete the next few activities, you need a different worksheet. The last one that you created was made up of just numbers. Here, you use some fictitious data for a candy store.

Follow these steps:

1. Click the New button on the toolbar.

2. Save the file in the Discover Excel folder as Sweets.

3. In B1, type **Sally's Sweet Shoppe** and press Enter.

4. Click B1, and click the Bold button and the Underline button on the toolbar. All the text in the cell is bold and underlined. Don't be concerned that the text runs over into C1.

5. In B3, type **Quarterly Sales by Store** and press Enter.

6. Continuing entering the data as shown in Figure 10-9. AutoFit Column A. Column E and row 12 should contain formulas. Format the values as Currency with two decimal places.

	A	B	C	D	E
1		Sally's Sweet Shoppe			
2					
3		Quarterly Sales by Store			
4					
5	Store Location	January	February	March	Total
6					
7	Denver	$1,532.00	$1,680.00	$2,348.00	$ 5,560.00
8	Seattle	$2,605.00	$3,115.00	$1,785.00	$ 7,505.00
9	Kansas City	$2,995.00	$1,992.00	$3,326.00	$ 8,313.00
10	Phoenix	$2,779.00	$1,304.00	$1,761.00	$ 5,844.00
11					
12	Total	$9,911.00	$8,091.00	$9,220.00	$27,222.00

Figure 10-9 The worksheet values are entered, and the cells are properly formatted.

7. Save the workbook, and leave it open for the next activity.

Creating Custom Views

Excel's View Manager allows you to create and save different views of your worksheet. For example, Figure 10-9 shows Sally's monthly sales by location. If she wants to print only the Phoenix data, she can select row 10 as her print area and print only that data; however, she then loses the title of her worksheet and the column headings. All that prints is row 10. (Remember, if she selected row 1 and row 10, which are noncontiguous areas, they would print on two different pages.)

A better way to print individual ranges within a worksheet is to create different *views* by using the View Manager. A view is a set of print and display settings that you can name and apply to a workbook. You can create multiple views of the same workbook. To create a view, you can hide any data that you do not want displayed and then save the way the screen looks as a *view*. Figure 10-10 shows Sally's data after she hides the unnecessary rows (rows 7 through 12, except row 10). She can then select this view, and Excel prints only the visible data.

	A	B	C	D	E
1		Sally's Sweet Shoppe			
2					
3		Quarterly Sales by Store			
4					
5	Store Location	January	February	March	Total
6					
10	Phoenix	$2,779.00	$1,304.00	$1,761.00	$ 5,844.00

Figure 10-10   By using View Manager, Sally can print Phoenix's data while retaining the column names and the worksheet title.

Hiding your data

To hide parts of your worksheet, follow these steps:

1. Select rows 7 through 9 by clicking and dragging through the appropriate row indicators. Excel highlights rows 7 through 9.

2. Press Ctrl and select the row 11 and row 12 indicators. Rows 11 and 12 are also highlighted.

3. Right-click any of the selected row indicators, and choose Hide from the resulting pop-up menu. Excel hides the highlighted rows.

4. Save the workbook and leave it open for the next activity.

Naming a view

When you are satisfied with the worksheet's appearance, you can give the view a name. This allows you to switch between different views without having to repeatedly hide and unhide data.

To add custom views to your file, follow these steps:

1. Choose **View** → **Custom Views**. As shown in Figure 10-11, Excel opens the Custom Views dialog box. Currently, there are no views.

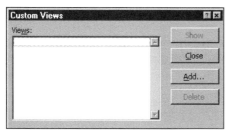

Figure 10-11   Use the Custom Views dialog box for quickly switching between views.

2. Click Add. The Add View dialog box, shown in Figure 10-12, is displayed.

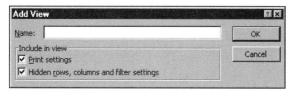

Figure 10-12   The Add View dialog box is used to add a named view to the available custom views.

3. Type **Phoenix Store Report** in the Name text box, and click OK. The worksheet is again displayed.

4. Select rows 5 through 13. Remember, to unhide all of the rows, you must select rows *above and below* the hidden rows.

5. Right-click the selected row indicators, and choose **Unhide**. All the rows are again displayed. In the following steps, you save your workbook (which saves the custom view that you created) and then create a custom view for *all* stores.

6. Click A1, and then save the workbook.

7. Choose View → Custom Views . Excel displays the Custom Views dialog box, which now includes the Phoenix Store Report.

8. Click Add. Excel displays the Add View dialog box.

9. In the Name text box, type **All Stores Report**.

10. Click OK.

TIP **After creating each of the following custom views, instead of selecting and unhiding all the rows to return the worksheet to normal, open the Custom View dialog box, choose All Stores Report, and click Show.**

11. Using the skills that you acquired in the previous activities, create custom views for the other three stores: Denver, Kansas City, and Seattle. Now you can display the data using any of the existing views.

12. Choose View → Custom Views . Excel displays the Custom Views dialog box.

13. Double-click Denver Store Report. The worksheet is again displayed, with only the Denver store data visible. Rather than double-clicking, you could have clicked Denver Store Report and then clicked Show .

14. Display the All Stores custom view.

15. Save the workbook, and leave it open.

BONUS

Creating and Printing Ranges

In addition to printing views and selected print areas, Excel also allows you to select and name a group of data that you often need to print. Once you name this group, you can use Excel's Go To command or select the range from the Name box (the box on the left side of the Formula bar, which normally displays the cell address) to quickly find the group and print it.

For example, if you regularly need to print a store's monthly figures, you may name each month's column so that you could use the Go To command when you want to access a specific column and print it.

This activity demonstrates using the Go To command and printing a named group of data.

Follow these steps:

1. Select B5 through B12.

2. Choose **Insert** → **Name** → **Define**. As shown in Figure 10-13, Excel displays the Define Name dialog box.

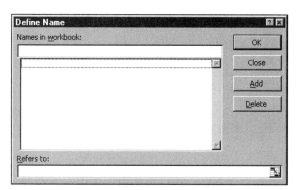

Figure 10-13   The Define Name dialog box is used to assign a name to each data series.

3. Type **January** in the Names in workbook text box, and click OK. Notice that *January* now appears in the Name box in the formula bar.

4. Select C5 through C12.

5. As a shortcut to naming this range, click the Name box (at the left edge of the Formula Bar), type **February**, and then press Enter. *February* now appears in the Name box.

If you don't press Enter after typing the name in the Name box, the range is not named. When you highlight a named range, the range name appears in the Name box.

6. Name the March and Total columns by using the same procedure.

7. Choose **Edit** → **Go To** or press Ctrl+G. Excel opens the Go To dialog box, as shown in Figure 10-14.

TIP   Pressing F5 is another shortcut for opening the Go To dialog box.

8. Select January, and click OK. Excel highlights B5 through B12 on the worksheet. This is the January range.

9. Choose **File** → **Print Area** → **Set Print Area**. A dashed line encloses the print area.

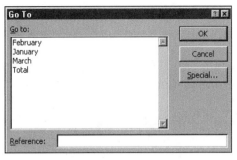

Figure 10-14 The Go To dialog box.

10. Choose File → Print , and click the Selection button. Excel prints the selected area. As demonstrated in the next step, you can also go to named ranges by using the Name box.

11. Click the drop-down arrow at the right edge of the Name box, and choose Total. Excel highlights the Total range. Although this may not seem helpful on a small worksheet, imagine its uses on a large one.

12. Save your work, and close the workbook.

13. Exit Excel.

Summary

Learning to effectively use Excel's print features can save you (and your employer) money by reducing the amount of paper that ends up in the recycling bin as well as the number of ink or toner cartridges that you waste on misprints. Mastering the print options can also decrease the number of print jobs that you have to send to the printer by ensuring that everything is correct *the first time* that you print your data (or at least the second time!).

Creating custom views allows you to quickly change the look of your worksheet to match your needs and allows quick printing of customized views. Naming a cell or group of cells allows you to quickly go to that named range. This also lets you quickly set a new print range.

NUMBERS DO LIE! CHECKING YOUR WORK

IN THIS CHAPTER YOU LEARN THESE KEY SKILLS

M ost of us have become comfortable with the huge role that computers play in our daily routine. Whether you're withdrawing money from the ATM, waiting for the traffic light to change, or simply clicking the remote at the television, you depend on computers to perform many functions that you tend to take for granted. You can easily overlook the fact that every computer in the world was designed and programmed by a human being, and that this opens up the possibility for *incorrect* design or programming. This holds true for spreadsheets just as it does for every other type of computer software.

Unfortunately, human error — whether in the data entry process or in the software design — can wreak havoc with a spreadsheet. The term *Garbage In, Garbage Out* (GIGO) summarizes the idea that if you don't enter the correct data or if you use an incorrect formula, the computer gives you an answer that does not conform to your data (although the computer thinks it is correct!). By checking your work manually, you can greatly reduce the number of errors that occur within your spreadsheet.

TIP Remember that the only thing worse than no data is bad data. Incorrect data can lead people to draw the wrong conclusions, so always check your data.

Checking Your Results

Looking back to high school, we remember our Algebra II teacher always telling the class to check our work. We also remember thinking, "Why should we do it again when we know it's right?" Unfortunately, it was always about that time that she would point out a step that we had missed or an equation that we had gotten wrong.

 Blaming your high school algebra teacher is not a good way to explain to your boss why the data that you provided was incorrect. Bosses don't want excuses or explanations; they only want accurate results — immediately.

Checking the data and the formulas in your spreadsheet is always a good idea. When checking your results, always review the steps that you have taken to create the worksheet and then ask the following questions:

* Could anyone who understands the basics of Excel use my spreadsheet?
* Are all my formulas correct? Do they produce the correct answers?
* Did I enter the data correctly? What steps have I taken to reduce data entry errors?
* Do the charts help viewers understand the data, or do they cause confusion?
* What conclusions can be drawn from the data that the spreadsheet presents? Are they the conclusions that I intended?

SIDE TRIP When we are involved in a project, we sometimes wonder, "If we got hit by a bus on the way home, could someone else understand what we were trying to accomplish and finish the task?" (This is not to suggest that finishing a data analysis project ranks higher on our list of priorities than avoiding large, potentially flattening objects.)

Once you know that the basics of your worksheet are sound, you need to run a couple of tests to ensure that the formulas and the data that you have entered produce the correct results.

The first step in checking your work is to make sure that your formulas are correct. Most errors in formulas result from forgetting the order in which Excel performs the various operations in an equation. When using a formula, Excel first solves those parts of the formula that are enclosed in parentheses. Next Excel calculates exponents, and it then proceeds to multiplication, division, addition, and finally, subtraction.

TIP The phrase *Please Excuse My Dear Aunt Sally* provides an easy way to remember the order of operations. The first letter in each word of the phrase corresponds with the first letter in an operation: parentheses, exponents, multiplication, division, addition, subtraction.

When checking your formulas for the correct order of operations, pay careful attention to the use of parentheses in multiplication and division statements. For example, you may think that the formula =10-3*8 would generate the answer 56 (10 minus 3 is 7, and 7 times 8 is 56). However, this is *not* the answer that Excel produces. Using the order of operation, Excel performs multiplication before it performs subtraction and thus comes up with – 14 (3 times 8 is 24, and 24 subtracted from 10 is – 14). As you can probably imagine, your boss isn't going to be too happy when you submit a report that says you have – 14 products in stock when you actually have 56.

Manually confirming answers

The next way to proof your worksheet is by manually checking the answers that Excel produces. You can do this by checking the answers for several (at least three) separate series of data. By using the data to complete the formulas manually, you can ensure that your worksheet performs the functions correctly.

TIP Excel offers you limited ways to check your work without breaking out the old calculator. For example, if you want to add the contents of a series of cells, you can write a formula (or use Excel's AutoSum feature) and check the work by verifying that AutoCalculate's running total matches the value that Excel produced. You can also use AutoCalculate to check your averages.

To manually verify that your formulas and data are correct, follow these steps:

1. Open Excel and a new workbook.

2. Save the workbook in your Discover Excel folder as Inventory.

3. In A3, type **Store 1**.

4. Drag the AutoFill handle from A3 through A12.

5. Type **Total** in A13.

6. Type **Nuts** in B2.

7. Type **Bolts** in C2.

8. Type **Washers** in D2.

9. Type **Screws** in E2, and then press Enter. To supply some data for this activity, you can fill the empty cells with random numbers.

10. Choose Tools → Add-Ins , make sure that the Analysis Toolpack is selected, and then click OK.

11. Select B3, type **=Randbetween(0,100)**, and press Enter.

12. Drag the AutoFill handle from B3 through E3 and then from E3 through E12. Your worksheet should resemble Figure 11-1.

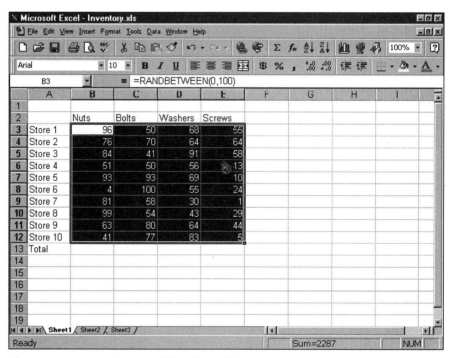

Figure 11-1   Drag the AutoFill handle to fill the empty cells with random numbers.

Because you used the Randbetween function, your numbers do not match the numbers that are shown in Figure 11-1. This does not affect this activity.

13. Choose Edit → Copy , and then choose Edit → Paste Special . Excel displays the Paste Special dialog box.

14. Select Values, and then click OK. Excel pastes the values into the cells, replacing the random number formulas.

15. Press Esc to remove the marquis.

TIP After using the Randbetween command, always remember to paste the values. Otherwise, Excel randomizes the cell values every time you enter new data.

16. Highlight B13, and click the AutoSum button *twice* to generate the total number of nuts in inventory. Excel totals the values in B3 through B12.

17. To check your work, highlight B3 through B12 and verify that the AutoCalculate total matches the sum that AutoSum provides, as shown in Figure 11-2.

Do not AutoCalculate C13 through E13 at this time.

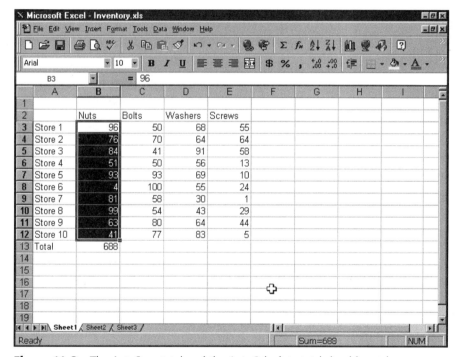

Figure 11-2   The AutoSum total and the AutoCalculate total should match.

CAUTION Make sure that your AutoCalculate is set to sum. If you need to compare averages, make sure that AutoCalculate is set to average.

18. Save your workbook, and leave it open.

Avoiding Potential Problems with Insert and Delete

Inserting data into a cell or deleting data from a cell can have an adverse effect on the rest of your worksheet. Before inserting or deleting data, you must make sure that you don't need the data that the cell currently contains. Inserting new data into a cell removes any existing data from the cell and deleting data . . . well, deletes it (as if we had to explain that).

When you insert or delete rows and columns, remember to check your *entire* worksheet to make sure that you aren't deleting important data. You may place formulas and links to other workbooks on the far right side of the worksheet because they are not part of your main data. However, you lose these important components if you delete the row or column that contains them.

Excel for Microsoft Office 97 allows you to undo *multiple* actions. If you delete data from a cell, you can *undelete* it by clicking the Undo button on the toolbar. Excel can now undo as many as the last 16 procedures that you have completed.

Understanding the Auditing toolbar

The Auditing toolbar, shown in Figure 11-3, helps you determine whether deleting a cell may have negative effects on your worksheet. For example, assume that you want to delete a cell in your worksheet but you aren't sure how its deletion is going to affect the rest of the worksheet. By using the Auditing toolbar, you can find any other cells that depend on that cell for information (called *dependents*) as well as which cells give information to the cell that you plan to delete (called *precedents*).

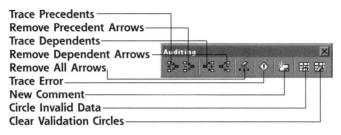

Trace Precedents
Remove Precedent Arrows
Trace Dependents
Remove Dependent Arrows
Remove All Arrows
Trace Error
New Comment
Circle Invalid Data
Clear Validation Circles

Figure 11-3 The Auditing toolbar can help you determine whether the deletion of a cell affects the rest of your worksheet.

Understanding precedents

Precedents are those cells that supply data to another cell. In Figure 11-4, for example, B13 contains a formula that totals the sum of the values in B3 through B12. Consequently, each cell in B3 through B12 is a precedent, because it provides a value that the dependent cell (B13) needs.

Precedent cells
Dependent cell

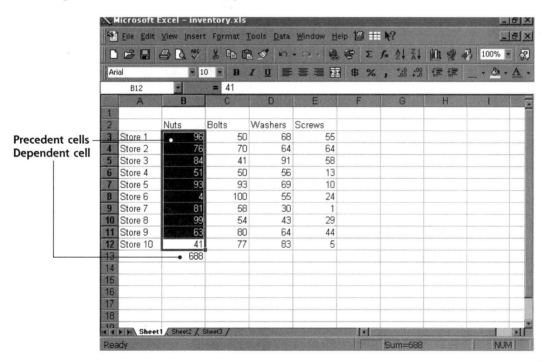

Figure 11-4 The cells to be totaled are called *precedents;* they supply information to the *dependent* cell (the sum).

Understanding dependents

Dependent cells are those cells that collect the data from the precedent cells. In the preceding example, the cell that holds the sum (B13) is the dependent cell, because it depends on the precedent cells to provide the information that it needs for calculating and displaying the total of the cells.

Using the Auditing toolbar

This activity shows how to use the Auditing toolbar to determine whether a cell is a *precedent* or a *dependent* to other cells.

Follow these steps:

1. Use the AutoSum feature to total columns C, D, and E, as shown in Figure 11-5.

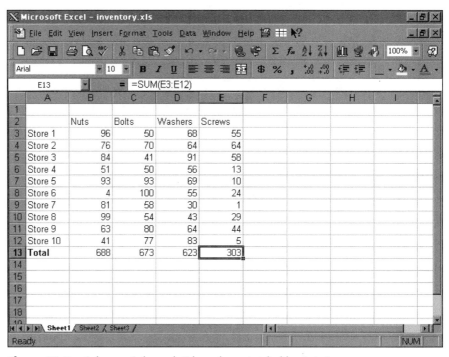

Figure 11-5 Columns C through E have been totaled by AutoSum.

 N O T E Remember that the values in your worksheet probably do not match those reflected in the figures because you used the Randbetween function to create random numbers.

2. In A17, type **Total Number of Units**.

3. Select D17, and click (the Paste Function button) on the standard toolbar. Excel displays the Paste Function dialog box.

4. In the Function name panel, choose Sum and click OK. Excel displays the Sum dialog box.

5. In the Number 1 box, click the Collapse button. Excel temporarily collapses the dialog box so that you can select the cells that you want to sum.

6. Select B13 through E13. Excel places a marquis around the selected range.

7. Click the Collapse button again to expand the Sum dialog box to full size, and then click OK.

8. Click OK to close the Sum dialog box. Excel places the total of cells B13 through E13 in cell D17.

TIP **You can verify that the total is correct by selecting B13 through E13 and comparing the AutoCalculate results to the sum in D17.**

9. Open the Auditing toolbar by choosing `Tools` → `Auditing` → `Show Auditing Toolbar`.

10. Select D17, and click ⊞ (the Trace Precedents button) on the Auditing toolbar.

    Excel places a blue border around B13 through E13 and an arrow from B13 to D17. This means that the sum of B13 through E13 (the precedents) is reflected in D17 (the dependent). With this information, you can see that deleting any or all of the cells in B13 through E13 would change the total that is reflected in D17.

NOTE **You can also find out which cells are dependent on B13 through E13 by selecting that range and then clicking the Trace Dependents button. Any blue trace lines remain on the screen until you save the worksheet; they then vanish.**

11. Close the Auditing toolbar.

12. Save your workbook, but leave it open for the next activity.

Beware of the Three Spreadsheet Assumptions!

People often make three assumptions about worksheets:

* Data entry was complete and correct.
* The spreadsheet designer checked for flaws.
* The report must be accurate.

Assumptions are dangerous things. Whenever I make an assumption, I'm usually wrong, and someone usually points out my error. I hate that! Think of the three spreadsheet assumptions like the seven deadly sins — avoid them like the plague (or the plaque, if you're really into dental hygiene).

Making any of the three assumptions can result in faulty data. All three combined can create a chain reaction. The last reaction in this chain may be the loss of your job!

 TIP **Taking precautions to avoid these three assumptions can be time consuming but well worth the effort. The guidelines in this section can help you develop a routine for checking your data and thus avoid falling prey to the consequences of these assumptions.**

Ensuring complete, correct data entry

When creating and maintaining a spreadsheet, you usually work with large amounts of raw data. To ensure that your data entry is complete, you need to manage the data both before and after you input it.

Prior to the data entry process, you should inventory your data. Document how much raw data you have as well as its source and the role that it plays in your worksheet. You can use this inventory when you check your spreadsheet for errors. Many spreadsheets require huge amounts of data, and the loss of even a small part of that data could be detrimental to the accuracy of the worksheet and any related reports.

Once you begin entering data, have *at least* one other person check to ensure that the data entry is correct. No matter how proficient you are at whatever data entry method you use, always remember that you are human and you could make a mistake. The more eyes that check the data, the less chance of missing an error.

Once the data is entered, you should inventory it again. If the two inventories match, you can be sure that the necessary data is now entered in your worksheet.

Taking time to inventory your data can save you a great deal of time and anxiety. The first time that we lost a major piece of data, we spent two days searching our desk, drawers, and every file folder in our cabinet, only to find that the data that we thought we needed wasn't even relevant to our project. If we had inventoried the data, we would have know that this piece of data was unrelated and didn't need to be entered.

Guarding against flaws in the spreadsheet's design

When you work with a spreadsheet that someone else designed, you should be alert for potential errors. In addition to checking your own work, you must ensure that the designer entered everything correctly.

The best way to do this is by checking your results. If the spreadsheet's author forgot to add parentheses to a formula, the answer that Excel produces differs from the answer that your calculator yields.

If you find errors in the worksheet, inform the author (in the most polite way possible) so that the errors can be corrected for future users.

If you gloat about all the bugs in someone else's spreadsheet, you will soon find yourself creating all your own spreadsheets (and being subjected to much gloating when others detect your errors).

Ensuring the accuracy of your reports

Even if your data is entered correctly and the formulas produce the correct results, your reports *still* may be wrong. Many factors go into the creation of your report, including the view of the worksheet, the headers and footers, and the page layout. Errors in any of these elements could adversely affect the presentation of your data.

For example, assume that you printed an inventory for your South store, but you forgot to change the header, which says *North store.* Anyone comparing the two sheets would wonder which is the true data for the North store and ask what you did with the data for the South store. An IRS auditor may wonder why you have two sets of books with different figures for the North store.

TIP   Once again, the most effective way to avoid inaccurate reports is to have someone else check your work. Check for errors in areas such as spelling, formatting, and page layout. By having someone else review your report, you can feel more assured that your data isn't misinterpreted.

Sampling Your Data

Although you should thoroughly check your data, you don't always have time to check every equation and every data series. The best way to approach this problem is by *sampling* your data. By taking multiple samples of data and checking each sample for errors, you get a good idea of whether your worksheet contains errors.

Sampling does *not* guarantee that all your data is correct. The purpose of sampling is to get a general idea as to the integrity of your worksheet. If possible, it is still best to check *all* your data for errors.

The first step in sampling is to check your worksheet for data entry errors. Because most problems in worksheets result from data entry mistakes, you should sample as many data series as possible, even though this is the most time-consuming task in checking your worksheet.

TIP You can sample data by checking every other row or column for data entry errors.

The next step in testing your data is to confirm that the selected formulas return the desired results. If your sample formulas are incorrect, you should check *every* formula in the worksheet for errors.

After you have confirmed that your sample data and formulas are correct, you need to examine the elements of your report. Use Print Preview to examine the headers and footers, the page layout, and the formatting of your worksheet. If your data, formulas, and report elements are correct, you are ready to print your worksheet.

BONUS

Using Data Validation

To make sure that data is entered correctly into your worksheet, you can use Excel's data validation feature. Choose **Data** → **Validation** to open the Data Validation dialog box that is shown in Figure 11-6. Use this dialog box to limit the type of data that can be entered into a cell. For example, if you know that all of the cells in a column should contain only whole numbers (that is, no decimals), you can choose Whole number in the Allow box, and Excel limits the cells in the selected column to whole numbers.

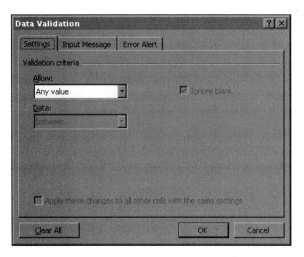

Figure 11-6 Use the Data Validation dialog box to specify the type of data that can be entered into a cell.

When limiting cells to numeric values, you can also specify the range of numbers that can be entered. For example, if you know that all your data falls between 0 and 50, you can limit the cells so that any number greater than 50 is considered to be invalid data.

 If you choose a column and limit the entire column to numeric values, Excel sees any column headings as invalid data because they are text data. If your worksheet has column headings, select the *cells* that you want to limit, not the entire column.

Once you limit a cell to a certain data type, set up a box that warns the user that the cell is limited to a certain data type. Click the Input Message tab in the Data Validation dialog box, and enter a message that Excel can display whenever you select the cells. For example, Figure 11-7 shows a data validation message that we created for the highlighted cell.

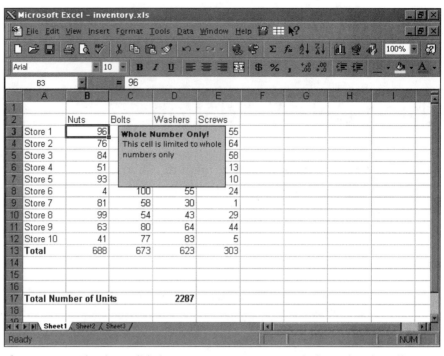

Figure 11-7 The data validation message pops up to remind you that the cell can contain only a certain type of data.

After you specify the type of data that a cell can contain and warn the user of that limitation, you need to tell Excel what to do when someone enters invalid data into the cell. As shown in Figure 11-8, the Error Alert tab in the Data Validation dialog box allows you to choose which type of alert you want Excel to display.

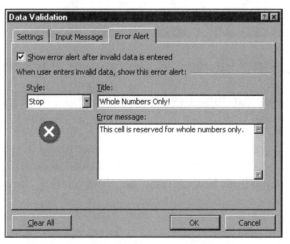

Figure 11-8 Use the Error Alert tab to specify what happens when someone enters incorrect data into a cell.

In the Style drop-down box, Excel offers you three choices of actions: Stop, Warning, and Information:

✷ **Stop** tells Excel that you do not want the user to continue entering the data if it is the incorrect type. As shown in Figure 11-9, if you choose Stop and someone enters an incorrect data type, Excel opens an error box telling the user that the data is incorrect and allowing the user to choose Retry or Cancel.

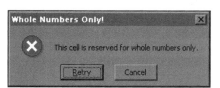

Figure 11-9 The Stop box prevents the user from continuing to input an incorrect data type.

✷ **Warning** tells Excel to display a warning box when a user enters incorrect data, as shown in Figure 11-10. However, this warning box offers the user the option to continue entering the data into the cell even though the data does not match the data type that is specified for the cell.

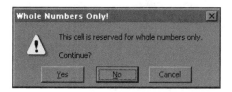

Figure 11-10 The Warning box warns users that the data type is incorrect but allows them to continue if they want.

✷ **Information** causes an information box to open when the user enters an incorrect data type. As shown in Figure 11-11, the Information box tells users that the data is incorrect but allows them to continue if they want.

Figure 11-11 The Information box tells users that their data is the wrong type but allows them to continue.

The Title and Error Message boxes allow you to customize the message that Excel displays when the user enters incorrect data.

Setting up cells with data validation helps to ensure that data is not entered into your worksheet incorrectly. By specifying the types of data that can be entered (as well as their value limitations), you can make Excel your *data watchdog* instead of having to monitor all entries yourself.

TIP If you have Office 97's Office Assistant running, the Assistant informs you when you enter an incorrect data type.

To limit the data that can be entered into a cell, follow these steps:

1. Select B3 through E13 in the inventory worksheet.

2. Choose **Data** → **Validation** . Excel displays the Data Validation dialog box.

3. Click the Settings tab.

4. Click the drop-down arrow in the Allow box to see a list of data types.

5. Choose Whole number, as shown in Figure 11-12.

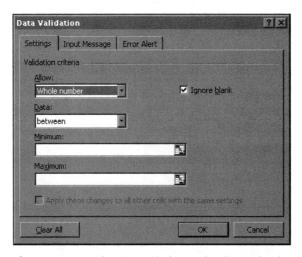

Figure 11-12 Choosing Whole number limits the data entry type to whole numbers only.

6. In the Data drop-down list, choose between.

7. Type **1** in the Minimum box.

8. Type **1000** in the Maximum box.

9. Click the Input Message tab.

10. In the Title box, type **Whole Numbers Only**.

11. In the Input Message box, type **This cell is limited to whole numbers only**.

12. Click the Error Alert tab.

13. In the Style drop-down box, choose Stop.

14. In the Title box, type **Whole Numbers Only**.

15. In the Error Message box, type **This cell is restricted to whole numbers only.**

16. Click OK.

17. Select B3. As shown in Figure 11-13, the input message warns you that the cell is restricted.

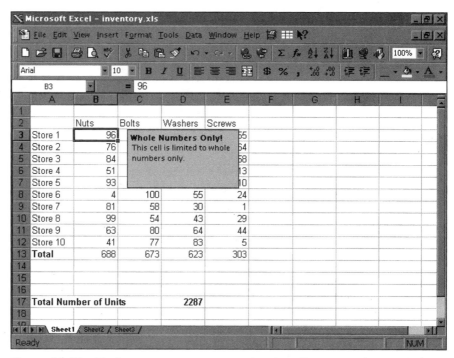

Figure 11-13   The input message warns you that the cell must contain a particular data type.

18. Type **Hi** in B3, and press Enter. Excel opens a Stop box telling you that this cell is limited to whole numbers only.

19. Click Retry.

20. Type **50** and press Enter. Excel accepts the entry, because 50 is a whole number and therefore fits the data entry style.

21. Save and close the workbook.

22. Exit Excel.

Summary

nfortunately, errors occur in almost every worksheet. However, the tactics that we describe in this chapter can greatly reduce the time that you spend tracking down errors and increase the accuracy of your worksheet. Remember that the time you spend preventing errors can save you the frustration and anxiety of having to figure out why your worksheet isn't functioning properly. In addition, error prevention and double-checking your results can save you the embarrassment of turning in an inaccurate report.

MULTIPLICITY: WORKING WITH MORE THAN ONE WORKSHEET

IN THIS CHAPTER YOU LEARN THESE KEY SKILLS

I n many ways, managing your data with Excel is much like coaching a sport. Some sports, such as running or cycling, require the effort of only one participant. Others, such as football or soccer, require the combined efforts of a team.

Various Excel projects also differ in the number of participants needed. In many cases, a project needs only one worksheet or one workbook to store the data. In other cases, a project requires multiple worksheets and workbooks to produce the desired result.

Think of yourself as the coach of your spreadsheet team. You must decide how many worksheets and workbooks your project needs. Then you need to tell the members of your team — the individual worksheets or workbooks — what to do and how to work together.

NOTE Buying a coach's whistle and blowing it while working on your worksheets will noticeably decrease your popularity with your coworkers.

Evaluating User Needs

Before you dive in and start entering your data, take the time to analyze the resources that the project requires. Then take a look at what you have. If you are using a workbook created by someone else, enter some test data to make sure the workbook suits your needs. Making modifications to the workbook *before* entering your data saves you time and confusion in the long run.

If you are developing your own workbook, consider the following questions:

* How many users need access to the data?
* How much data do you need to process?
* Can you fit all of the data on one worksheet?
* Should you segment the data into separate worksheets or even into separate workbooks?
* Do you need multiple worksheets or workbooks?
* If you need multiple workbooks, how will the multiple workbooks interact with one another?

By asking these questions *before* you enter data, you can avoid many future problems.

SIDE TRIP

Before you get too far into a project, find out whether anyone else has completed a similar project. For one of my first Excel projects, I had to create an inventory of the computers in our department. I spent almost two days collecting serial numbers from the equipment and entering this data into my worksheet. Once I was finished, I proudly showed my results to a coworker, who asked why I hadn't gotten the information from the Asset Control department, which maintained an up-to-date inventory of all equipment.

How many people will use the workbook?

Try to determine how many people will use your workbook. It also helps to have an understanding of their Excel skill levels. If you are the only person using your workbook, you don't need to consider issues such as password protection and shared lists. However, if more than one person will use your workbook, you must decide who needs access to specific data. You also need to ensure that data is not accidentally overwritten. By knowing who will modify or view your project, you can design a workbook or a series of workbooks that minimizes the risk of lost data and maximizes your productivity.

How many workbooks do I need?

Even if you are the only person working on a project, you may need to organize your data into more than one workbook. Segmenting the data into separate workbooks can provide a more organized method of accounting. In other cases, however, putting data into separate workbooks merely creates an organization nightmare.

Assume that you are the owner of a business with four stores. If each store maintains the same inventory as the others, dividing the stores into a separate workbooks might require reentering duplicate data for each store. You can solve this problem by creating one workbook with multiple worksheets. This enables you to easily cut and paste the duplicate data without having to worry about maintaining the accuracy of four different workbooks.

However, if each store maintains a different inventory, creating a separate workbook for each store might be the better choice. Keeping each store's data separate from the others may help you analyze the individual stores' strengths and weaknesses. You can also create a summary worksheet that contains the important information from each workbook and enables you to see the role each store plays within the company.

How do the workbooks interact with one another?

If you need multiple workbooks to better organize your data, you have to evaluate how each workbook should interact with the others and define the role each workbook should play in your overall project. For example, as the owner of the four stores, you need a summary worksheet that combines the incomes from the four stores to show total income for the business. Rather than manually enter each total, you can create *links* to the other workbooks and thus automatically update any changes in the specified cells. Using tools such as links can save you time and reduce the number of potential errors by eliminating the need for reentering data when changes occur.

Inserting and Deleting Worksheets

You can customize your workbooks by inserting and deleting worksheets. When you create a new workbook in Excel, the new workbook automatically includes three worksheets. If you find that you need only one worksheet, you can delete the other two; if you need more, you can insert the necessary number of worksheets.

Inserting worksheets

Inserting worksheets into a workbook is similar to inserting columns in a worksheet. When you insert a worksheet into a workbook, Excel places the new worksheet *before* the one you have selected.

To insert a worksheet into your workbook, follow these steps:.

1. Open Excel and a new worksheet.

2. In your Discover Excel folder, save the worksheet as **Stores.** In the following steps, you rename Sheet1.

3. Right-click the Sheet1 tab and choose Rename from the resulting pop-up menu, shown in Figure 12-1. Excel highlights the name tab.

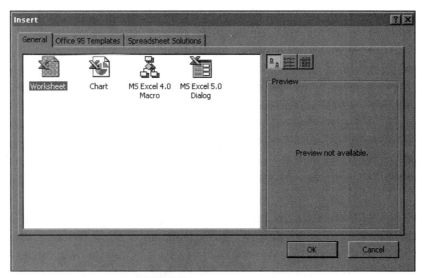

Figure 12-1   Choosing Rename on the pop-up menu enables you to change the name of your worksheet.

4. Type **Store 1** and press Enter.

5. In the same manner, rename Sheet2 as **Store 2** and Sheet3 as **Store 3**.

TIP You can also rename a worksheet by double-clicking its tab and then typing the new name.

6. Select the Store 3 tab and choose **Insert** → **Worksheet**. Excel inserts a new worksheet called Sheet1 *before* the Store 3 tab that you selected.

7. Rename this new worksheet **Store 4.**

8. Insert another worksheet before Store 3. Excel names this worksheet Sheet 2.

9. Rename Sheet 2 as **Summary Sheet.** You now have five worksheets, as shown in Figure 12-2. They are currently out of order.

10. Save your workbook and leave it open for the next activity.

TIP You can also insert a worksheet by right-clicking a worksheet tab and choosing **Insert** from the pop-up menu. Excel opens the Insert dialog box, which lets you choose the type of sheet to insert. Excel then inserts the new worksheet *before* the worksheet you selected.

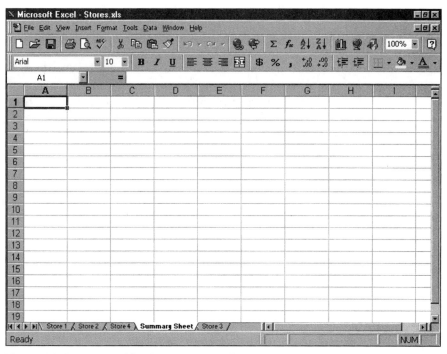

Figure 12-2 Your workbook now contains five worksheets.

Deleting worksheets

Deleting worksheets works similarly to deleting columns within a worksheet. Select the worksheet you want to delete and choose [**Delete**] from the pop-up menu to remove the worksheet.

Deleting a worksheet from your workbook is *permanent*. All data and formulas in the worksheet are deleted. Any cells in other worksheets or workbooks that depend on the deleted data now reflect incorrect information.

You *cannot* use the Undo command to recover a deleted worksheet. The only way you can recover a deleted worksheet is to close the file *without saving* and then reopen the workbook. You lose any data you have entered since you last saved the workbook.

To delete a worksheet from your workbook, follow these steps:

1. In the Stores.xls workbook, click the Store 3 tab.

2. Right-click the Store 3 tab and choose [**Delete**] from the pop-up menu. Excel displays a warning box to tell you that this worksheet and all its data will be deleted.

3. Click OK. Excel deletes the Store 3 worksheet.

4. Click the Store 4 tab and choose | Insert | → | Worksheet |. Excel inserts a new worksheet called Sheet3.

5. Rename Sheet 3 as **Store 3.** The worksheets are not in the correct order. You reorganize the worksheets in the next activity.

6. Save your workbook and leave it open.

Moving and Copying Worksheets

Moving and copying worksheets within your workbook gives you the flexibility to modify your workbooks as your project evolves. As with the Insert and Delete commands, moving and copying within a workbook works similarly to the way you move or copy data within your worksheet.

Moving a worksheet

Move a worksheet within the same workbook by simply dragging the worksheet's name tab to the desired destination and dropping it.

To move a worksheet within your workbook, follow these steps:

1. In the Stores.xls workbook, click and hold the Summary Sheet tab.

TIP As you hold the left mouse button, a blank page appears above your cursor to let you know that you are moving the entire sheet. A black pointer (an upside down triangle) appears in the upper left corner of the selected worksheet tab. This pointer lets you know where the worksheet will be placed when you let release the mouse button.

2. Drag the black pointer to the left of the Store 1 tab.

3. Release the mouse button. Excel places the Summary Sheet before the Store 1 worksheet.

4. Save your workbook and leave it open.

TIP You can also move a worksheet by right-clicking the tab of the worksheet and choosing | Move or Copy | from the resulting pop-up menu. In the Move or Copy dialog box, select the destination for the worksheet and then click OK.

Copying a worksheet

Like copying data from one cell to another, Excel can make an *exact* duplicate of your worksheet that you can then paste to another location. Copying the worksheet enables you to avoid the hassle of reentering and reformatting identical worksheets. For example, you might be able to use the same basic worksheets for the four stores in the previous example, even though they might have different data.

To copy a worksheet from one location to another, follow these steps:

1. Right-click the Summary Sheet tab in the Stores.xls workbook.

2. In the resulting pop-up menu, choose Move or Copy . Excel displays the Move or Copy dialog box.

3. Choose the Stores.xls workbook as your destination, and choose (move to end) in the Before sheet box.

4. As shown in Figure 12-3, make sure that the Create a Copy box is checked, and then click OK. Excel places an exact copy of the Summary Sheet at the end of the workbook. Your workbook now contains two Summary Sheets.

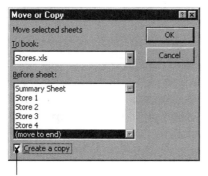

The Create a copy box.

Figure 12-4 The Create a copy box must be checked or the worksheet will be moved (not copied) to the selected destination.

> **TIP** When Excel makes a copy of a worksheet, the new worksheet has the same name as the original. To distinguish between the original and the copy, Excel places (2) after the first copy, (3) after the second copy, and so on.

5. Delete the original Summary Sheet (the first worksheet) from your workbook. You may have to click the Previous Sheet button (located to the left of the worksheet tabs) to see it.

6. Rename Summary Sheet(2) as **Stores Summary** and press Enter.

7. Save your workbook and leave it open.

Creating a Summary Sheet

As the owner of four furniture stores, you have created a worksheet for each store showing sales, expenses, and profits. However, you are also interested in monitoring the performance of your entire business. A Summary Sheet compiles all the data from your separate worksheets and displays it in one comprehensive worksheet.

To use a Summary Sheet, you must utilize the skills discussed in this chapter to create the worksheet, move it to the desired location within the workbook (usually first or last), and then tell it how to communicate with the other worksheets within the workbook.

To create a Summary Sheet within your workbook, follow these steps:

1. The Stores Summary worksheet should still be active.

2. Type **Sales** in B2 and press Tab.

3. Type **Expenses** in C2 and press Tab.

4. Type **Profit** in D2 and press Enter.

5. Type **Store 1** in A3 and press Enter.

6. AutoFill A3:A6.

7. Type **Total** in A8 and press Enter. Your worksheet should look like Figure 12-4.

8. Save your workbook and leave it open.

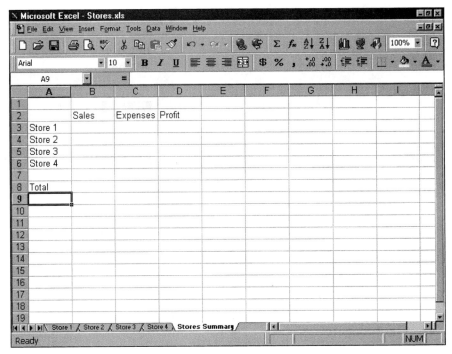

Figure 12-4 The completed worksheet

Working with Grouped Worksheets

Grouping worksheets is another way to save time and avoid the hassle of reentering the same data numerous times. When you group worksheets, you tell Excel that the data you enter into one of the worksheets should also be entered into the rest of the sheets in the group. To group worksheets, select the worksheets you want to group, and then enter the data.

Grouping contiguous worksheets

You can group worksheets that are next to one another (*contiguous* worksheets). To group contiguous worksheets, click the first worksheet's name tab, press Shift, and click the worksheet name tab for the last worksheet to be included in the group.

To create a group of contiguous worksheets within your workbook, follow these steps:

1. In the Stores.xls workbook, select the Store 1 tab.

2. Press Shift while you click the Store 4 tab.

The previous steps tell Excel that you want to group all worksheets from Store 1 to Store 4. As shown in Figure 12-5, the tabs for Stores 1 through 4 are now white, indicating that they are grouped. Notice that a Group message is now displayed in the Title bar.

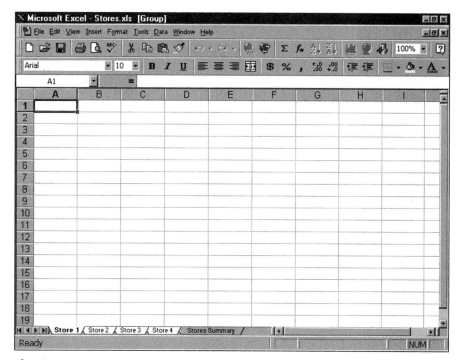

Figure 12-5   Grouped worksheet tabs change to white.

3. In B2, type **January** and press Enter.

4. AutoFill B2:G2.

5. In A4, type **Sales** and press Enter.

6. In A5, type **Expenses** and press Enter.

7. In A6, type **Profit** and press Enter.

8. In H2, type **Total** and press Enter.

9. Click the Store 3 tab. Store 3 now has the same data as Stores 1, 2, and 4.

10. Click the Stores Summary worksheet tab.

Because the Stores Summary worksheet is not part of the group, Excel did not enter data into this worksheet.

11. Save your file.

Grouping noncontiguous worksheets

You can also group worksheets that are not next to one another (*noncontiguous worksheets*). To group noncontiguous worksheets, click the first worksheet's name tab, and then press and hold Ctrl while you click each additional worksheet name tab that you want to include in the group.

To create a group consisting of noncontiguous worksheets within your workbook, follow these steps:

1. Click the Store 1 tab in the Stores.xls workbook.

2. Press Ctrl while you click the Store 4 tab.

   The previous steps tell Excel that you want to group only Stores 1 and 4. The tabs for Stores 1 and 4 are now white, signifying that they are grouped.

3. In B4, type **300** and press Enter.

4. AutoFill B4:G4.

5. In B5, type **100** and press Enter.

6. AutoFill B5:G5.

7. Select B6:G6.

8. Type **=B4-B5** and press Ctrl+Enter. Pressing Ctrl + Enter inserts the subtraction formula into each highlighted cell.

9. Select H4:H6 and click the AutoSum button on the toolbar. Because the cells are selected, clicking the AutoSum button *once* fills all the selected cells with the correct formula.

10. Click outside the selected area to deselect it.

11. Click the Store 2 tab. Notice that no data was entered into this worksheet. This is because the Store 2 worksheet was not included in the group.

12. Click the Store 4 tab. As you can see, this worksheet has the same new data as Store 1.

13. Save your workbook and leave it open.

Sharing Data Among Multiple Worksheets

O nce you create separate worksheets within your workbook, you need to understand how these worksheets can communicate with each other. Without using Excel's communication tools, your file is merely a collection of data in *separate* worksheets. However, when you tell your worksheets how to communicate effectively, you create a workbook in which the worksheets work together like a team.

Linking worksheets

One of the most important communication tools in Excel is linking. You link worksheets when you want one worksheet (for example, your Summary Sheet) to reflect the exact information contained within another worksheet (such as one of your stores).

To link worksheets, follow these steps:

1. In the Stores.xls workbook, select the Stores Summary tab.

2. In B3, type =**'Store 1'!H4**. Don't forget the single apostrophe before and after the worksheet name. This tells your Stores Summary worksheet that you want the current cell to reflect the data in H4 of the Store 1 worksheet.

3. Press Enter. The value of H4 on the Store 1 worksheet is entered into B3 of the Stores Summary worksheet.

 TIP In the preceding link formula, 'Store 1' identifies the worksheet that contains the data, the ! indicates the end of the worksheet name, and H4 tells Excel which cell contains the data.

4. In C3, type =**'Store 1'!H5** and press Enter. In the next step, you learn a new way to link worksheet cells.

5. In D3, type =. Then choose the Store 1 worksheet, click H6, and press Enter. The current cell — D3 on the Stores Summary worksheet — now contains a link to H6 on the Store 1 worksheet. In the following steps, you see how these links work:

6. Select the Store 1 worksheet.

7. In D4, type **0** and press Enter. Notice that your profit in D6 changes and the totals in H4 and H6 also reflect the change.

8. Select the Stores Summary worksheet. Notice that your totals here have also changed. Because your Stores Summary worksheet is now linked to Store 1, any changes you make in the Store 1 worksheet are reflected in the Stores Summary worksheet. This saves you reentering data and reduces the likelihood of incorrectly entered data.

9. Save your workbook and leave it open.

Creating multiple worksheet formulas

You can include links to worksheets in a formula and thus create a powerful linking tool. For example, suppose you want your Summary Sheet to reflect totals of cells from numerous worksheets. Using links, you can write a formula to total the cells of multiple worksheets.

Your Stores workbook should calculate the combined totals from all the stores. You can accomplish this by creating a formula that adds each store's total and displays the total in the Stores Summary worksheet.

NOTE You can also compile the totals from your worksheets by linking each cell (as you did in the preceding section) and then using the AutoSum feature to total the cells.

To create a formula that totals cells from multiple worksheets follow these steps:

1. Select the Stores Summary tab in the Stores.xls workbook.

2. Select D8.

3. Enter the following formula: ='Store 1'!H4+'Store 2'!H4+'Store 3'!H4+'Store 4'!H4. This formula tells Excel to total the values in H4 on each of the Store worksheets.

4. Press Enter.

5. Save your workbook and close it.

TIP You can also create this formula by typing =, selecting cell H4 in the Store 1 worksheet; typing +, selecting cell H4 in the Store 2 worksheet; typing +; and so on, until your formula is complete. When the formula is complete, press Enter. This is a much easier method to use when you are creating complex formulas.

TIP Multiworksheet formulas are just like normal formulas in that they can perform addition, subtraction, multiplication, and division, as well as numerous other complex mathematical functions.

Saving Your Workspace as a File

I f you often work with more that one workbook at a time, you should create a *custom workspace.* A workspace is a group of workbooks that open at the same time. For example, if you work with your sales reports, your financial records, and your employee records at the same time, you can add them to a workspace. You can arrange the workbooks in the desired display, and Excel opens them together each time you open the workspace. This saves you from opening each workbook separately.

 TIP   **Excel saves workspaces with the .XLW extension.**

To create a custom workspace, follow these steps:

1. Create a new workbook and save it in the Discover Excel folder as **Employees.**

2. Type **Number of Sales** in B1 and press Enter.

3. Type **Couches** in B4 and press Tab.

4. Type **Chairs** in C4 and press Tab.

5. Type **Tables** in D4 and press Enter.

6. Type **Jim** in A5 and press Enter.

7. Type **Sally** in A6 and press Enter.

8. Save your workbook.

9. Open the Stores.xls workbook.

10. Choose `Window` → `Arrange`. As shown in Figure 12-6, Excel displays the Arrange Windows dialog box, offering the following four options:

    * **Tiled:** Arrange the workbooks in a grid-like pattern.
    * **Horizontal:** Arrange the workbooks horizontally.
    * **Vertical:** Arrange the workbooks side by side.
    * **Cascade:** Arrange the workbooks in a cascading pattern, with each workbook below and to the right of the preceding one.

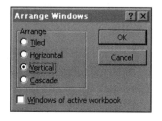

Figure 12-6   Use the Arrange Windows dialog box to change the way Excel displays your open workbooks.

11. Choose Vertical and click OK. Excel now displays your two workbooks side by side, as shown in Figure 12-7.

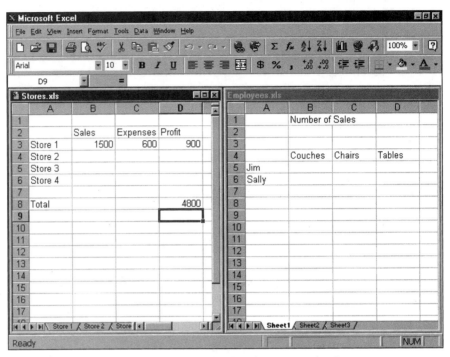

Figure 12-7 Your workbooks are now displayed next to each other.

12. Choose File → Save Workspace . As shown in Figure 12-8, Excel displays the Save Workspace dialog box.

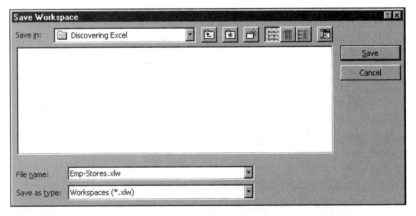

Figure 12-8 Use the Save Workspace dialog box to save multiple workbooks as a workspace.

13. Enter **Emp-Stores.xlw** in the File name box, and then click Save.

14. Close the Employees workbook and the Stores workbook.

15. Choose `File` → `Open`. Excel displays the Open dialog box.

16. Choose Emp-Stores.xlw and click Open. Excel opens both the Employees.xls workbook and the Stores.xls workbook. The workbooks are arranged vertically, as they were when you last closed the workspace. Leave the workbooks open for the next activity.

 TIP You can store many workbooks within a single workspace file.

BONUS

Linking Workbooks

Now that you know how to link worksheets within your workbook, you can apply the same principles to linking workbooks. You won't always find it practical to store all the data you need in one workbook. However, you may still need to reference data, even though you store it in another workbook. Creating a link between workbooks is similar to creating links between worksheets, except you must complete an additional step.

To link workbooks, follow these steps:

1. Make sure that Emp-Stores.xlw is open.

2. Select B5 in the Employees workbook.

3. Type **20** and press Tab.

4. In C5, type **10** and press Tab.

5. In D5, type **13** and press Enter.

6. In B6, type **19** and press Tab.

7. In C6, type **26** and press Tab.

8. In D6, type **6** and press Enter.

9. In A7, type **Total** and press Enter.

10. Highlight B7:D7, click the AutoSum button on the toolbar, and press Enter.

11. Click in any other cell to deselect B7:D7.

12. Create a new Excel workbook and save it as **Business Summary.xls**.

13. In C2, type **This Year** and press Tab.

14. In D2, type **Next Year** and press Enter.

15. In A3, type **Total Profits** and press Enter.

16. In A4, type **Couches Sold** and press Enter.

17. In A5, type **Chairs Sold** and press Enter.

18. In A6, type **Tables Sold** and press Enter.

19. AutoFit Column A.

20. In C3, type =, choose `Window` → `Stores.xls`, highlight D8 in the Stores.xls workbook, and then press Enter. Notice that C3 in the Business Summary workbook now reflects the same data as D8 in the Stores workbook.

21. Click C3. This cell contains the following formula: ='[Stores.xls]Stores Summary'!$D$8. This reference to a cell in another workbook begins with a single quotation mark followed by the workbook name enclosed in brackets. The worksheet name follows the closing bracket, and the reference concludes with a single quotation mark, an exclamation point, and the absolute cell address. If desired, you can continue setting the various workbook links.

22. Save the workbook and close all workbooks.

23. Exit Excel.

Summary

Learning how to add, remove, or change the worksheets in your workbook can help you customize your workbooks and save time. By learning how to link both worksheets and workbooks, you can save yourself the hassle of reentering data.

ENHANCING YOUR SKILLS

THIS PART CONTAINS THE FOLLOWING CHAPTERS

By the time you reach Part IV, you should be feeling fairly comfortable using Excel. Now it's time to move on to some of the truly innovative features of Excel 97. You're ready to work with three Excel features that can all increase your productivity — macros, templates, and styles. By understanding these features, you gain three more tools for making your work easier.

In addition to its primary role as a spreadsheet program, Excel 97 can act as a database. In this mode, you can use Excel to sort and select specific data. For example, you can keep an inventory, and then sort the inventory by part number, location, vendor, or any other categories you choose.

In Part III, you discovered how to share information with others. However, you may not always want other users to make changes to your data, or you might want to hide certain parts of the worksheet from prying eyes. In Part IV, you find out how to protect your worksheets and workbooks, as well as how to accept or reject changes suggested by other users.

Jackie always liked to read; even as a child, while other children were playing with Barbies or Hot Wheels (or Barbies and Hot Wheels), she enjoyed acting as a librarian in her large collection of books. She made cards for each book, and on the cards she would write the due date whenever neighborhood kids or various stuffed animals checked out books such as *The Cat in the Hat* or *Harriet the Spy*. Seldom did Jackie need to collect late fees; the personal attention that she paid her customers was usually returned to her in the form of punctual returns.

It's no surprise that as Jackie grew up, she continued reading with a passion. Throughout high school, college, and into her adult life, she devoured books, consuming them like a fire consumes wood. Her love for reading finally prompted Jackie to take a large, scary chance — opening her own bookstore. But in the age of the superstore and its bulk-rate pricing, Jackie knew that she had to offer her potential customers something special if she wanted to earn her place in the market. One of her Excel files, booklist.xls, helped her find that something. Booklist.xls is a spreadsheet that Jackie started about five years ago. In it, she lists important facts about every book that she's read, including author, ISBN, other books of similar topic, a paragraph of comments, and, finally, a letter grade ranging from A to F.

Looking over her list one day, Jackie had a thought. She wished that she had known ahead of time about each book that she had graded D or F, so that she could have avoided it and gone after another A or B title. What if she could offer that foresight to her customers? If she could provide objective analyses, reviews, and additional information about each title that she stocks, wouldn't she be providing a unique service to the book-buying community? With that thought, the Examined Life Bookstore was born. Socrates said that "an unexamined life is not worth living." The goal of the Examined Life Bookstore is to provide broad, objective insight into the vast supply of books available, thus helping each customer use books to fully examine his or her own life.

Jackie quickly compiled data for more books. For the titles that she had not read herself, she relied on reviews and information from several sources: published book reviews, friends, and the Internet. She always has the data available behind the counter. If someone likes books by Amy Tan, for example, Jackie's Excel sheet can advise the reader on other authors that write about similar themes. She encourages customers to contribute to the database, too, which makes them feel like part of a community. That and a strong cup of coffee have made the Examined Life Bookstore a successful new business.

CHAPTER THIRTEEN

MACROS AND TEMPLATES AND STYLES (OH, MY!)

IN THIS CHAPTER YOU LEARN THESE KEY SKILLS

WHAT IS A MACRO?   PAGE 296

RECORDING A MACRO   PAGE 301

PLAYING A MACRO   PAGE 303

DELETING AND EDITING MACROS   PAGE 309

WORKING WITH TEMPLATES   PAGE 310

DEFINING AND USING STYLES   PAGE 314

BONUS SECTION: ADDING MACROS TO EXCEL'S
TOOLBARS AND MENUS   PAGE 319

W ouldn't it be nice if you could press a key on your computer and have your house cleaned from top to bottom? In the future, you may be able to press a single button and have automated appliances carry out multiple instructions. Even now you probably use several such shortcuts. Consider the following:

* **Speed dial.** After programming a speed dial number on your telephone, you can automatically dial the entire phone number (including any long distance carrier codes) by simply pressing the designated speed dial button.

* **Time bake.** You tell the oven what time to start cooking, what temperature you want, and when to stop cooking. The oven automatically carries out those instructions.

* **Automated coffee brewing.** You set the pot to turn on at a specific time and to stay on for a specific amount of time, and your coffee is ready when you get up in the morning.

295

* **VCR taping.** If you figured out how to set yours (I haven't), you can program daily or weekly TV shows at various times and channels for your VCR to record. It automatically turns on and off and changes channels, all according to your instructions.

Like the devices in this list, Excel can automatically carry out a series of instructions — a *macro* — that you record. The instructions that make up an Excel macro might include numerous keystrokes, commands, and mouse clicks. By recording instructions in the form of a macro, you can automate an entire process — letting Excel perform the necessary keystrokes and commands for you. For example, you may often want to insert your company logo into your worksheets. You could do this by completing the following steps:

1. Choose Insert → Picture .

2. Click the folder or series of folders where the logo file is stored.

3. Click the logo file and click OK.

Instead, you can create a macro that incorporates all these steps and places a macro button on your toolbar. Whenever you need to insert the logo, you simply click the correct cell and click the macro button on the toolbar. Thanks to your macro, the logo is automatically inserted, saving you time and keystrokes.

This chapter introduces you to Excel macros. Entire books have been written about macros, so don't expect to become an expert by the end of this chapter. However, you will learn enough to increase your productivity when you use Excel.

In addition to macros, Excel offers other productivity features, such as templates and styles. A *template* is a workbook with some formatting and formulas already in place. Templates save you time by allowing you to customize a workbook rather than create one from scratch. *Styles* can include various character and paragraph attributes, including number, alignment, and font information. You can assign a style to any cell in a worksheet, and Excel automatically formats the selected cell(s) with the attributes of that style. Styles not only enhance your productivity, but also ensure consistency of formatting from worksheet to worksheet and from workbook to workbook.

What Is a Macro?

I could tell you that a macro is simply a collection of VBA code, but then you might want to know what *that* is. VBA is an abbreviation for Visual Basic for Applications, the Microsoft macro programming language. Now that you don't know much more than you did before, I'll start with a short discussion of macros, and then examine Visual Basic later on in this chapter.

What benefits do macros offer?

Macros offer several benefits, such as the following:

* Increasing productivity by requiring fewer keystrokes to complete a task (automating the task)
* Automating a complex *series* of tasks
* Ensuring accuracy by consistently repeating exactly the same keystrokes and commands in the same sequence
* Speeding up routine editing and formatting
* Combining multiple commands
* Making a dialog box option more accessible

NOTE **Unfortunately, macros do not offer such benefits as holidays, paid vacations, and health insurance.**

What's in a macro?

A macro can contain formatting commands, values, formulas, functions, and virtually anything you can accomplish by using the keyboard or the mouse.

A macro is actually a bunch of Visual Basic commands stored (by default) in the current workbook. (*Bunch* is a highly technical term meaning group.)

Do you have to be a programmer to write a macro? Well, to a certain extent, the answer is yes. If you want to actually *write* a macro, you must know the Visual Basic language. However, to make things easier for you, Excel includes a *macro recorder*. To create a macro, you turn on the recorder, perform your keyboard and mouse tasks, and then turn off the recorder. Excel automatically generates the Visual Basic code required to repeat the tasks you performed. Once the macro code is created in Excel, choosing a few commands or clicking a button *executes* the macro (meaning Excel duplicates your original keystrokes and mouse movements, not that it kills your data).

SIDE TRIP

The following is a list of the Visual Basic code for a simple macro. This macro inserts my name in the upper-right section of the header, and Page *X* of *Y* in the right section of the footer. It also changes all margins to 1 inch. Although this may look complex, Excel wrote all of the code — I didn't need to write any of it. Take a close look at the code, and see if you can get an idea of how it works. Later in this chapter, you will record your own macro and then explore its finer points.

(continued)

(continued)

```
Sub Head_Foot_Mar()
' Head_Foot_Mar Macro
' Macro recorded 11/13/96 by John R. Nicholson
With ActiveSheet.PageSetup
 .PrintTitleRows = ""
 .PrintTitleColumns = ""
 End With
 ActiveSheet.PageSetup.PrintArea = ""
 With ActiveSheet.PageSetup
 .LeftHeader = ""
 .CenterHeader = ""
 .RightHeader = "John R. Nicholson"
 .LeftFooter = ""
 .CenterFooter = ""
 .RightFooter = "Page &P of &N"
 .LeftMargin = Application.InchesToPoints(1)
 .RightMargin = Application.InchesToPoints(1)
 .TopMargin = Application.InchesToPoints(1)
 .BottomMargin = Application.InchesToPoints(1)
 .HeaderMargin = Application.InchesToPoints(0.5)
 .FooterMargin = Application.InchesToPoints(0.5)
 .PrintHeadings = False
 .PrintGridlines = False
 .PrintComments = xlPrintNoComments
 .PrintQuality = 300
 .CenterHorizontally = False
 .CenterVertically = False
 .Orientation = xlPortrait
 .Draft = False
 .PaperSize = xlPaperLetter
 .FirstPageNumber = xlAutomatic
 .Order = xlDownThenOver
 .BlackAndWhite = False
 .Zoom = 100
 End With
End Sub
```

Where do macros live?

By default, Excel stores your macros in the current workbook. They are on a hidden worksheet, which you can view by choosing `Tools` → `Macro` → `Macros`. In the resulting dialog box, click the name of the macro you want to examine, and then click Edit. Excel responds by displaying the Visual Basic code.

When you begin to record a macro, the Record Macro dialog box, shown in Figure 13-1, enables you to designate where Excel should store the macro. You learn more about this dialog box later in this chapter.

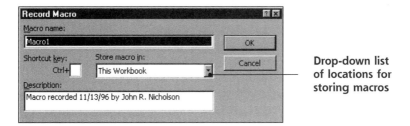

Drop-down list of locations for storing macros

Figure 13-1 The Record Macro dialog box

The Store macro in drop-down list offers the following three locations for storing the macro:

* This Workbook
* New Workbook
* Personal Macro Workbook

As detailed in the following sections, there are advantages and disadvantages to each of these options.

THIS WORKBOOK

Storing the macro in the current workbook adds a *hidden* Visual Basic worksheet to the workbook. This worksheet contains all of the macros for the current workbook. You can store as many macros as needed on a single worksheet in the workbook. Any macros stored in the current workbook work only under one of the following two conditions:

* You run the macro from within the current workbook.
* The workbook is open but inactive while you are working in another workbook.

The advantage to storing macros in the current workbook is that all macros available for use in that worksheet are kept together. This makes finding, troubleshooting, and editing somewhat easier. On the other hand, if you decide you want to use the macro in another workbook, you must either open both workbooks, or copy the macro to the new workbook.

NEW WORKBOOK

If you plan to use specific macros on a regular basis in multiple worksheets, but not often enough to have them loaded (and taking up memory) all of the time, you can save them in a separate workbook. When you want to use any of the macros stored in this workbook, you must first open it and then run the desired macro from the active workbook.

With this method, the workbook doesn't continually take up space in your computer's memory. And when you have the workbook open, the macros it contains can be run from any other open workbook. However, you must open the new macro workbook any time you want to use the macros it contains.

PERSONAL MACRO WORKBOOK

Each time you open Excel, a hidden workbook called *Personal.xls*, stored in the Excel Startup folder (C:\Program Files\Microsoft Office\XLStart\), automatically opens. When you record a macro, you can choose to store the macro in your Personal Macro Workbook. Because this workbook automatically opens *every time* you open Excel, any macros it contains are available to any open workbook.

If a particular macro works only in a *specific* workbook, you usually don't want to store it in your Personal Macro Workbook. On the other hand, if you write a macro that is designed to work in any workbook — for example, the company logo macro — store it in your Personal Macro Workbook so that the macro is always available.

How do you name a macro?

You must assign a name to each macro you create. When naming a macro, you must follow these rules:

* The first character of the macro name *must* be a letter.
* Other characters in the macro name are restricted to letters, numbers, and underscores.
* A macro name *cannot* include spaces. An underscore works well as a word separator (for example, John_Footer).
* Macro names can contain as many as 64 characters.

A dialog box can only display about 30 to 50 characters, thus you may want to limit the length of the macro name. You can add a description when you create your macro.

Recording a Macro

Recording a macro is as simple as turning on your video cassette recorder (VCR for the enlightened). Of course, for those of you who are like me — VCR-challenged — it may take a little more practice.

The best way to learn how to record a macro is by doing it. In this activity, you record a macro that changes the default column width to 10. Although it is easier to simply change the default column width, recording this macro gives you a starting place for understanding macros.

1. Open Excel. Excel displays a blank workbook.

2. Choose Tools → Macro → Record New Macro . Excel displays the Record Macro dialog box, shown previously in Figure 13-1.

3. In the Macro name text box, type **Default_Width.** Leave everything else at the default; your dialog box should be similar to Figure 13-2. A default description is automatically generated. You may edit it to make it more meaningful.

Remember, you can't use spaces, periods, or other punctuation in macro names. Use underscores instead.

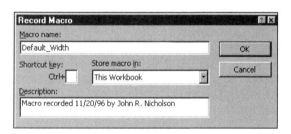

Figure 13-2 The Record Macro dialog box with the Default_Width macro name

4. Click OK to begin recording the macro. The Stop Recording toolbar appears in the center of the screen. (If someone has moved the toolbar, it reappears in its previous position.) Figure 13-3 displays the Stop Recording toolbar, which includes a button to stop the recording of the macro.

The Stop Recording toolbar (shown in Figure 13-3) is rather strange and deserves a few words of explanation. The Title Bar displays *Stop Re*. The toolbar contains only the following three buttons:

✳ **Stop Recording.** Click the left-hand button on the Stop Recording toolbar to end recording of the current macro.

✳ **Relative Reference.** Click the right-hand button on the Stop Recording toolbar to toggle the relative or absolute reference of cell addresses.

✳ **Close box.** Click the Close box in the upper-right corner of the Stop Recording toolbar to close the toolbar.

Like any other toolbar, the Stop Recording toolbar can be toggled on and off by choosing │ View │→│ Toolbars │ and selecting the toolbar to be displayed or hidden. If the toolbar is displayed, you can hide it by clicking the Close box. You can also move the toolbar by dragging it to a new position. Unlike most toolbars, however, it *can't* be resized. If you accidentally close the toolbar while recording a macro, display it again by choosing │ View │→│ Toolbars │→│ Stop Recording │.

 TIP If the Stop Recording toolbar doesn't appear, right-click anywhere on a toolbar, and click the │ Stop Recording │ option.

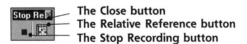

The Close button
The Relative Reference button
The Stop Recording button

Figure 13-3 The Stop Recording toolbar

5. Choose │ Format │→│ Column │→│ Standard Width │. Excel displays the Standard Width dialog box.

6. Type **10** and click OK.

7. Click the Stop Recording button in the lower-left corner of the Stop Recording toolbar. It appears as though nothing has happened, except that your columns are slightly wider. If you accidentally clicked the Close box, you can reopen the Stop Recording toolbar by right-clicking any toolbar and then choosing │ Stop Recording │. Then click the Stop Recording button.

8. Save the workbook as **Macro Samples** in the Discover Excel folder. Leave the workbook open.

9. Click the New button on the toolbar to create a new workbook.

10. Choose Format → Column → Standard Width . Excel displays the Standard Width dialog box. Notice that the Standard column width is set to 8.43. In the next section of this chapter, you change this setting by running your new Default_Width macro.

11. Click Cancel to close the dialog box. For now, leave both workbooks open.

Playing a Macro

There are several ways to play a macro, as you learn in the following activities, and later in the Bonus Section of this chapter. In order for a prerecorded macro to be available, one of the following two conditions must be met:

* The workbook containing the macro must be open. (The workbook doesn't have to be the active workbook, and it doesn't have be saved to disk.)

* The macro must be stored in the Personal Macro Workbook, which opens automatically as a hidden workbook whenever you open Excel.

If the macro you want isn't available, you either didn't save it to any of the open workbooks, or you didn't save it to the Personal Macro Workbook. If you saved the macro in a workbook other than the Personal Macro Workbook, you can make it available to the current workbook by opening the workbook that contains the macro. If you didn't save it to the Personal Macro Workbook, and you didn't save the workbook in which the macro was recorded, you have to record the macro again.

TIP If you want to create macros for special situations — in other words, you don't want them always available — save them in a workbook called My Macros.xls (or any other name). When you want to run a particular set of macros, open the workbook that contains them. The number of macros that you can save in a single workbook is limited only by the available memory of your computer.

There are several ways to play (or run) a macro. The following activity describes one of the more common ways to run a macro.

1. Create a new workbook.

2. Choose Tools → Macro → Macros . Excel displays the Macro dialog box, which lists all of the currently available macros.

3. Select the Default_Width macro.

4. Click Run. The macro runs behind the scenes.

5. Choose `Format` → `Column` → `Standard Width` to check the results of running your macro. The Standard Width dialog box is displayed. If your macro worked, the standard column width should be set to 10.

Assigning keyboard shortcuts

In addition to running a macro as described in the preceding section, you can assign the macro to a shortcut key, add the macro to a menu, or place a macro button on a toolbar, which can be done when you create the macro or at a later time.

When you assign a keyboard shortcut to play the macro, you can use Ctrl+*letter* or Ctrl+Shift+*letter*, where *letter* is any letter key on the keyboard. While the workbook containing the macro is open, the shortcut key overrides any default Microsoft Excel shortcut keys.

This activity shows how to assign a shortcut key to an existing macro. To assign a shortcut key while recording the macro, type the key in the Shortcut key box in the Record Macro dialog box, shown earlier in Figure 13-2. Currently, you should have a blank workbook displayed on your screen, and the Macro Samples workbook should still be open.

To assign a shortcut key to an existing macro, follow these steps:

1. Choose `Tools` → `Macro` → `Macros`. Excel opens the Macro dialog box, shown in Figure 13-4.

2. Select the Default_Width macro.

3. Click Options. Excel displays the Macro Options dialog box, shown in Figure 13-5.

4. Type **w.** I chose *w* as the shortcut key because the macro is named Default_Width, and the letter reminds you of the first letter of the designated action: width. This is called a *mnemonic* association.

5. Click OK to return to the Macro dialog box, and click Cancel to close it.

6. Press Ctrl+w to run the macro.

7. Choose `Format` → `Column` → `Standard Width`. Width is now set to 10. Before you ran the macro, it was set to 8.43.

8. Click OK.

9. Close both workbooks, saving the changes to the Macro Samples workbook and discarding the changes to the blank workbook.

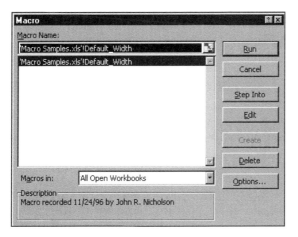

Figure 13-4 Use the Macro dialog box to select a macro to run (play) or edit.

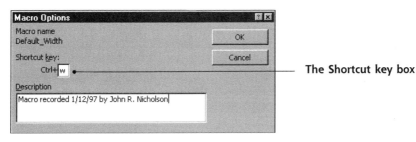

The Shortcut key box

Figure 13-5 Use the Macro Options dialog box to assign a shortcut key to an existing macro.

Choosing between relative and absolute macro settings

As you learned in Chapter 6, references to cell addresses can be either relative or absolute. For example, assume that C1 is the active cell and it contains the formula **=A1**. In English, this *relative* reference translates to, "retrieve the value that is located two cells to the left." If you copy this formula from C1 to C2, the formula in C2 is **=A2** (again, "retrieve the value that is located two cells to the left"). On the other hand, the formula **=$A$1** uses an absolute reference. This means that the cell references don't change, regardless of where you copy the formula. Remember that an absolute reference contains one or more dollar signs ($). If you copy the formula **=$A$1** to any other cell, the reference is always to cell A1.

Like references in formulas, macro references can be either absolute or relative. Unlike formulas, where the *default* reference is relative, the default macro references are absolute. For example, if the active cell is B2, a macro that types "Workbook Name" in A1 and then presses Enter is as follows:

```
Sub Workbook_Name()
' Workbook_Name Macro
' Macro recorded 11/24/96 by John R. Nicholson
 Range("A1").Select
 ActiveCell.FormulaR1C1 = "Workbook Name"
 Range("A2").Select
End Sub
```

As you can see in the fourth line of the macro, the selected range is set to A1, and when Enter is pressed, the specified location of the active cell is listed (A2). Regardless of the location of the active cell when this macro is run, "Workbook Name" is always entered in A1.

To record a macro as a relative macro, rather than as an absolute macro follow these steps:

1. Begin the recording procedure.

2. On the Stop Recording toolbar, click the Relative Reference button, shown in Figure 13-6.

Excel continues to record this and any additional macros with relative references until you close Excel or until you click the Relative Reference button again.

Relative Reference button.

Figure 13-6 The Relative Reference button on the Stop Recording toolbar

TIP   When it is active, the Relative Reference button appears depressed (physically, not emotionally).

If you create the previous macro with relative references, Excel enters "Workbook Name" in the cell one column to the left and one row above the active cell. In this case, "Workbook Name" appears in A1 if the active cell is B2. With relative references, the macro looks like this:

```
Sub Workbook_Name()
' Workbook_Name Macro
' Macro recorded 11/24/96 by John R. Nicholson
 ActiveCell.Offset(-1, -1).Range("A1").Select
 ActiveCell.FormulaR1C1 = "Workbook Name"
```

```
ActiveCell.Offset(1, 0).Range("A1").Select
End Sub
```

Notice that the fourth and sixth lines include references to cell *offsets*, rather than actual cell addresses. The first offset (-1,-1) means back one column and up one row from the address of the active cell. Therefore, if the active cell is C4 when you run the macro, the text is entered in B3 and the active cell is then changed to B4. The second offset (1,0), in line six, means to move down one cell.

Recording a macro with absolute or relative references

The following activity records a macro that inserts the current date in A1 using an absolute reference, and then replaces that macro with one that uses relative references.

1. Open the Macro Samples workbook. As shown in Figure 13-7, Excel *may* display a warning box with the following options:

   Tell Me More offers additional information about macro viruses.

   Disable Macros opens the workbook and disables all macros.

   Enable Macros opens the workbook and makes the macros in that workbook available.

   Do Not Open cancels the Open command.

TIP If you open a workbook containing macros, Excel may display this warning box. You can disable the warning by clicking the check box labeled Always ask before opening workbooks with macros.

CAUTION With the advent of Windows 95, a new type of virus appeared — a macro virus. (A *virus* is a small program that may be merely annoying, or one that may totally destroy your data.) If you don't know where the macros in a workbook originated, make sure that you use an antivirus program to check your workbooks for macro viruses.

2. For this activity, click Enable Macros.

WEB PATH Clicking Tell Me More offers a direct link to information about the macro viruses. For additional information, access the Microsoft Network at the following address:

```
http://www.microsoft.com
```

Click the Search button, and search for *macro viruses*.

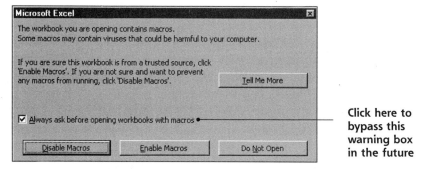

Microsoft Excel

The workbook you are opening contains macros.
Some macros may contain viruses that could be harmful to your computer.

If you are sure this workbook is from a trusted source, click
'Enable Macros'. If you are not sure and want to prevent
any macros from running, click 'Disable Macros'.

Tell Me More

☑ Always ask before opening workbooks with macros ●——————

Click here to
bypass this
warning box
in the future

Disable Macros   Enable Macros   Do Not Open

Figure 13-7 The Macro Virus warning box

3. Click the New button on the toolbar to create a new workbook.

4. Click B2 to make it the active cell.

5. Choose Tools → Macro → Record New Macro. Excel displays the Record Macro dialog box.

6. Name the macro **Current_Date** and click OK. Make sure the Relative Reference button on the Stop Recording toolbar *is not* depressed. (Maybe you could sing to it.)

You can't name your macro simply *Date*, because *Date* is a reserved word. That is, Excel won't let you use it when naming macros.

7. Click A1, type **=now()**, and press Enter. This enters the date and time in A1, and changes the active cell to A2.

8. If necessary, AutoFit the column.

9. Click the Stop Recording button.

10. Click A1 and press Delete.

11. Click C3 to make it the active cell.

12. Choose Tools → Macro → Macros, and run the Current_Date macro. Notice that the date and time appear in A1. Because you recorded the macro using absolute references, running the macro always inserts the current date and time in A1, regardless of which cell is active when you run the macro.

13. Click A1 and press Delete.

14. Click B2 to make it active. In the following steps, you replace the Current_Date macro with a new version that uses relative references.

15. Choose Tools → Macro → Record New Macro. Excel displays the Record Macro dialog box.

16. Name the macro **Current_Date** and click OK.

17. In the information box Excel displays, click <u>Y</u>es to record over the existing macro.

18. Click the Relative Reference button on the Stop Recording toolbar.

19. Click A1, type **=now()**, and press Enter. Again, Excel displays the date and time in A1.

20. Click the Stop Recording button on the Stop Recording toolbar.

21. Click C3 to make it the active cell.

22. Choose ╎ Tools ╎ → ╎ Macro ╎ → ╎ Macros ╎, and run the Current_Date macro again. Because this version of the macro uses relative references, Excel places the date and time in B2, and changes the active cell to B3 (rather than A2).

23. Save your work and leave the workbooks open.

If you want to record a macro with relative references, make sure you correctly select the active cell *before* you begin to record the macro.

Deleting and Editing Macros

You might want to delete a macro for one of two reasons:

* You don't need the macro any more.
* You made a mistake while recording the macro, and it's easier to correct by just deleting it and recording it again.

If you make a minor error in the macro, you can correct the error by editing the macro. (If the error was a fairly major one, it's easier to record the macro again.)

To delete a macro, follow these steps:

1. Choose ╎ Tools ╎ → ╎ Macro ╎ → ╎ Macros ╎. Excel displays the Macro dialog box.

2. Select Current_Date.

3. Click Delete. Excel asks for confirmation that you want to delete the macro.

You cannot *undelete* a macro by clicking the Undo button. You must record the macro again if you delete it.

4. Click <u>Y</u>es to delete the macro (or <u>N</u>o to cancel the deletion).

5. Save your work and close both workbooks.

 NOTE Editing macros is beyond the scope of this book. However, if you want to see what your macro looks like after you have recorded it, choose Tools → Macro → Macros , select the macro, and click Edit. This is an excellent way to learn some of the Visual Basic commands used in writing macros. After some experimenting, you may want to try to slightly modify the Visual Basic code for a macro and replay it to see the effect on the workbook.

 TIP If you make errors while recording the macro, it may be easier just to stop the recording and start recording the macro again.

Working with Templates

A *template* is a workbook that you use as the basis for developing other workbooks. It may contain prerecorded macros, specialized formatting, labels, formulas, and even charts. Rather than create a workbook from scratch, you can open a template, fill in the basic information, and save the template as a file of your own.

Excel comes with several workbook templates to help automate your work.

To create a new workbook based on an Excel template, follow these steps:

1. Choose File → New and click the Spreadsheet Solutions tab.

2. Select the template you want to use and click <u>O</u>pen. The new workbook opens without a name so you can't accidentally change the template.

Visiting Excel templates

To see a list of available templates, choose File → New and click the Spreadsheet Solutions tab. Microsoft also offers free templates at the Microsoft Network.

 WEB PATH To find additional templates on the Internet, choose Help → Microsoft on the Web → Free Stuff . If you have problems, you can also go to:

`http://www.microsoft.com`

Click the Search button and search for *Excel Free*. Follow the onscreen directions.

Creating a workbook based on an Excel template

You can easily create your own workbook based on an existing Excel template. This gives you a jump-start on completing your work. Using a template to create your workbook not only saves time, but it also ensures consistency (because everything in the template is already configured, you don't need to start from scratch).

This activity shows how to create a new workbook based on an Excel template. If the template is not available, it may not have been installed when Excel was installed.

(If templates weren't installed on your hard disk when Excel was installed, it's usually because you didn't have enough hard disk space. If you have enough space, run the Office Setup program again and add the templates.)

1. Choose File → New . Excel displays the General tab of the New dialog box. Excel uses the Workbook template to create a blank workbook when you click the New button on the toolbar.

2. Click the Spreadsheet Solutions tab. Several additional templates are displayed, as shown in Figure 13-8.

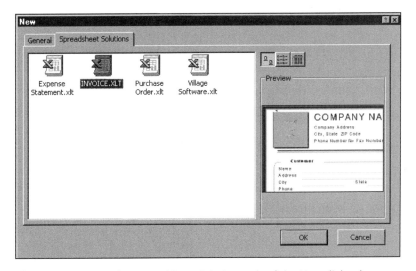

Figure 13-8   Use the Spreadsheet Solutions tab of the New dialog box to create a workbook based on an existing template.

3. Double-click the Invoice template to open it. If Excel displays the Virus Warning box, click Enable Macros. (Because Microsoft supplied the template, you can assume that the macros are not infected.)

4. Click the Customize Your Invoice worksheet name tab.

5. Fill in your name in the company name cell, and add your complete address and phone number.

6. Choose File → Save As. The default name changes to Invoice1 and the folder is set to Discover Excel.

7. Save the workbook in the Discover Excel folder as **My Invoice.** Notice the .xls extension, rather than the original .xlt.

8. Click the Invoice tab. Your invoice should be similar to Figure 13-9.

The Customize button

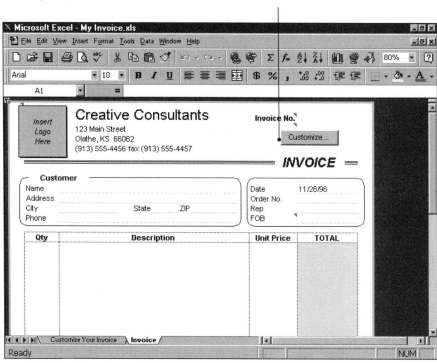

Figure 13-9   The Invoice worksheet displays your name and address.

9. Click the Customize button to make additional changes to your invoice. The Customize button displays the Customize Your Invoice tab again, as shown in Figure 13-10, so that you can further modify your invoice.

10. Change the first tax name to Kansas and the Rate to 8.00%.

11. Click the check box to turn off Apply tax on local purchases only.

TIP   **Move the cursor onto any of the red triangles on the screen to get additional help about the nearest information.**

12. Click the Invoice worksheet tab.

13. Type **2** in the Qty column.

1st tax name, Rate

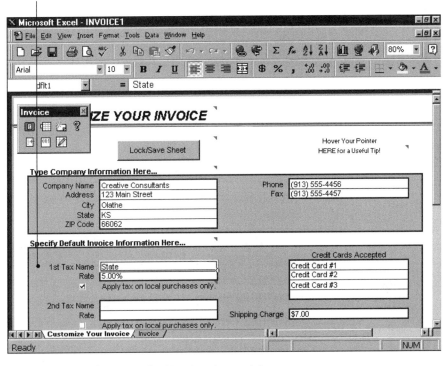

Figure 13-10   The Customize Your Invoice worksheet

14. Type **Widget** in the Description column.

15. Type **7.45** in the Unit Price column.

16. Scroll down the invoice. Note that the tax and the shipping charge have been automatically calculated.

17. Print a copy of the modified invoice.

18. Save the workbook with the changes you made, and then close the workbook.

19. Choose ⟦ **File** ⟧ → ⟦ **Save** ⟧. As shown in Figure 13-11, Excel displays the Template File — Save to Database dialog box. This is used to keep the data in an Access database format.

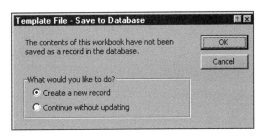

Figure 13-11   The Control Panel provides more than two dozen utilities for customizing and controlling Windows NT.

20. Select Continue without updating and click OK.

21. Save your work and leave the workbook open.

Saving Excel templates as your own templates

If you want to save a modified Excel template as your own template and then use your template to create new workbooks, you must do the following:

1. Load the template.

2. Make the changes.

3. Save the file *as a template* to the Solutions folder in C:\Program Files\Microsoft Office\Templates\Spreadsheet.

To open the modified template, choose `File` → `New` and double-click the modified template to open it as an Excel workbook. Save it immediately to the desired location with the appropriate name and the .xls extension.

Saving Excel workbooks as templates

You can also save an Excel workbook that you create as a template:

1. Choose `File` → `Save As`.

2. Select the C:\Program Files\Microsoft Office\Templates\Spreadsheet Solutions folder and save the file with an .xlt extension.

The next time you choose `File` → `New`, the new workbook template is available.

Defining and Using Styles

A style in Excel is a collection of formatting instructions. Styles offer three main benefits:

* They save time.
* They ensure consistency.
* They make it easy to change the formatting of your worksheet. (If you modify a style, Excel automatically updates the formatting of any cells that use that style.)

You can apply styles to individual cells, a range of cells, or an entire worksheet. When you apply a style to one or more cells or a worksheet, Excel automatically formats the selected area according to the specifications of that style.

The Style dialog box, show in Figure 13-12, enables you to change the formatting specifications for any style you create.

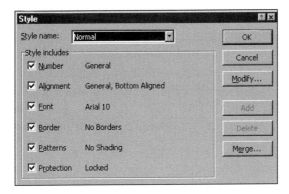

Figure 13-12 Use the Style dialog box to specify exactly how selected cells are formatted.

Each style is saved with its own name. It can contain formatting specifications for Numbers, Alignment, Font, Borders, Patterns, and Protection.

Creating a style

To create a new style, simply choose Format → Style to open the Style dialog box, shown in Figure 13-12. Notice that the default style is Normal. Enter a name for the new style, change the formatting specifications as desired, and click OK to close the dialog box.

As the following activity shows, creating and assigning a style is simple. When this style is applied, the selection is formatted as a heading for your new worksheet.

1. Create a new workbook.

2. Choose Format → Style. Excel displays the Style dialog box.

3 In the Style name list box, type **Worksheet_Title.**

4. Click Modify to open the Format Cells dialog box. You used this dialog box in previous chapters of this book.

5. Click the Font tab.

6. Choose Century Schoolbook as the font. If for any reason you don't have Century Schoolbook, choose a different font.

7. Set the Font Style to Bold, and set the Size to 18 points.

8. Click the Alignment tab, and set the Horizontal alignment to Center Across Selection.

9. Click the Border tab and choose the double-line border (second column, last row).

10. Click <u>O</u>utline.

11. Click OK twice to return to the worksheet. Notice that Excel automatically applies the new style to the current cell.

If you click the <u>O</u>utline button before you click the double-line border, Excel applies the *single-line* border, which is the default border when a border is selected. You must first select the border and then click <u>O</u>utline.

12. Select A1:H1.

13. Type **1997 Sales Report.** Don't worry that the text stays in column A and wraps strangely.

14. Press Enter. Notice that although Excel applied the font, size, and bold attributes, the text is not centered across the selection.

15. To cure this, choose | **F<u>o</u>rmat** | → | **Style** |, select Worksheet_Title from the <u>S</u>tyle name drop-down list, and then click OK. The text is now formatted correctly.

16. Save your work and leave the workbook open.

Assigning a style

To assign a style to one or more cells, simply select the cells to be formatted, and then choose the desired style. You can type the text or formula for a cell either before or after assigning a style to a cell or group of cells.

To style the headings in the other two worksheets in the current workbook, follow these steps:

1. Click the Sheet2 tab.

2. In A1, type **1998 Projected Sales** and press <Enter>.

3. Select A1:H1.

4. Choose | **F<u>o</u>rmat** | → | **Style** |. Excel displays the Style dialog box.

5. Select Worksheet_Title from the <u>S</u>tyle name drop-down list and then click OK. Excel automatically applies the formatting to the selected cells.

If you don't press Enter after entering data in a cell, the | **F<u>o</u>rmat | → | **Style** | option is grayed out. Press Enter and reselect the cell or cells to assign the style.**

6. Click the Sheet3 tab.

7. In A1, type **1999 Projected Sales** and press Enter.

8. Select A1:H1 and choose | Format | → | Style |. Excel displays the Style dialog box.

9. Select Worksheet_Title from the Style name drop-down list and click OK.

10. Click the Sheet1 tab again.

11. Click A1.

12. Save your work and leave the workbook open.

Modifying a style

By modifying a style, you get a chance to see the full potential of using styles. When you modify a style, Excel automatically changes the formatting of *all* cells or groups of cells to which you assigned that particular style. This saves time and ensures consistency in your worksheets and workbooks.

To modify a style, follow these steps:

1. Choose | Format | → | Style | → | Modify |, and click the Font tab in the Format Cells dialog box.

2. Change the Color of the font to red.

3. Click the Patterns tab.

4. Choose the lightest gray color and click OK twice to return to the worksheet.

5. Click the Sheet2 tab. Because A1:H1 is still selected, you can't see the actual color of the font or the background.

6. Click A1 to turn off the selection.

7. Click the Sheet3 tab and then click A1 to turn off the selection. Notice that the single change in style automatically changes *all* cells that are assigned that style.

8. Click the Sheet1 tab again.

9. Save your work and leave the workbook open.

Deleting a style

You delete a style by choosing [F**ormat**] → [**Style**], selecting the style to be deleted, clicking Delete, and then clicking OK. All cells that have been assigned the deleted style in *all* worksheets are then returned to the Normal style.

You are not asked for confirmation when you delete a style. The style is instantly deleted, and the Undo option will not replace it. You will need to recreate and reapply the style to the desired cells.

In the following activity, you delete a style and see how this affects the entire workbook.

1. Make sure that A1 on Sheet1 is still the active cell, and then choose [F**ormat**] → [**Style**]. Excel displays the Style dialog box. The Worksheet_Title style should already be selected in the Style name list box.

2. Click Delete.

3. Click OK. Look at all three sheets. All of the cells that were assigned the Worksheet_Title style are returned to the Normal style.

4. Close the workbook. You don't need to save the changes.

BONUS

Adding Macros to Excel's Toolbars and Menus

In addition to creating shortcut keys for macros, you can save time by placing frequently used macros on a toolbar or in a menu. This bonus section shows you how to do both.

To add a macro to a toolbar, run the macro, and then remove it from the toolbar, follow these steps:

1. Open the Macro Samples workbook.

2. Click **E**nable Macros, if the virus warning box is displayed.

3. Create a new workbook.

4. Choose **Tools** → **Customize** and click the Commands tab. If this is the first time you have used the Customize dialog box, the Office Assistant asks if you want help with this feature. Click No, don't provide help now. If you have used the dialog box before, the Office Assistant won't appear. The Commands tab is displayed in Figure 13-13.

Figure 13-13 The Commands tab in the Customize dialog box

5. If necessary, reposition the dialog box by dragging its title bar down until the Formatting toolbar is visible.

6. In the Categories drop-down list, choose Macros. You may need to scroll down through the list.

7. Drag the Custom Button from the Commands panel onto the Formatting toolbar, just to the right of the Spell Check button. Depending on your monitor and resolution, the toolbar may expand to take up two lines if there isn't enough room to fit all of the buttons on a single line.

TIP If you prefer a different icon instead of the Happy Face, you can click Modify Selection, highlight Change Button Image, and choose a new icon.

8. Click Close to return to the worksheet.

9. Click the custom button you placed on the toolbar. As shown in Figure 13-14, Excel displays the Assign Macro dialog box.

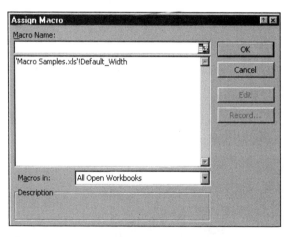

Figure 13-14 The Assign Macro dialog box is used to assign a macro to a custom button.

10. Select the Default_Width macro and click OK.

11. Choose Format → Column → Standard Width . The dialog box shows the current setting: 8.43. (If it's set to 10, you are in the Sample Macros worksheet instead of the new one you created.)

12. Click OK.

13. Click the custom button you installed on the toolbar again. Nothing seems to happen.

14. Choose Format → Column → Standard Width . Notice that the default column width is now set to 10. Whenever the workbook containing the assigned macro is open, you can use it to change the default width to 10 in any new worksheet.

15. Click OK. In the following steps, you delete the custom button from the toolbar.

16. Choose Tools → Customize . Excel displays the Customize dialog box. Make sure the Commands tab is still selected.

17. Drag the custom button from the toolbar onto the worksheet. Excel removes the button from the toolbar.

18. Click Close. Remember, you cannot undo the deletion.

Adding a macro to a menu

To assign the macro to a menu, rather than adding a button to the toolbar, follow these steps:

1. Create a new workbook.

2. Check the standard column width. It should be 8.43.

3. Choose Tools → Customize . Excel displays the Customize dialog box. Make sure the Commands tab is still selected.

4. Choose Macros from the Categories list.

5. Drag Custom Menu Item from the Commands panel onto the Tools menu. Do not release the mouse button! As you drag the Tools menu down, you see a black bar.

6. Drag the bar to just below Tools , and then release the mouse button. Do not close the Customize dialog box.

7. Right-click Custom Menu Item . Excel displays a pop-up menu similar to the one shown in Figure 13-15.

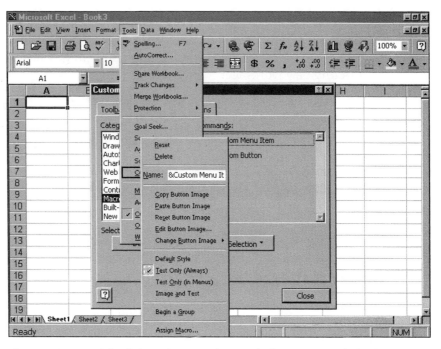

Figure 13-15 Right-clicking the menu item with the Customize dialog box open gives you several options, including changing the name of the new menu item.

8. Click in the Name box to rename the custom menu item. Place the ampersand (&) immediately before the letter you want underlined.

9. Delete the ampersand and the default name and type **&Default Column Width**.

10. Click any visible cell in the worksheet to close the menus.

11. Close the Customize dialog box.

12. Choose Tools → Default Column Width . Excel displays the Assign Macro dialog box.

13. Click Macro Samples.xls'Default_Width and then click OK. This attaches the macro to the menu command.

14. Run the macro by choosing Tools → Default Column Width again.

15. To make sure the macro worked, choose Format → Column → Standard Width . Notice that the width is set to 10.

16. Click OK to close the dialog box. To remove an item from a menu, the Customize dialog box must be open.

17. Choose Tools → Customize . The Customize dialog box opens, displaying the Commands tab.

18. Click Tools in the Categories panel.

19. Choose `Tools` → `Default Column Width`.

20. With the `Default Column Width` item highlighted, drag it down onto the worksheet.

21. Close the Customize dialog box, and make sure that the item has been removed from the `Tools` menu.

22. Close all workbooks without saving.

23. Exit Excel.

Summary

The main purpose in having a computer is to increase your productivity and effectiveness. You can best do that in Excel by learning how to use the macro, template, and style features. Macros are, perhaps, the most effective time-saving device in Excel. They are a powerful feature, which at times may seem too complex. Learn to use them, however, and you will benefit greatly. For additional information about macros, see *Excel 97 Bible* and *Excel 97 Secrets*, both published by IDG Books Worldwide.

13

CHAPTER FOURTEEN

MAKING A LIST: EXCEL'S DATABASE FEATURES

IN THIS CHAPTER YOU LEARN THESE KEY SKILLS

D ata entry is one of the most important tasks in any project. If your data is input incorrectly, your files and reports will also be incorrect.

To make data entry a little easier (and hopefully more error-free), Excel has adopted some basic database features. Features such as data entry forms, sorting, and filtering all simplify the process of entering and manipulating your data.

Choosing a Spreadsheet or a Database: How Do You Decide?

Before using Excel's database features, ask yourself, "Would I be better off using a database?" This section reviews some of the basic differences between spreadsheets (such as Excel) and databases (such as Access, Paradox, and dBASE) to help you determine which type of program best suits your needs.

A database is your best bet when you need to store large amounts of data and quickly retrieve, sort, and test data to determine whether it meets specific criteria. For example, a database containing a grocery store's inventory records allows the grocer to see exactly how many kumquats (I've always wanted to use that word) the store has in stock and compare that number to the quantity on order.

Use a spreadsheet when you need to solve a problem that you can express in mathematical terms. Spreadsheets are particularly effective for solving problems that you must repeatedly calculate after changing the values of variables. Unlike databases, spreadsheets allow the grocer to evaluate what-if scenarios such as, "What if I order 2,000 kumquats this month? Based on past sales, will they sell?" Spreadsheets provide the capability to see what happens when you manipulate variables. For example, the grocer might use a spreadsheet to forecast how a failed orange crop might affect the store's profits.

TIP **If you want to store large amounts of data for reference (for example, your address book, inventory records, or checking account transactions), you should use a database rather than a spreadsheet.**

So far, you have used Excel as a spreadsheet. In this chapter, you take a look at Excel's database features. Before I get into the basic terminology of databases, you must understand the difference between a flat-file database and a relational database. This will help you decide whether to use Excel's flat-file database features or a relational database, such as Access.

Working with flat-file databases

When you use a flat-file database, you can access only one database file at a time. For example, if you use Excel as a database for processing orders, you have to enter all of the information about a customer — name, address, city, state, zip code, and telephone number — every time you process an order for that customer. A flat-file database can access only one database file at a time. With a flat-file database, you must enter each order totally separate from any other order (even other orders from the same customer).

Working with relational databases

The power of relational databases lies in the fact that they can access data from multiple database files at the same time. To continue the order processing example from the preceding section, you might use Access to create a database file containing customer information. Each customer has a unique customer identification number such as a phone number or a social security number. The file also contains each customer's name, address, city, state, zip code, and telephone number.

Another file holds all the information about the items being ordered. For example, this file contains a unique product number for each item in inventory, as well as a product description and the product's price.

When you need to process an order, you enter the customer identification number. Access automatically retrieves all the information about that customer and displays it on the screen. Next, you enter the product number. Access retrieves the product description and the price of the item. You enter the quantity, and Access multiplies the unit price by the quantity to determine the total cost.

Relational databases have several advantages over flat-file databases:

* They require less typing.
* They reduce the likelihood of data entry errors.
* They speed up the data entry process.
* They offer advanced reporting features (for example, automatically generating an order form for objects sold, using the vendor information in yet another file).

If you don't have Access or another relational database, you must rely on Excel's flat-file database features. Actually, Excel can handle most simple database tasks. (In fact, it's probably easier to use, at least for beginners.)

If you need to dig one or two postholes, a shovel is probably adequate for the job. If you have to dig hundreds of holes, you need a powerful posthole digger. Such is the difference between using a spreadsheet as a database and using a full-featured database. For simple database tasks, Excel can handle the job.

Starting with the Basics

After determining that using your spreadsheet as a flat-file database is acceptable for the current job, your next step is to learn some of the terms that describe Excel's database functions. I use these terms throughout this chapter:

* **List.** A collection of information. For example, as shown in Figure 14-1, a feed store might have a list of the types of animal food it carries.

* **Field.** A column in a database list. A field displays a category of information, such as product name, quantity, or cost.
* **Record.** A row in a database list. A record consists of all the fields for one object in the database (for example, one item or one person).

Field names

Records

Fields

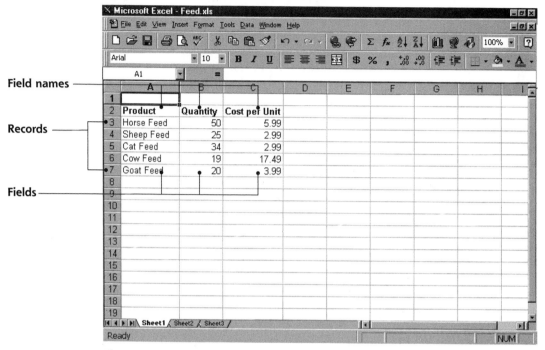

Figure 14-1 A sample list is shown in Excel. Each column is a field; each row is a record.

 TIP Before you create a list, take the time to plan how you want it to look. This will save you time and frustration in the long run.

Deciding How to Enter Raw Data

You can enter data into a new list by typing it directly into your worksheet or by creating a data entry form. Entering the data directly into the work-sheet (as you've done in previous exercises) is the most common data entry method and allows you to enter data into as many fields as you want. As shown in Figure 14-2, however, a data entry form offers a more organized, precise way to input your data. Unfortunately, Excel limits the number of fields to 32.

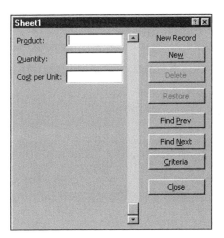

Figure 14-2 A data entry form provides a simple means for entering your data.

TIP If more than one user must enter data into the same worksheet, create a data entry form so that each user knows exactly which data to input.

Setting Up a Data Entry Form

Before you can create and use a data entry form, you must select a cell or a range of cells in your list and then name this selection *Database*.

By naming the range *Database*, you tell Excel which cells you want to show on your data input form.

Naming a database range

To highlight a range for the data entry form, follow these steps:

1. Open Excel and a new worksheet.

2. Save the worksheet in your Discover Excel folder as **Feed**.

3. Type **Product** in A2 and press Tab.

4. Type **Quantity** in B2 and press Tab.

5. Type **Cost per Unit** in C2.

6. Select A2 through C10.

7. Choose **Insert** → **Name** → **Define**. Excel displays the Define Name dialog box.

8. Enter **Database** as the name and then click OK.

9. Save your work, and leave the workbook open.

After you assign the name *Database* to a range, Excel uses *that* range as the basis for your data entry form. If you want to include another column (field) in your form, you must complete the following steps:

1. Choose Name → Define . Excel displays the Define Name dialog box.

2. Select Database and click Delete.

3. Click OK to return to the worksheet.

4. Highlight the *entire* new range.

5. In the Name box (on the Formula bar) type **Database** and press Enter. This resets the database range to include the new column. Once you select a range, you can create a data entry form.

Creating and using a data entry form

To create and use a data entry form, follow these steps:

1. In the Feed.xls file, choose Data → Form . Excel displays your Sheet 1 data entry form.

2. Type **Horse Feed** in the Product box and press Tab.

TIP You can move to the next box or *field* by pressing Tab. Pressing Shift+Tab moves you to the previous field.

3. Type 50 in the Quantity box and press Tab.

4. Type **5.99** in the Cost per Unit box and press Enter.

TIP After entering the data into the last field in a record, press Enter to go to the first field of a new record. You can also move backward or forward through existing records by pressing the up- or down-arrow key.

5. Type **Sheep Feed** in the Product field and press Tab.

6. Type **25** in the Quantity field and press Tab.

7. Type **2.99** in the Cost per Unit field and press Enter.

8. Enter the rest of the data, as listed in Table 14-1.

TABLE 14-1 Data for the Feed.xls Worksheet

Product	Quantity	Cost per Unit
CAT FEED	34	2.99
COW FEED	19	17.49
GOAT FEED	20	3.99
LLAMA FEED	3	15.99
HAMSTER FEED	12	1.99
WILD BIRD FEED	54	8.99
CHICKEN FEED	71	11.59
HOG FEED	13	19.59
RABBIT FEED	90	6.99
DOG FEED	98	5.99
TURKEY FEED	6	13.99

9. Click Close.

NOTE When you close the data entry form, notice that Excel has placed the data in the appropriate cells of your worksheet.

10. AutoFit all three columns.

11. Save your work and leave the workbook open.

TIP Using the data entry form, you can manage the records in your worksheet by adding new records, deleting unwanted records, or searching for information within records. When you add new records by using the data entry form, Excel automatically extends the Database range specifications. To see this, drop down the Name box (at the left end of the Formula bar) and choose Database. The entire range is automatically highlighted.

If you manually add records to the end of an existing database range, you must manually reset the range name. For this reason, you should use the data entry form to input data.

Sorting Information

Excel has powerful capabilities for sorting data. Because Excel allows you to sort by as many as three fields, you can be very specific about how you want your data sorted. For example, you might have an extensive customer list. Using a three-field sort, you could group customers by Zip Code, Last Name, and First Name.

Remember, when Excel sorts your data, it sorts *by records*. In other words, the data in each row always stays together.

 Always save your data before sorting. If Excel returns unexpected results, you can always close the file without saving, reopen the file, adjust your sort criteria, and try again. The Undo button usually works, but as a safety measure, always save before sorting.

You can sort in either ascending or descending order. In ascending order, Excel sorts from A to Z and from 0 through 9. In descending order, Excel sorts from 9 to 0 and Z to A.

 FEATURE FOCUS Remember, Excel for Office 97 offers multiple levels of undo (16 by default). If a sort doesn't produce the results you want, click the Undo button.

To sort your data, follow these steps:

1. Choose `Data` → `Form` to open the data entry form in the Feed.xls worksheet.

2. Click New to go to a new record. The feed store now carries two sizes of horse feed.

3. Type **Horse Feed** in the Product field and press Tab.

4. Type **75** in the Quantity field and press Tab.

5. Type **8.99** in the Cost per Unit field.

6. Click Close. Make sure that the active cell is part of your database list by clicking anywhere within the range you named Database.

NOTE You should now have two records for horse feed in your data.

7. Choose [Data] → [Sort]. As shown in Figure 14-3, Excel displays the Sort dialog box.

Figure 14-3 The Sort dialog box is used to specify how Excel should display your data.

8. If necessary, choose Product from the Sort by drop-down list.
9. In the Then by drop-down list, choose Cost per Unit.

Because your data has a header row, be sure that the Header Row radio button is marked.

10. Make sure that Ascending is chosen in both boxes.

11. Click OK.

As shown in Figure 14-4, Excel sorts the data alphabetically, placing the two types of horse feed together and then ranking them from least expensive to most expensive. This allows you to compare the differences in your data.

Finding Data by Using Filters

By using Excel's filters, you can find data that meets specific criteria. For example, suppose you want to determine the per-unit cost of cow feed. You *could* sort all your data and then find cow feed, but this becomes impractical if your spreadsheet has hundreds of records. By using filters, you can tell Excel exactly which data you want to see. Excel displays the data that fits your criteria and hides the rest.

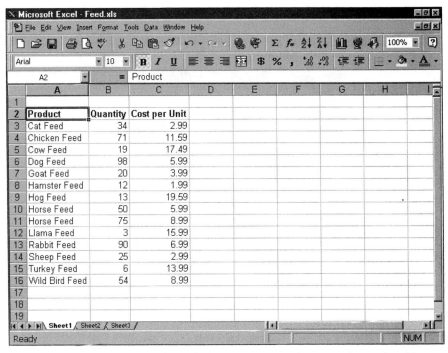

Figure 14-4 Excel sorts the data, placing common products together and ranking them by price.

Using AutoFilter to display specific data

Use AutoFilter to filter your spreadsheet based on unique data. When you use the AutoFilter feature, Excel lists all the unique data in the selected data field and offers you such options as a Top 10 list or a custom list. You can then have Excel filter out all data that does not meet the criteria you specify.

To find data by using the AutoFilter option, follow these steps:

1. In the Feed.xls worksheet, choose [Data] → [Filter] → [AutoFilter]. Excel places drop-down arrows in your column header rows, as shown in Figure 14-5.

2. Click the drop-down arrow in the Product header. Excel displays a list of criteria, as shown in Figure 14-6. You want to see how much llama feed costs.

3. Choose Llama Feed. Excel hides all data that does not match the criterion, Llama Feed, as shown in Figure 14-7. Think of this as a view of all the data for which the Product field equals Llama Feed.

Drop-down arrows

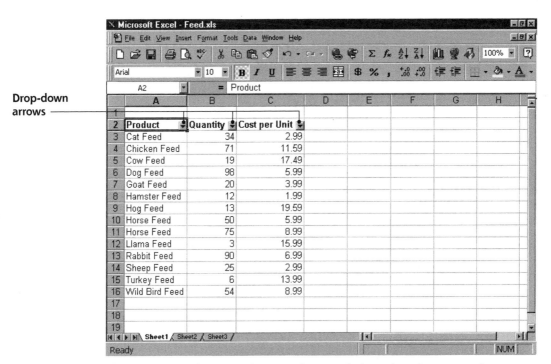

Figure 14-5   When you select AutoFilter, Excel places drop-down arrows in your column header rows.

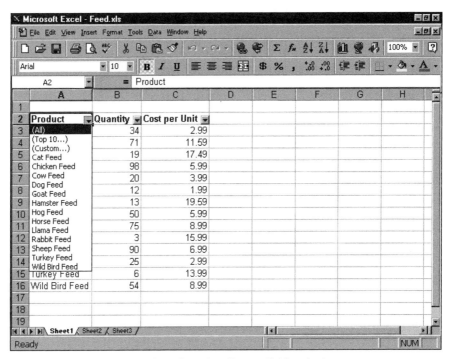

Figure 14-6   The Product drop-down box lists available criteria.

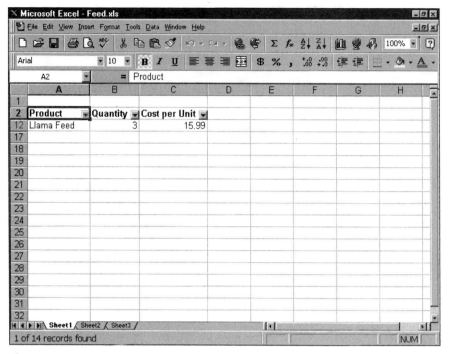

Figure 14-7 Excel displays only the Llama Feed record.

4. Click the drop-down arrow in the Product heading and choose All. This returns you to the view that shows all your data.

5. Save your work and leave the workbook open.

TIP When you turn off AutoFilter, your view automatically returns to normal.

Using the Top 10 AutoFilter

Use Excel's Top 10 AutoFilter to show the highest values for a specified data field. For example, suppose you want to find the five most expensive types of feeds. The Top 10 AutoFilter examines all data in the specified field and displays only the five highest values.

Although Microsoft named this feature the Top Ten AutoFilter, you can use the Top Ten AutoFilter to show as few as two and as many 500 highest or lowest values in a field.

The Top Ten AutoFilter can filter *only* numeric values.

To find data by using the Top 10 AutoFilter option, follow these steps:

1. In the Feed.xls worksheet, choose Data → Filter → AutoFilter . Excel turns on the AutoFilter.

2. Click the drop-down arrow in the Cost per Unit field.

3. Select Top 10. As shown in Figure 14-8, Excel displays the Top 10 dialog box. Top values is already chosen.

Figure 14-8   The Top 10 AutoFilter dialog box offers several filter options.

4. Highlight the default value of 10 and type **5**, to specify that you want to see the five most expensive feeds. You can also use the spin buttons to set this value.

5. Press Tab and make sure Items and not Percentages is chosen.

6. Click OK. Excel filters out all data except the top five values in the specified data field.

7. Save your work and leave the workbook open.

NOTE   Notice that the drop-down arrow in the Cost per Unit field is now blue. This indicates that the data in this data field is filtered.

Using the Custom AutoFilter

Use the Custom AutoFilter feature to specify the value that you want Excel to filter. For example, suppose you want to know which feeds have a per-unit price of 5.99. You can use the Custom AutoFilter to hide all records that do not meet the 5.99 criterion.

To use the Custom AutoFilter feature (AutoFilter is still activated.), follow these steps:

1. Click the drop-down arrow in the Cost per Unit field. All unique values are available for selection.

2. Select Custom. As shown in Figure 14-9, Excel displays the Custom AutoFilter dialog box.

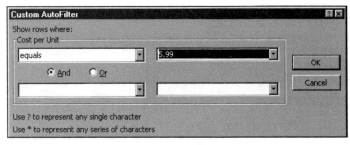

Figure 14-9 The Custom AutoFilter dialog box allows you to set strict criteria for filtering your data.

3. Using the drop-down lists, select **equals** in the top-left text box and **5.99** in the top-right text box.

TIP You have many choices for defining your custom filter. For example, you might want to find everything that is greater than or less than a specific value. To do this, specify the desired comparison operation — *is greater than* or *is less than* — in the top-left box, and then click the drop-down arrow and choose the comparison value.

FEATURE FOCUS Excel for Office 97 even allows you to perform custom filtering on text fields. For example, the *begins with* and *ends with* functions can sort your data based on the beginning or ending letter(s) of your fields.

4. Click OK. As shown in Figure 14-10, Excel shows you that Dog Feed and Horse Feed match the filter criterion: a per-unit price of 5.99. Excel hides all data that does not meet the criterion.

5. Save your work and leave the workbook open.

If you filter one category and then filter a second category, the second filter affects only the displayed data, *not* all data.

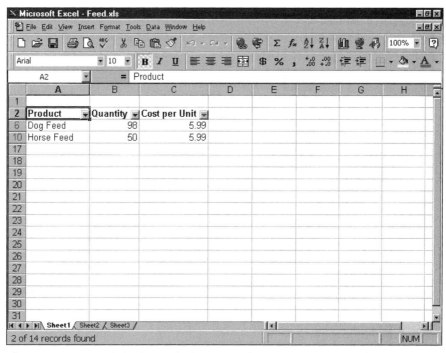

Figure 14-10 Excel displays only those records with a cost per unit of exactly 5.99.

Running Advanced Filters

In most cases, sorting your data or running a filter displays the information you need. In some cases, however, you need a more complex search to select specific data. If so, use Excel's Advanced Filter. To use this feature, you must insert at least three blank rows above the list. You use these rows — known as the *criteria range* — to define your criteria. In the criteria range (the three or more blank rows you insert), you must enter a header row and at least one row defining your search criteria.

The criteria range must contain a header row that matches the header row of your list. To ensure that they match exactly, copy the header row of your list and paste it into the header row of your criteria range.

Remember, if you enter criteria in the same row, Excel displays only those records that match *all* the criteria. If the criteria are in different rows, Excel displays all the records that meet *any one* of the criteria.

Within the criteria range, you can define your search criteria in the following ways:

* Specifying three or more conditions in one column. For example, if you want to display only Turkey Feed, Horse Feed, and Dog Feed, type these

in A2 through A4, respectively. When you type values (or text) in multiple cells of one column in the criteria range, Excel displays all records that meet *any* of those criteria.

✳ Entering criteria in two or more columns. If you enter criteria in two or more columns of the same row, Excel displays only those records that meet *all* the criteria. For example, if you type **Horse Feed** in the Product cell of the criteria range and **5.99** in the Cost per Unit cell of the same row, Excel displays only those records that meet *both* conditions.

✳ Combining criteria. For example, you might type **Horse Feed** in A2, **>50** in B3, and **<6.00** in C4. Because you entered the criteria in *different rows*, Excel responds by displaying all Horse Feed, plus all items with quantities greater than 50, plus all items with prices less than 6.00.

If you type **Horse Feed** in A2, **>50** in B2, and **<6.00** in C2 (all in the *same row*), Excel displays only those records that have Horse Feed in the Product column, more than 50 in the Quantity column, and a per-unit cost of less than 6.00.

To use the Advanced Filter to select records, follow these steps:

1. Choose Data → Filter → AutoFilter , to turn off the AutoFilter.

2. Highlight rows 1–3 in the Feed.xls worksheet.

3. Right-click the highlighted area and choose Insert . Excel inserts three new rows into your worksheet, as shown in Figure 14-11.

4. Copy the headings in row 5, and paste them into row 1.

5. Press Esc to turn off the selection.

6. Type **Horse Feed** in A2 and **8.99** in C3. This tells Excel that you want to see all records in which horse feed is the product, *as well as* all products with a per-unit price of 8.99.

7. Choose Data → Filter → Advanced Filter . Excel displays the Advanced Filter dialog box, shown in Figure 14-12.

8. Set the criteria range as **$A$1:$C$3**. You can do this by typing the range addresses in the Criteria range box (as shown in Figure 14-12), or by clicking the Collapse button at the end of the Criteria range box, selecting the cells on the worksheet, and then clicking the Collapse button again.

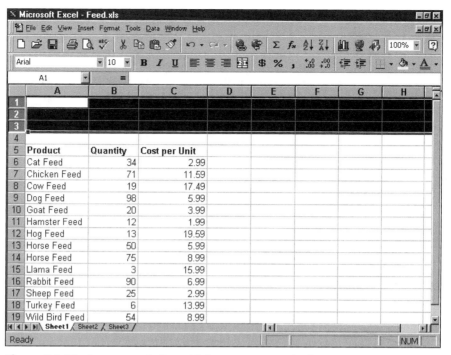

Figure 14-11 Insert rows 1, 2, and 3 for use as your criteria range.

Collapse button

Figure 14-12 The Advanced Filter dialog box allows setting a criteria range.

You must specify the *absolute* addresses of the criteria range.

9. Click OK. Excel displays all records in which the Product is Horse Feed or the price is exactly 8.99.

If you set the criteria range to extend from $A$1 to $C$4, *all* records are selected, because all records meet the *no-criteria* condition set in row 4 (row 4 is blank). Make sure that at least one cell in each row of your criteria range contains data.

Printing Lists

Printing the results of your sorts or filters works similarly to printing the different views of your data. (Chapter 10 shows how to print different views of your data.) After you complete your filter or sort, preview your document, ensure that the page layout is correct, and then print.

NOTE Excel prints only data that is *not* hidden. Therefore, until you tell Excel to Show All, it considers only the unhidden data to be your print area.

To print your data once it has been filtered, follow these steps:

1. Click the Print Preview button on the toolbar.

2. Click Margins and ensure that your margins are adequate.

3. Click Print.

4. Make sure that the number of copies is set to one, and click OK.

5. Save and close your workbook.

TIP If you used an advanced filter, Excel prints both the results *and* the criteria range. To print just the results, highlight the results and set the print area.

BONUS

Sorting Your Excel Workbook Files

Excel allows you to sort not only your data but also your workbook files. You can arrange files by name, extension, file size, and even the last date the files were modified.

Sorting by name is the most common way to organize files. When sorting by name, Excel places the files in alphabetical order. Sorting files by the date is helpful for finding recently used files. Sorting by extension can help distinguish your workbooks from your other files, such as Word or Access files. Sorting files by size does not usually help identify a file, but it does allow you to determine how much room a file takes up on your hard disk. This can be helpful for determining whether old files should be deleted or *archived* (copied to a floppy disk, a tape, or a removable hard disk cartridge).

To sort your files, follow these steps:

1. Click the Open button on the toolbar. Excel displays the Open dialog box.

2. Click the Commands and Settings button (the right-most button) on the Open dialog box toolbar.

3. Choose **Sorting** from the drop-down menu. Excel opens the Sort By dialog box shown in Figure 14-13.

Figure 14-13 Use the Sort By dialog box to specify how you want Excel to display your files.

4. Choose Modified from the Sort files by drop-down list. This sorts files according to the date on which you last modified them.

5. Click OK. If you don't see the dates, click the Details button on the toolbar (the fourth button from the right). Although your files and dates will differ from those shown in Figure 14-14, they should be similar. In addition to the File Name, Excel shows the Size, the File Type, and the Modified Date.

6. Click Cancel.

7. Exit Excel.

**Details
button**

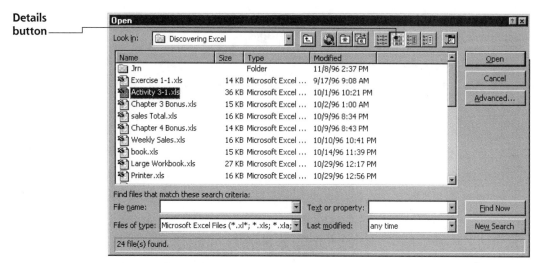

Figure 14-14   The files have been sorted in ascending order by the date that
they were last modified.

Summary

By using Excel's database features, you can simplify your data entry chores
and search your lists for valuable information. Features such as data
entry forms, sorting, and filtering can quickly reduce the amount of time
you spend entering and analyzing your data.

SHARING THE WORKLOAD: GROUP PROJECTS

IN THIS CHAPTER YOU LEARN THESE KEY SKILLS

Group projects are commonplace, and programs such as Excel offer data-sharing features that enable groups to transfer data between users with relative ease. However, data sharing can cause such problems as unauthorized access or improper data entry and file modification. By protecting data and limiting file access to specific users, you can help to prevent these problems.

By using Excel's sharing and workbook protection features — such as passwords, limited write access, and custom views — you can increase the productivity of group members while reducing the possibility of data loss.

Controlling Access to Your Files

The current emphasis on working in groups increases the importance of protecting your workbooks. If other people can access your data, you may want to prevent them from changing or deleting your data. You can restrict access to your files and protect your data by setting up passwords for your files.

Setting a password for opening a workbook

If your data includes sensitive information (such as Social Security numbers or salaries), you probably don't want everyone in your company accessing the data. You can protect this data by establishing a password that a user must enter to open the workbook. Once you set the password, a user is allowed access to your data only after entering the proper password.

To set a password for opening a workbook, follow these steps:

1. Open Excel and a new workbook.

2. Save the workbook in your Discover Excel folder as **Sharing**.

3. Type **Last Name** in A1.

4. Type **First Name** in B1.

5. Type **Social Security Number** in C1.

6. Type **Start Date** in D1.

7. AutoFit the columns.

8. Choose File → Save As . Excel displays the Save As dialog box.

9. Click Options. Excel displays the Save Options dialog box, shown in Figure 15-1. The Save Options dialog box allows you to enter two types of passwords: Password to open and Password to modify. A *to open* password allows the user to view the workbook without adding, deleting, or modifying the data. A *to modify* password gives the user full access to the data.

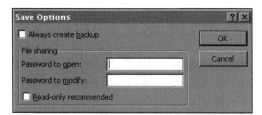

Figure 15-1 The Save Options dialog box allows you to set two types of passwords.

10. Type **cooperation** in the Password to open text box. Be sure to type the password accurately; you do not see it on the screen. Excel displays asterisks in place of the characters that you type.

11. Click OK. Excel opens the Confirm Password dialog box, shown in Figure 15-2. In this dialog box, you must confirm your password by reentering it *exactly* as you did in the Save Options dialog box.

Excel and other Microsoft products use *case-sensitive* passwords. In other words, a password that includes a capital *A* is not the same as one with a lowercase *a* in that position. Therefore, when you type your password, make sure that you remember whether you use any capital letters.

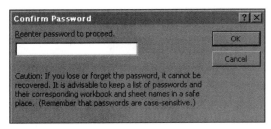

Figure 15-2   The Confirm Password dialog box verifies that the password you typed is correct.

Even though the Confirm Password dialog box warns you of password dangers, the following point is worth repeating: If you lose or forget your password, your data is locked *forever* (under normal circumstances). You cannot access your data without the proper password. Therefore, make sure you write down your password and put it somewhere safe.

12. Type **cooperation** in the Reenter password to proceed text box. Again, asterisks appear as you type.

13. Click OK. Excel returns you to the Save As dialog box.

If you incorrectly enter the confirmation password, Excel displays an error message similar to the example shown in Figure 15-3. (Your message box may look different, depending on the Office Assistant you have selected.) When you click OK, Excel returns you to the *original* Save Options dialog box to reenter the password. You are then asked to confirm the new password.

14. In the Save as dialog box, click Save. Excel asks you if you want to replace the existing file.

15. Click Yes.

16. Choose File → Close . Excel closes the Sharing.xls file. Now you can try out your new password.

Figure 15-3 Excel warns you if you incorrectly enter the confirmation password.

17. Choose `File` → `Open` and open the Sharing.xls file.

18. When prompted to enter the password, type **none**. Without the proper password, Excel denies access to the workbook.

19. Click OK.

20. Open Sharing.xls once more, and this time type **cooperation** in the password text box. With the correct password, Excel grants you access to the file.

TIP To remove a password from a file, you must first open the file. Then open the Save As dialog box, click Options, and delete the password from the text box. Click OK two times to save the file.

Setting a password for modifying a workbook

You can also establish a password that users must enter if they want not only to view the data but also to modify your workbook. In this way, some users can view your data, whereas others can enter an additional password and then modify the file.

To set a password that allows the user to modify the workbook, follow these steps:

1. In the Sharing.xls workbook, choose `File` → `Save As`. Excel displays the Save As dialog box.

2. Click Options. Excel displays the Save Options dialog box.

3. Enter **share** in the Password to modify text box and then click OK. Excel displays the Confirm Password dialog box.

4. Type **share** and then click OK. Excel returns you to the Save As dialog box.

5. Click Save. Excel asks if you want to replace the existing file.

6. Click Yes.

7. Close the Sharing.xls file.

8. Reopen the file.

TIP Remember, if you forget your password, you are denied access to the file. If your data is very important, you can purchase a program to unlock your password-protected file. For additional information, visit the following Web site:

WEB PATH `http://www.crak.com`

The program costs approximately $100, but if your data is important, this may be a worthwhile investment.

9. In the Password dialog box, type the password **cooperation** to open the file. As shown in Figure 15-4, Excel opens a second Password dialog box that asks you to enter the password for write access.

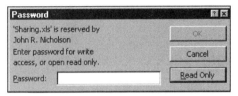

Figure 15-4 Excel differentiates between the password for opening a file and the password for modifying that file.

TIP To view your data without being able to modify it, click Read Only in the second Password dialog box.

10. Type **share** in the Password text box and click OK, because you want to modify the workbook.

11. Leave the workbook open for the next activity.

Sharing Files

Whether you work for a large corporation or small company, your computer is probably part of a network that lets you share data and exchange e-mail with other users. Small groups of networked users, known as *workgroups*, can share access to the same worksheets or workbooks, and thus group members can efficiently examine and modify one another's work. By sharing your files, you can let other people read the data in your files and, if necessary, make changes to the data.

You can share files within Excel in several ways, depending on the amount of access you want to allow each user. Before setting up your shared files, you need to determine which access privilege each member of your workgroup requires:

* Members who need to view the data but don't need to change it or add to it should have *read-only* privileges. This means they cannot modify the file in any way.

* Members who need to make additions or changes to the data should have *read/write* privileges.

When working with one file, you must limit the access privileges of those users who don't need to modify the file. Few things are more frustrating than having your data or formulas accidentally deleted or changed by someone who shouldn't have write privileges. You can avoid unnecessary problems by limiting access privileges.

Letting many workers access one copy

For the simplest approach to sharing data within a workgroup, create one file that everyone can access. If you use a network, you can store this file in a central location (such as a network drive) and each user can access it simply by opening the file.

NOTE Remember, just because each user has *access* to the file does not mean that everyone needs to modify the data.

To allow multiple users to work on the same workbook, set up a *shared list*. This list identifies which users can access the workbook and make changes to the file.

To create a shared list so that multiple users can work on a single workbook at the same time, follow these steps:

1. In the Sharing.xls workbook, choose `Tools` → `Share Workbook`. Excel displays the Share Workbook dialog box, shown in Figure 15-5.

2. Click to place a check in the Allow changes . . . box. This tells Excel that you want to let more than one person modify the workbook at the same time.

FEATURE FOCUS This is a new command. In previous versions of Excel, you create a shared workbook by choosing `File` → `Share List`.

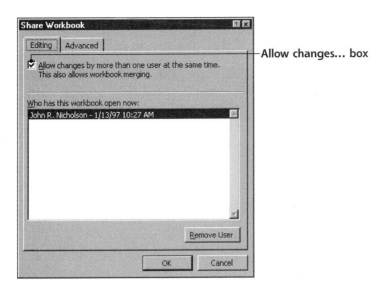

Figure 15-5 The Share Workbook dialog box is used to set up access privileges for your workbook.

NOTE If you don't check the Allow changes . . . box, the first user to open the workbook has both read and write privileges. Every user who opens the file after that has read-only privileges. Then, after the first user exits the workbook, the second user is given the option of taking the read-write privileges.

3. Click OK. Excel displays the message "This action will now save the workbook. Do you want to continue?"

4. Click OK. As shown in Figure 15-6, Excel now displays the word *Shared* next to the filename in the Program title bar, indicating that this workbook is part of a shared list.

Giving each worker a copy of a file

You can also share data by making copies of the workbook and distributing them to individual users. This method is especially useful for situations in which one or more users need to work on the file away from their networked computers.

For example, if you need to take your workbook home and enter data, you won't have access to the file you stored on the network. Additionally, any changes you make to the workbook won't be reflected in the file stored on the network. For these reasons, Excel allows you to distribute multiple copies of the same workbook. Once the various users have entered their data, you can merge their files into one complete workbook.

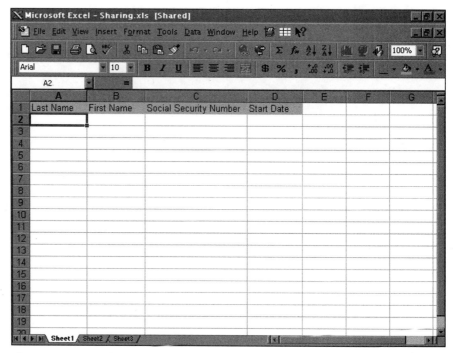

Figure 15-6   Excel places the word *Shared* next to your filename, to show that the file is part of a shared list.

If you distribute copies to multiple users, make sure that all users have identical copies of the original workbook. Additionally, the users *must* understand that if they make changes to the *format* of the workbook, the files will not merge correctly.

To prevent users from accidentally changing their copies of the workbook, lock any cells that they don't need to access (such as headings). By locking these cells, you prevent users from making changes that might prevent merging their copies with the other workbooks.

To distribute copies of a workbook to multiple users, follow these steps:

1. Choose File → Save As . Excel opens the Save As dialog box.

2. Type **Sharing Original** in the File name text box, and click Save.

If you make errors in the following activities, you can delete the three Sharing files you create in the following steps and make a copy of the Sharing Original by opening Sharing Original, renaming the copy Sharing.xls, and beginning this activity again. If you don't save a copy as Sharing Original, and you make any mistakes in the following activities, you must delete Sharing, Sharing 2, and Sharing 3, return to the first Hands-On activity in this chapter, and begin again. This is a very exacting process, so follow the steps closely.

3. Choose [File] → [Save As] again. Excel opens the Save As dialog box.

4. Type **Sharing2** in the File name text box, and click Save.

TIP It is always a good idea to store a copy of your original file on a floppy disk. That way if something happens to the original, you can restore the file.

5. Choose [File] → [Save As] again, and save the file as **Sharing3**. Notice that only the most recently named file remains open.

NOTE At this point, you would distribute copies of the files to other members of your workgroup so that they can enter their data. To simulate this process in the next few steps of this exercise, you make changes to the individual worksheets, so that you can see how data is entered. In the following section, "Combining workbooks," you learn how to merge the various copies.

6. Open the Sharing.xls workbook and the Sharing2.xls workbook. You have to enter the passwords to open these files. (The passwords are **cooperation** and **share**.) All three workbooks should now be open.

7. Choose [Window] → [Arrange]. Excel displays the Arrange Windows dialog box.

TIP Because Sharing2.xls and Sharing3.xls are *exact* copies of Sharing.xls, they have the same passwords. Remember to enter **cooperation** as your password to open and **share** as your password to modify.

8. Click the Vertical radio button and then click OK. This displays the workbooks side by side.

9. Type **Kremers** in A2 of the Sharing.xls file, and press Tab.

10. Type **Lynn** in B2 and press Tab.

11. Type **333-44-5555** in C2 and press Tab.

12. Type **08-15-90** in D2 and press Enter.

13. Save the Sharing.xls file.

14. Type **Taylor** in A2 of the Sharing2.xls file, and press Tab.

15. Type **Steve** in B2 and press Tab.

16. Type **111-22-3333** in C2 and press Tab.

17. Type **05-19-92** in D2 and press Enter.

18. Save the Sharing2.xls file.

19. Type **Cashatt** in A2 of the Sharing3.xls workbook, and press Tab.

20. Type **Drew** in B2 and press Tab.

21. Type **222-33-4444** in C2 and press Tab.

22. Type **03-09-95** in D2 and press Enter. Your screen should look similar to Figure 15-7.

23. Close Sharing3.xls and save the changes.

24. Close Sharing2.xls and save the changes.

25. Save the changes to Sharing.xls, and leave this file open for the next activity.

Combining workbooks

After the members of your workgroup have entered their data into the individual copies of the workbook, you need to combine the various copies. Excel makes combining the workbooks easy by allowing you to *merge* the individual workbooks into a *host* workbook.

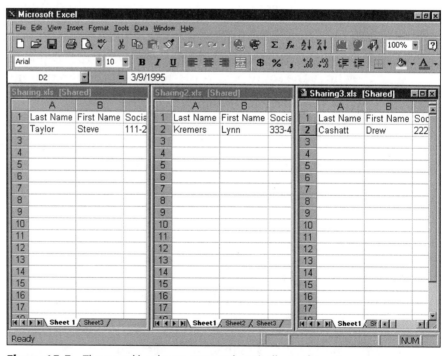

Figure 15-7 Three workbooks are arranged vertically on the screen.

To merge multiple copies of the same workbook, follow these steps:

1. Maximize the Sharing.xls workbook by clicking the maximize button in the upper-right corner of the *worksheet* window.

Excel does *not* merge open files. When you merge files, only your *host* file — in this case, Sharing.xls — should be open.

2. Choose Tools → Merge Workbooks . Excel displays the Select Files to Merge Into Current Workbook dialog box, shown in Figure 15-8.

If Merge Workbooks is grayed out, you forgot to place a check mark in the Allow changes . . . text box in the Editing tab of the Share Workbook dialog box. To correct the problem, choose Tools → Share Workbook and place a check mark in the appropriate box.

You want to merge Sharing2.xls *into* Sharing.xls.

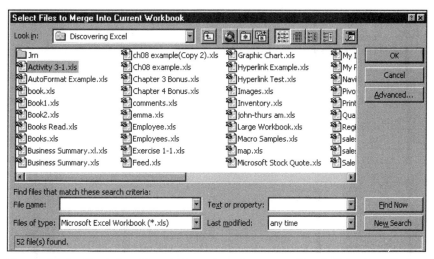

Figure 15-8 The Select Files to Merge Into Current Workbook dialog box displays available files.

3. Select Sharing2.xls and click OK. As shown in Figure 15-9, Excel inserts the data and places a blue marker in the upper-left corner of each inserted cell. When you place the cursor on any of the inserted cells, the change information appears.

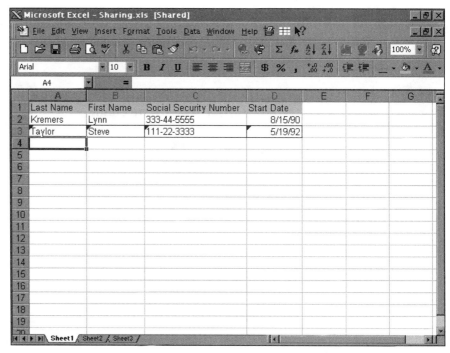

Figure 15-9 Excel places blue change markers in those cells that have been modified elsewhere.

NOTE The blue notation markers remain in the cells of the most recently entered data. They disappear when you merge newer data into the workbook.

4. Choose **Tools** → **Merge Workbooks** again. Excel displays the Select Files to Merge Into Current Workbook dialog box.

5. Select Sharing3.xls and click OK. Once again, Excel inserts data into the host sheet and places blue markers in the most recently merged cells.

TIP To merge more than one workbook at a time, in the Select Files to Merge Into Current Workbook dialog box, hold Shift while you select contiguous files, or Ctrl to select files that are not adjacent.

6. Save the Sharing.xls file and leave it open.

Tracking Changes

When a workbook is shared, each user must know what changes the other users have made. Excel offers two ways for you to track and review the modifications made by other users.

The default method for tracking changes is *highlighting*. When you create a shared list, Excel automatically assigns a different color to each user. Whenever a change is made, Excel highlights the modified cells by using the color assigned to the user who changed them.

For the highlighting option to work properly, you must set up your workbook as a shared workbook *before* changes are made. Excel does not highlight any changes made prior to setting the workbook as shared.

You can also track changes by creating a separate *history worksheet*. For easy review, this worksheet tracks all changes made within the workbook. The history worksheet allows you to filter out certain types of changes. For example, you may want to see only the changes that were made by a certain user. Using the history worksheet's filter, you can hide all other changes.

Highlighting changes in a workbook

Follow these steps to set up your workbook so that you can use highlighting to track the changes made by other users.

1. In the Sharing.xls workbook, choose Tools → Track Changes → Highlight Changes . Excel displays the Highlight Changes dialog box, shown in Figure 15-10.

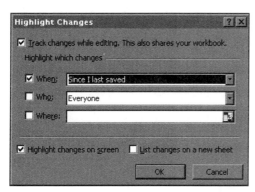

Figure 15-10 The Highlight Changes dialog box helps track the changes in your workbook.

2. Make sure the Track changes while editing box is checked.

3. Make sure the When box is checked.

4. In the When drop-down box, choose All.

5. Check the Who box, and choose Everyone from the Who drop-down box.

6. Make sure the Highlight changes on screen box is checked.

7. Click OK. Because you have merged data into this workbook, Excel places blue markers in the cells that have been merged.

8. Highlight cells A4 through D4. Excel places a yellow border around the selected cells. Excel highlights any changes you make in yellow.

9. Save the workbook and leave it open.

Creating a history worksheet

To set up a history worksheet to track all changes made to your workbook, follow these steps:

1. In the Sharing.xls workbook, choose Tools → Track Changes → Highlight Changes . Excel displays the Highlight Changes dialog box.

2. Check the List changes on a new sheet box, and then click OK. Excel creates a separate worksheet in your workbook and names it History. As shown in Figure 15-11, this worksheet documents all changes, who made them, and when they were made.

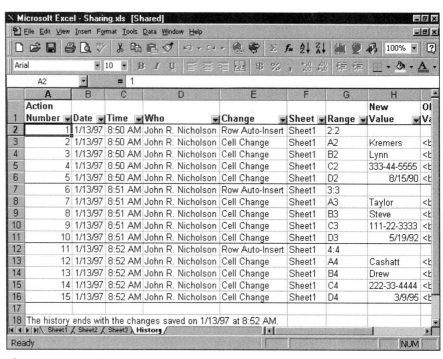

Figure 15-11 The History worksheet documents all changes made to your workbook.

In many cases, you need to see only the changes made to a specific cell or range of cells. To view only the changes made to D2, click the Range column's filter drop-down arrow and then choose D2 from the drop-down list. As shown in Figure 15-12, Excel filters out all data except the changes made to D2.

3. Return the History worksheet to the normal view by dropping down the filter arrow in the Range column and choosing (All).

4. Save your file. When you save the file, the History sheet disappears and your workbook returns to its normal view.

TIP   Excel automatically updates the history worksheet and does not let anyone modify it. This prevents other users from hiding any changes they make.

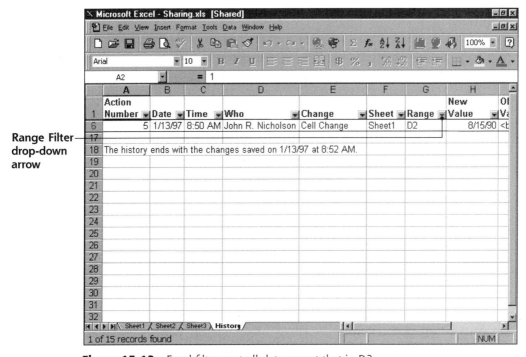

Figure 15-12   Excel filters out all data except that in D2.

Accepting or rejecting the changes in your workbook

For the final step in tracking changes to a workbook, the project leader decides whether to accept the changes made by others. The leader should regularly review all changes and decide whether they are correct.

TIP   You can reject unwanted changes. Excel restores the changed cells to reflect their previous values, even if they were previously empty.

Once you decide whether the changes are valid, you can accept them and Excel will remove them from your History worksheet. Once you accept the changes, they become a *permanent* part of your workbook.

To accept or reject the changes to your worksheet, follow these steps:

1. In the Sharing.xls workbook, choose Tools → Track Changes → Accept or Reject Changes . Excel opens the Select Changes to Accept or Reject dialog box.

2. Check the When box, and choose Not yet reviewed from the When drop-down list.

3. Check the Who box, and choose Everyone from the Who drop-down list.

4. Click OK. As shown in Figure 15-13, Excel opens the Accept or Reject Changes dialog box.

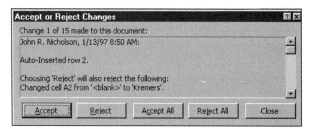

Figure 15-13   Use the Accept or Reject Changes dialog box to choose the changes you want to keep and reject those you don't want.

TIP   **The Accept or Reject Changes dialog box allows you either to accept or reject the changes one at a time or accept all changes or reject all changes.**

Because *you* made the changes to Sharing.xls during this activity, you know they are correct. Right? Aha! Caught you! That's one of the three terrible assumptions that users make about their spreadsheets. If this weren't just a practice activity, you would want to be sure to check all your changes for accuracy.

5. Click Accept All. If you had rejected any of the changes, Excel would replace the contents of those cells with the original data.

6. Save your work and leave the workbook open.

BONUS

Setting Independent (Personal) Views and Print Options

When sharing a workbook, you may not want certain users to see or print parts of your workbook. For example, if you are sharing a workbook that contains employee information, you may not want anyone else seeing employee salaries.

Excel allows you to limit specific users to specific views. Limiting the view also limits the data that can be printed.

To change the view that users can access, follow these steps:

1. In the Sharing.xls workbook, rename Sheet 1 as **Primary**.

2. Rename Sheet 2 as **Secondary**.

3. On the Primary worksheet, copy cells A1 through B4.

4. Select the Secondary worksheet.

5. Click A1 and click the Paste button on the toolbar. Cells A1 through B4 are filled with the data from the Primary worksheet.

6. Type **Annual Pay** in C1.

7. Type **95,000** in C2 and press Enter.

8. Type **92,500** in D2 and press Enter.

9. Type **96,300** in E2 and press Enter. As long as you are making up salaries, you may as well make them good ones! You do not want other users to access the Secondary sheet.

10. Choose `Format` → `Sheet` → `Hide`. Excel hides the Secondary sheet from view.

11. Select `View` → `Custom Views`. As shown in Figure 15-14, Excel displays the Custom Views dialog box.

12. Click Add. Excel opens the Add View dialog box.

13. Type **Sam's View** in the Name box.

15

Figure 15-14 The Custom Views dialog box is used to limit the views of other users.

14. Click the Print settings box to turn off the check mark. This restrict the user's ability to make changes to the print settings of the view.

15. Check the Hidden rows . . . box, to turn off the check mark. This restricts the user's ability to unhide any hidden rows, columns, or sheets.

If you don't remove the check mark from the Hidden rows . . . box, the user can simply unhide any hidden rows, columns, or sheets and then print or change them.

16. Click OK.

17. Choose `Format` → `Sheet` → `Unhide`. Excel displays the Unhide dialog box.

18. Highlight the Secondary sheet and click OK. Your view returns to normal, with the Secondary sheet again visible.

19. Choose `View` → `Custom Views`. Excel displays the Custom Views dialog box.

20. Select Sam's View and click Show. This shows the view you created for Sam; Excel automatically hides the Secondary sheet.

21. Save your work and close all open workbooks.

22. Exit Excel.

TIP To restrict a user's view, simply create the view that you want the user to have, copy the shared file, and distribute the file to the user *with that view only*. Using the Custom Views dialog box, you can remove any views that you don't want the user to have.

One final warning is in order: If you give Sam the read/write password, he can still unhide the hidden worksheet, if he knows that it exists.

Summary

By learning how to share workbooks among multiple users, you can provide a more efficient means for transferring and modifying data and thus increase the productivity of your workgroup. And by using Excel's protection features, you can avoid accidental modification of data, by restricting access to your workbooks, worksheets, and specific data.

REAL-LIFE SOLUTIONS

This part of the book examines some common problems that you may encounter, and suggests solutions. You find out how to link your worksheet charts and files with other documents.

The major new feature in Excel 97 is its capability to *hyperlink*, or jump, from one part of the worksheet to another at the click of a button. But hyperlinking doesn't stop there — you can also click to other workbooks, to other spots on your company's Intranet, or to a site on the World Wide Web. Hyperlinking offers an easy method for sharing data with other users throughout the world.

No worksheet is without errors, and in this part you find out how to troubleshoot those errors and correct them. Because we can't cover all possible errors in a book of this size, you also find out where to go for additional help.

"The main trick here is knowing how to set up the data. In your head, you know what you want the numbers to tell you, but it's not always easy to tell the computer how to do it."

You might expect those words from your boss or maybe from a computer instructor. But when you look at Tim Norris, you probably wouldn't think of sorting data. It's not that Tim looks dumb or anything; he just looks like he has better things to do. After all, he's a teenager. "Well, almost," Tim corrects. "I'm twelve and a half."

So why is Tim sorting columns when he could be out on the football field? Actually, he has time for both, and his love of sports and computing are closely related. Earlier this year, Tim sprained his knee in the middle of the football season, which forced him to miss the last four games of the season. He couldn't bear to miss the games, however.

He quickly found a solution. No one was keeping the statistics for his team, and he had always had an interest in numbers. Problem solved. "I enjoyed keeping the statistics," Tim recalls, "but when the game was done, the numbers were just sitting there. I knew they could tell me more, but I didn't know how to get them to talk." That's where Excel came in.

Tim's mother, an accountant, suggested that he enter the game's statistics into Excel. "Tim had used the computer many times before for games and Internet topics," she remembers, "but this time, he was using it like an adult would. I taught him how to use formulas once or twice, and he immediately caught on."

"All season long," Tim says, trying to change the subject, "our third downs were really unreliable. We punted way too much, and our punter wasn't very good. I thought that if I could figure out why our third downs are so poor, maybe we wouldn't end up punting so much, which means not as many turnovers."

That sounds logical, but how can a software program and a Nintendo jockey do all that? "It's really pretty simple," Tim replies. "For every play of the game, I have an Excel column for the following things: The down, yards to go, what yard line we're on, what play we run, who carries the ball, how many yards we get, and a few more things." What he found was remarkable. "First, I sorted the data to find third-down plays. From that group, I found the plays where we got six or more yards on the play. Nine times out of ten, that play was either a bootleg pass or an option around the short side of the field."

Needless to say, Tim's coach was impressed. "We've done better ever since," Tim says, "and next year, we're going to have two student statisticians." Neither of which will be Tim. "I'll look at the data, but not until after the game. Next year, I'm on the field!"

HYPERLINKING: THERE AND BACK AGAIN

IN THIS CHAPTER YOU LEARN THESE KEY SKILLS

I f only J.R.R. Tolkien's Hobbit hero, Bilbo Baggins, had the ability to hyperlink, his life would have been amazingly simplified. He could have hyperlinked to Smaug's cave, plucked the treasure from under the dragon's fire-belching nose, and hyperlinked home. Of course, then Tolkien would have written a short story, rather than the adventure-packed novel, *The Hobbit*.

Luckily for you, Excel 97 adds the capability to *hyperlink* (jump) among worksheets, workbooks, computers on your Intranet, or even Internet sites. This capability can transform your workload from a novel of perplexing proportions into a simple short story.

Hyperlinking is rather like the transport room aboard a starship (if you're a Trekker, you understand this; if not, just ignore this sentence). You set the coordinates for where you want to go, and you are immediately taken to that place. This is a much faster method of navigation than manually typing each reference, as you see later in this chapter.

T I P   If you haven't yet experienced the Internet, this chapter is probably *not* the best way to learn about it. A better way is by using an Internet-specific guide, such as *Internet For Dummies*™, by John Levine and Carol Baroudi. (Notice that I never hesitate to plug an IDG book!) If you have at least surfed the Internet using a commercial or not-for-profit provider, you already have a knowledge base from which you can expand. Surfing the Internet without a guide is similar to using a remote control on a television that receives, oh, about 40 or 50 million channels; you will find what you need only by luck. With so many channels to choose from, it's probably best to limit yourself to those sites that you find helpful.

Excel 97 is laden with tools for working with the Internet. Actually, Excel doesn't have its own tools but is tightly integrated with Microsoft Internet Explorer. You can easily retrieve information, such as stock quotes, by following very simple instructions. You can also place your own work on the Internet so that others can view it, or even so that they can download information from your worksheet directly into their own worksheets.

To complete some of the more complex hands-on activities in this chapter, you need an Internet connection. You also need a *browser* (a piece of software specifically designed to access the Internet) to view data. Microsoft Excel 97 comes with Microsoft Internet Explorer, one of the three most popular browser programs (the other two are Netscape and Mosaic).

Creating and Using Hyperlinks: Beam Me Up

Before I get any further into this Internet discussion, you need to understand how hyperlinking works. Hyperlinks are brand new to Excel 97. They can be links to locations on the current worksheet, on other worksheets within the workbook, in other workbooks, or even to other computers (through an Internet or Intranet connection). Inserting hyperlinks is straightforward, as long as you know where you want to go.

Creating internal workbook hyperlinks

You can use hyperlinks to move the cursor to any position in the current worksheet or workbook. All hyperlinks (internal or external) have a specific syntax. However, Excel includes an Insert Hyperlink button ▣ on the toolbar to automate the task of creating a hyperlink.

Using the Insert Hyperlink dialog box, shown in Figure 16-1, you can create either an *external* hyperlink reference (a reference to a source outside the current workbook) or an *internal* hyperlink reference (a reference to another location within the current workbook). I cover the Link to file or URL drop-down box later in this chapter. First, you need to learn how to create internal hyperlink references.

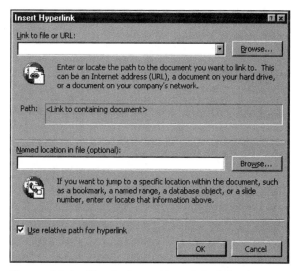

Figure 16-1 Use the Insert Hyperlink dialog box to create links easily.

The easiest way to learn about hyperlinks is to use them. You begin by creating a link to a specific cell in the current worksheet, and then to a named range.

When creating a hyperlink, to make things easier, use the Insert Hyperlink dialog box, rather than manually creating the formula. The first part of the following activity is fairly long, because you create a workbook with five worksheets. However, you continue to use this workbook throughout the rest of this chapter.

1. Open Excel and a new workbook. *Don't* save the workbook yet; you do that in a few minutes. Make sure the Web toolbar is turned *off*. (Right-click any toolbar and make sure that there isn't a check mark next to **Web** in the toolbar list.)

2. Click Sheet3.

3. Choose **Insert** → **Worksheet**. Sheet4 is added.

4. Repeat the preceding command (this gives you a total of five worksheets).

5. From the left (Sheet1), rename the worksheets **First Qtr, Second Qtr, Third Qtr, Fourth Qtr**, and **Navigation.**

6. Choose **Tools** → **Add-Ins**. Excel displays the Add-Ins dialog box.

7. Make sure the Analysis ToolPak has a check mark next to it, and then click OK. As usual, you're going to create a series of random numbers.

8. Click the First Qtr worksheet tab to make it active.

9. Press Shift and click the Fourth Qtr tab. This groups the worksheets, so whatever you enter on one is replicated on the other worksheets. (You *didn't* select the Navigation tab, because you don't want to create data on it.)

10. Type **January** in B1.

11. AutoFill February and March in C1 through D1.

12. Type **Total** in E1.

13. Type **North, South, East,** and **West** in A2 through A5, respectively.

14. Type **Total** in A6.

15. In B2, type **=RANDBETWEEN(5000,10000).**

16. AutoFill B2 through D2.

17. With B2 through D2 still selected, drag the AutoFill handle down to row 5. Excel fills B2 through D5 with random numbers between 5,000 and 10,000.

18. Click the Copy button on the toolbar.

19. Choose Edit → Paste Special , click the Values radio button, and then click OK.

20. Press Esc to turn off the marquis.

21. Click E2 and then double-click the AutoSum button.

22. AutoFill E2 through E5.

23. Click B6 and then double-click the AutoSum button.

24. AutoFill B6 through E6.

25. Select B2 through E6, click the Currency Style button, and then click the Decrease Decimal button twice.

26. Right-click the First Qtr tab and choose Ungroup Sheets from the resulting pop-up menu.

27. In the Second, Third, and Fourth Qtr sheets, change the names of the months to reflect the correct months for each quarter. D1 on the Fourth Qtr sheet should be December.

28. Click the First Qtr tab and then click A1. Your workbook should be similar to the one shown in Figure 16-2. Your values will differ from those shown in the figure.

29. Click the Navigation worksheet tab.

30. With A1 as the active cell, click the Insert Hyperlink button on the Standard toolbar. It looks like a globe with chain links across the bottom. You are prompted to save the document.

Insert
Hyperlink
button

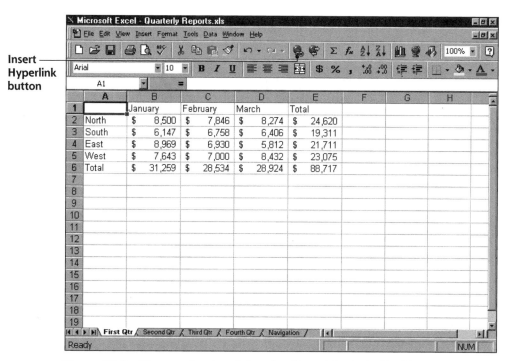

Figure 16-2 The completed worksheet for this activity looks like this.

31. Click Yes. Excel displays the Save As dialog box.

32. Double-click the Discover Excel folder, and type **Quarterly Reports** in the File name text box.

33. Click Save. Excel displays the Insert Hyperlink dialog box, shown earlier in Figure 16-1.

34. Click Browse. This is the *lower* of the two Browse buttons, used for internal references. As shown in Figure 16-3, Excel displays the Browse Excel Workbook dialog box.

35. Make sure the Sheet name radio button is active.

36. Type E6 in the Reference box. In the lower panel, you see the names of all worksheets in the current workbook.

37. Make sure the 'First Qtr' sheet *name* is selected, and then click OK. The Insert Hyperlink dialog box is again displayed. Notice that Named location in file (optional) box contains 'First Qtr'!E6. This points the link to the First Qtr worksheet (the worksheet name is in single quotes, followed by an exclamation point), at the appropriate cell reference (E6).

38. Click OK. 'First Qtr'!E6 is inserted in A1.

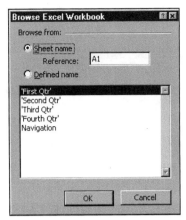

Figure 16-3 The Browse Excel Workbook dialog box is used to set a hyperlink reference within the current workbook.

39. Click C2 so that you can see how the hyperlink appears in your worksheet. Your worksheet should look like Figure 16-4. The hyperlink appears in blue and is underlined.

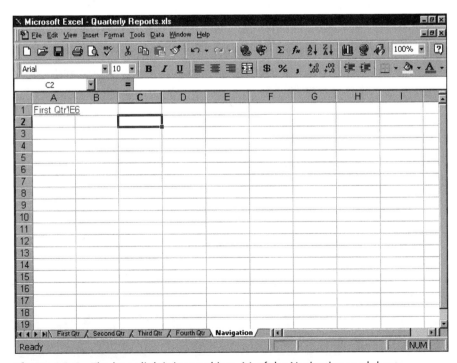

Figure 16-4 The hyperlink is inserted into A1 of the Navigation worksheet.

40. Use the mouse to move the cursor onto A1. The mouse cursor changes to a pointing finger.

41. Click the hyperlink. The active cell becomes E6 on the First Qtr worksheet. Notice that Excel automatically displays the Web toolbar, shown in Figure 16-5. By hyperlinking locations, you can navigate using the Web toolbar.

42. Click the Back button on the Web toolbar. You are immediately returned to A1 on the Navigation worksheet. The link color changes to purple, showing that you have already used this link. You can use the link again; the color simply reminds you that you have visited that site.

43. Save the workbook and leave it open.

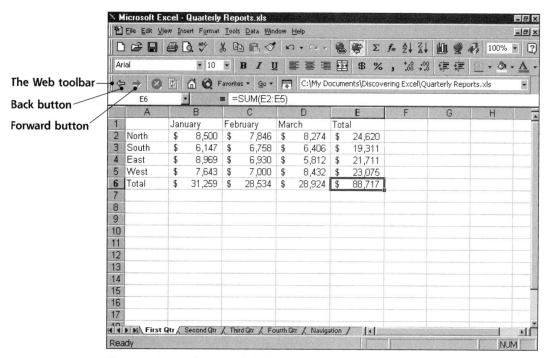

The Web toolbar

Back button

Forward button

Figure 16-5 When you click the hyperlink, Excel takes you to the linked location and displays the Web toolbar.

Changing the hyperlink name

If you click the cell containing the hyperlink, the active cell changes to the linked location. To edit the hyperlink, you need to sneak up on it. Because you can't click it without going to the linked location, you need to click any empty cell and then use the arrow keys on the keyboard to highlight the hyperlink you want to edit.

As you saw in the previous activity, Excel displays the hyperlink entry in a location format (for example, 'First Qtr'!E6). This doesn't make it easy to navigate if you have a large worksheet. Here, you give the link a friendly name that is easier for you to understand. A1 on the Navigation worksheet should still be active.

1. Type **First Quarter Total** and press Enter. A2 becomes the active cell. The name of the link is changed, but its association with E6 on the First Qtr worksheet is maintained.

2. To make sure that your renamed hyperlink still works, click it. Then click the Back button on the Web toolbar to return to the Navigation worksheet.

3. Now, in A2 through A4, create hyperlinks for the totals for each of the other three quarters.

4. Rename them on the Navigation worksheet as **Second Quarter Total**, **Third Quarter Total**, and **Fourth Quarter Total.** Remember, you must use the keyboard arrow keys to highlight the cell you want to change.

5. Check each of your links. Remember to use the Back button to return to the Navigation worksheet.

6. AutoFit column A on the Navigation worksheet.

7. Save the workbook and leave it open.

Deleting a hyperlink

You shouldn't delete any of the hyperlinks that you just created. Just so you know, here's how to delete a hyperlink:

1. Click any cell that doesn't contain a hyperlink.

2. Using the *arrow keys,* move to the hyperlink you want to delete.

3. Choose Edit → Clear → All .

Creating hyperlinks using range names

Previously, you learned to hyperlink to a specific cell in a worksheet. You can also easily create a hyperlink that moves to a named range within a worksheet. This is particularly helpful if you want to print several ranges.

To create a named range and then reference it in a hyperlink, follow these steps:

1. Click the First Quarter Total hyperlink (in A1). Excel displays the First Qtr worksheet.

2. Select A1 through E6. You need to define a range name for the selected cells.

3. Choose [Insert] → [Name] → [Define]. Excel displays the Define Name dialog box, shown in Figure 16-6. You use this dialog box to assign a name to the selected range. Notice that the selected range is shown in the Refers to text box at the bottom of the dialog box.

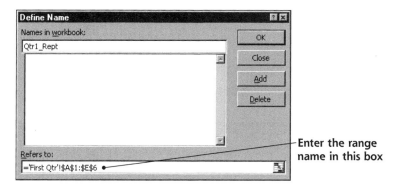

Figure 16-6 The Define Name dialog box allows you to name a selected cell or group of cells.

4. In the Names in workbook text box, type **Qtr1_Rept**.

5. Click OK. The Range name of the selected range is displayed in the Name box on the Formula toolbar.

6. Click A1 to remove the selection.

7. Click the Back button, to return to the Navigation worksheet.

8. Click A7 on the Navigation worksheet.

9. Click the Insert Hyperlink button on the toolbar. Excel displays the Insert Hyperlink dialog box.

10. Click Browse. Make sure you click the lower of the two Browse buttons.

11. In the Browse Excel Workbook dialog box, click the Defined name radio button. All defined names in the *workbook* are displayed, as shown in Figure 16-7.

Each range name can exist only once in a single workbook. If you define a range named "Test" on Sheet1, and then define a range named "Test" on Sheet3, the reference is simply changed from Sheet1 to Sheet3. Make sure that each range in a workbook has a unique name.

12. Click OK, because Qtr1_Rept is already highlighted. If the current workbook contained additional named ranges, all would be listed in the dialog box. The named range, "Qtr1_Rept," is inserted in the Named location in file (optional) box in the Insert Hyperlink dialog box.

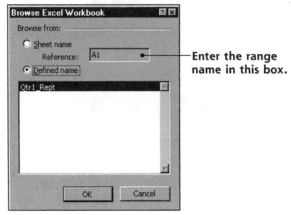

Enter the range
name in this box.

Figure 16-7 The <u>D</u>efined name
option displays all
defined names in
the workbook.

13. Click OK to return to the active worksheet. A7 contains the underlined range name.

14. Click A8.

15. Press the up-arrow key, to make A7 the active cell.

16. Type **First Quarter Report** and press Enter.

17. Click the newly created link in A7. Your screen should be similar to Figure 16-8.

18. Create range names and hyperlinks to the other three worksheets.

TIP Here's a shortcut for naming ranges: Select the range you want to name, click in the Name Box at the left of the Formula toolbar (it normally contains the address of the current cell), and type the range name. It must be a legal range name (no spaces), and you *must* press Enter after you type the name of the range. If you have done everything correctly, the new range name appears in the Name box.

19. Save the workbook and close it.

20. Turn off the Web toolbar.

21. Leave Excel open.

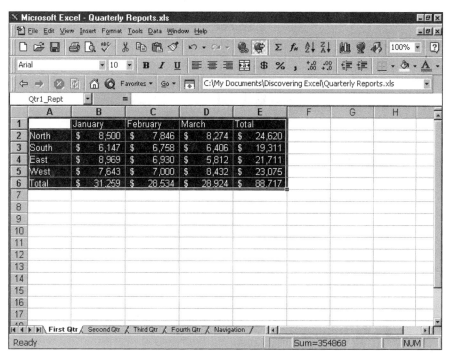

Figure 16-8 The range named Qtr1_Rept is automatically selected.

Creating external workbook hyperlinks

Now that you understand how to create internal workbook hyperlinks, you'll find that creating external hyperlinks is just as simple. In the next hands-on activities, you create links to external workbooks using both cell references and named ranges. Most of the skills you used when creating internal hyperlinks transfer directly to creating external ones.

Because you have already developed the Quarterly Reports workbook, you can use this as the external reference for this activity.

1. Click the New button on the toolbar, to create a new workbook.

2. Save the workbook in the Discover Excel folder as **Navigation.** You will use this workbook much like a table of contents, using it to locate and open multiple files and to move easily between them.

3. With A1 as the active cell, click the Insert Hyperlink button to open the Insert Hyperlink dialog box. In previous activities, you have used the lower Bro<u>w</u>se button to specify the hyperlink destination. Now you use the upper <u>B</u>rowse button.

4. Click <u>B</u>rowse. Excel displays the Link to File dialog box, shown in Figure 16-9. (If you know the exact name and location of the destination file,

you can simply enter the file path in the Link to file or URL drop-down box, rather than clicking Browse.)

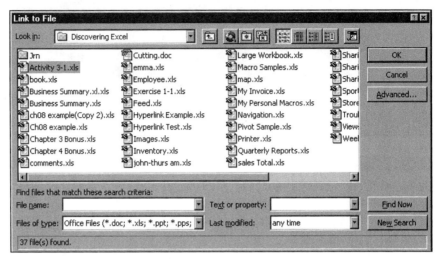

Figure 16-9 The Link to File dialog box allows you to create a hyperlink to an external file.

5. Select the Quarterly Reports workbook and click OK. Alternatively, you could just double-click the filename. The Insert Hyperlink dialog box is again displayed. Notice in Figure 16-10, the Link to file or URL drop-down box displays the entire path, *not* just the filename. Excel inserts the filename in the Path panel. You cannot modify this in any way.

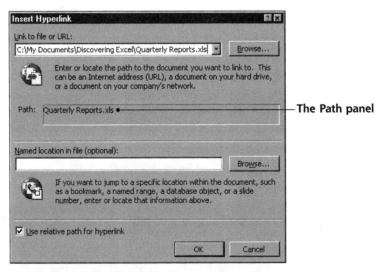

The Path panel

Figure 16-10 The Link to file or URL drop-down box contains in the entire path for the external workbook.

6. Click OK. A1 now contains a hyperlink to the external file. To make sure it works, move the cursor over the link. When the cursor changes to a pointing finger, click the mouse button. The Quarterly Reports Workbook is automatically opened.

7. Close the workbook. The hyperlink in A1 is now purple, indicating it has been used.

8. In A1, type **Quarterly Reports Workbook** and press Enter.

   Remember, editing the contents of a cell containing a hyperlink doesn't change the hyperlink; it only changes the text that is actually displayed. To *modify* the hyperlink, you need to reopen the Insert Hyperlink dialog box.

9. If necessary, right-click any toolbar and choose Web to display the Web toolbar.

10. Save the Navigation workbook and leave it open.

Creating a cell-specific, external workbook hyperlink

You can also easily create a link to a specific cell in an external workbook. In addition to creating the file hyperlink, you hyperlink to a specific cell.

This activity shows how to create a hyperlink to a specific cell in an external workbook. The Navigation workbook should still be open.

1. Click A3.

2. Click the Insert Hyperlink button. Excel displays the Insert Hyperlink dialog box.

3. To see how to use the drop-down list in the Link to file or URL box, click the down-pointing button on the right edge of the box. You see a list of the files or URLs you have recently visited.

4. Click *C:\My Documents\Discover Excel\Quarterly Reports.xls*.

5. Click Browse (the lower of the two Browse buttons). In the Browse Excel Workbook dialog box, make sure that the Sheet name option is chosen.

6. Type **E6** in the Reference box.

7. Click *'Second Quarter'* in the list of sheet names.

8. Click OK.

9. Click OK again, to close the Insert Hyperlink dialog box. A3 is still selected.

10. Type **Second Quarter Total** and press Enter.

11. Click the hyperlink in A3. The active cell should become E6 on the Second Qtr sheet of the Quarterly Reports.xls workbook, as shown in Figure 16-11.

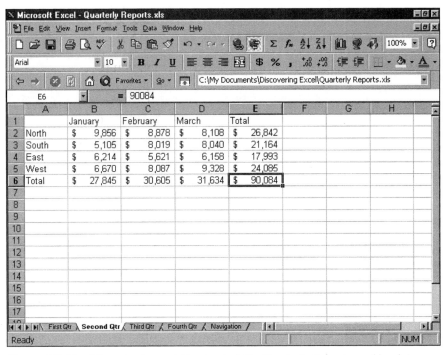

Figure 16-11 E6 on the Second Qtr sheet of the Quarterly Reports workbook is now the active cell.

12. Close the Quarterly Reports workbook once again. Leave the Navigation workbook open.

Creating a hyperlink to a named range in an external workbook

One final way to navigate between workbooks on your computer is by hyperlinking to a named range in a specific workbook. This works essentially the same as hyperlinking to a specific cell, with the following exceptions:

1. After clicking Bro<u>w</u>se in the Insert Hyperlink dialog box — which opens the Browse Excel Workbook dialog box — click <u>D</u>efined name (rather than <u>S</u>heet name).

2. Select the defined range name that you want to use as the hyperlink destination.

3. Click OK until you are back in the original worksheet.

Taking a Peek at the Internet

If you haven't yet heard of the Internet, you really should get out of your cave more often. Take your spouse or significant other (or that mouse in your pocket) to any public location, and you're bound to overhear comments about the Internet. (Mother said it isn't polite to eavesdrop, but you learn a lot of interesting things that way.) Many compare the introduction of the Internet into society as an event ranking with of the invention of the printing press. James Burke, author of *The Day the Universe Changed* (Boston: Little, Brown and Co., 1995) thinks it is even more important.

When the printing press was first invented, only the very rich could afford to own books. The content of the books was often controlled by the powerful. The Internet is nearly the antithesis of the first books. You can access the Internet from a wide variety of locations. Most libraries and colleges (and many high schools) now offer free Internet access to their patrons or students. If you have a computer and a modem, Internet providers can allow you access from your home or work. And, if you have a laptop, you can surf the Net from almost anywhere! You not only have access to a vast ocean of information, but you, too, can easily publish an article, a booklet, a magazine, or even a complete book on the Internet.

Beware when you first venture onto the Internet. There is something out there to offend *everyone*. But for purposes of this book, you don't need to know all the dark secrets; you'll stumble across them soon enough.

Excel fits into the Internet by letting you create catalogs, phone directories, price lists, stock quotes, as well as a multitude of other publications, and make the information available to millions of people. Before Excel 97, you could only share data with others who had a spreadsheet program (although you could give them a hard copy of your data). Now you can easily share worksheets and other information with users from all over the world.

You need to know some terms when using Excel on the Internet:

* **HyperText Markup Language (HTML).** The language used by most programs to interact with other data sources on the Internet. Excel doesn't support all HTML codes, but it does support enough to allow you to do most of what you need to accomplish.

* **Hyperlink.** A cell or other object in Excel that users can click to transport them to some other place, within the current worksheet, in a different worksheet, in a different workbook, or even to another computer.

* **Web query.** A short program that is specifically written so that Excel can extract data from other Internet or intranet sites. An *intranet* is like the Internet, except it is only available locally; for example, an intranet may be specific to people working within a certain company. An intranet is used the same as an Internet (the same browsers can be used), but it is more locally confined. Excel comes with several examples of Web queries, and you learn to create simple ones a little later in this chapter.

Hyperlinking to Your Network and the Internet

This section shows you how to create hyperlinks to your local network as well as to Web sites on the Internet. Again, these skills are an extension of those you have already acquired.

Linking to a server on your network

To create a destination hyperlink to a server on your network, you use Universal Naming Convention (UNC) addresses. These addresses start with "\\" (two back-slash characters) and supply the server name, the share name, and the full path to the file. Here's an example of a UNC address:

```
\\myserver\myfiles\excel\workbook.xls
```

For additional information on accessing the files on your network, speak to your network administrator.

Linking to an Internet site

To create a hyperlink to a site on the Internet, you must know the address (URL) of the destination. *URL* is an abbreviation for Uniform Resource Locator. It is simply an Internet address. This is the address of the Web site you are accessing. Most URLs begin with *http://*. The URL for the Microsoft home page is

WEB PATH

```
http://www.microsoft.com
```

For example, you might want to create a hyperlink to the Microsoft Knowledge Base. Clicking this hyperlink would automatically activate your Web browser and display the appropriate page.

Creating a hyperlink to Microsoft's Knowledge Base

To complete this activity, you must have an active account with an Internet Service Provider and be logged on to the Internet. The Navigation workbook is still open.

1. Click A5 in the Navigation workbook.

2. Click the Insert Hyperlink button. Excel displays the Insert Hyperlink dialog box.

3. In the Link to file or URL text box, type **www.microsoft.com/kb**, and then press Enter. Excel automatically completes the entry by adding *http://*, as shown in Figure 16-12. (I moved the active cell to A7, so that you better see the hyperlink.)

4. Click A5, to try your new hyperlink.

5. After exploring the site, close the browser.

6. Close and save the workbook. Leave Excel open.

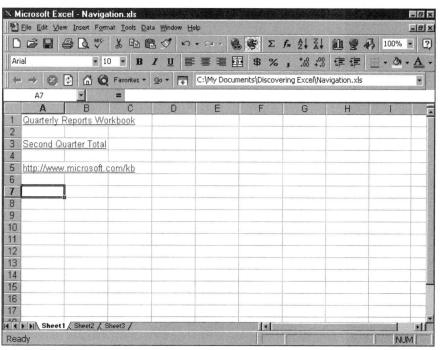

Figure 16-12 Excel automatically adds *http://* to the hyperlink.

Creating Web Queries

O ne of the most powerful new features in Excel for Microsoft Office 97 is the capability to go to a specific site (on another worksheet on your computer, on your local Intranet, or on the Internet) and retrieve data that can be entered directly into your worksheet. Microsoft calls this new capability *Web queries*.

What is a Web query?

A Web query is simply a text file containing a few lines of text, each separated by a hard carriage return (Enter). You can create the text for a Web query in NotePad, WordPad, or Word, as long as you save the query as a text file with an .IQY extension. A Web query contains these instructions:

* Type of query (optional)
* Version of query (optional)
* URL (required)
* Parameters (required to get information from the user)

A Web query can access the Internet and retrieve information from an Excel workbook posted there, and enter the data into your worksheet.

Retrieving information from the Internet

As with the previous activity, you must have an Internet connection open to complete the activity. In this activity, you use WordPad to create the query.

1. Minimize Excel.

2. Click the Windows Start button.

3. Choose | Programs | → | Accessories | → | Word Pad |.

4. Click in the WordPad window to make sure it is active.

5. Type **WEB** and press Enter.

6. Type **1** and press Enter.

7. Type **http://webservices.pcquote.com/cgi-bin/excelget.exe?TICKER=msft**.

TIP If you want to check a different stock, replace *msft* with the appropriate ticker code.

8. Choose | File | → | Save As |. The Save As dialog box is displayed.

9. Type **"S_Quote.iqy"** in the File name box. Don't forget the quotation marks.

10. From the Save as type drop-down list, choose Text Document.

11. From the Save in drop-down list, click the C drive icon, double-click the My Documents folder, and then double-click the Discover Excel folder.

12. Click Save.

13. Close WordPad.

14. Maximize Excel and create a new workbook.

15. Choose `Data` → `Get External Data` → `Run Web Query`.

16. In the Run Query dialog box, select the Discover Excel folder.

17. Double-click S_Quote.iqy. Excel displays the Returning External Data to Microsoft Excel dialog box, as shown in Figure 16-13.

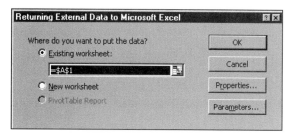

Figure 16-13 The Returning External Data to Microsoft Excel dialog box is used to define the location of the returned query data.

18. Click OK.

   If your Internet connection is already open, Excel retrieves the data; otherwise, you are prompted by Internet Explorer (or whichever browser you use) to open the connection (or you may just get an error message). After a few seconds, your screen should be similar to Figure 16-14. In the figure, the zoom value has been decreased to 85 percent so that you can see all of the data, and the External Data toolbar has been moved to the upper-right corner of the worksheet. If the External Data toolbar is not displayed, right-click any toolbar and choose `External Data`.

19. Save the file in your Discover Excel folder as **Microsoft Stock Quote.**

20. Close the file.

TIP Once you run the query, the original query is no longer needed. It is embedded in the worksheet. To update the information, click the Refresh button (it looks like an exclamation point) on the External Data toolbar. You must be connected to the Internet for the Refresh to work.

The External
Data toolbar

Refresh button

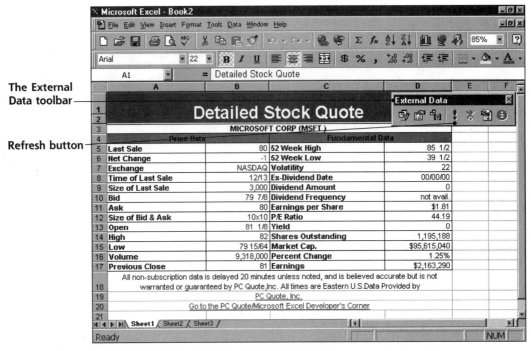

Figure 16-14 The Web query has retrieved the requested data.

BONUS

Saving a Workbook as an HTML File

Luckily for you, it isn't necessary to learn HTML code to make your worksheet available on the Internet or on your intranet. Simply save the file in HTML format, and then upload it to your Web site. Although you learn to save the file in HTML format in the next hands-on activity, the actual process of transferring it to your Web site goes beyond the scope of this book. In general, you use a File Transfer Protocol (FTP) to copy the file to its destination, and you need to make some modifications to your Web site so that others can get to the data. Check with your local Webmaster (network administrator) for details on how to transfer the file.

Changing your workbook to an HTML file is just a matter of saving it in HTML format. This activity steps you through the procedure and then shows you the results.

1. Open the Quarterly Reports workbook, and select the First Qtr worksheet tab.

2. Select A1 through D5.

3. Click the Chart Wizard.

4. In Step 1 of the Chart Wizard, accept the default and click Next.

5. Click Next in Step 2.

6. Type **First Quarter Sales** in the Chart title box.

7. Click Next.

8. In Step 4, choose *As object in* and leave it as **First Qtr.**

9. Click Finish. Excel displays the chart.

10. Drag the chart down, so that it doesn't cover the data.

11. Click A1. Your screen should be similar to Figure 16-15.

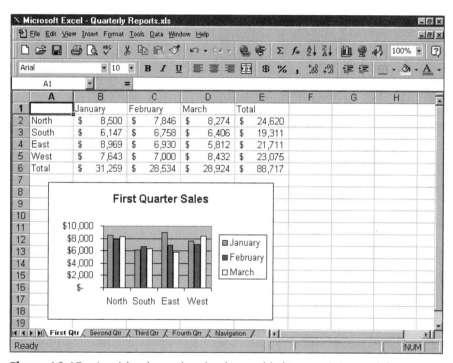

Figure 16-15 A quick column chart has been added to an existing worksheet.

12. Choose File → Save As HTML .

 TIP If this is the first time the Save As HTML command has been used, the Office Assistant asks if you want help with this feature. If you see this message, click No, don't provide help now.

As shown in Figure 16-16, Excel displays Step 1 of the Internet Assistant Wizard. In addition to the current range of data, *all charts* in the workbook are listed. If you want to add another range, click Add. To remove any listed range or chart, highlight it and click Remove. To change the order of the ranges and charts, select the one to move and click the Move Up or Move Down button.

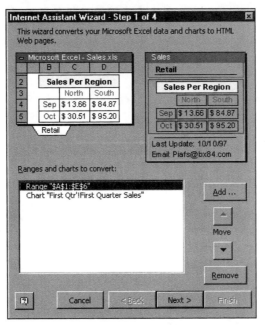

Figure 16-16   Step 1 of the Internet Assistant Wizard lists charts in the current workbook.

13. For now, leave the single range and chart as is, and click Next. The next step, shown in Figure 16-17, allows you to decide if you want this to be a new HTML page, or if you want to add it to an existing one. This time, you want to create a new document.

14. Leave the default setting, and click Next. The third step, shown in Figure 16-18, helps you lay out your HTML document. You can change the title of the Web page and its header. You can type a description of the document and choose to insert a horizontal line before and after the converted data. The other text boxes allow you to change the last update date and the person who updated the document. Finally, if desired, you can add your e-mail address; this is a good idea, because others may want to contact you.

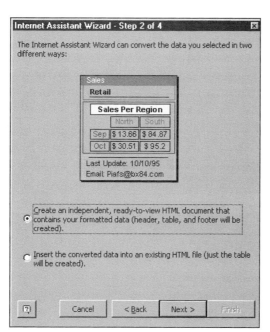

Figure 16-17   Step 2 of the Internet Assistant Wizard allows you to create a new document or add your selection to an existing HTML document.

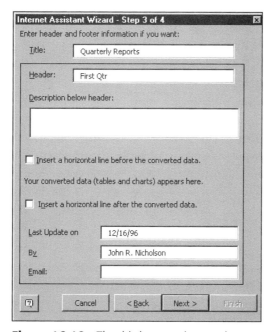

Figure 16-18   The third step assists you in laying out your document page.

15. Click Next to display the final step of the Wizard. The fourth step allows you to choose the type of code you want to generate (if you aren't sure, just use the default). You can choose to save the page as a separate document, or if you are using Microsoft Front Page, you can add it to an existing page.

16. Click Browse and save the file in your Discover Excel folder as **Qtrrept1.htm**, as shown in Figure 16-19.

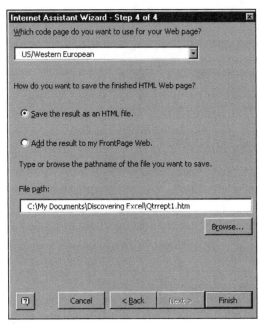

Figure 16-19 The final step allows you to choose the type of code page you want, and the name and file destination.

TIP Remember to limit your filenames to eight characters or fewer, no spaces, and use only the underline or a hyphen as punctuation (no spaces, periods, commas, and so on). Save the file with an .HTM extension.

17. Click Finish to complete the save. At this point, you would normally use an FTP program to upload your Web page onto the Internet. However, FTP is beyond the scope of this book, and you need to fine-tune your Internet skills before you try this.

18. Save the workbook.

19. Drop-down the URL address list on the right side of the Web toolbar, and choose the Qtrrept1.htm entry. Your default Web browser opens, and the HTML document you created is saved. If necessary, maximize the browser.

20. To see what your HTML code looks like, choose View → Document Source in Netscape or View → Source in Internet Explorer.

NotePad opens (if you are using Internet Explorer; Netscape has a built-in program to read the code), and you see code similar to that shown in Figure 16-20. (Aren't you glad you didn't have to write it manually?)

```
Qtrrept1.htm - Notepad                                          _ □ ×
File  Edit  Search  Help
<HTML>
<HEAD>
<meta http-equiv="Content-Type" content="text/html; charset=windows-1252">
<TITLE>Quarterly Reports</TITLE>
</HEAD>
<BODY>
<H1><CENTER>First Qtr</CENTER></H1>
<!-- The following table was generated by the Internet Assistant Wizard for Mi
<!-- ------------------------ -->
<!-- START OF CONVERTED OUTPUT -->
<!-- ------------------------ -->
<Table border>
<TR VALIGN="bottom">
<TD ALIGN="right"><FONT FACE="Arial">
 </FONT></TD>
<TD ALIGN="left"><FONT FACE="Arial">
January</FONT></TD>
<TD ALIGN="left"><FONT FACE="Arial">
February</FONT></TD>
<TD ALIGN="left"><FONT FACE="Arial">
March</FONT></TD>
<TD ALIGN="left"><FONT FACE="Arial">
Total</FONT></TD>
</TR>
<TR VALIGN="bottom">
<TD ALIGN="left"><FONT FACE="Arial">
North</FONT></TD>
<TD ALIGN="right" STYLE="vnd.ms-excel.numberformat:_($* #,##0_)[semicolon]_($▸
```

Figure 16-20 Excel has generated HTML code for your worksheet and chart.

21. Close your browser and exit Excel.

Summary

This chapter offers a very brief introduction to using the built-in Excel hyperlinking capabilities and shows you how to view HTML documents located either on your hard disk or at a remote site. Remember that this is only the briefest of introductions to Excel's Internet features. Here, you developed hyperlinks between Excel worksheets and workbooks, but you can just as easily develop hyperlinks to Word documents, PowerPoint presentations, and even Access databases. The power of hyperlinking adds ease of navigation to Excel.

A BUG IN YOUR WORKSHEET: BASIC TROUBLESHOOTING

IN THIS CHAPTER YOU LEARN THESE KEY SKILLS

One of the most unpleasant aspects of project management is dealing with problems. Whether the issue involves lost data, computer hardware difficulties, or numerous other dilemmas, no one likes to deal with problems. Sometimes, however, knowing how to solve problems can avert the little emergencies that may determine the success or failure of your project.

NOTE Although previous chapters discuss some of the topics that this chapter covers, a second look at these troubleshooting tools can help you avoid and, sometimes, solve problems in your workbooks.

Fortunately, Excel comes with some built-in problem solvers. By using these tools, you can quickly locate and solve problems in your worksheet and workbook so that you can proceed to other aspects of your project.

> **NOTE** Throughout this chapter, I show you not only how to solve common problems, but also how to create them. Many times, understanding how a problem is created can help you solve the problem more quickly.

Using Excel's Validation Tools

As discussed in Chapter 11, you can restrict the types of data entered into your worksheet by using Excel's validation tools. By restricting data types, you can avoid problems that occur when users enter the wrong type of data. The validation tools also alert you and the other users of your workbook whenever an incorrect data type has been entered.

To create a data validation error and then eliminate the error once it occurs, follow these steps:

1. Open Excel and a new workbook.

2. Save the workbook in your Discover Excel folder as **Sports**.

3. Using Table 17-1 as a guide, create a worksheet, starting with **Footballs** in B1.

TABLE 17-1 A Sample Worksheet for the Data Validation Activity

	Footballs	Baseballs	Soccer Balls	Hockey Pucks
STORE 1	96	16	68	55
STORE 2	76	70	64	64
STORE 3	84	41	91	58
STORE 4	51	50	56	13
STORE 5	93	93	69	10
STORE 6	4	100	55	24
STORE 7	81	58	30	1
STORE 8	99	54	43	29
STORE 9	63	80	64	44
STORE 10	41	77	83	5
TOTAL	688	639	623	303

Total Number of Units   2253

To fill the worksheet with data, generate random numbers between 1 and 100, and then convert the random number formulas to values. Use AutoFill to complete cells A2 through A11. Use formulas for the totals in B12 through E12 and D14. AutoFit and format the headings and Total as indicated.

4. Highlight B2 through E11.

5. Choose ⎸ **Data** ⎹ → ⎸ **Validation** ⎹ . Excel opens the Data Validation dialog box.

6. Click the Settings tab, shown in Figure 17-1.

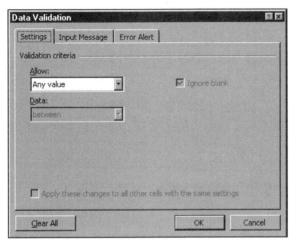

Figure 17-1   The Settings tab is used to specify the type of data that can be entered into a cell.

7. Choose Whole numbers in the Allow drop-down box. The Data box is no longer grayed out, and Minimum and Maximum boxes are added to the display.

8. In the Data drop-down box, choose between.

9. Enter **0** in the Minimum box.

10. Enter **100** in the Maximum box.

11. Click the Error Alert tab. The Error Alert tab is used to create the warning box that Excel displays when a user enters invalid data. Figure 17-2 shows the Error Alert tab.

12. Select Warning in the Style box.

13. In the Title box, type **Numeric Data Only**.

14. In the Error Message box, type **This cell is restricted to whole numbers only. Please click No and change the value in the current cell so that it is between 0 and 100. Clicking Yes overrides the data restriction.**

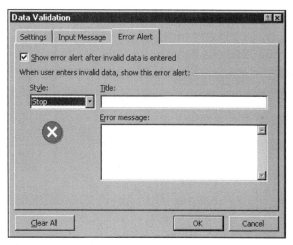

Figure 17-2   The Error Alert Tab allows you to create
a warning box.

15. Click OK. The Data Validation dialog box closes.

16. Highlight C2, type **text**, and press Enter. As shown in Figure 17-3, Excel
    displays your Numeric Data Only warning box.

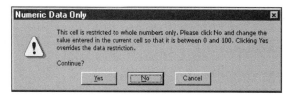

Figure 17-3   The Numeric Data Only warning box
alerts the user to data validation errors.

17. Because you should have entered numeric data and not text, click No.

 TIP   **If you need to enter text into a numeric-restricted cell, click Yes and
Excel overrides the restriction for that cell.**

18. Type **16** in C2, and press Enter.

19. Save your work and leave the workbook open.

Using the Auditing Toolbar

By allowing you to see the relationships between selected cells, the
Auditing toolbar shown in Figure 17-4 helps you avoid problems in your
worksheets. For example, you can determine which cells depend on one

another for data, and you can understand the effect that changing or deleting a cell would have on other cells.

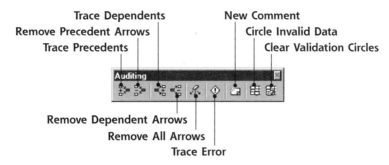

Figure 17-4 Use the Auditing toolbar to trace problems in your worksheet.

To trace and solve an error by using the Auditing toolbar, follow these steps:

1. Highlight C2.

2. Choose `Tools` → `Auditing` → `Show Auditing Toolbar`. Excel displays the Auditing toolbar.

3. On the Auditing toolbar, click the Trace Dependents button (the third button). An arrow shows any cells in the worksheet that depend on C2 for data. As shown in Figure 17-5, C12 depends on C2 to provide data for the sum of the column.

4. Again, click the Trace Dependents button on the Auditing toolbar. As shown in Figure 17-6, D14 also relies on C2. Therefore, changing or deleting C2 will affect the data in both C12 and D14. Clicking the Trace Dependents button again shows that no more cells depend on the data in C2.

5. Type **text** in C2 and press Enter. Excel displays the Numeric Data Only warning box.

6. Click Yes to continue. Excel replaces your numeric value in C2 with the text. Notice that the sums in C12 and D14 do not include the value from C2.

7. On the Auditing toolbar, click the Circle Invalid Data button (the second button from the right). As shown in Figure 17-7, Excel places a red circle around any cells containing invalid data. C2 is supposed to contain only whole numbers, but you entered text in this cell.

8. Type **16** in C2 and press Enter. After identifying the cell that causes the problem, simply replace the invalid data with the correct data; Excel automatically removes the red circle.

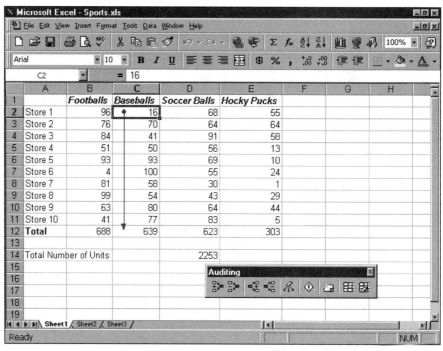

Figure 17-5 The blue arrows show that C12 depends on C2 for information.

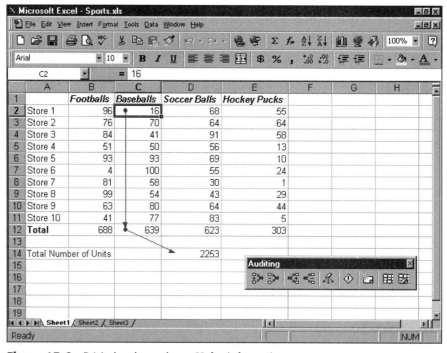

Figure 17-6 D14 also depends on C2 for information.

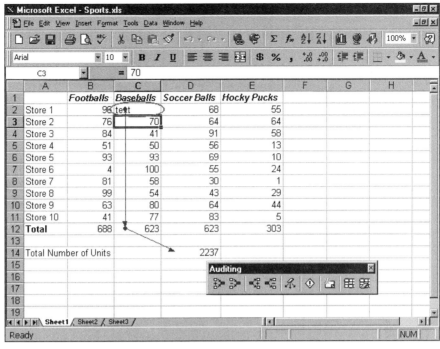

Figure 17-7 Excel places a red circle around any cells that contain invalid data.

9. On the Auditing toolbar, click the Remove All Arrows button (the fifth button).

10. Close the Auditing toolbar.

11. Save your work and leave the workbook open.

Identifying and Solving Circular Reference Errors

Circular reference errors occur when two or more cells depend on each other for information but neither cell has the data. To understand the term *circular reference error*, assume that Joe asks Sally what time it is. Sally then asks Fred and Fred, in turn, asks Joe. No one actually knows what time it is, so the answer cannot be found.

This type of error occurs in Excel when cell A relies on information from cell B and cell B relies on information from cell A.

TIP If the preceding sentence makes your head spin, don't worry. This concept becomes clearer when you complete the following activity. Circular reference errors aren't as hard to understand as they are to explain.

To identify and solve circular reference errors in your worksheet, follow these steps:

1. Highlight E12.

2. Type **=D14** and press Enter.

   As shown in Figure 17-8, Excel displays a Stop box, indicating that you cannot enter this data because it creates a circular reference. To sum B12 through E12, D14 must depend on E12 for data. Consequently, E12 cannot also depend on D14. Neither cell would have the data that the other requires, thus creating a circular reference problem.

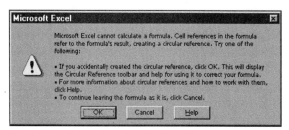

Figure 17-8   The Circular Reference stop box indicates that cells are depending on each other for data.

3. Click OK.

4. Choose [**View**] → [**Toolbars**] → [**Circular Reference**] to display the Circular Reference toolbar.

SIDE TRIP

You may occasionally create a circular reference error by including the answer cell in the formula to be calculated. For example, in E12, entering the formula =SUM(E2:E12) iresults in an error message. At times, for reasons I don't understand and can't always duplicate, instead of seeing the preceding formula as a circular reference, Excel may simply double the answer. Be careful when you are either writing formulas manually or dragging to identify a range in a formula.

---

5. Read the Help screen to find out more about circular references, and then close this screen. Excel places a blue arrow showing the flow of data between cells involved in the circular reference. As shown in Figure 17-9, a drop-down box lists the cells that are included in the circular reference. The offending cell is also listed in the status bar.

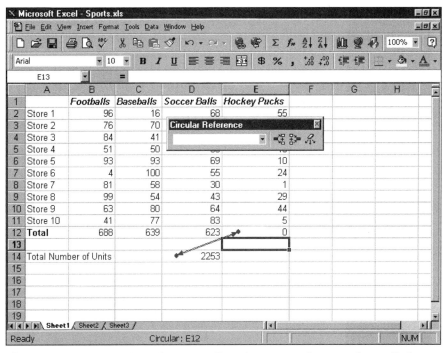

Figure 17-9 The Circular Reference toolbar places arrows between the conflicting cells so that you can identify the problem.

6. Click E12 and then double-click the AutoSum button. The blue lines disappear, as does the Circular Reference toolbar.

7. Save your work and close the workbook.

Troubleshooting Error Messages

Although you can hardly be expected to jump for joy when Excel displays an error message, Microsoft has taken much of the pain out of troubleshooting your worksheet by making error messages as helpful as possible. The cardinal rule of troubleshooting error messages is to read the *entire* message. Many of Excel's error messages actually tell you how to fix a problem. For example, Excel's circular reference error message tells you how to open the Circular Reference toolbar so that you can locate and fix the error.

TIP Sometimes, it even helps to write down the message. That way, if you have to seek help from other sources (such as the Microsoft Knowledge Base or Technical Support) you have the exact language of the error message. Having complete information about the error can save you lots of time.

Once you read the message and understand the nature of the error, try to locate the problem. Excel provides tools such as the Auditing toolbar and the Circular Reference toolbar for just this purpose. Once you locate the error, think about why the data or the formula is causing an error. Did you enter the wrong type of data? Did you make a mistake in the formula syntax? You'll be surprised how many of your errors occur because of little things that you can easily fix.

After you locate and fix the error, ask yourself, "Did I make the same mistake anywhere else in the worksheet?" Often, you can save time by forecasting other potential problem areas.

Fixing Common Errors in Excel Worksheets

The following sections describe some of the most common errors encountered by Excel users. Each section describes how the error originates and then gives the most common method for fixing the error.

TIP Remember, everyone makes mistakes, but not everyone can *fix* them. By understanding how these common mistakes occur and how to fix them, you'll be one step ahead of everyone else.

Order-of-operation errors

Most mistakes occur in formulas because the user forgot Excel's rules regarding the order of operation. Remember, when calculating your formula, Excel solves operations in parentheses first. Next it solves exponents, and then multiplication, division, addition, and subtraction. The phrase *Please Excuse My Dear Aunt Sally* can help you remember the order because the first letter in each word is the same as the first letter in an operation.

Unfortunately, order-of-operation errors are often difficult to locate. The only sure-fire method for finding the error is to calculate your data manually. This may be a time-consuming task, but it is the best method for checking your data.

After you locate the formula causing the error, rewrite the formula on paper and again check that the order of operations is correct. Add parentheses to any portions of the formula that need to be solved first, and recalculate the formula to make sure the results are correct. After you are sure the formula is correct, reenter it into your worksheet and check the results of any cells affected by the change.

Copying absolute addresses or relative addresses

Another common problem results from copying a formula using the wrong address. Remember that *relative addresses* are the default in Excel. For example, if B11 contains the formula =SUM(B6:B10), this means sum the contents of the five cells immediately above this one. If you copy this formula to C11, Excel *automatically* changes the formula in C11 to read =SUM(C6:C10). The problem arises when you really want C11 to reflect the sum of cells B6 through B10.

You solve this problem by using *absolute addresses* in the formula. Using the absolute address tells Excel that you want to copy the formula exactly as it reads. To create an absolute formula, place a $ before the cell row and another one before the cell column. To continue the example, the correct formula for C11 is =SUM($B$6:$B$10).

Formulas with incorrect cell references

Worksheet errors often involve a formula that includes an incorrect cell reference. Unfortunately, this can be one of the hardest problems to track down. When you make reference to a cell in a formula (such as =SUM(A1:B1)), you are telling Excel that you want those specific cells used in your formula. So, following your command, Excel calculates the result. But what happens if you intended =SUM(A1:A2)? This produces an entirely different result.

It's up to you, therefore, to make sure that each of your formulas references the correct cells. You can do this by keeping a running list of the formulas you include in your worksheet, their purpose, and the pertinent cell references. Remember to recheck your work manually. This can save a lot of troubleshooting time.

TIP If you want to see all the formulas on your worksheet, choose `Tools` → `Options` and click the View tab. In the Window Options panel, click the Formulas option. When you return to your worksheet, all formulas (rather than their answers) are visible. Because Excel automatically widens all columns, you may want to select the entire worksheet and choose `Format` → `Columns` → `AutoFit Selection` (the columns are usually much wider than required).

Formulas that fail to include inserted rows or columns

If you insert a row or a column into a range included in one of your formulas, Excel might not adjust the formula to include the new data. Whether Excel recognizes the data as part of your formula depends on where you insert the row or column. If you insert a column between the last data column and the total column, Excel doesn't include the data in the new column as part of the formula. If you insert the new column in the middle of the range of cells used in the formula, however, Excel incorporates the new data into the formula. Rows work the same way. When possible, insert them inside the range that the formula references.

To ensure that Excel recognizes inserted data in your formula, follow these steps:

1. Create a new Excel worksheet and save it as **Trouble**.

2. Type **5** in A1 and press Tab.

3. Type **7** in B1 and press Tab.

4. Type **10** in C1 and press Tab.

5. Type **2** in D1 and press Tab.

6. Highlight E1 and double-click the AutoSum button on the toolbar. Your answer should be 24.

7. With E1 highlighted, choose Insert → Columns . Excel inserts a column between columns E and F.

8. Type **10** in E1 and press Enter. Notice that your total in F1 doesn't change to include the value in E1.

9. Highlight F1. This cell still contains the formula =SUM(A1:D1).

10. Highlight Column E, right-click, and delete this cell from your worksheet.

11. Highlight C1.

12. Choose Insert → Columns . Excel inserts a new column between columns B and C.

13. Type **10** in C1 and press Enter. Because you inserted the new column in the middle of the range used by your formula, your total in F1 changes to include the new value.

14. Save your work.

 TIP The lesson to be learned from this exercise is to *always* insert any columns or rows into the inner area of the range specified in the formula. Otherwise, you run the risk that Excel won't include your new data in the results.

Using the same range name on different sheets within the same workbook

When naming cell ranges in Excel, you cannot use the same name for two different ranges of cells — even if they are on different worksheets. Unfortunately, if you do try to use the same name for two different ranges, Excel doesn't warn you that you can't do this. Instead, Excel assumes that you want to use the name to identify another range of cells and moves the name from the first range to the second range. This then leaves your first range unnamed.

To avoid this problem, *never* use a name more than once. Use numbers to distinguish your range names — for example, Store1, Store2, and Store3. This avoids not only naming problems but also confusion among the users of your workbook.

Common errors in Excel formulas

Table 17-2 describes common errors and their solutions.

TABLE 17-2 Common Error Messages and Their Solutions

Error	Description	Solution
#####	The numeric value or the result of a formula is too wide to display within the cell.	Resize the column by AutoFitting it or by dragging the boundary line, located between the column headings.
#VALUE!	You entered the wrong type of data — for example, the formula calls for true/false and you entered 432.	Make sure that all cells and range names have the correct data type designated.
#DIV/0!	Excel is asked to divide a value by zero or by an empty cell.	Check that no formula attempts to divide by 0 and that no division formula references a blank cell.
#NAME?	Excel doesn't recognize text in your formula.	Verify that any named ranges are spelled correctly and the names haven't been deleted.
#REF!	A formula contains an invalid cell reference.	Verify that the referenced cell is available. The Auditing toolbar can help you trace the problem.
#NUM!	The number entered is greater than or less than the specified maximum or minimum value for this cell.	Change the value of your number.

BONUS

Using a Microsoft Troubleshooter

Although the tool I describe in this section could easily be part of the chapter on finding additional help, it provides help of a specific type: Troubleshooting Excel worksheets. This step-by-step process helps you find the causes of errors. To take advantage of this service, you must have an Internet connection. If you don't currently have one, consider adding this service. You will probably find it to be a worthwhile investment. A great deal of technical support is available on the Internet 24 hours a day.

The following activity gives you a chance to see how automated help can assist you in solving your Excel problems. Again, you must have an Internet connection before you can complete this exercise.

1. Minimize the Excel program and establish the Internet connection with your provider. When you are connected, maximize Excel again.

2. On the Excel Standard toolbar, click the Web toolbar button. The Web toolbar, shown in Figure 17-10, lets you access the Internet while you're working in Excel (providing you have an account with an Internet Service Provider).

The Address box

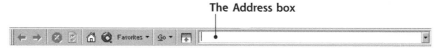

Figure 17-10   The Web toolbar connects you to the Internet from within Excel.

3. Click in the Address box.

4. Type **http://www.microsoft.com** and press Enter. After a few moments, you should see Microsoft's home page. You may have to maximize your Browser window.

 TIP   Always make sure that you type Web addresses exactly as shown. No spaces are allowed. The case of all characters must be correct. However, you can skip typing **http://** if you want. Internet Explorer uses that as the default.

5. On the Microsoft Home Page, click Support. The Support Wizard is displayed.

6. Click Select a Troubleshooter in the left column. A list of Troubleshooters is displayed.

WEB PATH ➡ **The direct address to the Troubleshooter page is**

`http://www.microsoft.com/support/tshooters.htm`

Links to specific pages change often. If this doesn't work for you, go to the Microsoft home page and proceed from there.

7. Click the Excel Workbook Troubleshooter radio button.

8. Click Next. The Microsoft Excel Workbook Troubleshooter is displayed.

9. Select the type of problem you are having. For this exercise, click *The formulas in my workbook return incorrect values or are missing values.*

10. Click Next.

11. Continue through the Troubleshooter, making up the problem as you go along.

12. When you are finished, close your Browser.

Summary

In many ways, understanding how errors occur and what you can do to prevent them is just as important as knowing what to do when an error occurs. Excel's troubleshooting features not only help you anticipate potential problems but also offer easy-to-understand solutions.

INSTALLING EXCEL 97

If Excel came with your computer, you may not need to worry about installing it (assuming that the person who installed it actually put *all* of the Excel files on your hard disk). In the following sections, I tell you about the different types of installation you can accomplish in Microsoft Office.

If Excel Is Already Installed

If Excel 97 is already installed on your computer, you probably have all of Microsoft Office (either the Standard or the Professional edition) installed on your computer. If you have the Professional edition, you have Microsoft Access 97 in addition to the other Office programs — the Standard edition does not include Access.

If Excel is already installed, you should have the Microsoft Office 97 CD-ROM. You need the CD-ROM if you want to change the way in which Excel is set up. If the software is already installed on your computer but you don't have the CD-ROM, contact the seller of your computer and get a copy of the CD. In some cases, dealers have installed the software on a computer and then didn't give the buyer the disk. This is illegal; buyers should always be supplied with a disk. If you didn't receive the disks, contact Microsoft to see what can be done. It may be a case of piracy (installing software that has not been purchased), or just a mistake. In any case, make sure that you have the *original* disk.

To check which portions of Excel 97 are installed on your hard disk, refer to the section on installing Office from a CD-ROM.

Installing Excel from Diskettes

It's too late now, but if you have a computer powerful enough to run Windows 95 and Excel 97, you probably should have purchased the CD-ROM version of Excel 97, as it includes extra features and is much easier to install than the diskette version.

To install Excel using diskettes, follow these steps:

1. Place the first diskette of the set in the diskette drive (usually A) and click the Windows Start button.

2. Choose Settings→Control Panel. The Control Panel dialog box is displayed.

3. Double-click the Add/Remove Programs icon. Windows displays the Add/Remove Program Properties dialog box, shown in Figure 1.

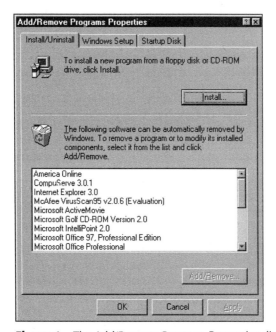

Figure 1   The Add/Remove Program Properties dialog box.

4. On the Install/Uninstall tab, click <Install>. The Install Program from Floppy Disk or CD-ROM dialog box is displayed.

5. Click <Next>. Windows automatically finds the Setup.exe file on the first diskette.

6. Follow the on-screen instructions. If you are given a choice between Typical and Custom, choose Custom, and select <Install All>.

7. Change to the second floppy disk when prompted. Continue to insert disks as prompted, until the installation is complete.

8. When Excel is completely installed, reboot your computer.

Installing Excel from a CD-ROM

f you *didn't* buy Excel 97 as part of Microsoft Office 97, follow these steps to install Excel using the Excel CD-ROM disk:

1. Place the CD-ROM in the drive and click the Windows Start button.

2. Choose `Settings` → `Control Panel`. The Control Panel dialog box is displayed.

3. Double-click the Add/Remove Programs icon. Windows displays the Add/Remove Program Properties dialog box, shown in Figure A-1.

4. On the Install/Uninstall tab, click <Install>. Windows displays the Install Program from Floppy Disk or CD-ROM dialog box.

5. Click <Next>. Windows automatically finds the Setup.exe file on the CD-ROM.

6. Follow the on-screen instructions. If you are given a choice between Typical and Custom, choose Custom, and select <Install All>.

7. When Excel is completely installed, reboot your computer.

Installing Excel 97 from the Microsoft Office CD-ROM

f you want to install only Excel from the Microsoft Office disk, complete these steps:

1. Place the CD-ROM disk in the drive and click the Windows Start button.

2. Choose `Settings` → `Control Panel`. The Control Panel dialog box is displayed.

3. Double-click the Add/Remove Programs icon. Windows displays the Add/Remove Program Properties dialog box, shown in Figure 1.

4. On the Install/Uninstall tab, click <Install>. Windows displays the Install Program from Floppy Disk or CD-ROM dialog box.

5. Click <Next>. Windows automatically finds the Setup.exe file on the CD-ROM. The Microsoft Office 97 Setup dialog box is displayed, as shown in Figure 2.

INSTALLING EXCEL 97   **411**

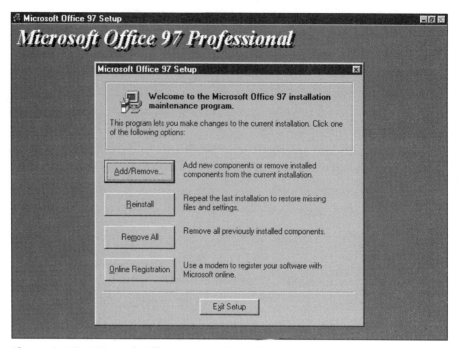

Figure 2   The Microsoft Office 97 Setup dialog box.

6. Click <Add/Remove>.

If you want to install only Excel, remove the check marks from all other boxes. You may still want to install the Web Page Authoring, Data Access, Office Tools, and Converters and Filters options. If you don't, you may find that Excel doesn't work as expected, and you get many error messages.

If you are given a choice between Typical and Custom, choose Custom, and select <Install All>. This installs all of the Office components on your hard disk. If your computer has a large hard disk (1 gigabyte or larger) install all of Office. It will make things easier later.

7. When Office is completely installed, reboot your computer.

 NOTE To check which components of Office are installed at any time, you can run the setup program. The Microsoft Office 97 Maintenance dialog box, shown in Figure 3, is displayed. Any option with a black check mark is completely installed. If the check mark is gray, only part of the option is installed. (To see all of the possible components of any option, click it in the Options panel and then click <Change Option>.) If there is no check mark in the Options panel, the option is not installed.

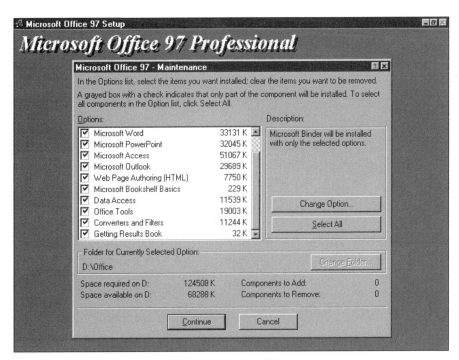

Figure 3   The Microsoft Office 97 Maintenance dialog box.

DISCOVERY CENTER

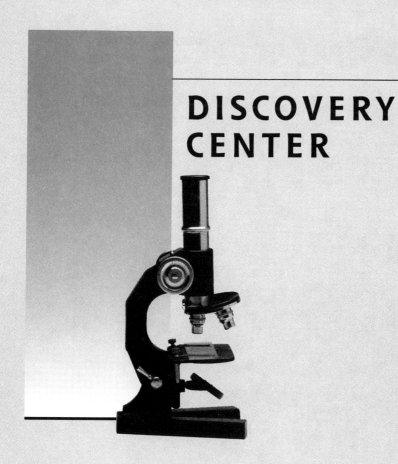

Like all books in the *Discover* series from IDG Books Worldwide, *Discover Excel 97* includes a feature called the Discovery Center. The Discovery Center acts as a visual guide to the most commonly performed actions in Excel. Turn to the Discovery Center when you want concise, step-by-step instructions for completing a task – especially when you aren't quite sure which Excel feature you use to perform that task. (If you already know the name of the Excel feature, you can easily find the information you need by using the book's index.) The Discovery Center also shows you where to turn in the book for more details about the task. Think of the Discovery Center as just one more method you can use to quickly accomplish your goals when using Excel 97.

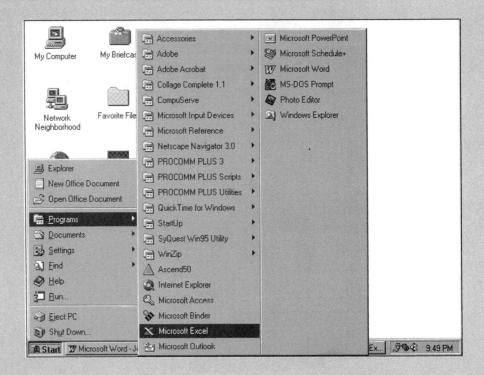

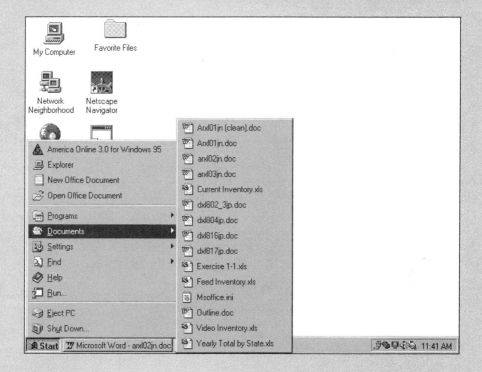

1. Click **Start**.
2. Highlight **Documents**.
3. Click the name of the workbook that you want to open.

To Create a Workbook Shortcut on the Windows Desktop (page 22)

1. Open Explorer.
2. Double-click the folder names until you can see the workbook for which you want to create a shortcut.
3. Click the workbook name.
4. Click Copy.
5. Close Explorer.
6. Right-click an empty area of the desktop and choose **Paste Shortcut** from the resulting pop-up menu.

To Choose Menu Commands by Using the Mouse (page 30)

1. Move the cursor to a menu command.
2. Click the highlighted command.
3. If a submenu appears, repeat Step 2 until you have completed the task. Enter information in a dialog box if necessary.

To Choose Menu Commands by Using the Keyboard (page 31)

1. Press Alt, and type the underlined letter of the desired command.
2. Release Alt.
3. Type the underlined letter for the desired option in the menu that opens.
4. If a submenu appears, repeat Step 3 until you have completed the task. Enter information in a dialog box if necessary.

To View Hidden Toolbars (page 32)

1. Choose View → Toolbars .
2. Click the name of the desired toolbar.

To Save a File for the First Time (page 34)

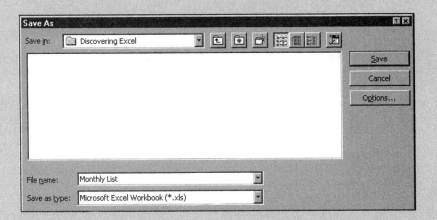

To Save an Existing File (page 34)

* Click the Save button on the toolbar, or

* Press Ctrl+S, or

* Choose File → Save.

To Display the Office Assistant (page 36)

* Press F1, or

* Click the Office Assistant button (the right button on the standard toolbar).

To Get Help by Using the Office Assistant (page 37)

1. Click the Office Assistant.

2. Type your question.

3. Click Search.

4. Click the button next to the topic that you want to review.

5. If the topic that you want is not visible, click More to see other topics.

To Get Help by Using the Help Command (page 39)

1. Choose Help → Contents and Index.

2. Choose the Index or Find tab.

3. Type the topic in the Index tab, or the phrase in the Find tab.

4. Highlight the topic that you want to view.

5. Press Display.

To Create a Formula (page 57)

1. Click in the cell where you want to enter the formula.

2. Begin the formula by typing an equal sign (=).

3. Type the cell references, numbers, and mathematical manipulators that make up the formula.

4. End the formula by pressing Enter or Tab.

To Change the Alignment of Text and Numbers (page 56)

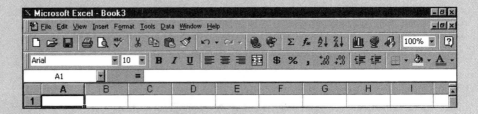

To Create a Simple Function (page 58)

1. Select the cell where you want to enter the function.
2. Begin the function by typing an equal sign (=).
3. Type the name of the function (such as **SUM**).
4. Type a left parenthesis.
5. Enter the appropriate cell references.
6. End the function by typing a right parenthesis.

To Insert a Worksheet (page 64)

Choose Insert → Worksheet .

To Insert Multiple Worksheets (page 65)

1. Specify how many worksheets you want to insert by selecting the corresponding number of tabs. For example, to insert three worksheets, select three existing worksheet tabs.
2. Choose Insert → Worksheet .

To Create a New Workbook with a Specified Number of Worksheets (page 65)

1. From an existing workbook, choose Tools → Options . Excel displays the Options dialog box.
2. Click the General tab.
3. In the Sheets in new workbook box, specify how many sheets you want the new workbook to contain.
4. Click OK to return to the existing workbook.

5. Click ⬜ on the toolbar.

Excel creates a new workbook with the specified number of worksheets. Until you reset the number of sheets in the Options dialog box, Excel opens all new workbooks with this number of sheets.

To Delete Worksheets (page 66)

1. Select the worksheet that you want to delete. To select multiple worksheets, hold Ctrl and click the tabs of the worksheets to be deleted.

2. Choose [Edit]→[Delete Sheet].

3. At the warning dialog box, click OK to delete the selected worksheets.

To Rename a Worksheet (page 67)

1. Double-click the worksheet's tab.

2. Type the new name for the worksheet.

3. Press Enter to complete the name change.

To Group Worksheets (page 68)

✳ Group contiguous worksheets by clicking the first sheet's tab, pressing Shift, and clicking the last sheet's tab.

✳ Group nonconsecutive worksheets by clicking the first sheet's tab, pressing Ctrl, and clicking the tabs for the other sheets that you want to group.

Anything that you enter on a grouped set of sheets appears on all sheets in that group.

To ungroup the worksheets, right-click the tab of any grouped worksheet and then choose [Ungroup Sheets] from the resulting pop-up menu.

To Copy a Worksheet (page 69)

1. Click the worksheet's name tab.

2. Choose [Edit]→[Move or Copy Sheet].

3. Click the Create a copy option box in the lower-left corner of the resulting dialog box.

4. In the Before sheet panel, select the sheet that the copy is to precede. To insert the copy at the end of the workbook, choose (move to end).

5. Click OK.

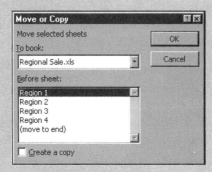

To Move a Worksheet (page 71)

1. Click the worksheet's name tab.

2. Choose Edit → Move or Copy Sheet . Excel displays the Move or Copy dialog box.

3. Make sure that the Create a copy option box is *not* checked.

4. In the Before sheet panel, select the worksheet that you want your worksheet to precede. To move the worksheet to the end of the workbook, choose (move to end).

5. Click OK.

To Back Up Your Data to a Floppy Disk (page 73)

1. Save the file to your hard disk.

2. Choose File → Save As . Excel displays the Save As dialog box.

3. In the File name text box, type **A:*MYFILE*** (where *MYFILE* represents the name of the workbook to be saved).

4. Click Save.

5. Close the workbook. To continue working with the file, make sure that you load it from the hard disk.

To Delete a Workbook (page 73)

1. Close the workbook. The workbook *must* be closed before you can delete it.

2. Choose File → Open .

3. Right-click the name of the file that you want to delete. A pop-up menu appears.

4. Choose **Delete**.

5. Click Yes to delete the selected workbook.

To Recover a Deleted Workbook (page 74)

1. Minimize Excel and any other programs.

2. Double-click the Recycle Bin.

3. Double-click the file that you want to restore.

To Password Protect a Workbook (page 78)

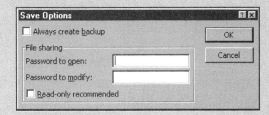

1. Choose **File** → **Save As**. Excel displays the Save As dialog box.

2. Click Options. Excel displays the Save Options dialog box. At this point you have the following options:

   ✳ Click the Always create backup box to create a backup of the current file.

   ✳ Enter a password in the Password to open box to require a password for opening the workbook.

   ✳ Enter a password in the Password to modify box to require a password for modifying the workbook.

   ✳ Click the Read-only recommended box to alert the user to open the file as a read-only file.

3. Choose the desired options for saving the workbook.

4. Click OK to close the Save Options dialog box.

5. Click Save to save the workbook with the new options.

1. Select the cells to be formatted.

2. Right-click any selected cell, and choose ⟨Format Cells⟩ from the resulting pop-up menu. Excel opens the Format Cells dialog box.

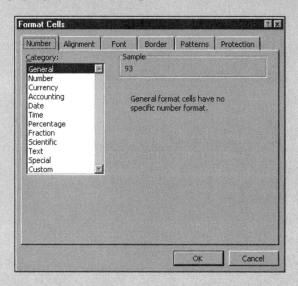

3. Select the appropriate tab: Number, Alignment, Font, Border, Patterns, or Protection.

4. Choose the desired formatting options.

5. Click OK to implement the changes.

1. Select the row or rows to be formatted.

2. Choose ⟨Format⟩ → ⟨Row⟩ → ⟨Height⟩. Excel displays the Row Height dialog box.

3. Enter the desired row height (in points). Note that 72 points equals one inch.

4. Click OK.

To Let Excel Choose the Height for Selected Rows (page 101)

1. Select the row or rows to be formatted.

2. Choose Format → Row → AutoFit. Excel sets the row height to the minimum possible height, based on the current font sizes of the entries in the row.

To Hide or Reveal Selected Rows (page 101)

1. Select the row or rows to be formatted.

2. Choose Format → Row → Hide if the selected rows are currently visible. Choose Format → Row → Unhide if the selected rows are currently hidden.

To Change the Width of One or More Columns (page 102)

1. Select the column or columns to be formatted.

2. Choose Format → Column → Width. Excel displays the Column Width dialog box.

3. Enter the value for the width.

   Choosing the correct width is tricky, because the value is based on an average of how many characters at the default font fit in the column. You may be better off using AutoFit or adjusting the column width manually.

4. Click OK.

To Set a Standard Column Width (page 102)

1. Choose Format → Column → Standard Width. Excel displays the Standard Width dialog box. The value that you enter in this dialog box sets the width for any columns that do not have a custom width.

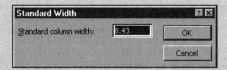

2. Enter a width value.

3. Click OK.

To Move Data From One Spot to Another in Your Worksheet (page 112)

1. Select cell(s) containing the data that you want to move.

2. Click ![cut] (the Cut button) on the toolbar (or press Ctrl+X, the quick-key command). A marquis (a flashing border) surrounds the data that you've cut.

3. Select the cell(s) in which you want to place the data.

4. Click ![paste] (the Paste button), or press Ctrl+V.

To Copy and Paste Data (page 112–113)

1. Select the data that you want to copy.

2. Click ![copy] (the Copy button) on the toolbar, or press Ctrl+C.

3. Select the cell(s) in which you want to paste the copied data.

4. Click ![paste] or press Ctrl+V.

To Limit the Range of Cells in Which You Can Enter Data (page 114)

1. Select all of the cells in which you want to enter data.

2. Enter the data for the upper-left cell in the selected range of cells.

3. Enter the data for the other cells in the range. To move right (one cell at a time), press Tab. To move left, press Shift+Tab. To move down, press Enter. To move up, press Shift+Enter.

To Use Excel's AutoCalculate Feature (page 117)

1. Select the cells to be calculated. Excel automatically keeps a running total in the status bar (found in the lower-right part of your screen).

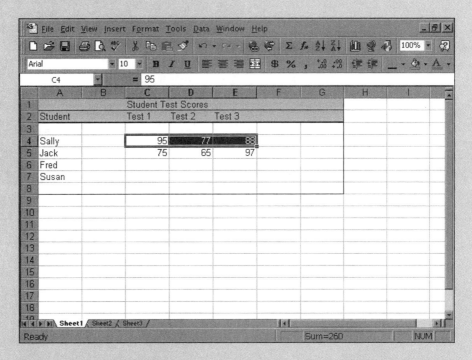

2. Right-click the running total to open the AutoCalculate menu, which offers options for performing various calculations.

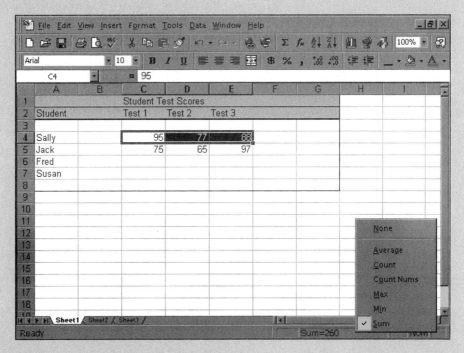

3. Choose the desired AutoCalculate option.

1. Simply enter your data. If AutoComplete finds any data within the current column to match the data that you are entering, it fills in the matching data.

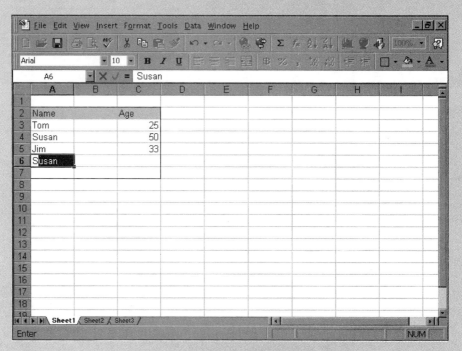

2. If you do not want to use the AutoComplete data, continue to type, and Excel replaces the AutoComplete data with your data.

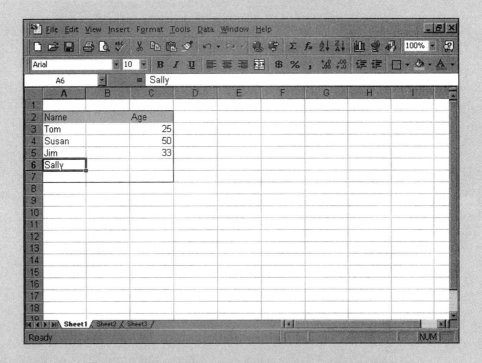

To Add a Commonly Misspelled Word to Excel's AutoCorrect Dictionary (page 121)

1. Choose Tools → AutoCorrect . Excel displays the AutoCorrect dialog box.

2. Enter both the misspelled word and the proper spelling.

3. Click OK. Excel automatically corrects any commonly misspelled words that you specify.

To Automatically Calculate a Sum (page 124)

1. Select the cell below or to the right of the data that you wish to total.

2. Click Σ (the AutoSum button) on the toolbar. Excel places a marquis (a flashing border) around the cells that are to be totaled.

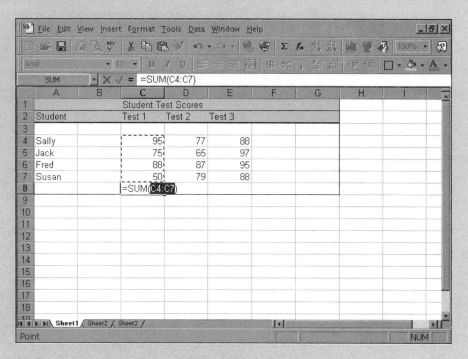

3. To complete the AutoSum process, either press Enter or click the AutoSum button a second time. The total appears in the selected cell.

To Automatically Fill Several Cells (page 125)

1. Select the data that you want to be continued into the following cells.

2. Click and hold the AutoFill handle, and drag it across the desired cells.

If the selected data continues in only one cell and it is not the name of a month or day, AutoFill simply copies the data into the target cells. If the data covers more than one cell or is the name of a month or day, AutoFill either continues the pattern in the target range of cells (for example, Store1, Store 2, Store 3) or inserts the month or day names in sequential order.

To Freeze Parts of the Screen (page 128)

1. Select the cell below the row that you want to freeze and to the right of the column that you want to freeze.

2. Choose [Window] → [Freeze Panes].

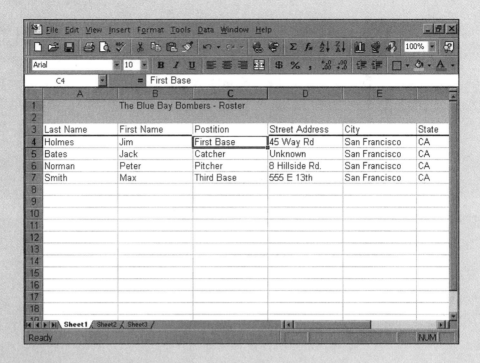

To Create a Label (page 138)

1. Click the cell in which you want to enter the label.

2. Type the label.

3. If the label doesn't fit within the current column width, AutoFit the label.

To Enter a Value (page 141)

1. Click the cell in which you want to enter the value.

2. Enter the value. A value is simply a number. Type it as you would a label. As a rule, do not include any punctuation or special symbols (such as the dollar sign).

3. Add any special symbols by formatting the cell that contains the value.

To Enter a Formula (page 144)

1. Click the cell in which you want to enter the formula. A formula always begins with an equal sign (=). A formula contains operands (such as values or cell references) and mathematical operators (such as +, –, *, and /).

2. Begin the formula by typing an equal sign (=). A formula can contain values, mathematical commands, or references to other cells within the same worksheet, other worksheets, or even other workbooks.

3. Finish entering the formula or point to each cell or group of cells to be referenced, and then type the appropriate mathematical operator.

In general, Excel evaluates the formula from left to right. However, Excel performs multiplication and division before addition and subtraction. Also, if the formula contains parentheses, Excel evaluates the elements within the parentheses *before* proceeding from left to right with the elements outside the parentheses.

Know the results of the formula before you depend on it. For example, the answer to the formula =10-6/2 is 7, *not* 2. Excel performs the division *before* evaluating the rest of the formula from left to right. To get 2 as the formula's result, you must type the formula as follows: =(10–6)/2.

4. Press Enter to complete the formula. The active cell displays the results of the formula; the formula bar displays the formula itself.

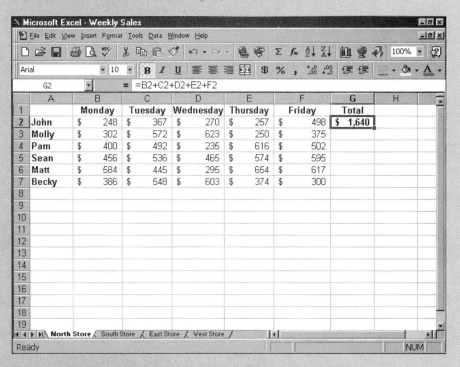

To Copy and Paste a Formula (page 147)

1. Highlight the cell containing the formula that you want to copy.

2. Click the Copy button on the toolbar. Alternatively, you can right-click the cell containing the formula and then choose 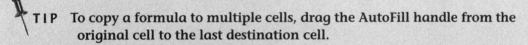 Copy from the pop-up menu.

TIP Remember that *copying* leaves the original data intact. *Cutting* deletes the original formula. To cut a formula, click the Cut button, or right-click the cell containing the formula and then choose Cut from the pop-up menu.

3. Click the cell in which you want to paste the formula.

4. Click the Paste button on the toolbar, or right-click the cell and choose Paste from the pop-up menu.

TIP To copy a formula to multiple cells, drag the AutoFill handle from the original cell to the last destination cell.

To Enter a Function (page 151)

1. Click the cell in which you want to enter the function.

2. Begin the function by typing an equal sign (=). Functions are a part of formulas and must begin with an equal sign.

3. Type the name of the function and a left parenthesis, followed by any required or optional arguments, and a closing parenthesis. If you are unsure of the syntax for a particular function, use the Formula Palette. Access the Formula Palette by clicking the equal sign in the formula bar.

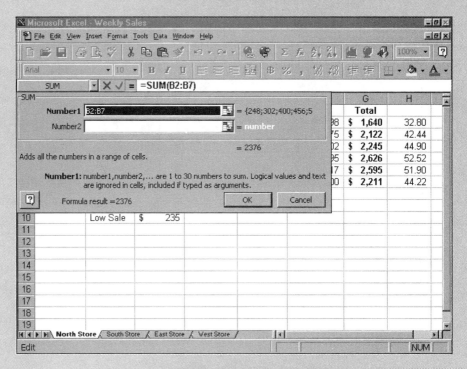

4. Press Enter to complete the function entry.

To Create a Chart by Using the Chart Wizard (page 165)

1. Enter your data into your worksheet.

Before you start the Chart Wizard, be sure that the active cell contains data. If you start the Chart Wizard and the active cell contains no data, Excel assumes that you want to incorporate that empty cell into your chart.

2. Click 📊 (the Chart Wizard button) on the toolbar. Excel displays the Chart Type dialog box (Step 1 of 4 in the Chart Wizard).

3. Choose a Chart type. Excel displays several options in the Chart sub-type box.

4. Select the Chart sub-type, and click Next to move to Step 2 in the Chart Wizard.

5. Make sure that Excel is building your chart based on your specific needs by choosing either columns or rows, and then click Next to move to Step 3.

6. Under the Titles tab, enter any titles (for example, chart, x-axis, y-axis) that you would like.

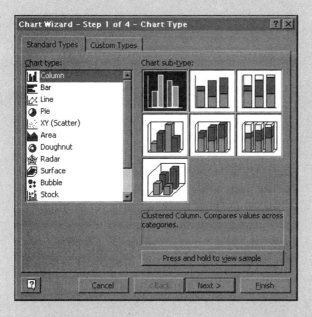

7. To modify or turn off the legend, click the Legend tab and make the necessary changes.

8. On the Data Labels tab, choose the labels that you want to display and then click Next to move to Step 4.

9. Select the destination for your chart, and click Finish. Excel builds your chart and places it in your worksheet.

To Change the Chart Type (page 183)

1. Right-click any white space in the chart. Excel displays a pop-up menu.

Make sure that you right-click the *white space.* If you right-click the data or the labels, Excel displays a different menu.

2. Select [**Chart Type**]. Excel displays the Chart Type dialog box.

3. Choose the chart type and sub-type that you want to use, and then click OK.

To Resize a Chart (page 184)

1. Click any white space in the chart.

2. Drag any sizing handle until the chart reaches the desired size.

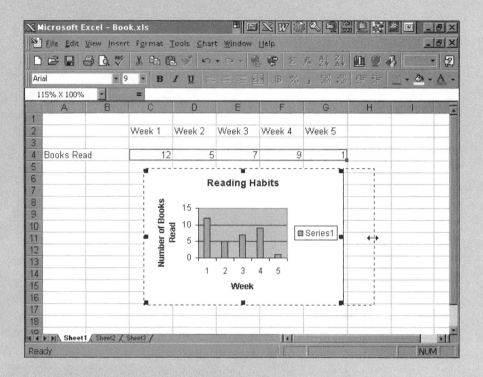

To Resize Objects Within a Chart (page 186)

1. Click to select an object (such as the title or the legend) within the chart.

2. Drag one of the sizing handles to the desired size.

To Add Data to a Chart (page 187)

1. Enter the data in your worksheet.

2. Click any white space in the chart. Excel places a blue border around the data that is currently represented in the chart.

3. Drag the AutoFill handle on the blue border so that it includes the new data. Excel automatically updates the chart.

To Display a Worksheet's Filename Extension in Excel's Title Bar (page 197)

1. Minimize any windows so that the Windows Desktop is visible.

2. Double-click the My Computer icon.

3. Choose   View → Options . Excel displays the Options dialog box.

4. Click the View tab.

5. Click the Show all files option button.

6. Make sure that a check mark appears next to the option entitled Display the full MS-DOS path in the title bar. If necessary, turn on this option by clicking its check box.

7. Make sure that the check box next to the option Hide MS-DOS file extensions for file types that are registered *does not* contain a check mark. If necessary, turn off this option by clicking its check box.

8. Click OK to close the Options dialog box.

9. Close the My Computer window.

10. Maximize Excel.

To Create Random Numbers (page 198)

1. Choose Tools → Add-Ins , and make sure that a check mark appears in the Analysis ToolPak option box.

2. Click OK.

3. Click the upper-left cell of the area where you want to insert the random numbers.

4. Type the formula =**Randbetween**(*X,Y*) (where *X* represents the minimum value and *Y* represents the maximum value for the random numbers), and press Enter.

5. Drag the AutoFill handle from the upper-left cell to be filled to the upper-right cell. Release the mouse button.

6. Drag the AutoFill handle from the right-most cell containing the formula down through the rows that you want to fill with random numbers. Excel fills the selected cells with random numbers, and the entire range of selected cells remains selected.

To Load a File That Was Created in a Supported Spreadsheet Program (page 201)

1. Choose File → Open . Excel displays the Open dialog box.

2. In the Files of type drop-down box, choose the file type that you want to open.

3. Double-click the file to be opened. The file is opened as an Excel file, but you must save the file to complete the conversion.

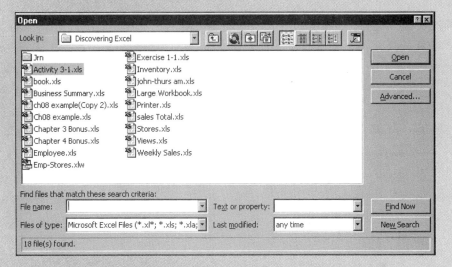

4. Save the file.

To Convert a File That Was Created in an Unsupported Spreadsheet Program (page 201)

1. In the program that created the file, save the file as a file type that is supported by Excel. You can usually choose to save spreadsheet files as text files, delimited files, DIF files, or SYLK files.

2. Close the original program.

3. Open Excel, and choose File → Open . Excel displays the Open dialog box.

4. Click the drop-down arrow in the Files of type list box, and click the file type that you want to convert.

5. Double-click the file to be opened. Depending on the file type, it may load directly into Excel without further intervention, or Excel may display a Conversion dialog box.

6. Follow the instructions in the Conversion dialog boxes, if displayed.

7. Click Finish to display the imported file.

To Copy a Table From Word to Excel (page 207)

1. Open Word and the document containing the table.

2. Highlight the table, and click the Copy button on the toolbar.

3. Open Excel, or click its button in the taskbar.

4. Click the New button to create a new workbook.

5. Click the Paste button on the toolbar. Excel pastes the table into your new worksheet.

6. Save the Excel workbook.

To Set Up Your Page (page 218)

1. Choose File → Page Setup to open the Page Setup dialog box.

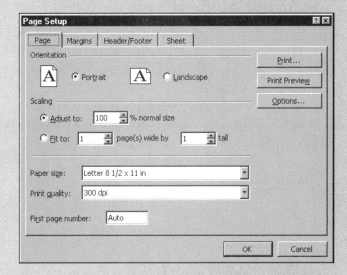

2. Click one of the four tabs: Page, Margins, Header/Footer, or Sheet.

3. Choose the desired page setup options on the selected tab.

4. If necessary, click another tab and continue to select page setup settings.

5. To accept the settings that you've entered, click OK.

To Change the Page options (page 220)

1. Choose File → Page Setup to open the Page Setup dialog box.

2. Click the Page tab in the Page Setup dialog box.

3. Set the orientation, scaling, paper size, print quality, and first page number options as desired.

4. Click OK.

1. Choose `File` → `Page Setup` to open the Page Setup dialog box.
2. Click the Margins tab in the Page Setup dialog box.

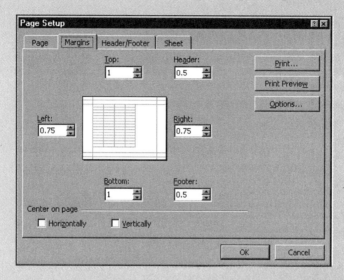

3. Set the four margins — Top, Bottom, Left, and Right — as desired. You can use the spin buttons or enter a value directly into the associated text box.
4. Set the position for the header and the footer.
5. Click a check box to center the worksheet horizontally and/or vertically on the page.
6. Click OK.

1. Choose `File` → `Page Setup` to open the Page Setup dialog box.
2. Click the Header/Footer tab in the Page Setup dialog box.
3. Drop down the Header or Footer list to choose from several preformatted headers and footers.
4. Click Custom Header or Custom Footer to create your own headers and footers.
5. Click OK.

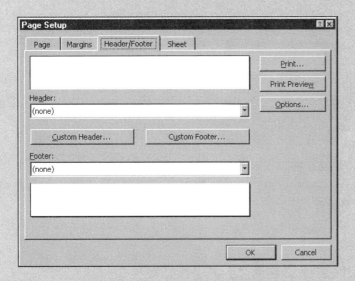

To Change the Sheet Options (page 228)

1. Choose `File` → `Page Setup` to open the Page Setup dialog box.

2. Click the Sheet tab in the Page Setup dialog box.

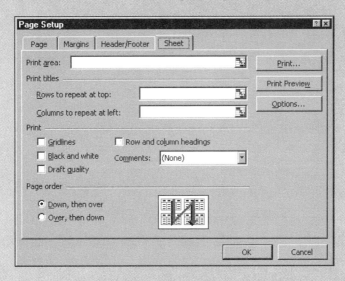

3. Click the Collapse box next to the Print area setting, and then drag to set the print area.

4. In the Rows to repeat at top box and the Columns to repeat at left box, set *repeating* rows and columns by using the same process as in the preceding step.

5. Choose the desired print options.

6. Set the page order for printing.

7. Click OK.

To Print your Worksheet (page 239)

1. Make sure that your printer is turned on.

2. Choose `File` → `Print`. Excel displays the Print dialog box.

 TIP You can click (the Print button) on your toolbar to print a single copy of the current worksheet at the default settings.

3. In the Name box, choose the printer that you want to use. The next two steps are optional.

4. Click Properties. Excel opens the Properties dialog box.

5. Make sure that the Page and Graphics settings are correct, and then click OK to return to the Print dialog box.

6. Specify which pages you want to print (all pages or a specified range) and the number of copies that you want.

 TIP For a bird's-eye view of how your worksheet is going to look when printed, click Preview. In response, Excel displays the Print Preview window. From the Print Preview window, you can do any of the following items:

* Click Margins and adjust your margins by dragging the margins to their proper places.

* Click Page Break Preview to adjust the page breaks.

✳ Click Print to send your worksheet to the printer.

7. When you have entered all the desired settings in the Print dialog box, click OK. Excel prints your worksheet.

To Print a Specific Area (page 247)

1. Highlight the area that you want to print.

2. Choose `File` → `Print Area` → `Set Print Area`.

Excel places a dashed box around the new print area. When you print the worksheet, Excel prints only the specified print area, not the entire worksheet.

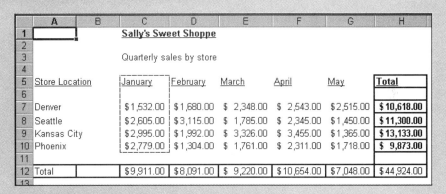

	A	B	C	D	E	F	G	H
1			Sally's Sweet Shoppe					
2								
3			Quarterly sales by store					
4								
5	Store Location		January	February	March	April	May	Total
6								
7	Denver		$1,532.00	$1,680.00	$ 2,348.00	$ 2,543.00	$2,515.00	$ 10,618.00
8	Seattle		$2,605.00	$3,115.00	$ 1,785.00	$ 2,345.00	$1,450.00	$ 11,300.00
9	Kansas City		$2,995.00	$1,992.00	$ 3,326.00	$ 3,455.00	$1,365.00	$ 13,133.00
10	Phoenix		$2,779.00	$1,304.00	$ 1,761.00	$ 2,311.00	$1,718.00	$ 9,873.00
11								
12	Total		$9,911.00	$8,091.00	$ 9,220.00	$10,654.00	$7,048.00	$44,924.00
13								

3. Choose `File` → `Print` to print the selected area.

To Print Nonconsecutive Ranges (page 250)

1. Select the first range that you want to print.

2. Press *and hold* Ctrl while you select any additional print ranges using the mouse. Don't release Ctrl until you have selected all of the ranges that you want to print.

3. When all ranges have been selected, choose `File` → `Print Area` → `Set Print Area`.

4. Click 🖨 (the Print button) on the toolbar. Excel prints the selected data.

To Create Different Views Within Your Worksheet (page 252)

1. Hide the rows or columns that you do not want to see by selecting them, *right-clicking* the row or column indicator, and choosing `Hide` from the pop-up menu.

2. When your worksheet shows only the desired data, choose ⎡ View ⎤ →
   ⎡ Custom Views ⎤. Excel displays the Custom Views dialog box.

3. Click Add.

4. Type a name for your custom view.

5. Click OK.

To Check Your Results (page 258)

1. Verify that you properly input your data.

2. Ensure that your formulas use the proper order of operations
   (parentheses, exponents, multiplication, division, addition, and
   subtraction).

3. Use AutoCalculate to calculate the answers to formulas, and thus
   confirm that Excel displays the correct answers.

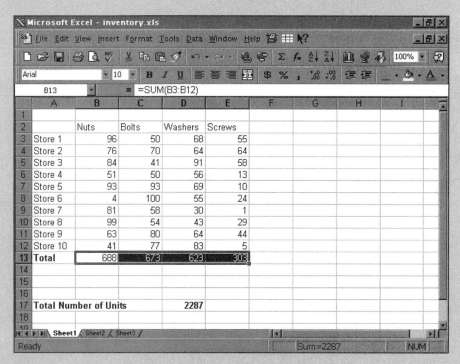

To Avoid Problems with Insert and Delete (page 262)

1. Select the cell that you want to modify.

2. Open the Auditing toolbar by choosing Tools → Auditing → Show Auditing Toolbar .

3. Determine whether the cell that you want to insert or delete is going to affect other cells by clicking the Trace Precedents button and the Trace Dependents button.

4. If Excel displays arrows showing either precedents or dependents, determine whether modifying the cell is going to adversely affect the rest of the worksheet.

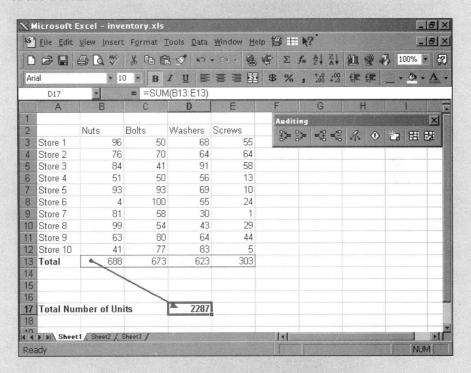

To Ensure Complete, Correct Data Entry (page 266)

1. Inventory your data before you enter it. Document how much data you have, its source(s), and the role that it plays in your worksheet.

2. After data entry, inventory the data that you entered into your worksheet.

3. Compare your pre-entry inventory to your post-entry inventory. If the inventories match, you probably entered your data correctly.

4. If the inventories differ, identify the differences and determine how to resolve them.

To Protect Against Flaws in a Spreadsheet's Design (page 267)

1. Pay careful attention to any formulas that another user has entered. Check them as thoroughly as any formula that you create.

2. If you find an error in a spreadsheet that someone else created, report the error *to the spreadsheet designer*, who can then correct the error for future users.

To Ensure the Effectiveness of Your Report (page 267)

1. Before printing your report, check for the correct page layout. Your headers and footers should accurately reflect the content of the report.

2. Check the formatting of the report.

To Check Multiple Sets of Data (page 268)

1. When time does not allow a complete analysis of all data, select various sets of data to be checked for errors.

2. Test the results of every formula in your sample sets of data.

3. Verify that the data was entered correctly into the sample sets of data.

To Use Data Validation (page 269)

1. Highlight the cell(s) that you want to restrict.

2. Choose `Data` → `Validation`. Excel displays the Data Validation dialog box.

3. Click the Settings tab.

4. Using the drop-down list in the Allow box, choose the type of data that should be entered into the selected cells.

 NOTE Depending on your choice, you may have additional text boxes to further limit the data. For instance, if you choose *Whole numbers* from the Allow list and *between* from the Data list, you must then specify the valid range of numbers by using the Minimum and Maximum boxes. Complete the Settings tab with the desired validation criteria.

5. Click the Input Message tab.

6. Enter the message that you want Excel to display when a user selects the cell.

7. Click the Error Alert tab.

8. Choose the type of error alert that you want to have displayed when a user enters an incorrect data type in the cell.

9. Enter the message that you want Excel to display when it performs that action.

10. Click OK.

To Insert a Worksheet (page 278)

1. Select a worksheet in your workbook.

   Excel will insert the new worksheet *before* this worksheet.

2. Choose | Insert | → | Worksheet |.

TIP You can also insert a worksheet by right-clicking any worksheet tab and choosing | Insert | from the resulting pop-up menu. When Excel displays the Insert dialog box, choose the type of worksheet you want to insert and then click <OK>. Excel inserts the worksheet tab *before* the tab you choose.

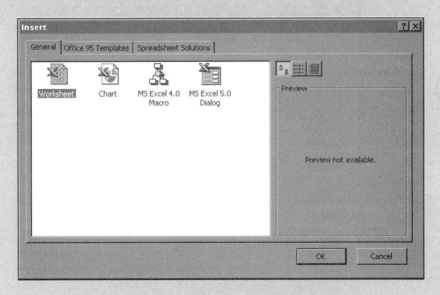

To Delete a Worksheet (page 280)

1. Right-click the tab of the worksheet you want to delete.

   Excel displays a pop-up menu.

Remember, when you delete a worksheet, you are deleting all data on that worksheet and any formulas the worksheet contains. Be sure to check whether cells in other worksheets depend on data in the worksheet you want to delete. Chapter 11 describes the process for finding precedent and dependent cells.

2. Choose $\boxed{\text{Delete}}$.

   Excel displays a warning: The selected sheet(s) will be permanently deleted.

3. Click <OK> to complete the deletion.

 TIP The only way to retrieve a deleted worksheet is to close the file *without saving* and then reopen it.

To Move a Worksheet (page 281)

1. Click the tab of the worksheet you want to move and hold down the mouse button.

   The mouse cursor changes shape and adds a blank page icon to the regular icon. A black triangle appears to the left of the worksheet name on the tab, indicating where the worksheet will be inserted when you release the mouse button.

2. Continue pressing the mouse button and drag the tab to the desired destination.

3. Release the mouse button.

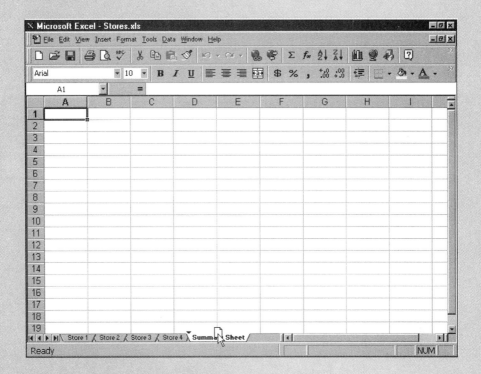

To Copy a Worksheet (page 282)

1. Right-click the worksheet you want to copy.

Excel displays a pop-up menu.

2. Choose Move or Copy .

Excel displays the Move or Copy dialog box.

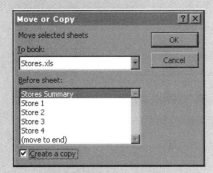

3. Select the destination workbook in the To book box.

TIP You can copy a worksheet to another workbook or to another location within the same workbook.

4. In the Before sheet box, specify the location for inserting the copy.

5. Make sure that the Create a copy box is checked.

6. Click <OK>.

To Create a Summary Worksheet (page 283)

1. Insert a new worksheet at the beginning or the end of your workbook.

2. Right-click the new sheet's tab and choose Rename from the pop-up menu.

Excel highlights the sheet tab.

3. Type **Summary Sheet** and press <Enter>.

4. Create the appropriate formulas by typing them or by using a combination of typing and mouse actions.

To Group Contiguous Worksheets (page 284)

1. Select the first worksheet you want to group by clicking its tab.

2. Press <Shift> and click the tab of the last worksheet to select the worksheet.

Excel selects all worksheets from the first worksheet you selected to the last worksheet you selected and changes all tab colors to white.

To Group Noncontiguous Worksheets (page 286)

1. Select the first worksheet you want to group by clicking its tab.

2. Press <Ctrl> while clicking the tabs for any other worksheets you want to group.

Excel changes all grouped worksheet tabs to white.

To Link Cells in Different Worksheets (page 287)

1. Select the cell in which you want to enter links to data in another worksheet.

2. Type the location of the linked data by using the following form: ='*XXX*'!$*Y*$*Z*, where *XXX* represents the name of the worksheet that contains the data and *YZ* represents the absolute address of the cell that contains the data.

Make sure you place single quotes around the name of the worksheet.

3. Press <Enter>.

To Create a Workspace File (page 289)

1. Open the files you want to save in your workspace.

2. Arrange the files on the desktop in the order you want them to appear when you open your workspace.

You can arrange the files by choosing Windows → Arrange and then selecting the desired arrangement.

3. Choose File → Save as Workspace .

Excel displays the Save Workspace dialog box.

4. Enter the name of your new workspace in the File name text box and then click <Save>.

To Record a Macro (page 301)

1. Choose Tools → Macro → Record New Macro .

Excel displays the Record Macro dialog box.

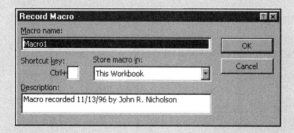

2. Enter a name for the macro and choose the location for storing the macro file.

If desired, assign a shortcut key to the macro.

3. Click <OK>.

Excel displays the Stop Recording toolbar.

4. On the Stop Recording toolbar, click the Relative Reference button, to record a macro with relative references.

Skip this step if you want to use absolute references.

5. Perform the keystrokes and the mouse commands you want to record as a macro.

6. Click the Stop Recording button on the Stop Recording toolbar.

To Play a Macro (page 303)

1. Make sure the workbook that contains the macro is open.

If you stored the macro in the Personal Macro workbook, the macro is already loaded, but hidden from view.

2. Choose Tools → Macro → Macros.

Excel displays the Macro dialog box.

3. Select the macro to play.

4. Click <Run>.

To Delete a Macro (page 309)

1. Choose Tools → Macro → Macros.

Excel displays the Macro dialog box.

2. Select the macro to be deleted.

 Once you delete the macro, you cannot undo the deletion.

3. Click <Delete>.

To Edit a Macro (page 310)

1. Choose Tools → Macro → Macros.

Excel displays the Macro dialog box.

2. Select the macro to be edited.

3. Click <Edit>.

4. Make any changes directly to the Visual Basic commands.

 Always run the macro after editing to make sure it performs properly.

5. Close the macro worksheet.

To Open a Template (page 311)

1. Choose File → New .

   Excel displays the New dialog box.

2. Choose a template from the General tab or the Spreadsheet Solutions tab.

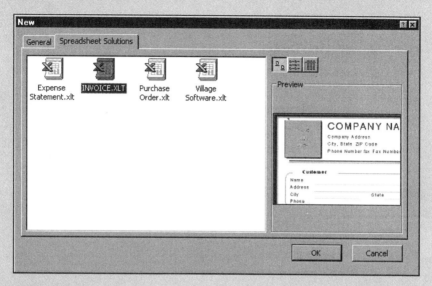

3. Click <OK> to open the template as a worksheet.

4. Modify the template, as necessary.

5. Save the template as a workbook, using the .xls extension.

To Create a Style (page 315)

1. Choose Format → Style .

   Excel displays the Style dialog box.

2. Enter a name for the style and click <Modify>.

3. In the Format Cells dialog box, choose the desired settings for the new style.

4. Click <OK> twice to return to the worksheet.

To Assign a Style (page 316)

1. Highlight the cell or cells that are to be assigned the new style.

2. Choose Format → Style .

Excel displays the Style dialog box.

3. Select the style from the Style name drop-down list, and click <OK>.

To Edit an Existing Style (page 317)

1. Choose ⌷ Format ⌷ → ⌷ Style ⌷.

   Excel displays the Style dialog box.

2. Select the style to be modified.

3. Click <Modify>.

4. In the Format Cells dialog box, make the needed modifications.

5. Click <OK> twice to return to the worksheet.

   Excel automatically updates all of the cells to which you assigned the modified style.

To Delete an Existing Style (page 318)

1. Choose ⌷ Format ⌷ → ⌷ Style ⌷.

   Excel displays the Style dialog box.

2. Select the style to be deleted.

 Once you delete a style, you cannot undo the deletion.

3. Click <Delete>.

To Add a Macro to the Toolbar (page 319)

1. Open the file containing the macro.

2. Choose ⌷ Tools ⌷ → ⌷ Customize ⌷.

   Excel displays the Customize dialog box.

3. Click the Commands tab.

4. In the Categories panel, choose Macros.

5. In the Commands panel, drag the Custom Button icon into the desired position on the toolbar.

6. Close the Customize dialog box.

7. Click the custom button on the toolbar.

   Excel displays the Assign Macro dialog box.

8. Select the macro you want to assign to the custom button and then click <OK>.

To Add a Macro to a Menu (page 321)

1. Open the file containing the macro that is to be added to a menu.

2. Choose `Tools` → `Customize`.

   Excel displays the Customize dialog box.

3. Click the Commands tab.

4. In the Categories panel, choose Macros.

5. In the Commands panel, drag the Custom Menu Item from the Commands panel onto the menu that is to contain your macro.

6. Drag the menu down until the solid bar is correctly positioned for your macro.

   Don't close the Customize dialog box.

7. Right-click the new menu item — it is called `Custom Menu Item`.

   Excel displays a pop-up box with many options.

8. Enter the new name in the Name box.

   If you want to underline one of the letters in the new name for quick-key selection, place an ampersand (&) *before* the letter you want underlined.

9. Close the Customize dialog box.

To Create a Data Entry Form (page 330)

1. Highlight a cell in your list, *or* select a range.
2. Choose **Insert** → **Name** → **Define**.

   Excel displays the Define Name dialog box.
3. Enter **Database** in the Names in workbook text box and then click OK.
4. Choose **Data** → **Form**.
5. Excel displays the current sheet's data entry form.

To Sort Your Data (page 332)

1. Save your file before sorting.
2. Choose **Data** → **Sort**.

   Excel displays the Sort dialog box.

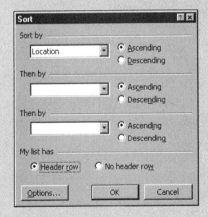

3. Specify which field(s) you want sorted.

   You can choose one, two, or three fields for your sort.
4. If your worksheet has a header row, make sure that the Header row option button is marked.
5. Click OK.

   Excel sorts your data. If the sort does not produce the desired results, check the criteria you specified in the Sort dialog box and then try again.

1. Choose Data → Filter → AutoFilter .

Excel places a drop-down arrow in the header of each field.

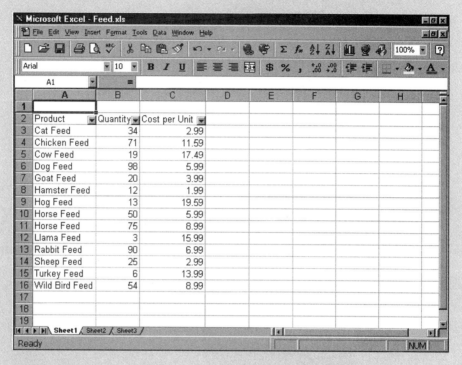

2. Click the drop-down arrow for the field you want to filter.

3. Select the unique data item to be used as your filter criterion.

Excel hides all data that does not meet the criterion.

4. To unhide all hidden data, click the same drop-down arrow and select All.

5. To toggle the AutoFilter off, choose Data → Filter → AutoFilter .

To Use the Top 10 AutoFilter (page 336)

The Top 10 function works only with numeric values.

1. Choose Data → Filter → AutoFilter .

Excel places a drop-down arrow in the header of each field.

2. Click the drop-down arrow for the *numeric* field you want to filter.

3. Select Top-10.

Excel displays the Top 10 AutoFilter dialog box.

4. Specify whether you want the Top values or the Bottom values.

5. Specify how many values you want Excel to display (for example, Top 2, Top 5, Bottom 10).

6. Indicate whether you want Excel to display the items or percentages.

7. Click OK.

To Use the Custom AutoFilter (page 337)

1. Choose `Data` → `Filter` → `AutoFilter`.

Excel places a drop-down arrow in the header of each field.

2. Click the drop-down arrow of the field you want to filter.

3. Select Custom.

Excel displays the Custom AutoFilter dialog box.

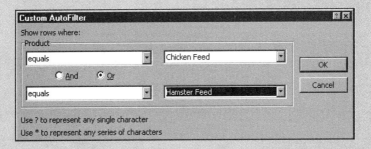

4. Choose an operation.

5. Enter the value you want Excel to use for the comparison or exclusion.

If necessary, choose either the And radio button or the Or radio button and then specify a second comparison operation.

6. Click OK.

To Use the Advanced Filter (page 340)

1. Insert *at least* three rows before your data for the criteria range.

2. Copy the column headers of your data and paste them into the first row of your criteria range.

3. Enter the criteria you want Excel to use in the row or rows beneath the header row of your criteria range.

4. Choose Data → Filter → Advanced Filter .

   Excel displays the Advanced Filter dialog box.

5. Click in the Criteria Range box and select the criteria range to be used.

6. Click again to restore the Advanced Filter dialog box to its full size.

7. Click OK.

To Print Your Reports (page 342)

1. Sort or filter your data.

2. Click 🔍 on the toolbar.

3. Check your margins and page setup to ensure that they are correct.

4. Click 🖨.

   Excel displays the Print dialog box.

5. Choose the range of pages to be printed and the number of copies.

6. Click OK.

To Set a Password for Opening a Workbook (page 346)

1. Choose File → Save As .

   Excel displays the Save As dialog box.

2. Click Options.

   Excel displays the Save Options dialog box.

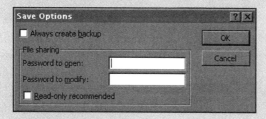

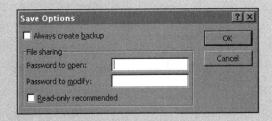

3. Enter a password in the Password to open text box and then click OK.

   Excel displays the Confirm Password dialog box.

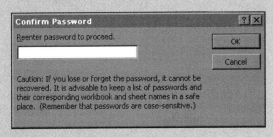

4. Reenter your password and click OK.

   Excel returns you to the Save As dialog box.

5. Click Save.

To Set a Password for Modifying a Workbook (page 348)

1. Choose File → Save As .

   Excel displays the Save As dialog box.

2. Click Options.

   Excel displays the Save Options dialog box.

NOTE If you want to prevent others from opening the file without proper authorization (a password), type the password in the Password to open text box. If you only want to keep them from modifying the file, type the password in the Password to modify text box.

3. Enter a password in the Password to modify box.

   Excel displays the Confirm Password dialog box.

4. Reenter your password and click OK.

5. Click Save to close the Save As dialog box.

To Create a Shared List (page 350)

1. Choose `Tools` → `Share Workbook`.

   Excel displays the Share Workbook dialog box.

2. Check the Allow changes . . . box.

3. Click OK.

   Excel displays a warning box asking you to save the workbook.

4. Click OK.

   Excel saves the file and places **Shared** next to your filename.

To Copy a Shared File for Distribution (page 352)

1. Choose `File` → `Save As`.

   Excel displays the Save As dialog box.

2. Enter a new name to make a copy of your workbook.

3. Click Save.

To Merge Copies of a Workbook (page 354)

1. Open the workbook into which you want to merge files.

2. Choose `Tools` → `Merge Workbooks`.

   Excel opens the Select Files to Merge Into Current Workbook dialog box.

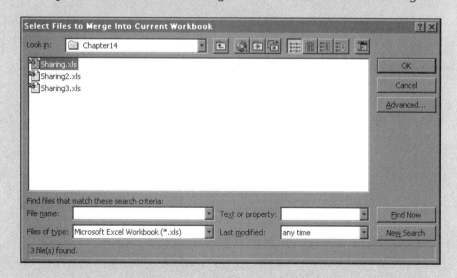

3. Select a file that you want to merge into the currently open file and then click OK.

4. Repeat this procedure until you have merged all necessary files.

To Highlight Changes in a Workbook (page 357)

1. Choose Tools → Track Changes → Highlight Changes.

Excel opens the Highlight Changes dialog box.

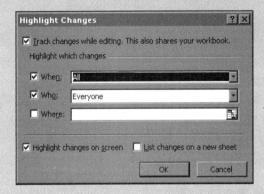

2. Check the Track changes while editing box.

3. Check the When box and select the time frame you want to track.

4. Check the Who box and specify whose changes you want to track.

 NOTE The Where box allows you to specify a range of cells to track, rather than the entire worksheet.

5. Click OK.

To Create a History Sheet (page 358)

1. Choose Tools → Track Changes → Highlight Changes.

Excel opens the Highlight Changes dialog box. If you choose Highlight changes on screen, when you place the cursor over any cell in your worksheet, Excel lists any changes made to the cells, the person who made them, and the time and date they were made.

2. Check the List changes on a new sheet box.

The List changes on a new sheet box is used to create a separate history worksheet listing all changes.

3. Click OK.

To Accept or Reject Changes (page 359)

1. Choose Tools → Track Changes → Accept or Reject Changes .

   Excel opens the Select Changes to Accept or Reject dialog box.

2. In the When drop-down box, choose Not reviewed yet.

3. In the Who drop-down box, select Everyone.

4. Click OK.

   Excel displays the Accept or Reject Changes dialog box.

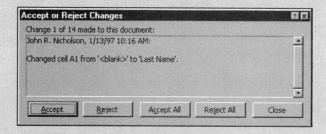

5. Click Accept or Reject for each change, or click Accept All or Reject All.

6. After accepting or rejecting the changes, click Close.

To Set an Independent (Personal) View (page 361)

1. Create the view you want by hiding any cells, columns, rows, or worksheets.

2. Choose Views → Custom Views .

   Excel opens the Custom Views dialog box.

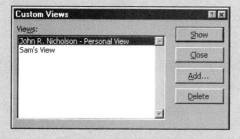

3. Add or Delete any views.

 TIP If you aren't sure you want to delete a view, click Show. Excel displays the view, and you can decide whether you want to keep it.

4. Click Close.

1. Click the Insert Hyperlink button on the toolbar.

   Excel displays the Insert Hyperlink dialog box.

2. Click Browse (the lower of the two Browse buttons), to create an internal hyperlink.

   Excel displays the Browse Excel Workbook dialog box.

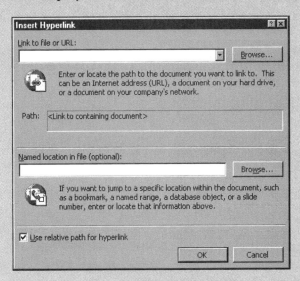

3. Make sure the Sheet radio button is active.

4. Enter the destination cell location in the Reference box.

5. In the lower panel, select the name of the destination worksheet.

6. Click OK.

   The Insert Hyperlink dialog box is again displayed.

7. Click OK.

1. Click in a blank cell near the hyperlink to be modified.

2. Using the *keyboard* arrow keys, highlight the cell containing the hyperlink.

3. Enter a new name for the hyperlink, in the cell containing the hyperlink.

To Delete a Hyperlink (page 374)

1. Click in a blank cell near the hyperlink to be deleted.
2. Using the *keyboard* arrow keys, highlight the cell containing the hyperlink.
3. Choose `Edit` → `Clear` → `All` .

To Create a Hyperlink Using a Named Range (page 374)

1. Highlight the destination range.
2. In the Name box of the Formula bar, enter a name for the range and then press Enter.
3. Move to the workbook, worksheet, and cell where you want to create the hyperlink.
4. Click the Insert Hyperlink button on the toolbar.

   Excel displays the Insert Hyperlink dialog box.
5. Click Browse (the lower of the two Browse buttons).
6. Click the Defined name radio button.
7. Select the named range you want to use as your destination.
8. Click OK to return to the Insert Hyperlink dialog box.
9. Click OK again to return to the worksheet.

To Create a Hyperlink to an Internet Address (page 379)

1. Click the Insert Hyperlink button on the toolbar.

   Excel displays the Insert Hyperlink dialog box.
2. In the Link to file or URL box, type the location (such as **www.microsoft.com**).

   You don't need to type **http://**. Excel inserts it automatically.
3. Click OK.

To Create a Web Query (page 384)

1. Use Notepad, WordPad, or Word to create the query.

   You create and store a Web query as a text file with the filename extension .IQY.

2. Save the query as a Text File, making sure you place double quotation marks around the name of the file to be saved (otherwise, .TXT is used as the extension).

To Run a Web Query (page 385)

1. Choose **Data** → **Get External Data** → **Run Web Query** .

   Excel displays the Run Query dialog box.

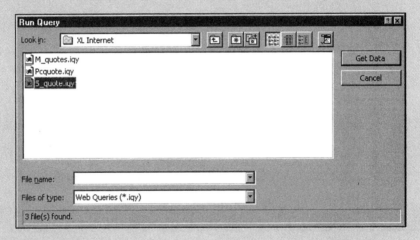

2. Enter the name of the query to be run.

3. Click Get Data.

4. Enter any parameters requested by the query.

   After the query runs, you can delete the .IQY file. To update the data, click the Refresh button on the Data toolbar. (It looks like an exclamation point.)

To Save a Worksheet as an HTML File (page 387)

1. Choose **File** → **Save As HTML** .

2. Follow the instructions in the four steps of the Internet Assistant.

3. Add any information, such as the title of the document, the date of the last update, your name, and an e-mail address.

To View the HTML Source Code (page 391)

1. From within your Web browser, choose View → Source (in Internet Explorer) or View → Document Source (in Netscape).

   Either Notepad (in Internet Explorer) or a special window (in Netscape) opens with the code displayed. If you are viewing a screen that you developed, you can use Notepad to make changes to the source code.

2. Save the file after any changes have been made.

To Restrict Data by Using Excel's Validation Tools (page xx)

1. Highlight the cells you want to restrict.

2. Choose Data → Validation .

   Excel displays the Data Validation dialog box.

3. Click the Settings tab and then select a data type in the Allow drop-down box.

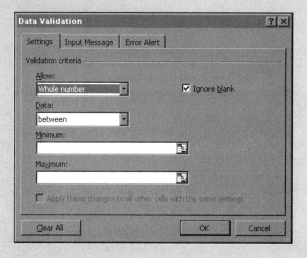

4. Choose the desired data restrictions in the Data drop-down box.

5. Enter the Minimum and Maximum, if required by the data type.

6. Click the Input Message tab.

7. Enter a title in the Title text box and type the message you want users to see when they highlight the restricted cells.

8. Click the Error Alert tab.

9. Choose a style for your error message in the Style box.

10. Enter a title in the Title text box and type the message you want displayed in the Error message box.

11. Click OK.

To Forecast Potential Errors by Using the Auditing Toolbar (page 396)

1. *Before* deleting or changing a cell's contents, open the Auditing toolbar by choosing | Tools | → | Auditing | → | Show Auditing Toolbar |.

2. Highlight the cell you plan to delete or change.

3. On the Auditing toolbar, click the Trace Precedents button.

   If this cell is dependent on any other cells for information, Excel places an arrow *from* the precedent cell *to* the highlighted cell.

4. On the Auditing toolbar, click the Trace Dependents button.

   If any other cells depend on this cell for information, Excel places an arrow *from* the highlighted cell *to* the dependent cell.

5. Click the Circle Invalid Data button.

   Excel places a red circle around any cells containing data that violates the cell's data validation restriction. Based on any precedents, dependents, and invalid data cells, you can now determine how any deletion or change will affect your worksheet's performance.

To Identify Circular Reference Errors (page 399)

1. If Excel displays a warning box to alert you that the data you entered creates a circular reference error, click OK.

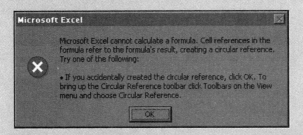

In place of the formula you entered in the highlighted cell, Excel inserts a 0 value. Excel also places a blue arrow between the two cells involved in the circular reference error.

2. Click the Trace Precedents and Trace Dependents buttons to examine each formula and its role in your worksheet. Decide which formula incorrectly references the other.

3. Enter the corrected formula into your worksheet.

To Troubleshoot Error Messages (page 401)

1. When an error message occurs in your worksheet, read the *entire* error message carefully.

2. Write down the exact language of the error message, in case you need it when getting help from other sources.

3. Follow the error message instructions to solve the problem.

To Troubleshoot Order-of-Operation Errors (page 402)

1. Write down the formula on a piece of paper.

2. Work through the formula and determine where the order-of-operation error occurs.

3. Rewrite the formula to correct the error.

4. Enter the corrected formula into your worksheet.

To Copy a Formula with Absolute Addresses (page 403)

1. Select the formula you want to copy.

2. Insert a dollar sign ($) before each column reference and each row reference in your formula.

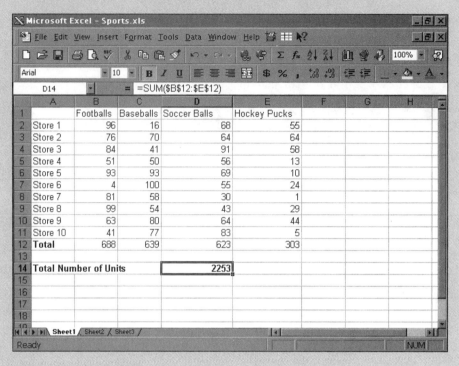

3. Choose Edit → Copy .

4. Select the destination for the formula.

5. Choose Edit → Paste .

To Insert a Column or a Row into a Range That Your Formula References (page 404)

1. Select a cell in the middle of the area that your formula references.

2. Choose Insert → Columns or Insert → Rows .

Excel adds a new column or row to your worksheet.

3. Enter your data into the new column or row.

4. Make sure that the cell containing the total accurately reflects the addition of the new data.

To Access the Microsoft Knowledge Base (page 405)

1. Open Excel.

2. Right-click any empty area of any toolbar, and choose to display the Web toolbar.

You could also start your Web browser (such as Netscape or Mosaic) manually.

3. In the Address bar, type **www.microsoft.com/kb**.

Make sure you enter the address with no spaces and all lowercase text.

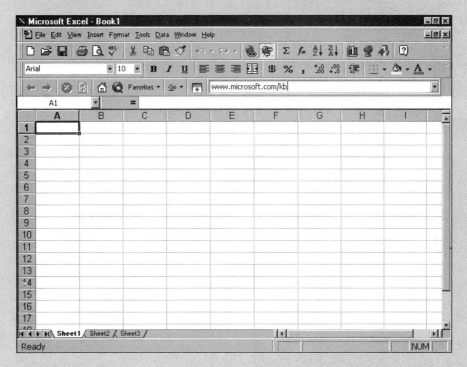

4. Press Enter.

After a few seconds, the Knowledge Base main screen appears.

5. From the Choose a product or technology drop-down list, choose *Excel for Windows or Macintosh*.

6. Click in the Search Phrase box.

7. Enter the search word or phrase.

8. Click the Show titles with brief excerpts radio button.

9. Click Next>.

The Knowledge Base search results screen is displayed.

10. Browse the list of articles and click any you want to read.

You can print an article by choosing File → Print and clicking OK.

VISUAL INDEX

How to use the AutoFill feature
Chapter 5

How to align text
Chapter 5

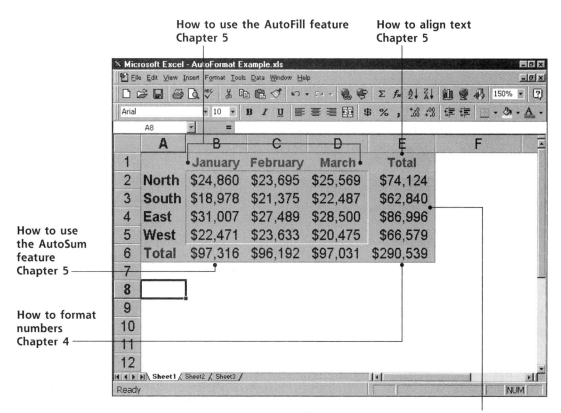

How to use
the AutoSum
feature
Chapter 5

How to format
numbers
Chapter 4

How to apply AutoFormat to a range of data
Chapter 4

How to create formulas
Chapter 6

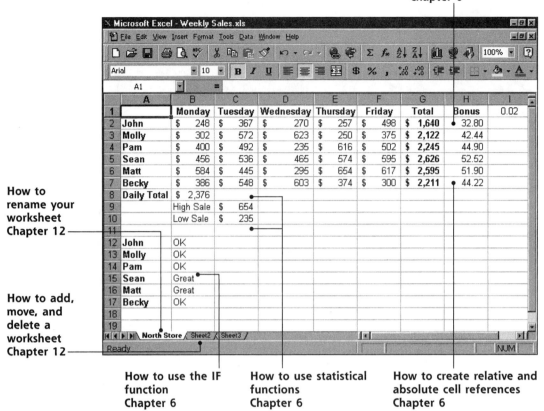

How to rename your worksheet
Chapter 12

How to add, move, and delete a worksheet
Chapter 12

How to use the IF function
Chapter 6

How to use statistical functions
Chapter 6

How to create relative and absolute cell references
Chapter 6

How to create charts
Chapter 7

How to add titles to charts
Chapter 7

How to add pictures as markers on your chart
Chapter 7

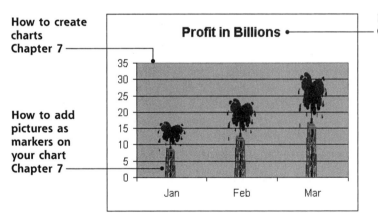

How to create
headers
Chapter 7

How to set
the page
orientation
Chapter 7

How to set
margins
Chapter 9

How to create
footers
Chapter 7

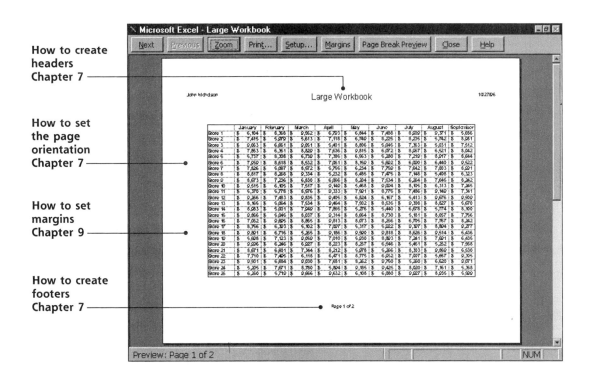

How to adjust
page breaks
Chapter 10

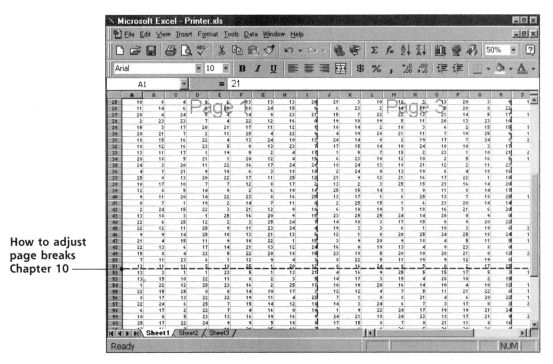

How to start a Wizard
Chapter 13

How to choose a template
Chapter 13

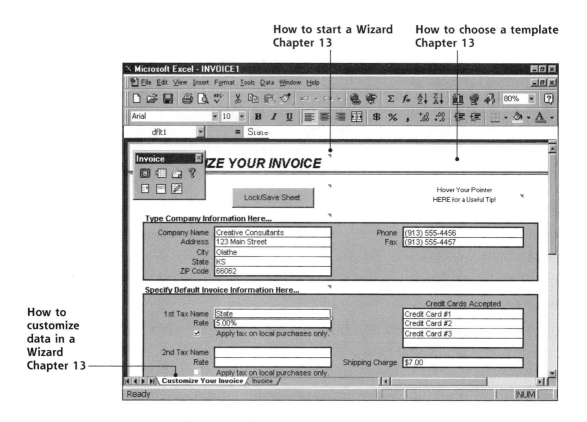

How to customize data in a Wizard
Chapter 13

How to AutoFit a column
Chapter 4

How to create a top ten AutoFilter list
Chapter 14

How to format text
Chapter 14

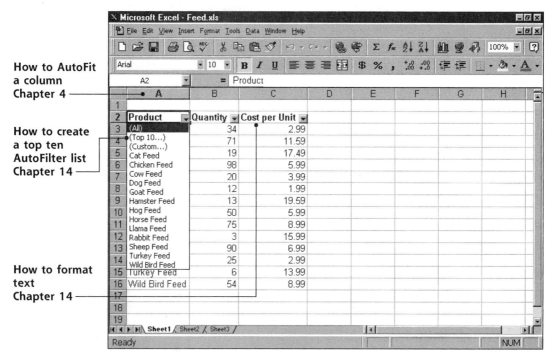

How to arrange multiple windows
Chapter ?

How to mark workbooks as shared
Chapter 15

How to merge shared workbooks Chapter 15

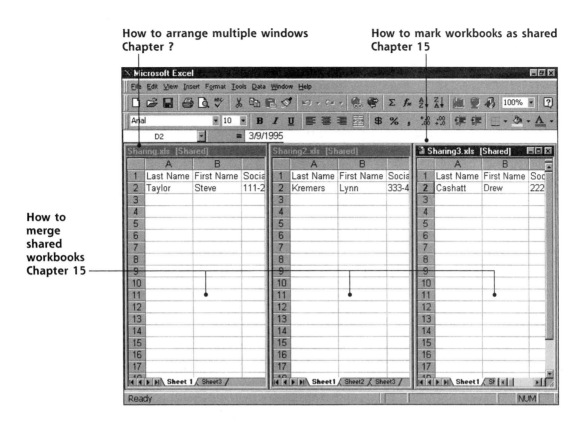

How to apply the AutoFilter feature Chapter 14

How to create a sheet listing all changes made to a shared workbook Chapter 15

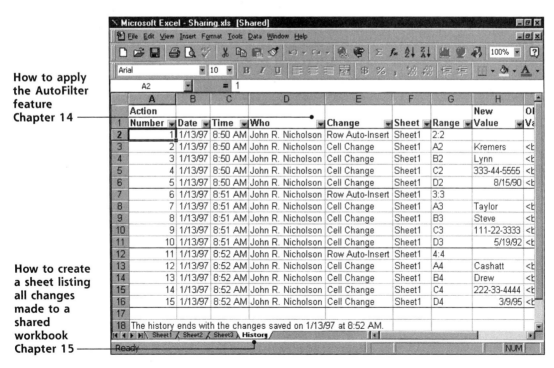

How to find cell precedents and dependents Chapter 17

How to use the Auditing toolbar to troubleshoot worksheet errors Chapter 17

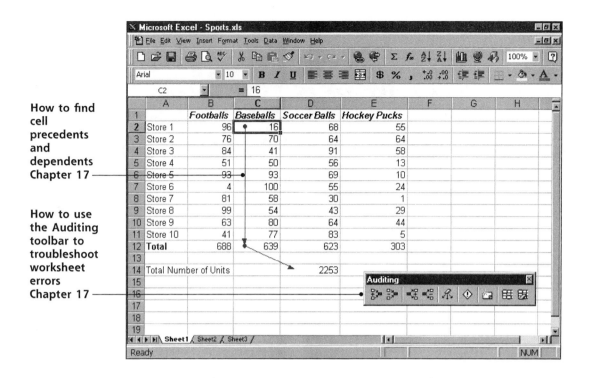

INDEX

(continued)

Merge cells option, Text control panel, 92
Merge and Center button, 92-93
merging workbooks to hosts, 354-356
Microsoft Excel. See Excel
Microsoft Office 97 Maintenance box, checking Office components for installation, 412, 413
Microsoft Office CD-ROMs, installing Excel from, 411-412
Microsoft Office shortcut bar. See Office shortcut bar
Microsoft Word, importing/exporting tables from, 207-209
Microsoft's Knowledge Base, hyperlinks to, 383
minimizing Excel, 26-27
misspellings, AutoCorrect feature, 121-123
monitors. See screen display
Mother Nature Assistant, Office Assistant, 43
mouse, 2-3
  clicking with, 2
  double-clicking with, 2
  dragging with, 2
  left-handed instructions, 3
  menu commands and, 30-31
moving
  between pages with Print Preview, 243
  charts, 186
  worksheets, 71, 281
multiple worksheets. See workbooks
My Macros.xls, saving macros, 303

N

name box, screen display, 28
named ranges. See range names
names
  See also labels
  Program title bar, 26
  saving files with existing, 34-35
  worksheet, 6
naming
  database ranges, 329-330
  Define Name dialog box (creating ranges), 255
  filename rules, 35-36
  hyperlinks, 373-374
  macros, 300
  renaming shortcuts, 24
  renaming worksheets, 67-68, 279
  views with View Manager, 253-254
networks, hyperlinking to Internet, 382-383
noncontiguous pages, printing, 250-251
noncontiguous worksheets, grouping, 286
nonproprietary formats, converting worksheets, 200, 201-202
notation markers, combining workbooks, 355-356
numbers, 55-56
  aligning, 56
  formatting, 85-90
  hyphenated, 55
  random, 141-143
Numeric Data Only warning box, validation tools, 396
numeric values, limiting cells to, 269, 272-273

Shrink to fit option, Text control panel, 92

sizing charts, 184-186

sizing handles, 185, 186

slanted text, Orientation panel, 92

sorting database records, 332-333
  See also AutoFilter; filters (database)
  Sort dialog box, 333

sorting workbook files, 342-344

special characters
  filename rules, 35-36
  menu commands and, 30

spelling, AutoCorrect feature, 121-123

Spreadsheet Solutions tab, creating workbooks based on templates, 311

spreadsheets, 45-61
  See also worksheets
  assumptions about, 266-267
  contents of, 53-54
  customer contact lists, 50, 51
  data types, 54-56
  databases comparison, 53, 326-327
  design flaws, 267
  design questions, 59-61
  formulas, 48, 57, 144-150
  functions, 48, 57-59
  history of, 18
  importing. See converting worksheets
  inventory control, 47-50
  overview, 45-46
  personnel information, 52
  printing, 14-15, 235-256
  sales information, 52, 53
  tasks, 47-52

word processors and, 46

standard toolbar, shortcuts and, 27-28

Standard Width dialog box, formatting columns, 102

starting Excel, 3-4, 20-24

statistics
  About Statistical Functions dialog box, 161
  football anecdote, 366

status bar, screen display, 29

Stop boxes, Data Validation dialog box, 271

Stop Recording toolbar, recording macros, 302

styles, 314-318
  assigning, 316-317
  border, 96
  creating, 315-316
  defined, 296
  deleting, 318
  modifying, 317
  Style dialog box, 315

Summary Sheets, 283

SYLK (Symbolic Link) files, converting worksheets, 202, 206-207

syntax
  defined, 150
  formula, 146-150
  function, 155-159

T

tab-delimited files
  See also delimited files
  importing, 203-206
  saving Excel worksheets as, 202-203

IDG BOOKS WORLDWIDE REGISTRATION CARD

Visit our Web site at http://www.idgbooks.com

ISBN Number: 0-7645-3047-x

Title of this book: Discover Excel 97

My overall rating of this book: ❏ Very good [1] ❏ Good [2] ❏ Satisfactory [3] ❏ Fair [4] ❏ Poor [5]

How I first heard about this book:

❏ Found in bookstore; name: [6]

❏ Advertisement: [8]

❏ Word of mouth; heard about book from friend, co-worker, etc.: [10]

❏ Book review: [7]

❏ Catalog: [9]

❏ Other: [11]

What I liked most about this book:

What I would change, add, delete, etc., in future editions of this book:

Other comments:

Number of computer books I purchase in a year: ❏ 1 [12] ❏ 2-5 [13] ❏ 6-10 [14] ❏ More than 10 [15]

I would characterize my computer skills as: ❏ Beginner [16] ❏ Intermediate [17] ❏ Advanced [18] ❏ Professional [19]

I use ❏ DOS [20] ❏ Windows [21] ❏ OS/2 [22] ❏ Unix [23] ❏ Macintosh [24] ❏ Other: [25]

(please specify)

I would be interested in new books on the following subjects:

(please check all that apply, and use the spaces provided to identify specific software)

❏ Word processing: [26]

❏ Data bases: [28]

❏ File Utilities: [30]

❏ Networking: [32]

❏ Other: [34]

❏ Spreadsheets: [27]

❏ Desktop publishing: [29]

❏ Money management: [31]

❏ Programming languages: [33]

I use a PC at (please check all that apply): ❏ home [35] ❏ work [36] ❏ school [37] ❏ other: [38]

The disks I prefer to use are ❏ 5.25 [39] ❏ 3.5 [40] ❏ other: [41]

I have a CD ROM: ❏ yes [42] ❏ no [43]

I plan to buy or upgrade computer hardware this year: ❏ yes [44] ❏ no [45]

I plan to buy or upgrade computer software this year: ❏ yes [46] ❏ no [47]

Name: _____ Business title: [48] _____ Type of Business: [49] _____

Address (❏ home [50] ❏ work [51]/Company name: _____)

Street/Suite#

City [52]/State [53]/Zip code [54]: _____ Country [55] _____

❏ **I liked this book!** You may quote me by name in future
IDG Books Worldwide promotional materials.

My daytime phone number is _____

**IDG
BOOKS
WORLDWIDE**

THE WORLD OF
COMPUTER
KNOWLEDGE®

❏ YES!

Please keep me informed about IDG Books Worldwide's World of Computer Knowledge. Send me your latest catalog.